**EMERGING
TECHNOLOGIES**

To Julie

EMERGING INFORMATION TECHNOLOGIES
Improving Decisions, Cooperation, and Infrastructure

Kenneth E. Kendall
Editor

SAGE Publications
International Educational and Professional Publisher
Thousand Oaks London New Delhi

Copyright © 1999 by Sage Publications, Inc.

All rights reserved. No part of this book may be reproduced or utilized in any form or by any means, electronic or mechanical, including photocopying, recording, or by any information storage and retrieval system, without permission in writing from the publisher.

For information:

SAGE Publications, Inc.
2455 Teller Road
Thousand Oaks, California 91320
E-mail: order@sagepub.com

SAGE Publications Ltd.
6 Bonhill Street
London EC2A 4PU
United Kingdom

SAGE Publications India Pvt. Ltd.
M-32 Market
Greater Kailash I
New Delhi 110 048 India

Printed in the United States of America

Library of Congress Cataloging-in-Publication Data

Main entry under title:

Emerging information technologies: Improving decisions, cooperation, and infrastructure/edited by Kenneth E. Kendall.
   p. cm.
Includes bibliographical references and index.
ISBN 0-7619-1748-9 (cloth; alk. paper)
ISBN 0-7619-1749-7 (pbk.)
  1. Information technology—Social aspects. 2. Decision support systems. 3. Management information systems. 4. Information technology.   I. Kendall, Kenneth E., 1948–
  HC79.155 E435   1999
  658.4′038′011—dc21   99-6076

01 02 03 04 05 7 6 5 4 3 2

Acquiring Editor:	Harry Briggs
Editorial Assistant:	Maryann Vail
Production Editor:	Wendy Westgate
Production Assistant:	Nevair Kabakian
Typesetter/Designer:	Marion Warren
Indexer:	Molly Hall
Cover Designer:	Candice Harman

Contents

Preface — viii

1. **Emerging Information Technologies: Information Technologies That Support Decision Making, Facilitate Cooperation, and Enable the Information Infrastructure** — 1

   Kenneth E. Kendall

Part I. Decision-Supporting Technologies

2. **Recommendation Systems: Decision Support for the Information Economy** — 21

   Edward A. Stohr
   Sivakumar Viswanathan

3. **Animation in User Interfaces Designed for Decision Support Systems: The Effects of Image Abstraction, Transition, and Interactivity on Decision Quality** — 45

   Cleotilde González
   George M. Kasper

4. **The Emergence of Hypertext and Problem Solving: An Experimental Investigation of Accessing and Using Information From Linear Versus Nonlinear Systems** — 75

   Narender K. Ramarapu
   Mark N. Frolick
   Ronald B. Wilkes
   James C. Wetherbe

5. **Data Warehousing: Three Major Applications and Their Significance**   99

    Paul Gray

6. **Artificial Intelligence: A Short History and the Next 40 Years**   117

    Phillip Ein-Dor

PART II. COOPERATION-FACILITATING TECHNOLOGIES

7. **Media Appropriateness: Effects of Experience on Communication Media Choice**   143

    Ruth C. King
    Weidong Xia

8. **Group Support Systems, Power, and Influence in an Organization: A Field Study**   177

    Susan Rebstock Williams
    Rick L. Wilson

9. **An Empirical Investigation Into Factors Relating to the Adoption of Executive Information Systems: An Analysis of EIS for Collaboration and Decision Support**   205

    Arun Rai
    Deepinder S. Bajwa

10. **Virtual Teams Versus Face-to-Face Teams: An Exploratory Study of a Web-Based Conference System**   241

    Merrill Warkentin
    Lutfus Sayeed
    Ross Hightower

PART III. INFRASTRUCTURE-ENABLING TECHNOLOGIES

11. **Web Pull and Push Technologies: The Emergence and Future of Information Delivery Systems**   265

    Julie E. Kendall
    Kenneth E. Kendall

12. **Structure and Macro-Level Impacts of Electronic Commerce: From Technological Infrastructure to Electronic Marketplaces** — **289**

    Vladimir Zwass

13. **Client/Server System Success: Exploring the Human Side** — **317**

    Tor Guimaraes
    Magid Igbaria

14. **Knowledge Work Productivity: Features and Functions of Information Technologies** — **343**

    Gordon B. Davis
    J. David Naumann

Index — **359**

About the Editor — **365**

About the Contributors — **367**

Preface

Two Lenses for Viewing Emerging Technologies

There are several different lenses with which we can view emerging information technologies. This volume uses two different lenses, alternating between them to give you the richest and most colorful panorama of outlooks possible. One lens that I use is the life cycle of technological advancement; a second lens is how the emerging information technologies are being used.

The technological advancement life cycle has five phases: technological invention or discovery; technological emergence; technological acceptance; technological sublime; and technological surplus. All of the authors whose chapters are included in this book are examining the second phase, that of technological emergence.

To show how the lens of technological advancement life cycle is relevant to emerging information technologies, the analogy of the invention and use of the light bulb is chronicled briefly below.

Phase 1: Technological invention and introduction. Although the first light bulb was a vacuum tube invented by the German chemist Herman Sprengel in 1865, the first practical light bulb was demonstrated in 1878 by English chemist Joseph Swan. Thomas Edison demonstrated his incandescent lamp 11 months later, but Edison beat Swan to the patent, thus ensuring his place in history (Trager, 1994).

Phase 2: Technological emergence. Parts of London (30 buildings) and New York were lit with electric light bulbs in 1882, but kerosene, candlewax, and whale oil continued to light the rest of the world until the development of dynamos and standardized sockets. Electric lights were installed in the White House in 1889, but "neither President Harrison nor his wife will touch the switches. An employee turns on the lights each evening, and they remain burning until the employee returns in the morning to turn them off" (Trager, 1994).

Phase 3: Technological acceptance. By 1901, the general public realized the beauty and potential of the incandescent light bulb, and electricity was chosen as the central theme for Buffalo's Pan-American exhibition. The electric tower, with 40,000 small bulbs, and the Grand court, with another 200,000 bulbs, turned the exhibition grounds into a work of art. The cost of electric lighting continued to decrease, and in 1903, a new bottle-blowing machine permitted volume production of electric light bulbs, thus encouraging the widespread use of electric lighting (Trager, 1994).

Phase 4: Technological sublime. During the first half of the 20th century, the general public not only accepted electric lighting but also valued it. In his book *The American Technological Sublime,* Nye (1996) notes that "by World War I the electrified skyline was a defining characteristic of the large city and usually a source of civic pride" (p. 189).

Phase 5: Technological surplus. The public views electrical lighting as a free good, and lighting becomes omnipresent. The middle of the 20th century welcomes the "push technology" era for electric lighting. Lights are used commercially in the fantasy worlds of Las Vegas or Disneyland with both positive and negative implications.

As mentioned at the outset, all of the authors here are examining information technologies that are in the second phase (technological emergence). For each of the chapters in this book, the reader might try drawing an analogy between the development of the technology addressed in the chapter with that of electrical lighting. It is worthwhile to reflect on what will happen to the technology as it progresses from one phase to another.

Another powerful lens that can be used to view the information technologies covered in this volume concerns how they are being used. To that end, this book is divided into three parts: decision-supporting technologies, cooperation-facilitating technologies, and infrastructure-enabling technologies.

Decision-supporting technologies. Chapters 2-6 are concerned with decision-supporting technologies. Chapter 2, by Stohr and Viswanathan, examines recommendation systems. Chapter 3, by González and Kasper, looks at animation for decision support. In Chapter 4, Ramarapu, Frolick, Wilkes, and Wetherbe explore the use of hypertext and problem solving. In Chapter 5, Gray recounts the growth of data warehousing and cites its business value. In the final installment of this first part, Chapter 6, Ein-Dor covers the growth and development of artificial intelligence as a decision-supporting technology.

Cooperation-facilitating technologies. The second part of this volume, comprising Chapters 7-10, covers cooperation-facilitating technologies. Chapter 7, by King and Xia, examines media usage and choice. Chapter 8, written by Williams and Wilson, examines group support systems (GSS) and organizational context issues.

In Chapter 9, Rai and Bajwa explore the adoption and implementation of executive information systems (EIS). In Chapter 10, the final chapter in this part, authors Warkentin, Sayeed, and Hightower study web-based conferencing to understand differences between real and virtual teams.

Infrastructure-enabling technologies. The third and final part of this volume, composed of Chapters 11-14, develops insights on infrastructure-enabling technologies. Chapter 11, by Kendall and Kendall, details IDS, or information delivery systems, that are Web-based information systems that include push and pull technologies. In Chapter 12, Zwass explains the rise of E-commerce and its value. Guimaraes and Igbaria study client/server systems (CSS) to model implementation success in Chapter 13. In the final chapter in this volume, Chapter 14, Davis and Naumann explore knowledge work productivity systems.

The two lenses I have introduced are the life cycle of technological advancement and the uses to which the information technologies are being put. It is my hope that the reader finds these lenses useful in analyzing implications of the emerging technologies in this book.

I would like to thank my editor, Harry Briggs, for his encouragement. I would also like to thank the Board of the Decision Sciences Institute (DSI) for their endorsement of this endeavor. I would especially like to acknowledge the help of Professor Lee Krajewski, University of Notre Dame; Carol Latta, Executive Director of DSI; and Marian McCreery of the *Decision Sciences* journal. Their help and support with this project has been instrumental, and it is accurate to say that without them, this book could not have happened.

Kenneth E. Kendall, Editor
Rutgers University

References

Nye, D. E. (1996). *American technological sublime.* Cambridge: MIT Press.
Trager, J. (1994). *The people's chronology.* New York: Henry Holt.

CHAPTER
ONE

Emerging Information Technologies

Information Technologies That Support Decision Making, Facilitate Cooperation, and Enable the Information Infrastructure

KENNETH E. KENDALL

Many of us are fascinated when we read about the latest technological innovation. We imagine many of the potential benefits, and often, we want to use the new technology at once. The optimist within us dreams about how the innovation can make our lives more meaningful, easier, or just more enjoyable.

To be fair, many authors have chronicled the darker side of technology and the evils that it is bound to visit upon unsuspecting people (Dery, 1996; Slouka, 1995; Stoll, 1996). Negroponte (1995) offers a more exhilarating vision of what the potential for "being digital" offers.

Unfortunately, there is often a lag between the invention or discovery of a new technology and the practical application of that technology. For instance, Teflon™ became an emerging technology when no-stick frying pans were first sold in the United States at Macy's department store in 1960. Teflon was (accidentally) discovered in 1938 by the Du Pont chemist Roy Joseph Plunkett, but the technology was not highly visible until it resonated with the American purchasing public. Of course, today, Teflon is used in countless products because it is an excellent electrical insulation material, stable over a wide range of temperatures, and resistant to most corrosive agents. We are so conversant with Teflon's physical properties that when the mass media apply the term "Teflon" in a figurative way, we instantly recognize that even the highly publicized blunders of politicians will not "stick" to them.

For the purpose of discussion, I will describe the life cycle of technology in the following five, somewhat overlapping phases of technological advancement: (a) technological invention or discovery, (b) technological emergence, (c) technological acceptance, (d) technological sublime, and (e) technological surplus. The

---

AUTHOR'S NOTE: This chapter was adapted from an article originally published in *Decision Sciences,* Volume 28, Number 4, Fall 1997.

term *sublime* has the greatest positive connotation, and deservedly so. This is the phase in which a technology is fully understood, appreciated, and put to its best uses.

The intent of this volume is to present and survey research being conducted on emerging information technologies, which occur in the second phase of technological advancement. To emerge means "to come forth from obscurity" (*The American Heritage™ Dictionary of the English Language,* 1992). All of the technologies described in this volume are known by researchers. Their invention or creation was some time ago. Decision makers and other end users, however, may be unaware of the details, the inherent potential they offer, or how to make use of these technologies. In that sense, they are emerging.

Why should researchers study and write about emerging technologies? The basic possibilities include advancing the field in order to (a) improve or promote the technology to gain its wider acceptance and use; (b) distribute the technology to a wider set of end users; and (c) understand how to implement, use, and value the technology. These possibilities correspond to the technological acceptance, technological surplus, and technological sublime phases in the model presented.

The first reason for researching emerging technologies is to improve the technology so that it achieves acceptance. An article aligned with this purpose might be more suitable for a scientific or trade publication. The second reason for researching new technology is to understand it better so that it can be distributed or disseminated to a growing set of end users. The third reason to study and research technology is to understand how to implement, use, and value the technology. This research benefits the fourth phase, the one referred to as the technological sublime. All of the chapters contained in this volume serve as supports for the building of bridges from technological emergence to the technological sublime.

In the technological emergence phase, managers learn how to employ technology to its fullest, including such functions as using decision support models, computerizing procedures, and facilitating communication. In the process, managers are educated and also train others in the use of information technology (IT). Additionally, managers learn about planning for IT, and how to avoid unique organizational problems created by newly adopted technology. In an in-depth study of IT managers and technological changes, Benamati, Lederer, and Singh (1997) chronicled common problems faced by IT managers in this phase. Additionally, they identified and classified the coping mechanisms that managers use to address problems created by emerging information technologies, which include "education and training, inaction, internal support, vendor support, new procedures and persuasion" (p. 275).

The 13 emerging technology chapters are classified as to whether they examine decision-supporting technologies, cooperation-facilitating technologies, or infrastructure-enabling technologies. Chapters are thus arranged according to one of those three classifications. The contributions made by the authors of each of the 13 chapters are then presented.

Five Phases of Technological Advancement

As noted earlier, the life cycle of technology is described in the following five, somewhat overlapping phases of technological advancement:

1. Technological invention or discovery
2. Technological emergence
3. Technological acceptance
4. Technological sublime (in which its value is fully appreciated)
5. Technological surplus

The fifth phase could result in a continual use of, and perhaps overindulgence in, the technology (e.g., the wheel and the overabundance of vehicles); additional higher order inventions; or the discontinuance or decrease of the technology (such as the fountain pen) when it is replaced by an improved technology (such as the ballpoint pen).

The remaining chapters in this volume all study and report on emerging technologies (Phase 2). The upcoming section explores the 13 chapters by classifying them on three dimensions as to whether they examine decision-supporting, cooperation-facilitating, or infrastructure-enabling technologies.

Classification of Research on Information Technology

All of the following chapters in this volume focus on the second phase. Now, it is appropriate to examine the differences among them. The chapters differ in their orientation. Some are decision-supporting, meaning that the technology enables tasks to be accomplished more efficiently and decisions to be made more effectively. Others are cooperation-enabling, encouraging communication or cooperation. The final group of chapters can be called infrastructure-enabling, because they make it possible to use more efficiently the information resources we possess.

Decision-Supporting Technologies

Some technologies are aimed directly at solving problems. A decision-supporting technology implies that the emerging technology directly affects the capacity of an individual, organization, or team to create models efficiently, make more effective decisions, or develop alternatives and solutions. The promise of increased productivity, rationalization, or an extension of the limit of bounded design rationality motivates the development and use of decision-supporting technologies. Typical elements of decision-supporting information technologies are GUI interfaces (to improve user interaction with decision models), speech recognition (to make data entry more efficient), and hypertext (to organize and retrieve information more effectively). The use of these decision-supporting technologies will result in more effective decisions, better service to customers, and more effective management of information.

Cooperation-Enabling Technologies

A cooperation-enabling technology means that the technology provides ways to enable, intensify, or expand the interactions of multiple agents (i.e., organizational members) in the execution of a planning, design, decision, or implementation task. Use of cooperation-enabling technologies is motivated by users' bounded rationality and accrued higher costs of coordination and communication. Sometimes, technologies can be used to help reduce geographical and/or time constraints. Cooperation-enabling technologies cover control technologies that are means of enforcing rules, policies, or priorities over development activities and resources (Orlikowski, 1991); and cooperative technologies, which are ways for improving the sharing and exchange of information that can affect the concept, process, or product of information systems (IS) development (Chen, Nunamaker, & Weber, 1989). Examples of cooperation-enabling technologies are group support systems (cooperation); Executive Information Systems (control, cooperation, and planning); email (communication); and video conferencing (cooperation). The use of these cooperation-enabling technologies will result in better managerial planning and group decision making.

Infrastructure-Enabling Technologies

The purpose of an infrastructure-enabling technology is to make everything come together. These technologies form procedures, standards, and practices that determine the broader environment in which decision-supporting and cooperation-enabling technologies are put into practice. Their use is motivated by the increased effectiveness, visibility, and organizational and societal efficiency gained from standardized organizational and societal behavior. Infrastructure-enabling technologies include support functions that provide help to users (hypertext help systems), ways to conduct international and personal business (E-commerce), approaches to seeking and storing information (using search engines), and personal and organizational productivity (improved office automation). Use of infrastructure-enabling technologies will allow individuals, organizations, and society to accomplish typical tasks more efficiently and effectively.

Contributions From Research on Emerging Decision-Supporting Technologies

Research that can be classified as possessing a decision-supporting technology is considered first. This classification includes the following five chapters in this book: the first chapter by Stohr and Viswanathan, on using recommendation systems; the

TABLE 1.1 Contributions From Research Relating to the Emerging Decision-Supporting Technologies

Authors	Emerging Technology	Contributions From This Research on Technological Emergence
Stohr and Viswanathan	Recommendation systems	The authors demonstrate that recommendation systems can be used to help users with major decisions, such as purchasing equipment for corporations, or for deciding on other major personal or corporate purchases. They provide an original classification of recommendation systems based on the source of expertise underlying the recommendation.
González and Kasper	Animation	Decision quality of subjects exposed to parallel navigation interactivity was greater than that of those exposed to sequential interactivity; image realism/abstraction and transition effects require further research.
Ramarapu et al.	Hypertext	When doing perceptual problems, users of the hypertext, or nonlinear, system were able to make decisions more quickly and accurately; this translated into superior problem solving as well as higher user satisfaction.
Gray	Data warehousing	Gray derives nine characteristics of a data warehouse: the data are subject oriented, integrated, nonvolatile, time series not current status, summarized, larger due to the attributes of time series data, not normalized, metadata (data about data), and partially derived from input that is from legacy systems.
Ein-Dor	Artificial intelligence	Ein-Dor discusses two important and currently popular approaches: neural networks and genetic algorithms. State-of-the-art applications—such as the latest in human-computer interfaces, developments in expert systems, a variety of autonomous intelligent machines, and the future of data mining—are all discussed and meticulously evaluated for their usefulness in advancing the AI field and for their potential to help humankind.

second chapter by González and Kasper, on animation for decision support systems (DSS) user interfaces; the third chapter by Ramarapu, Frolick, Wilkes, and Wetherbe, researching the use of hypertext for learning; the fourth chapter by Gray, on the characteristics of data warehousing; and the fifth chapter by Ein-Dor, on artificial intelligence (AI). The research contributions of these five chapters are summarized in Table 1.1.

Taking the group of five decision-supporting technology chapters as a whole, it is possible to see that the emerging technologies of recommendation systems, animation, hypertext, data warehousing, and AI cover a wide range of technologies designed to affect the way that many users in many different tasks are supported in decision making with the help of recommendation systems based on a variety of inputs, making decisions through the use of animated interfaces, solving problems with the enabling capacities of hypertext, making decisions with high-quality data culled from a data warehouse, and using AI in expert systems to solve organizational problems.

Recommendation Systems

Stohr and Viswanathan provide an insightful overview of recommendation systems, highlighting their increasingly important role in the information economy. They survey the field and attempt to understand where such systems fit into the support of decision making in electronic commerce. They go on to explore the technical foundations of recommendation systems, suggesting original implications of their use for managers and raising the critical issues that surround how such systems will be deployed and adopted in organizations.

The authors make a distinction between a narrowly defined *recommender* system and their preferred terminology, *recommendation systems,* which indicate systems that make recommendations by any means, whether human or automated (in full or part). Stohr and Viswanathan make a credible case for why recommendation systems should not be relegated to small or medium matters of decision support, such as ranking films, restaurants, books, and so on. Rather, they demonstrate that recommendation systems can be used to help users with major decisions, such as purchasing equipment for corporations, or for deciding on other major personal or corporate purchases. They provide an original classification of recommendation systems based on the source of expertise underlying the recommendation. This results in utility-based systems, content-based systems, collaborative systems, and expert consultation. Within the complicated and burgeoning demand for electronic commerce applications, the authors see a huge potential market for recommendation systems that collect and analyze user tastes and needs, on one hand, and on the other hand flag the quality of products and services.

Animation for Decision Support

González and Kasper take an imaginative approach to the emerging technology of animation by explicitly linking animation and its role in DSS user interfaces. This is innovative in at least two important regards: the first is the opening of an entire realm of possibility with the use of animation in DSS interfaces; the other is their systematic examination of the effect of animation on decision quality via the development and testing of an original framework. González and Kasper define animation as it pertains to the use of DSS interfaces as "images presented dynamically that change, guided by the user, in ways that improve decision quality."

The authors used a laboratory experiment to compare differences in the quality of decisions made by a sample of 89 student subjects who used differing animation designs in DSS interfaces to accomplish two different decision tasks. In this way, they empirically tested three hypotheses that arose via their original framework.

González and Kasper are able to contribute some useful results, building on their premise that decision quality is affected by the design of animation. The authors examine interactivity (whether it was parallel or sequential) and find that parallel navigation interactivity translates to superior decision quality. They also examine variables of image abstraction, in other words, whether the images presented to decision makers in DSS should be realistic or abstract. With several caveats concerning the type of decision task, they recommend more realistic images for better decision quality. González and Kasper also examine whether transitions among images should be gradual or abrupt, and (although the results differed depending on the task and were not compelling) they recommend using gradual rather than abrupt transitions between animated images if quality of decision is important.

Hypertext for Problem Solving

Ramarapu et al. study hypertext and problem solving to assess empirically whether problem solving using nonlinear links would have better results than would problem solving using conventional, or linear, links. Their study makes a contribution by empirically substantiating relationships that have been part of our intuitions only prior to this time.

Ramarapu et al. used 64 graduate business students to study whether problem solving and user satisfaction were better under linear or nonlinear experimental problem-solving treatments. They used both analytical and perceptual tasks. Interestingly, their findings indicate that the hypertext, or nonlinear system, translated into superior problem solving as well as higher user satisfaction than did the experimental treatment with the linear system. Users were able to make decisions more quickly and accurately when doing perceptual problems using the nonlinear system.

However, when doing analytical-type tasks, users were able to perform more rapidly using the experimental nonlinear system. Accuracy of problem solving for the analytical task was seemingly not influenced by whether the system was hypertext or linear.

The authors move us to further question the importance of the World Wide Web hypertext-based structure for problem solving, and they also give rise to questions about the criticality of evaluating the type of decision task (analytical or perceptual, or some combination thereof) to be supported by a linear or hypertext system.

Data Warehousing

Gray recounts the phenomenon of data warehousing as a major information systems development of the 1990s. He uses an original historical/critical approach to define the meaning of data warehouse, and he discusses how a data warehouse works, how it is being applied in decision support systems, data mining, and database marketing. Additionally, he offers an insightful appraisal of the significance of warehouses for managers.

Gray notes that data warehousing has origins in the need to improve the data underlying DSS and executive information systems (EIS). There are high standards of quality necessary to fill a data warehouse with data that will be useful for a variety of managerial and strategic decision systems. The data included must be clean, validated, and properly aggregated. Gray derives nine characteristics of a data warehouse—the data are (a) subject oriented, (b) integrated, (c) nonvolatile, (d) time series not current status, (e) summarized, (f) larger due to the attributes of time series data, (g) not normalized, (h) metadata (data about data), and (i) partially derived from input that is from legacy systems. Gray proceeds to provide insights on the data warehousing industry, indicating that the total world market is currently estimated to be in the 6 to 8 billion dollar range. Additional analysis reveals three popular applications of data warehousing in industry, and the final part of the chapter provides a well-grounded managerial perspective on the use and future of data warehouses for organizations. Gray urges the reader to put the data warehouse in the context of its business value for the organization, rather than focus on technological aspects alone.

Artificial Intelligence

Ein-Dor provides a fascinating tour of the history of artificial intelligence. He deftly chronicles a variety of paradigms prevalent in AI. He characterizes the AI field as an emerging technology and identifies the major obstacles to the further development of artificial intelligence.

Additionally, Ein-Dor discusses two important and currently popular approaches: neural networks and genetic algorithms. State-of-the-art applications—such as the latest in human-computer interfaces, developments in expert systems, a variety of autonomous intelligent machines, and the future of data mining—are all discussed and meticulously evaluated for their usefulness in advancing the AI field and for their potential to help humankind. Several specific predictions for the future are ventured, including the widespread use of softbots and immobots on the Web, real-time vision systems, and the emergence of domain-dependent systems for natural language processing. Ein-Dor puts all of his predictions within a time frame, making the usually difficult task of comparing AI development with other predictions for the future of information technology relatively effortless.

Contributions From Research on Emerging Cooperation-Facilitating Technologies

The second group of chapters can be classified as possessing a cooperation-facilitating technology. The emphasis here is on supporting a multitude of capabilities for use by multiple participants so that the capabilities are strengthened in their interactions. Cooperation-facilitating technologies span control capabilities that

TABLE 1.2 Contributions From Research Relating to the Emerging Cooperation-Facilitating Technologies

Authors	Emerging Technology	Contributions From This Research on Technological Emergence
King and Xia	Communication Media	Individual differences and individual experience with a communication medium may be better explanations of media choice phenomena than the prevailing theories of rationality and media appropriateness.
Williams and Wilson	Group support systems (GSS)	Respondents perceive that GSS serve as an equalizing force on the power and influence exercised by others in the organization. GSS increase users' participation in decision making, seem to improve access to information and people in the company, and allow users an increased opportunity to influence the opinions of other people in the organization.
Rai and Bajwa	Executive information systems (EIS)	Organizations adopting EIS faced greater environmental uncertainty, possessed more heterogeneity, and were more hostile than were organizations that did *not* adopt EIS.
Warkentin, Sayeed, and Hightower	Web-based conferencing	Teams using this Web-based computer-mediated communication system could not outperform face-to-face groups that experienced the same problem-solving task. Group cohesion may be difficult to develop in a virtual environment, the usual ways in which groups control members are not available in cyberspace, and losing members might be a common and unfortunate occurrence.

help enforce policies and procedures to which their users are subject as well as supporting cooperative endeavors. The four chapters included in this classification are the chapter by King and Xia, who examine usage of different communication media; the chapter by Williams and Wilson, who examine group support systems (GSS); the chapter by Rai and Bajwa, who study EIS; and the chapter by Warkentin, Sayeed, and Hightower, who explore Web-based conferencing. The research contributions of these four chapters are shown in Table 1.2.

The four cooperation-facilitating technology chapters show us that the communication media choices of email, voice mail, and fax—as well as group support systems, executive information systems, and Web-based conferencing—are emerging information technologies that feature aspects of cooperation and control for individuals and teams. Taken as a group, the results of these studies also reflect that researching the cooperation-facilitating technologies and their capabilities is critical to further our understanding of how they are currently functioning in work situations. Additionally, this type of research demonstrates how cooperation-facilitating technologies can be designed better in the future. Not only can they fully support the functions necessary for individuals and teams to reach their goals, but they can also promote the building of relationships to help achieve those goals. Furthermore, cooperation-facilitating technologies can facilitate the embedding of organizational responses (often codified in policies, practices, strategies, and tactics) that foster learning, implementation, and use of emerging information technologies far beyond the work life of any one particular employee.

Communication Media Choices

King and Xia tackle the complex issue of how organizations can help their employees realize early benefits from the adoption of new information technologies by examining how learning experiences with nine different communication media (an electronic meeting system [EMS], email, voice mail, fax, telephone, group meetings, face-to-face communication, letters, and handwritten notes) effect perception of media choice appropriateness. They find that in order to receive desired benefits of new information technology, organizations must do more than simply adopt the technology. They must provide organizational opportunities for individuals to learn new communication media.

Additionally, the research contribution of King and Xia is useful to many IS and communication researchers who are currently formulating their research strategies based on popular and prevalent theories of media richness or social presence. King and Xia find that individual differences and individual experiences with a communication medium may be better explanations of media choice phenomena than the prevailing theories of rationality and media appropriateness. As such, the contribution of this chapter may be considerable in altering the course of research into media choice.

King and Xia conducted a longitudinal, quasi-experimental study using 295 MBA students to answer the question of whether "the individuals' perception of media-task appropriateness remains stable over time as experience changes." Media appropriateness was measured by abstract schemes of tasks, and self-report measures were used to capture an individual's experience with a medium. The authors found that learning experience affected an individual's perception of media appropriateness, particularly as it pertains to use of a new medium. They also found that use of an old medium may dwindle as a new medium is used. They concluded that organizations can mediate effectively the use of communication technology by providing systematic training and experience for individuals when introducing new communication technologies.

Group Support Systems

In their study of group support systems (GSS), Williams and Wilson use in-depth interviews, observation, and documents to examine organizational context issues in light of the perceptions of GSS users. Their work addresses the notable absence of other reported research examining the use of GSS, power, and influence in organizations. The Williams and Wilson chapter begins to address this lack in the literature.

The authors purposefully chose 15 users from a division of a major U.S. software development company specializing in the development of business software tools for desktop PCs. These users formed a cross-section of all GSS users in the company. Their rich qualitative evidence suggests many avenues for future research that can be investigated with other techniques, including modeling of organizational variables in a quantitative correlation model.

Williams and Wilson confirm the existence of some of the user perceptions that early GSS developers had hoped to evoke in the initial development of GSS. They found that their respondents perceived that group support systems increase users' participation in decision-making processes in the organization, and also seem to improve access to information and people in the company by making them more approachable. GSS users also report that using the group support system allows them an increased opportunity to influence the opinions of other people in the organization. All of these are made possible by the perception that GSS serve as an equalizing force on the power and influence exercised by others in the organization.

Executive Information Systems

The research conducted by Rai and Bajwa develops a theoretical model to examine how a particular set of contextual factors affects the adoption and implementation of executive information systems (EIS) in organizations. Their findings confirm much of what has become part of our best practices in systems implementation, and they mirror much of what we already know about how to conduct successful implementations of other information technology. They also provide practical guidelines for organizations attempting to adopt and implement this emerging technology.

Using a survey methodology, Rai and Bajwa collected data from 210 organizations. Overall, they have found that EIS are not broadly in place in the organizations they surveyed, and that the levels of implementation fluctuate across different managerial functions. Rai and Bajwa examine the low level of EIS diffusion in the organizations represented. They found that numerous environmental and organizational complexities serve to ensure that EIS will be adopted successfully to serve managerial functions such as communication, coordination, control, and planning.

The authors call for a more thorough study of what it means to support executives with information, asserting that focusing on executive information will enable developers to create systems that address urgent needs in an appealing way.

Penetration of the emerging technology of EIS is limited at this time. Only one third of the organizations surveyed had adopted EIS, with communication being the most frequently supported managerial function. The authors found that organizations adopting EIS were faced with greater environmental uncertainty, possessed more heterogeneity, and were more hostile than were organizations that did *not* adopt EIS.

Web-Based Conferencing

Warkentin, Sayeed, and Hightower conducted an exploratory study of Web-based conferencing using a customized version of Meeting Web™, which is a software product developed by CitySource, Inc. Teams using this Web-based computer-mediated communication system (CMCS) could not outperform face-to-face groups that experienced the same problem-solving task.

This result notwithstanding, the authors make an important contribution to our understanding of real versus virtual teams. They wonder whether the advantages of virtual teams (efficiency, time shifting, automatic documentation, support of geographic dispersion, masking of [irrelevant] social cues) may not be outweighed by some serious disadvantages that surfaced throughout the study. Group cohesion may be difficult to develop, and virtual team members may not develop the strong bonds that can actually improve group communication. They also note that the usual ways in which organizations control team members are not available in cyberspace, and that losing members might be a common and unfortunate occurrence.

Warkentin et al. assert that virtual team communication alters the rules under which we normally communicate. Fortunately, teams can be supported by companies in strengthening the relationships among virtual team members. One of the many suggestions coming out of this study is the idea of combining interactive media during different phases of a relationship. For instance, during early formative meetings, people who will be members of virtual teams should be encouraged to meet face-to-face to set up implicit and explicit norms, share expectations, and begin working together to fashion a relationship flexible enough to withstand the vagaries of virtual meetings.

Contributions From Research on Emerging Infrastructure-Enabling Technologies

The third group of chapters can be classified as possessing an infrastructure-enabling technology. The emphasis here is on technology that provides ways to enable, intensify, or expand the interactions of multiple agents (i.e., organizational members) in the execution of a planning, design, decision, or implementation task. The four chapters included here are the chapter by Kendall and Kendall, on information delivery systems (IDS); the chapter by Zwass, on electronic commerce (E-commerce); the chapter by Guimaraes and Igbaria, on client/server technology; and the final chapter in the volume, by Davis and Naumann, which covers knowledge work productivity systems. The research contributions of these four chapters are shown in Table 1.3.

When surveying the four chapters on infrastructure-enabling technologies as a whole, it is clear that the technologies provide great power—through the use of IDS that feature search engines for use in seeking and storing information, via the use of E-commerce for users to conduct personal and international business, through

TABLE 1.3 Contributions From Research Relating to the Emerging Infrastructure-Enabling Technologies

Authors	Emerging Technology	Contributions From This Research on Technological Emergence
Kendall and Kendall	Information delivery systems (IDS)	The authors identify and classify eight types of information delivery systems (four Web pull and four push technologies). They predict that pull technology will use an evolutionary agent to obtain what the user needs, and push technology will use data mining to deliver what users need. Future technologies that may overcome some of users' frustration with current IDS are described.
Zwass	E-commerce	The author develops an original hierarchical framework to assist in understanding E-commerce. This hierarchy consists of three metalevels, designated as infrastructure, services, and products and structures, which in turn consist of seven functional levels.
Guimaraes and Igbaria	Client/server	Developers' skills and organizational support were found to be the most important factors affecting the success of implementing the client server technology according to user perceptions. The skills demonstrated by the client/server systems developers appeared to have the strongest effect on the satisfaction of end users.
Davis and Naumann	Knowledge work productivity systems	The authors note that individual knowledge workers bear great responsibility for increasing their own productivity by applying productivity principles and developing technology skills. For their part, organizations have managerial responsibility for providing appropriate technology infrastructure, along with establishing organizational forms and suitable training and help facilities where new information technologies can be learned and embedded into the organizational culture.

approaches to planning and implementing systems available with client/server technology, and through the use of knowledge work productivity systems to improve personal and organizational productivity.

Information Delivery Systems

Kendall and Kendall have created the term *information delivery systems,* or IDS, to denote an entire class of Web-based emerging information systems that include push and pull technologies. The providers of these technologies are intent on enabling users to receive, access, analyze, and handle Web information such as news, audio, video, and music in ways that will be useful on a personal or corporate level. The authors identify and classify eight types of IDS that they label as alpha-, beta-, gamma-, and delta-*pull* technologies, as well as alpha-, beta-, gamma-, and delta-*push* technologies. Each of these categories addresses successively refined capabilities of pull and push.

Throughout the chapter, as Kendall and Kendall name each technology, they also describe it, provide a predominant metaphor being used in conjunction with the technology, and then indicate which aspects of user wants or needs the technology addresses. Each level of pull and push technology is illustrated with current examples of content from Web providers.

Early IDS technologies helped users find information by surfing the Web (pull technology), followed by Webcasters delivering content in the form of channels, subscriptions, streaming video, and event reproduction (push technology). Early pull and push technologies were unsatisfactory because users could not find or pull the information they needed very easily, nor did users feel that the content being pushed was what they wanted.

Kendall and Kendall predict that future information delivery systems will continue to develop. Delta-pull technology will use an evolutionary agent to observe user decision-making behavior and seek the information the user actually needs. Delta-push technology will use techniques similar to data mining so that Webcasters deliver precisely what users need.

Current corporate applications of pull and push technologies are provided, and original managerial and social implications of higher-level IDS are elaborated, along with a preview of future technologies that are predicted to overcome some of users' frustration with current IDS.

E-Commerce

The topic of electronic commerce (or E-commerce) is skillfully explored by Zwass, who defines it as sharing business information, maintaining business relationships, and conducting business transactions by means of telecommunications networks.

Zwass stresses as critical the arrival of the commercial use of the Internet via the Web as the driving force of the new E-commerce since 1993. He analyzes the present structure of E-commerce and also looks forward to future developments in E-commerce. Zwass develops an original hierarchical framework to assist in understanding E-commerce. This hierarchy consists of three metalevels that are designated as infrastructure, services, and products and structures, which in turn consist of seven functional levels. These levels of E-commerce development range from wide-area telecommunications infrastructure to electronic marketplaces and electronic hierarchies. Products and structures of E-commerce cover its three categories of consumer-oriented commerce, business-to-business commerce, and intraorganizational business. Zwass highlights the problems inherent with the existence of E-commerce on the Web, and he also contemplates thoughtfully the stage of rapid and sustained development that E-commerce has now entered.

Client/Server Systems

Client/server systems (CSS) were studied by Guimaraes and Igbaria, who develop a model to examine the success of CSS implementation. One important contribution they make is based on their assertion that past models of successful implementation of information systems should be tested using new client/server technology as the focus. The Guimaraes and Igbaria model centers around people in their interactions with client/server systems, and specifically, they test the relationships among management support, end-user characteristics, developer skills, and end-user involvement in the CSS development process, with three measures of system success that they call end-user satisfaction, usage of the system, and impact on end-users' jobs.

The methodology used by Guimaraes and Igbaria was to construct a questionnaire incorporating questions about previously validated models of human factors and their relationship to system implementation. The questionnaire was sent to 500 IS seminar participants, with 148 usable questionnaires returned by IS managers and end-user department managers who were involved with a client/server system project that had been operational for at least 1 year. The authors used structural equation modeling to test the relationships they had hypothesized among the variables.

Guimaraes and Igbaria found that developers' skills and organizational support were the most important factors affecting the success of implementing the client/server technology. The skills demonstrated by the CSS developers appeared to have the strongest effect on the satisfaction of end users. The authors correctly estimate that the significance of their results will grow in importance as more organizations adopt Web-based systems that feature information-pull applications.

Knowledge Work Productivity Systems

Davis and Naumann describe the productivity problem in knowledge work by noting that there are large productivity differences among individuals, and that this is amplified by an increasing percentage of workers in the knowledge work class. They discuss methods for improving productivity in knowledge work by organizing knowledge work around effectiveness and efficiency strategies. A whole handful of information technologies can improve and support knowledge work, including tools that enhance productivity of individual knowledge workers, system management utility software, and group-oriented software. The authors describe the features and functions of information technologies that support knowledge work activities and then provide a creative mapping of them to the strategies for improving knowledge work effectiveness and efficiency.

Davis and Naumann note that knowledge work productivity has important and far-ranging implications for individuals and organizations. Individual knowledge workers bear great responsibility for increasing their own productivity by applying productivity principles and developing technology skills. For their part, organizations have managerial responsibility for providing appropriate technology infrastructure, along with establishing organizational forms and suitable training and help facilities where new information technologies can be learned and embedded into the organizational culture.

Conclusion

As you read through this volume, you will notice that each emerging information technology appears to encounter a different barrier that must be overcome, and each obstacle carries implications for future research. When all of the barriers are removed the technology can be said to have advanced to the technological sublime phase. Nye (1996) summarized the impact of achieving this phase succinctly when he stated:

> The sublime underlies this enthusiasm for technology. One of the most powerful of human emotions, when experienced by large groups the sublime can weld society together. In moments of sublimity, human beings temporarily disregard divisions among elements of the community. (p. xiii)

The chief barriers encountered along the way of advancing to the phase of the technological sublime are conceived of as uncertainty concerning the value of the emerging information technology; the resistance or difficulty with use of it; and the complexities of implementation, as illustrated in Figure 1.1. Each of the emerging technologies researched in this book has met or will meet certain obstacles in moving from the emergence phase into the technological sublime.

Honestly appraised, our progress through phases of technological advancement is anything but a smooth ride. Moving by fits and starts, greeted with disheartening setbacks and exhilaratingly great leaps, we struggle as information systems researchers to understand what is happening, how, and why. We ask, "Who will be involved in the complex processes of moving to the next phase of information technology?" all the while fretting over who *should* be involved in moving toward the technological sublime. We question and query, anxiously wondering what roles we are to play—as researchers, as organizational members, as humans in society—as we witness an explosion of technology undreamed of even in the past generation.

The answer echoes back to us through the research presented here: *We* are the ones who must understand how to implement new information technology; *we* must comprehend its uses; *we* must make the determinations of how best to value it. And although the invention or discovery of new technologies seems at times to be tinged with an aura of inevitability, our reactions and creations as researchers must not be.

Indeed, the authors whose work is represented here were not satisfied to let information technology just happen, sans chronicling, sans examination. Their contributions have made it possible to carry forward an enlightened dialogue about

Emerging Information Technologies 17

```
Information Technology  →  Uncertainty Concerning the Value of
                            Emerging Information Technologies

Information Technology  →  The Resistance or Difficulty with Use
                            of Emerging Information Technologies

Information Technology  →  Complexities of Implementing
                            Emerging Information Technologies
```

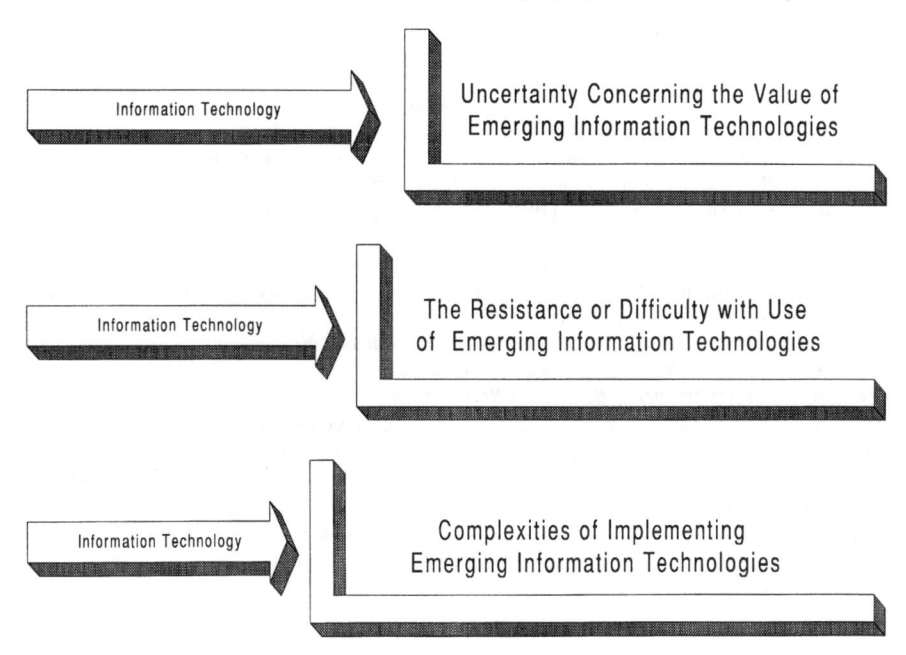

Figure 1.1. Barriers That Have To Be Faced by Emerging Information Technologies

emerging information technologies. Derry and Williams (1993), in their book *A Short History of Technology*, were cautiously optimistic about human technological advancements made thus far, stating:

> But to the more searching question, whether technological progress has on balance added to the happiness of the individual, we can at best offer no more than an affirmative answer hedged with qualifications, rejecting the temptation to pretend to weigh imponderables. (p. 710)

But even acknowledging this careful assessment, we are now empowered to ask discerning questions, refine our hypotheses, reconstitute our samples, supplement our methods, and examine our results with confidence that the answers we derive will help shape our future in ways that will benefit whole societies, not just individuals. This last is critical, for as Harrington (1962) observed, "If there is technological advance without social advance, there is, almost automatically, an increase in human misery, in impoverishment." Information systems researchers can be instrumental in preparing the way for a transition to the technological sublime that is mirrored by our corresponding development as a society.

References

The American heritage™ *dictionary of the English language.* (3rd ed.). (1992). Boston: Houghton Mifflin. Electronic version licensed from InfoSoft International, Inc.

Benamati, J., Lederer, A. L., & Singh, M. (1997). Changing information technology and information technology management. *Information & Management, 31,* 275-288.

Chen, M., Nunamaker J., & Weber, S. (1989, Spring). Computer-aided software engineering: Present status and future directions. *Data Base, 1,* 7-13.

Dery, M. (1996). *Escape velocity: Cyberculture at the end of the century.* New York: Grove.

Derry, T. K., & Williams, T. L. (1993). *A short history of technology: From the earliest times to A. D. 1900.* New York: Dover.

Harrington, M. (1993). The other America. In *The Columbia dictionary of quotations* (Appendix, sec. 1) [CD-ROM]. New York: Columbia University Press.

Negroponte, N. P. (1995). *Being digital.* New York: Vintage.

Nye, D. E. (1996). *American technological sublime.* Cambridge: MIT Press.

Orlikowski, W. (1991). Integrated information environment or matrix of control? The contradictory implications of information technology. *Accounting, Management and Information Technologies, 1*(1), 9-42.

Slouka, M. (1995). *War of the worlds: Cyberspace and the high-tech assault on reality.* New York: Basic Books.

Stoll, C. (1996). *Silicon snake oil.* New York: Anchor/Doubleday.

PART ONE

DECISION-SUPPORTING TECHNOLOGIES

CHAPTER TWO

Recommendation Systems

Decision Support for the Information Economy

EDWARD A. STOHR
SIVAKUMAR VISWANATHAN

It is five years hence, the dawn of the new millenium. The World Wide Web serves 500 million people and is inhabited by several billion software agents. A large part of the world economy is on-line. Organizations are networked in a constantly changing kaleidoscope of relationships—some fleeting, others mutating slowly. Competition is for the intelligent and agile—those organizations that have mastered the arts of discovering new value propositions, nurturing customer relationships, and executing their core functions rapidly and faultlessly. Human beings in the developed nations are totally dependent on the electronic world for their education, entertainment, communication, and commerce.

Is such a world possible? Simple extrapolation of current exponential growth trends indicates that the above human and software agent population figures are not unreasonable. The feasibility of such a vision, however, rests on issues of system stability and human benefits. Can an electronic economy making millions of decisions per minute and executing billions of transactions and transferring trillions of dollars per day remain stable? Or, will there be an electronic world financial crisis that will make the recent Asian crisis seem like a minor blip? Will the evolving electronic society actually benefit mankind? Will it create an elite of whiz-kid millionaires controlling vast electronic financial resources and a huge underclass of the less fortunate or less able? We are already experiencing an almost unbearable flood of information and communication requirements that sap our time—thus making it increasingly valuable—and make leisure more difficult. How can we realize the benefits of the increased productivity that we feel instinctively can be provided by the information revolution?

The questions raised in the previous paragraph probably can be answered only in practice as new markets, organizational forms, and lifestyles evolve from the maelstrom of electronic commerce. In this chapter, we will concentrate on only one

22 EMERGING INFORMATION TECHNOLOGIES

```
┌─────────────────────────┐
│ Information search and  │──────────┐
│ discovery technologies  │          │
└─────────────────────────┘          ▼
┌─────────────────────────┐   ┌──────────────────────────┐
│ Technologies for        │──▶│ Decision support and     │
│ understanding information│   │ decision-making technologies│
└─────────────────────────┘   └──────────────────────────┘
┌─────────────────────────┐          ▲
│ Technologies for controlling│──────┘
│ and filtering information  │
└─────────────────────────┘
```

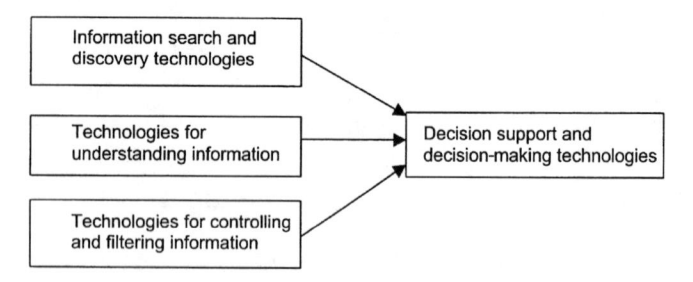

Figure 2.1. A Classification of Technologies for Coping With the Information Explosion

necessary condition for the existence of such an electronic world. Our thesis is that we need new technologies to help individuals and firms cope with the evolving information ecology—coping technologies to manage the information-producing technologies (which, if unchecked, could actually become disabling technologies). The emphasis in information technology research and practice must turn from producing information to controlling and managing it. The emphasis needs to be on shaping the information into forms that are more useful and accessible, condensing it, filtering out noisy elements, finding useful nuggets of information on demand, analyzing them, and creating new knowledge—using every means at our disposal to make the new information universe friendly, understandable, and useful. The technologies for doing this are exciting and challenging. Some have been around since the early days of computer and management science, and others are emerging in response to the new electronic realities.

The technologies fall into four groups (see Figure 2.1). The first group consists of technologies for discovering information: search engines, directories, electronic markets, and electronic auctions. The second group is technologies for controlling and restricting the flow of information to which we are subject: filtering and alerting systems. The third group is technologies for understanding information: knowledge representation, visualization, data mining, and the tools of statistics and management science. Finally, the fourth group consists of technologies to assist decision making: recommender systems and "electronic butler" systems (Tuzhilin, 1998). The first three categories of technology—those for discovering, controlling, and understanding information—provide support for the fourth category—that of decision support and decision making.

In this chapter, we will concentrate on the fourth set of technologies and, within that, only on a new class of systems that has been called recommender systems. Our objective is to provide an overview of recommender systems and their role in the information economy. We look at where they fit in the panoply of technologies that have been developed to support decision making in electronic commerce, their technical foundations, managerial implications, and issues that surround their deployment and adoption.

Recommendation Systems as a Decision Technology

Recommendation systems provide information about the relative merits of alternative courses of action. In everyday life, when faced with a choice for which we lack adequate information, we often turn to various guides such as *Consumer Choice* magazine, Zagat's restaurant guide, knowledgeable friends, experts, and so on. The function of these guides is to increase the probability that we will be satisfied with the results of our decision making. Recommendation systems are electronic versions of such everyday systems.

There is a subtle definitional issue. As originally conceived, and by common usage, recommender systems are automated systems in which people (recommenders) provide recommendations as inputs, which the systems then aggregate and direct to appropriate recipients (Resnick & Varian, 1997). This is narrower than the definition of the previous paragraph, which essentially says that recommender systems make recommendations (by any means). We prefer the broader definition—first, because it is more goal-oriented, and second, because the narrow definition seems unnecessarily restrictive. Strictly interpreted, for example, the narrow definition would not include the use of intelligent software agents as recommenders, nor would it include information filtering systems that make recommendations based on content analysis in which a user's interest profile is matched with document content profiles. Worse still, many recommender systems are really hybrids in which the source of the recommendations is both human and nonhuman (e.g., collaborative filtering plus content analysis). To distinguish between the broad and narrow definitions of recommender systems, we will call the former *recommendation* systems. Because this is a new area for computer support, it is worthwhile taking some pains to make the definitions as clear as possible. We move from the general to the particular (see Figure 2.2).

The objective of decision technologies in general is to overcome the limits of our bounded rationality—to help us make better decisions, more quickly, and with less expenditure of effort. Decision-making technologies automate the decision-making process and remove the human element. Automated inventory systems are a prime example. More recently, Tuzhilin (1998) has suggested that automated decision making be extended to include everyday activities such as shopping. He has proposed "electronic butler" services that use the past history of user purchases to infer a subset of purchases that can be made automatically without user consultation.

Decision support systems (DSS) were originally conceived as an alternative to computerized decision-making systems for use in situations in which the human inputs were necessary because the decision situation was not highly structured (programmable) and, therefore, required human judgment and intuition (Gorry & Scott Morton, 1971). The role of the computer was to provide information via databases or models to help in the decision-making process (Alter, 1977). An interesting consequence of the new information economy is that a decision situation

24   EMERGING INFORMATION TECHNOLOGIES

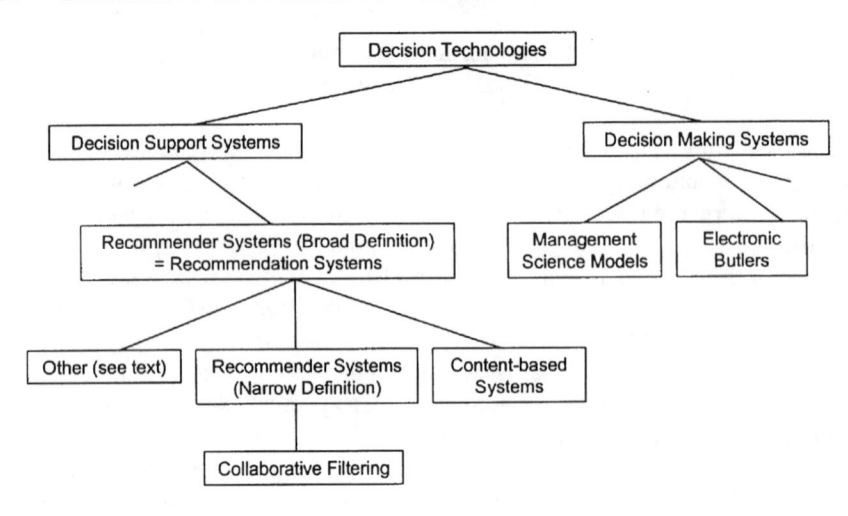

Figure 2.2. Partial Classification of Decision Technologies

can become unstructured as a result of a glut of information and the speed at which decisions have to be made. Users then need computer support, not only because of the complexity of a given decision (the original DSS concept) but also because they lack the processing speed and power to cope with an overload of information and the myriad decisions that demand attention.

Recommendation systems, systems that evaluate choices, fall into this category of decision support. Typical uses of recommendation systems have been to suggest the information that a decision maker might need (filtering systems), and to rank films, restaurants, books, and so on.[1] These are small decisions, in a way, but demanding in the aggregate. However, we do not mean to restrict recommendation systems to low or medium matters of importance to individuals or organizations. Systems to assist users in decisions of major consequence, such as equipment purchases for corporations and home or automobile purchases for individuals, can also be envisaged as outlined below. Recommendation systems may use all or any information from whatever source and make use of very different processing algorithms to form their recommendations.

Recommender systems (narrow definition), on the other hand, perform the same function as recommendation systems but involve other human beings as recommenders. The recommenders may or may not explicitly collaborate with the recipients of the information because the recommenders and recipients may not be known to each other (Resnick & Varian, 1997).

Finally, collaborative filtering systems are special purpose recommender systems that filter or restrict the information delivered to recipients. They are narrower in scope than recommender systems because the latter can suggest new items of interest rather than just filter out those that are presumed to have little or no interest (Resnick

& Varian, 1997). Typically, collaborative filtering systems have been used to filter information from Internet Usenet groups (as in Grouplens; Konstan et al., 1997), provide recommendations on books (as in Amazon.com), and so on. Collaborative filtering techniques can differ in their implementation and approach, but all incorporate the use of individuals to annotate or recommend items to others. Of course, the same individual can alternate between the roles of recommender and recipient at different times.

Recommendation Systems Within a Framework for Electronic Commerce

The World Wide Web has dramatically altered the availability of information for users, but most of this information is useless or of poor quality. Given the magnitude and diversity of content and its uncertain quality, familiar search engines, such as Lycos, Yahoo, and Alta Vista, have proved inadequate. Typically, these search engines employ a fairly traditional information retrieval (IR) paradigm augmented by software agents (spiders) that continuously examine and index the content of millions of Web sites. The metamorphosis of the World Wide Web from a digital library (where the focus was on retrieval) into an electronic marketplace (where the focus now is on transactions) alters the rules of the game, calling for a new perspective and a broad range of new capabilities, institutions, and control mechanisms. The following framework provides some pointers for future directions and some insights into the role of recommendation systems in the information economy.

The framework is based on the concept of *intermediation* in an economy. Just as the traditional economy is populated by physical intermediaries in various forms who serve to facilitate transactions, the information economy requires the service of "electronic intermediaries" serving similar roles[2] on the Web. Intermediaries, by nature of their role specialization, help to reduce the risks and uncertainties that plague transactions in a traditional economy. In addition, intermediaries add value by engaging in activities that help reduce coordination costs and provide economies of scale and scope. Similarly, the information economy could benefit greatly from intermediaries who can help facilitate transactions.

The framework in Figure 2.3 is an adaptation and expansion of that contained in Kambil (1997). The framework proposes a hierarchy of 10 levels of functionality. Whereas some of the levels of functionality focus primarily on the needs of customers, others serve the needs of suppliers/manufacturers. Note that these levels are not necessarily conceptualized as strict levels in a hierarchy, that is, we do not claim that higher levels of functionality, by themselves, add more value than do those below them. Although the higher levels of functionality indicate potentially greater benefit, they also rank higher in terms of complexity of implementation and execution, besides requiring human intervention and consensus among various players. The higher levels of functionality, being inherently more complex in nature,

EMERGING INFORMATION TECHNOLOGIES

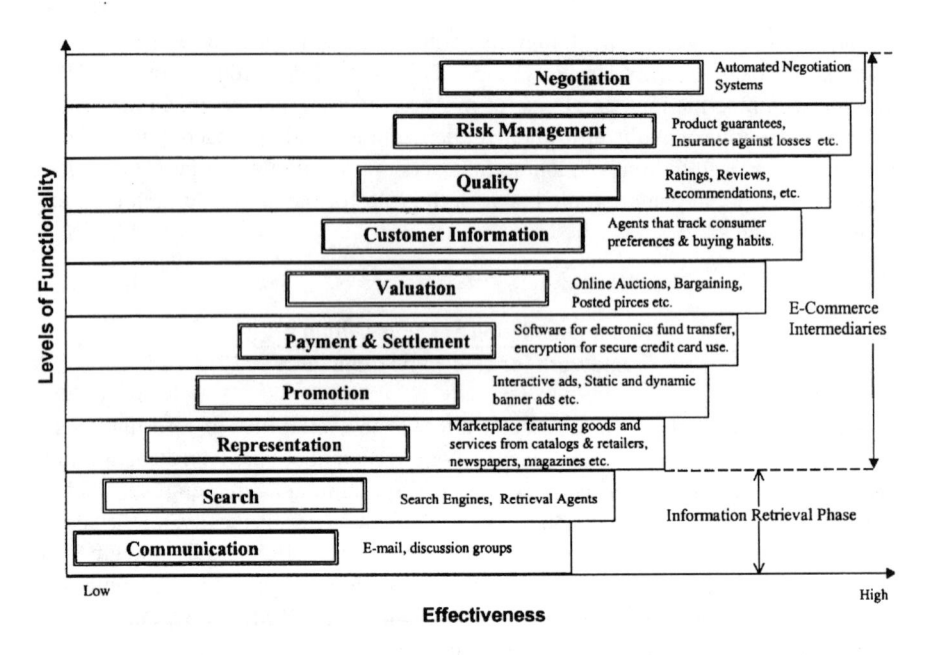

Figure 2.3. A Value Framework for Web-Based Agents

have been slower to evolve. Thus, the various levels in the framework may be conceptualized as stages in the evolution of E-commerce systems.

Web-based agents typically focus on one or more levels of functionality and strive to gain efficiencies in these. A more complete description of the framework and its implications for the design of Web-based agents and for electronic commerce in general is contained in Stohr and Viswanathan (1998).

The framework in Figure 2.3 highlights the role of recommendation systems in electronic commerce. Recommendation systems are software agents that attempt to incorporate the three functions of search and retrieval, eliciting customer information, and signaling quality. In addition, because they convey quality information, they help mitigate the risk of executing transactions on the Web.

The combination of the three functions of search and retrieval, eliciting customer information, and signaling quality in recommendation systems is ideally suitable for one-to-one marketing applications. In one-to-one marketing, firms seek to learn and satisfy the unique needs of each individual customer (Pine, Joseph, & Rogers, 1995). For example, Individual Inc.'s First! Service allows it to compete with wire, clipping, and information retrieval services (http://www.individual.com/). Clients such as MCI Telecommunications, McKinsey & Co., and Avon use the service to have customized information delivered to executives via fax, email, Lotus Notes, or their corporate Intranets. The executives first provide simple descriptions of the kinds of items in which they are interested. The system then fine-tunes these user profiles by asking the executives to rate each received article as being of high, medium, or low relevance. Over time, the ratio of medium plus highly relevant articles to the total number of articles received by the executives is reported to be as high as 80% (Pine et al., 1995). Firefly (http://www.firefly.com/) is another example of a commercial recommendation system that facilitates one-to-one marketing. The Firefly software enables businesses to create usercentric applications and services that manage personal profiles and personalize services for individual users. For example, Filmfinder (http://www.filmfinder.com/), a site that recommends movies, is enabled by Firefly. Other companies that have formed partnerships with Firefly include Barnes and Noble, Virtual Emporium, and Yahoo.

Other applications of recommendation systems on the Web include personalized recommendations of URLs; filtering of Usenet articles; blocking access to undesirable Web sites; one-to-one marketing of banking services; and shopping services for music, video, and books (Resnick & Varian, 1997). Some of these applications are discussed in more detail below. Within an organization, recommendation systems will be increasingly used in organizational learning applications in which employees share knowledge by commenting on and rating various company products, sales leads, and practices (Stein & Zwass, 1995).

Information Retrieval: The Underlying Technology for Recommendation Systems

To understand recommendation systems, it is useful to compare them with the information retrieval systems from which they have evolved. In this section, we provide a broad overview of IR as a background to the framework for recommendation systems that we develop in the next section.

An information retrieval system helps users find documents that best satisfy their need for information, or it helps them obtain information from knowledge sources for the purposes of problem management (Belkin & Croft, 1992). The term *information retrieval* is primarily associated with text retrieval. The three major areas of concern in IR research are depicted in Figure 2.4: representation of the individual's information needs, representation of the meaning of the texts/documents, and comparison of the two to find the most suitable match.

- *Information needs representation:* The information needs of a user are usually represented by means of a query consisting of a simple term or a set of terms. The query terms are usually keywords or phrases involving Boolean representation. However, given the richness of natural language, query terms are usually not accurately indicative of the user's true meaning.
- *Document representation:* Documents or texts produced by different sources are indexed (manually or automatically) to extract terms that are best representative of

28 EMERGING INFORMATION TECHNOLOGIES

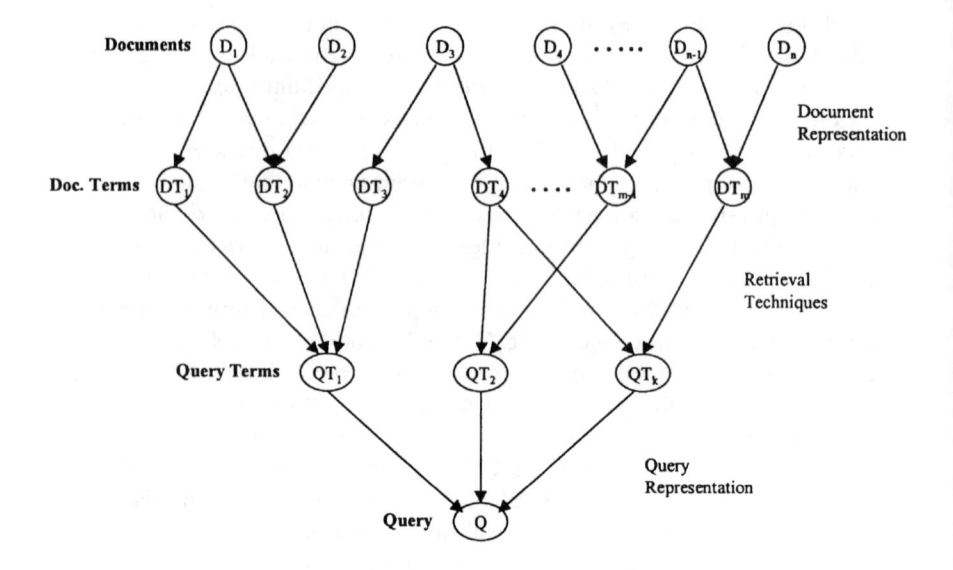

Figure 2.4. Basic Inference Network

the documents. As in the case of queries, these document terms also are not accurately indicative of the actual document meaning. Various indexing techniques (e.g., Probabilistic Indexing and TF-IDF; Salton & Buckley, 1988) have been developed in an attempt to characterize more accurately the information content of the document.

⋄ *Retrieval techniques:* The third area of concern is the comparison of the query terms with the document terms, which is the basis on which the relevant documents are retrieved. Most of the major IR models have been primarily concerned with this process of comparison.

It is inherently difficult to satisfy specific user needs with a document database indexed by librarians to serve the needs of a general audience. Associative search techniques based on probability, statistics, set theory, and logic (e.g., Boolean models, vector space models, and probabilistic retrieval models; Robertson, 1977) enable the retrieval of documents that are close, in some sense, to the user's query. These same measures of closeness can narrow the user's search for relevant documents by providing a system-determined relevance rating or ranking of retrieved articles in terms of their relevance to the user's request. In addition, relevance feedback techniques—continuously improving queries by asking the user to rate the relevance of retrieved articles—can greatly improve the performance of IR systems. IR systems that provide relevance ratings are a specialized form of recommendation system as we have defined the term.

Current IR systems depend on the "best-match" principle, that is, given a query, the best possible system response is the text whose representation most closely matches it (Belkin, Oddy, & Brooks, 1982). In turn, the best-match principle depends on the assumption of equivalence between the expression of need and the document text in that it treats the representation of the need as a representation of the document that is ideal for resolving that need. The best-match principle looks first for a document that is just like the expression of need (i.e., that is functionally equivalent to it; Belkin et al., 1982). If we know precisely what the user wants, and if we know what documents best satisfy this need, then the problem reduces to a simple matching process. Unfortunately, "noise" is inherent in each of the IR components in Figure 2.4. Users generally cannot specify precisely what information is needed to resolve a particular problem; documents are represented imprecisely by the document terms; and, although many different algorithms have been proposed, the retrieval process itself may be unsatisfactory.

Precision and recall are the two most common measures for evaluating IR effectiveness. *Precision* is defined as the percentage of items retrieved in a search that are relevant to the query, whereas *recall* is defined as the percentage of all relevant items that are retrieved in a search. Although one would like the IR system to consistently score high on both measures, there is an inherent trade-off between the two. The concept of *relevance* has, in itself, been a source of problems. Although there has been a lack of consensus regarding the concept, a system's view of relevance has dominated most of IR research. As stated by Saracevic (1975),

> The system's view of relevance was a result of thinking that relevance is mostly affected by the internal aspects and manipulations of the system. Relevance was conceived in terms of indexing, coding, classification, linguistic manipulations, file organization, and eventually question analysis and searching strategies. This thinking led to development of a myriad of schemes, and to attention to input processing and manipulation almost to the exclusion of other aspects. (p. 327)

Saracevic emphasized the need for a view of relevance that included the concept of pragmatic usefulness or "pertinence" to the needs of the user.

The problems and limitations of IR systems become acute as we move to the domain of Web-based commerce. Most of the early attempts at information retrieval on the Web (e.g., search engines and directories) have built upon the models of IR, not withstanding the fact that these systems performed best in narrow domains where the information was relatively well structured and homogeneous. The Web, though, is a very different information space, with vast differences in the structure, quantity, and quality of content. In particular, the development of electronic commerce, where the focus is on transactions involving consumer durables as well as informational items, demands a much higher level of functionality and a quite different view of relevance.

Recommendation Systems Architecture

The schematic in Figure 2.5 provides a framework for recommendation systems illustrating both their basic components and the change in perspective that differentiates them from traditional IR systems. The dotted lines in the figure encompass the areas of concern of IR systems (see Figure 2.5).

The major differences between IR and recommendation systems are, first, that the objects of interest may be general items (goods) as well as informational items, and second, that the pertinence, or relevance of the retrieved items to the user's actual needs (utility), is paramount. These two differences imply capabilities that are not found in IR systems.

Returning to our earlier discussion, recommendation systems provide information about the relative merits of alternative choices or courses of action. The objects of choice can be informational, such as articles, books, and Web sites. In this case, the recommendation system might produce a relevance ranking for the user query, as in IR systems, or it might choose from a large population of information items only those that should be of importance to the user, as in filtering systems. Alternatively, the objects of choice could be durables, such as cars and houses; consumable items, such as plays, movies, and concerts; or abstract entities, such as stocks and other investment vehicles. In the sequel, the various alternatives considered by the recommendation system will be said to belong to its choice domain. The choice domain may be constructed on the fly in answer to a particular user request, or it might be an index or database that is maintained by the system and continuously updated.

Given the broad range of possible applications of recommendation systems, it is of interest to see what minimal set of functions a recommendation system must perform. First, a recommendation system, like an IR system, must have search capabilities in order to access and process information about the available choices. In some cases, recommendation systems have been linked to Web search engines such as Alta Vista (http://altavista.digital.com/); in other cases, they have accessed and processed information in Usenet newsgroups. More generally, the recommendation system might access information in Web-based shopping malls, on-line auctions, or the homepages of car manufacturers.

Second, the recommendation system must ensure that the relevant information is available for each alternative in the choice domain. For information items, the relevant information might be annotations and rankings by other users (the recommenders) or a set of document terms, as in a traditional IR application; for durable goods, the information on each alternative will usually consist of a list of attribute values, including the price of the good, and so on.

Third, the evaluation system must have some notion of user preferences. In most systems, a user profile will be generated by asking the user to rank some typical alternatives or to state his or her preferences and requirements (e.g., for certain classes of subject matter). The user profile is usually updated on a continuous basis

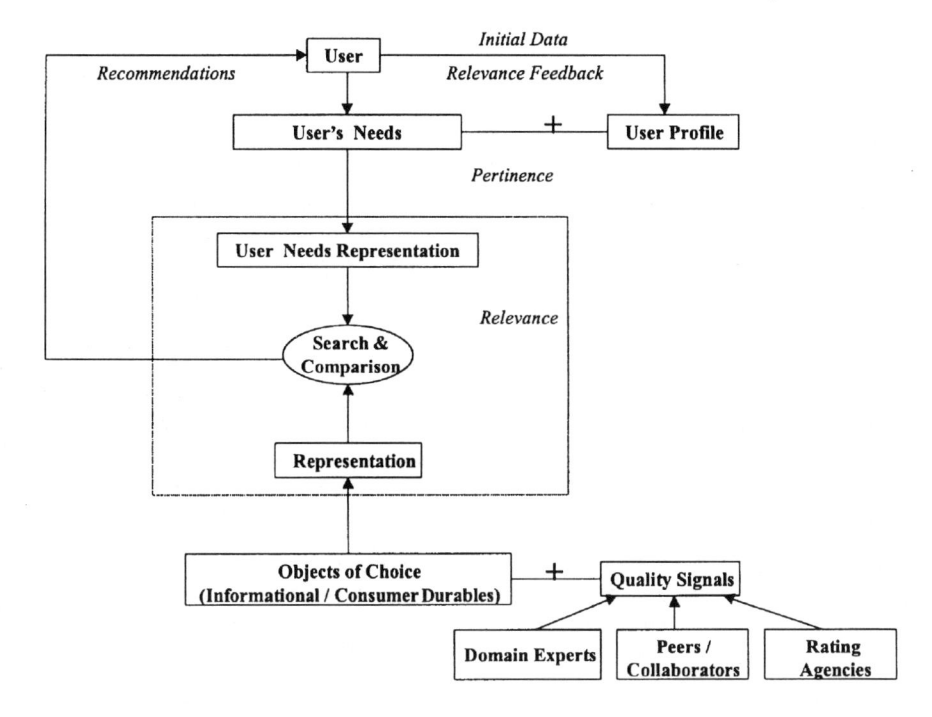

Figure 2.5. The Architecture for Recommendation Systems

using relevance feedback techniques. In other systems, those using rating agencies, it is tacitly assumed that the quality rankings of third-party experts can be used as a proxy for the user's own preferences.

Fourth, the recommendation system must be able to score the alternatives in its choice domain by assigning them an ordinal rank or cardinal rating that will signal their relative desirability to the user. The scoring mechanisms employed in recommendation systems differ depending on the source of expertise that is used to rank the alternatives, as explained in the next section.

Finally, the recommendation system must be able to present its results in an understandable and convenient fashion to the user. Again, there are many alternatives, depending on the type of scoring system used and the application domain. For example, in an IR system, information items are generally ranked in terms of their predicted relevance to the query—and this may be the only choice-oriented information offered by the system. However, especially in collaborative systems, much more elaborate information may be presented to the user. For example, in Amazon.com, the user may read the full text of book critiques by other users.

These five sets of capabilities are necessary in any recommendation system. Namely, the system must be able to seek out possibilities for user choice, generate

TABLE 2.1 Recommendation System Approaches

Recommendation System Technique/Philosophy	Source of System Expertise—Who Is the Recommender?	Example Choice Domains	Example System
Utility estimation	User introspection	Big ticket items such as houses and cars	No known examples
Content- or rule-based analysis	Descriptive information about alternatives and user interests; match alternative profile to user profile	Information items—information retrieval or filtering	Syskill & Webert (Pazzani, Muramatzu, & Billsus, n.d.) [*http://www.ics.uci.edu/pazzani/*] NewsWeeder (Lang, 1995)
Collaborative systems—consult peers	The judgments or opinions of a like group of peers	Choices involving tastes; alerting and filtering systems	Phoaks (Terveen, Hill, Amento, McDonald, & Creter, 1997) [*http://www.phoaks.com/phoaks/*]
Rating Agencies—consult domain expert(s)	The judgment or opinion of one or more experts in the choice domain	Problems in an organizational learning application; issues of high importance	Referral Web (Kautz, Selman, & Shah, 1997) Argus Clearing House [*http://www.clearinghouse.net/*]

or maintain relevant information about each alternative in its choice domain, elicit or infer the preference profile of each of its users, evaluate the choices in terms of the user's profile, and present its recommendations to the user. Although each recommendation system has these capabilities, there are major differences between them in philosophical approach, which will now be sketched.

Classification and Examples of Recommendation Systems

Recommendation systems can be classified according to the source of the knowledge, or expertise, on which the system bases its recommendations. The major alternatives are set out in Table 2.1 together with some example application domains and references to actual systems that have adopted each approach. As in real life, there are four sources of such expertise: the users themselves (utility approach), information about user preferences and about the choices (content-based systems), the recommendations of a peer group (collaborative systems), and the opinions of third-party experts or rating agencies (third-party expertise). Many existing Web-based systems combine the content-based and collaborative approaches (hybrid systems). In this section, we discuss each of these approaches, provide examples, and provide an overview of their relative advantages and disadvantages.

Utility-Based Techniques

In this approach, the expertise (on what the user requires) is assumed to reside only in the user. The system interacts with the user to construct an explicit representation of the user's utility function in terms of the features (attributes) of the choices. Utility estimation techniques are suitable for choices between extremely valuable items, such as cars and houses, for which attribute values such as price are readily available but for which the ultimate choice must be made by the user. The Prefcalc system (Jacquet-Lagrèze & Siskos, 1982),[3] for example, requests users to rank a subset (five or six items) from a much larger set of choices and uses the rankings to construct an additive piecewise linear utility function for the user. Given values for the attributes of each possible choice (such as the price, size, speed, and fuel consumption, in the case of automobiles), it is then a simple matter to rank all of the choices, even those for which the user had no prior knowledge. In a similar vein, users could interactively and implicitly indicate their utility for the various choice possibilities, as in multicriterion decision-making techniques (Zionts & Wallenius, 1976). Although a scoring approach based on utility theory is possible and even desirable in some situations, to our knowledge, no existing Web-based recommendation systems attempt to estimate user utility functions in this classical, decision theory sense.

Content-Based Systems

In this approach, the knowledge required to rank alternatives is embedded in a combination of descriptive information about the alternatives themselves (e.g., document terms or attribute values) plus an explicit user profile (e.g., keywords

---

Syskill & Webert is the name of a software agent that uses a content-based approach to recommender systems (Pazzani, Muramatzu, & Billsus, n.d.). Syskill & Webert learns the user's interests and preferences and then uses a Lycos (Web-based search engine) query to retrieve Web pages that match the user's profile. The user evaluates the retrieved Web pages, which are usually related to a narrow subject domain, and these preferences are then stored in the user's profile, which is updated as more evaluations are made. A simple Bayesian classifier is used to determine the probability that the user would like a Web page. The system uses a Boolean vector space model for learning "features" (document terms) that help discriminate between interesting sites and uninteresting ones.

indicating subject interest, or a past history of previous choices by the user). The content-based (or rule-based) approach has its roots in information retrieval (Balabanovic & Shoham, 1997). The techniques used for full-text searches of Web-based documents are similar to those used in IR. The key to improved performance of the content-based approach over traditional IR approaches is the use of user profiles containing information on user preferences and tastes. These may be explicitly elicited through questionnaires or built over time by observing and tracking users as they interact with the Web. Relevance feedback, an important component of content-based approaches, is used to update user profiles. One or more of the above-mentioned IR methods may be used for weighting words to represent documents and text. Similarly, several different methods exist for updating user profiles.

Content-based approaches build upon IR models and consequently inherit many of their limitations. In particular, given the diversity of resources on the Web, not all Web-based documents are amenable to proper representation using traditional IR indexing techniques, which are best suited for text-based documents. Second, content-based approaches rely heavily on prior feedback from users. This results in overspecialization, that is, the system performs best in restricted domains that the users have evaluated in the past (Balabanovic & Shoham, 1997). Third, obtaining proper feedback from users for retrieved items is time-consuming and frustrating; given their limited knowledge and experience, users cannot determine which documents best satisfy their needs without actually browsing through each and every one of them. More importantly, the user might not be in a position to evaluate satisfactorily the quality of the items retrieved. Collaborative recommender systems overcome some of the limitations of content-based systems, but they have some weaknesses of their own.

Collaborative Systems

In collaborative approaches, the opinions of people who have interests and tastes similar to those of the user provide the basis for the recommendations. This is the basic philosophy underlying recommender systems (narrow definition) and collaborative filtering applications. "Rather than compute the similarity of the items, the collaborative approach computes the similarity of users" (Balabanovic & Shoham, 1997, p. 67). In collaborative systems, the user profile does not represent the user's preferences over the various choices that are to be recommended. Rather, it helps determine the user's similarity to other users of the recommender system. The recommendations are then based on the choices made by users with similar profiles. For example, a user might simply indicate a set of keywords of interest and then be provided rankings by a subset of users with a similar profile. In this approach, the software agent finds other users whose preferences are similar to those specified by the user and then recommends items that they liked. Clusters of users with similar preferences are identified based on the correlation of their earlier evaluations of

> **PHOAKS** (*P*eople *H*elping *O*ne *A*nother *K*now *S*tuff) is a collaborative recommender system that mines Usenet newsgroups for mention of Web pages (URLs). Upon passing a number of tests, these pages are then classified as recommendations (Terveen et al., 1997). Some of the search, classification, and filtering techniques common to IR systems are used. URLs that are cross-posted to a number of newsgroups and have accompanying text that is suggestive of an advertisement or promotion are automatically discarded. URLs recommended by a large number of users were found to be of higher quality than were those with fewer recommendations. Additional information from FAQ (Frequently Asked Questions) databases was used to measure and improve the quality of the recommendations. One of the limitations of the PHOAKS system is that it does not distinguish between different evaluations, thus assigning them equal weights irrespective of their credibility.

items in the choice domain. However, this requires that the user have rated the same items for comparison. Scores for unseen items are predicted based on a combination of scores known from the nearest neighbors in a cluster (Balabanovic & Shoham, 1997).

Collaborative approaches can recommend a wide variety of items, not just those evaluated by the user. One of the most significant advantages of the collaborative approach is how little an individual user has to contribute to be able to retrieve relevant documents, because the approach relies less on the user's own evaluations and more on the evaluations of users with similar tastes. However, the success of such a system depends on the availability of a critical mass of users with similar profiles, the willingness of the users to contribute evaluations, and the credibility of their evaluations. Because some users who benefit from such systems have no incentive to contribute evaluations, there may be problems of free riding. Market mechanisms and pricing schemes for evaluations have been suggested to overcome some of these problems (Resnick & Varian, 1997).

Third-Party Expertise

In the fourth approach to producing recommendations, the system facilitates consultation with a domain expert. This approach might be indicated for problems and issues of major consequence. The referral web (Kautz et al., 1997), in which users are linked into communities around domain specialists, takes this approach.

> **The Argus Clearinghouse** (http://www.clearinghouse.net/) serves as a clearinghouse for topical guides that identify, describe, and evaluate Internet-based information sources. The topical guides are rated based on five criteria: (a) level of resource description (content, currency, access, technical performance, etc.); (b) level of resource evaluation (subject quality indicators, information on authors, document layouts, graphics, etc.); (c) guide design (images, layout, navigational aids, etc.); (d) guide organizational schemes; and (e) guide meta-information. Exceptionally good guides are also given a Digital Librarian's Award. Thus, rating agencies (or clearinghouses) can serve as a credible source of recommendations in different domains.

Rating agencies or third-party experts are useful in situations where special expertise is required to make the recommendations. A disadvantage is that the recommendations produced by such systems are not usually personalized to the user.

Hybrid Systems

Most existing recommendation systems take a hybrid approach involving some combination of content-based analysis and collaborative filtering. The Barnes and Noble implementation of the Firefly software mentioned earlier uses a combination of rule-based and collaborative filtering.

Hybrid systems overcome some of the limitations of content-based systems. By using group feedback, we potentially require fewer cycles to achieve the same level of personalization (Balabanovic & Shoham, 1997). In addition, individuals gain because the group can appraise more items and will usually provide a different viewpoint.

The application domains in Table 2.1 are suggestive only. Each technique could be applied in multiple domains. This is suggested by Table 2.2, which arranges the information just described around some typical problem domains. (The third row in the table lists the alternative approaches in each problem domain.)

Managerial Implications

From a firm's viewpoint, recommendation systems can be used in two ways: as a marketing tool to positively influence consumer perceptions and preferences, and/or as a tool for knowledge management and organizational learning. Table 2.2 shows sample problem domains in these two areas of concern. The first and second rows in Table 2.2 list the choice domain and characterize the type of problem to

> **The FAB system,** a part of the Stanford University digital library project, is a hybrid recommendation system (Balabanovic & Shoham, 1997). It is composed of three main components—collection agents, which find pages on a specific topic; selection agents, which find Web pages for a specific user; and the central router. Users receive items when the items score highly against their own profile, as well as when the items are rated highly by a user with a similar profile. Whereas the collection agent's profile represents its current topic, the selection agent's profile represents a single user's interests based on his or her evaluation. The central router forwards Web pages from the collection agent to users based on their profiles, which are stored in their personal selection agents. Collection agents specialize in narrow domains and adapt to a dynamically changing population of users. The FAB system uses Web-based, full-text search engines to retrieve pages that match the user's profile. The success of the system depends largely on how accurately the users' profiles reflect their true preferences.

TABLE 2.2 Problem Domains, Alternative Approaches, and Value Added

	Electronic Commerce		*Knowledge Management—Continuous Flow of Knowable Product (e.g., information)*
What Is Recommended?	*Durables—Known Attribute Values (such as price)*	*Consumables— Matters of Opinion*	
Typical choice domains	Cars, houses, vacations	Art, movies, books, CDs	News feeds, Usenets, problem databases, organizational learning
Problem type	Optimal selection from a relatively few big ticket items	Selection from many items of low value	Filtering, prevention of information overload, directing attention to important issues
Who is the recommender?	(a) Utility-based (User + decision aid) (b) Rating agencies	(a) Content-based (Rules + personal profile) (b) Collaborative (peer group) (c) Rating agencies	(a) Content-based (Rules + personal profile) (b) Collaborative (peer group) (c) Experts
Value added by recommendation system	Information gathering and presentation; one-to-one matching to personal preferences	Information gathering and presentation; one-to-one matching to personal preferences; save time and cost of sampling; align with opinions of others	Information filtering, evaluation, and presentation; alerting to new issues and ideas; match to personal information needs; save time by reading only items of direct interest

be solved by the recommendation system, the third row suggests alternative sources of recommendations, and the last row describes the value that the system provides its users.

As is to be expected, the design and deployment of recommendation systems should differ to reflect the concerns of the different problem domains. Columns 2 and 3 illustrate two contrasting decision situations in E-commerce—high-value, one-off decision making in which personal preferences are of overriding importance, and low-value decision making in which matters of opinion and taste are paramount. The level of trust, risk, validity, and performance expected in these two situations is vastly different. For example, as suggested in the third row of the table, the locus of decision making for high-value decisions should probably reside in the user, whereas in low-value decision-making situations, it is reasonable to rely on more automated approaches.

As organizations are overwhelmed by the information explosion, and as they become more knowledge intensive, organizational learning and knowledge management within the organization become important. Recommendation systems, using some of the techniques discussed earlier, can help firms in these areas. Column 4 in Table 2.2 lists information-filtering applications in which the chief concern is to bring only interesting or new (from the recipient's point of view) items to the attention of employees and to eliminate uninteresting or unimportant items.

Issues Surrounding the Use of Recommendation Systems

Space does not permit a review of the many interesting issues and problems involved in successfully implementing a recommendation system. Obviously, these issues span the gamut from the development of advanced software technologies to the care and nurturing of customers. In the case of recommender systems in particular, the developers must be concerned with how they can develop a community of people that will actively contribute to the common good. In this section, we briefly discuss only two questions: Why would a user accept the recommendations of a recommendation system? and How can the value of such systems be measured?

The major factors associated with user acceptance and use of recommendation systems are shown in Table 2.3. The issues of trust, validity, privacy, and risk are necessary preconditions for acceptance of recommendation systems, but ultimately, their success will depend on the performance factor—the utility they provide their users.

Trust

Possible bias in the recommendations due to the self-interest of either the owners or the users of such systems is a major issue, particularly for collaborative recommender systems. "If anyone can provide recommendations, content owners may

TABLE 2.3 Factors Influencing the Acceptance of a Recommendation System

Trust:	Authenticity of source—is the recommender who I think it is?
	Does the recommender provide an unbiased recommendation?
Validity:	Does the system have the correct information/expertise?
	Does the system understand my requirements and wishes?
	How does the system make its recommendations?
Privacy:	Is my personal profile kept secret?
	Are my inquiries and purchases private?
Risk:	What redress do I have if I act on a bad recommendation (e.g., money back if not satisfied)?
Performance:	What value do I derive from the recommendations—do I save money or time?

generate mountains of positive recommendations for their own materials and negative recommendations for their competitors" (Resnick & Varian, 1997, p. 57).

Validity

The question here is whether the system has the information and expertise to be helpful. Just as we associate more or less validity to the pronouncements of wine and food critics, or to human experts in any other walk of life, so too will computer recommendation systems acquire reputations for the relative usefulness or otherwise of their recommendations. The second question under this heading in Table 2.3 refers to the ability of the recommendation system to adapt its response to the needs of individual users. The third question emphasizes the need for recommendation systems to have accurate and reliable inference mechanisms—an active area of current research.

Privacy

Most recommendation systems rely upon the evaluations and ratings provided by different users to recommend items. Sharing the opinions of individuals with the society at large raises concerns relating to privacy. Although anonymity and the use of pseudonyms provide a partial solution to this problem, several alternatives have been proposed. For example, the Open Personalization Standard (OPS), also known as the Open Profiling Standard, is yet to be agreed upon by industry participants ("Web Marketing," 1998). Under OPS, users could choose to store personal information, hobbies, and interests on their PC hard drives and then decide whether to disclose that information to a particular Web site.

Risk

The risk assumed by users of recommendation systems varies with the choice domain. For users of filtered Usenet information, the risks are probably inconsequential, but for users of recommendation systems for large budget items or stock advisory services, the risks of acting upon computer-generated recommendations will be quite large. In traditional commerce, both competition and legal considerations have shaped the way risks are shared between sellers and consumers. We suspect that a proper understanding of the risks for both providers and users of recommendation services will be similarly shaped over a period of use.

Performance

The market for recommendation services will ultimately decide which ones survive and prosper. Performance will improve over time as the technology becomes more sophisticated and the surviving intermediaries reach and surpass critical mass. Size is especially important for recommender systems, which depend on evaluations and feedback from users and, hence, require a critical mass of recommenders and recommendations to be able to perform effectively.

This leads us to the interesting question of how the performance of recommendation systems can be evaluated. One possibility is to use the notions of recall and precision, which were defined earlier. More generally, we stated in the introduction that the role of a recommendation system is to increase the probability that its users will be satisfied by the choices that they make as a result of using the system.

From a similar viewpoint, we have the notion of *predictive utility* (Konstan et al., 1997). In other words, recommendation systems must be able to predict which items in their domain of choice will most satisfy each user. A simple cost-benefit analysis approach based on Konstan et al.'s work illustrates the need for a closer look at performance measures for recommendation systems. Table 2.4 shows the possible outcomes for a recommendation system that makes binary predictions as to whether an item will be useful to the user (good) or not useful (bad). Illustrative costs and benefits are provided for two different hypothetical recommendation systems: one that rates movies and a second that filters news items for financial analysts. To illustrate the kind of reasoning that might determine the values in each cell, the benefit of the correct prediction of a good movie (one that the user will enjoy) is listed as "medium," whereas the cost of a false positive (the prediction that the user will enjoy the movie, when he or she does not) is the cost of buying a ticket and wasting an evening, which has been judged to be "high." As another example, the value of a hit and the cost (opportunity cost) of a miss of a pertinent news item to a financial analyst are both rated as "high" in the table.

As discussed earlier, recall measures the number of relevant items (hits) divided by the total number of items in all four quadrants, whereas precision records the number of hits divided by the total number of hits plus false positives. But such ratios do little to reflect the costs and benefits of the various possible outcomes and

TABLE 2.4 Cost-Benefit Analysis for Recommendation Systems

	Predict "Good Item"	Predict "Bad Item"
Good Item	HIT	MISS
	Movie: Medium benefit	Movie: Low cost
	News item: High benefit	News item: High cost
Bad Item	FALSE POSITIVE	CORRECT REJECTION
	Movie: High cost	Movie: Medium benefit
	News item: Medium cost	News item: Low benefit

can therefore shed little light on whether a recommendation system is beneficial to an individual or an organization. A complete cost-benefit analysis, even in such simple applications, is quite difficult because it depends on a correct assessment of the utility of the various outcomes for each particular user as well as the probabilities of a given recommendation ending up in each of the four cells.[4] Nevertheless, a consideration of the issues raised by even an approximate cost-benefit analysis should provide useful guidance for the designers of recommendation systems. Further research on the costs and benefits of recommendation systems is urgently required.

Summary and Conclusions

To cope with the ever-increasing complexities of the information economy, we suggested in the introduction that research and development of a range of coping technologies is needed. In fact, we believe that we will need to develop support environments that will, among other things, monitor the environment; direct our attention to what is urgent, relevant, and important; increase our understanding of the world; and help us with our decision making. Recommendation systems are an important new technology that may help us in the decision-making aspect of our lives. We defined recommendation systems broadly as systems that provide recommendations by any means, reserving the term recommender systems for the important subclass of recommendation systems that makes recommendations based on the opinions of other people.

The explosive growth of the Internet and the World Wide Web has resulted in the proliferation of information of uncertain quality in widely varying formats, which has greatly reduced the effectiveness of traditional IR approaches. More importantly, the needs of electronic commerce extend far beyond those of information dissemination and retrieval. In this new world, we see a huge potential market for systems that collect and analyze user tastes and needs, on the one hand, and signal the quality of products and services on the other hand. Throughout the chapter, we discussed a number of examples of expert-based, content-based, collaborative, and hybrid recommendation systems. Some of these are research systems; others are already commercial successes.

The framework for recommendation systems clarifies the differences with IR systems and the general functions provided by recommendation systems. We also identified four general classes of recommendation systems based on the source of expertise underlying the recommendation: utility-based systems, content-based systems, collaborative systems, and expert consultation. Finally, we briefly discussed the issues of user acceptance of recommendation systems and the need for research on performance measures.

This brief survey and classification of recommendation systems has barely scratched the surface of a whole new technology of assisted decision making that we feel will grow in importance as electronic media become the main vehicles for human communication, education, and commerce. As we argued in the introduction, recommendation systems are a response to the need for individuals and organizations to manage the overwhelming flood of new information, products, and services and to make more and more decisions under increasing time pressure. For these reasons, we believe that recommendation systems are inevitable and that they will be part of a thriving new industry of Web-based intermediaries.

The social consequences of such systems are enormous. If recommendation systems fulfill their promise, they could make markets more efficient by providing consistent, valid, and credible quality signals, thereby reducing or eliminating the hassle associated with search and investigation of a wide range of goods and services. Recommendation systems also provide opportunities for one-to-one marketing, which, by catering to individual tastes, should increase overall welfare.

On the other hand, there are several dangers. First, individuals and organizations could become overly dependent on such systems, creating opportunities for unscrupulous companies, or even government agencies, to manipulate user tastes and decision making. Second, it is not at all certain whether widespread use of recommendation systems will lead to more diversity and freedom of expression or to the opposite—an economic and social system in which individual tastes and needs are satisfied on the margin but overall cultural and intellectual directions are dictated by the majority. Civil liberty groups, for example, are concerned by the power of filtering systems to limit free speech on the Internet (Harmon, 1998). In our opinion, the future economic and social consequences of these new technologies are a matter for urgent research and debate in academic, industrial, and governmental regulatory agencies.

Notes

1. Many existing examples of recommendation systems fit the narrow definition of recommender systems.

2. Because we are primarily concerned with electronic intermediaries in an information economy, we restrict our discussion to intermediary functions that lend themselves to automation.

3. Prefcalc is a stand-alone (rather than Web-based) Multiple Criteria Decision Making application.

4. A closed form solution for this problem was first proposed in the IR context by Verhoeff, Goffman, and Belzer (1961).

References

Alter, S. (1977). A taxonomy of decision support systems. *Sloan Management Review, 19,* 39-56.
Balabanovic, M., & Shoham, Y. (1997). Fab: Content-based, collaborative recommendation. *Communications of the ACM, 40*(3), 66-72.
Belkin, N. J., & Croft, B. W. (1992). Information filtering and information retrieval: Two sides of the same coin. *Communications of the ACM, 35*(12), 29-38.
Belkin, N. J., Oddy, R. N., & Brooks, H. M., (1982). ASK for information retrieval. Part I. Background and theory. *Journal of Documentation, 38,* 61-71.
Gorry, G. A., & Scott Morton, M. S. (1971). A framework for management information systems. *Sloan Management Review, 13*(1), 55-71.
Harmon, A. (1998, January 19). Technology to let engineers filter the web and judge content. *New York Times,* pp. D1, D4.
Jacquet-Lagrèze, E., & Siskos, M. (1982). Assessing a set of additive utility functions for multicriteria decision-making: The UTA method. *European Journal of Operational Research, 10,* 151-164.
Kambil, A., (1997, May). Doing business in the wired world. *IEEE Computer,* pp. 56-61.
Kautz, H., Selman, B., & Shah, M. (1997). Referral web: Combining social networks and collaborative filtering. *Communications of the ACM, 40*(3), 63-65.
Konstan, J. A., Miller, B. N., Maltz, D., Herlocker, J. L., Le, G. R., & Riedl, J. (1997). GroupLens: Applying collaborative filtering to Usenet news. *Communications of the ACM, 40*(3), 77-87.
Lang, K. (1995). Newsweeder: Learning to filter netnews. *Proceedings of the 12th International Conference on Machine Learning,* Tahoe City, CA.
Malone, T. W., Yates, J., & Benjamin, R. I. (1987). Electronic markets and electronic hierarchies. *Communications of the ACM, 30*(6), 484-497.
Pazzani, M., Muramatsu, J., & Billsus, D. (n.d.). *Syskill & Webert: Identifying interesting web sites* (http://www.ics.uci.edu/pazzani/).
Pine, B., Joseph, D. P., III, & Rogers, M. (1995, March/April). Do you want to keep your customers forever? *Harvard Business Review,* pp. 103-114.
Resnick, P., & Varian, H. R. (1997). Recommender systems. *Communications of the ACM, 40*(3), 56-58.
Robertson, S. E. (1977). Theories and models in information retrieval. *Journal of Documentation, 33,* 126-148.
Salton, G., & Buckley, C. (1988). Term-weighting approaches in automatic text retrieval. *Information Processing and Management, 24,* 513-523.
Saracevic, T. (1975). Relevance: A review of a framework for thinking on the notion of information science. *Journal of the American Society for Information Science, 26,* 321-343.
Stein, E., & Zwass, V. (1995). Actualizing organizational memory with information systems. *Information Systems Research, 6*(2), 85-117.
Stohr, E. A., & Viswanathan, S. (1998). *Web-based agents for electronic commerce.* Unpublished manuscript, Center for Research in Information Systems, Stern School of Business, New York University.
Terveen, L., Hill, W., Amento, B., McDonald, D., & Creter, J. (1997). PHOAKS: A system for sharing recommendations. *Communications of the ACM, 40*(3), 59-62.

Tuzhilin, A. (1998). *The e-butler service, or has the age of electronic personal decision making assistants arrived?* Unpublished manuscript, Center for Research in Information Systems, Stern School of Business, New York University.

Verhoeff, J., Goffman, W., & Belzer, J. (1961). Inefficiency of the use of Boolean functions for information retrieval. *Communications of the Association for Computing Machinery, 4,* 557-558.

Web marketing gets personal. (1998, January 12). *Infoworld,* pp. 93-94.

Zionts, S., & Wallenius, J. (1976). An interactive programming method for solving the multiple criteria problem. *Management Science, 22,* 652-663.

CHAPTER
THREE

Animation in User Interfaces Designed for Decision Support Systems

The Effects of Image Abstraction, Transition, and Interactivity on Decision Quality

CLEOTILDE GONZÁLEZ
GEORGE M. KASPER

Including animation in the design of user interfaces is a natural extension of graphical user interfaces. Moreover, animation seems particularly well suited for representing many real-world situations, and the conventional wisdom is that animation makes the user interface easier to use, more enjoyable, pleasurable, and understandable (Baecker & Small, 1990; Chang & Ungar, 1993; Robertson, Card, & Mackinlay, 1993; SIGGRAPH 94, 1994). Despite this evidence, very little is known about the efficacy of animation for decision support. In fact, the efficacy of animation in user interfaces designed for decision support systems has not been studied directly.

The term *decision support systems* (DSS) is used here as defined by Scott Morton (1984) to include all forms of information systems and technologies designed to assist one or more users in making better decisions. Although the nature of the decision support provided by DSS range from passive to active (Henderson, 1987; Humphreys, 1986; Keen, 1987; Luconi, Malone, & Scott Morton, 1986; Remus & Kotteman, 1986) and from individual to group (DeSanctis & Gallupe, 1987; Olson & Olson, 1991), the goal in designing all decision support systems is to improve "decision quality" (Ginzberg & Stohr, 1982, p. 12).

According to Daft (1991), a decision is "a choice made from among available alternatives" (p. 180). Choosing from among alternative courses of action lies at the heart of decision making (Payne, 1982). Decision quality is a measure of the goodness of this choice.

A user interface both supports the mechanics of the interaction and facilitates the broader notion of a dialogue between human and computer. As used here, a user interface is an "observable two-way exchange of symbols and actions between human and computer" (Hartson & Hix, 1989, p. 8). In this way, the study of

---

Reprinted by permission from *Decision Sciences,* Volume 28, Number 4, Fall 1997.

animation in user interfaces emphasizes the symbols and actions of images, the effects of images and images in action, and the user's actions and reactions to these images and their actions.

In the film industry, animation is defined as movement that brings characters to life (Solomon, 1983). In psychology, animation has been referred to as "apparent movement which is actually a series of still pictures" (Goldstein, 1989, p. 277). In education, animation is "a series of rapidly changing computer screen displays that represent the illusion of movement" (Rieber & Hannafin, 1988, p. 78). In the human-computer interface literature, animation is a "sequence of static images changing rapidly enough to create the illusion of a continuously changing picture" (Baecker & Small, 1990, p. 252). Some writers contend that animation must create the illusion of movement (Baecker & Small, 1990; Keller & Keller, 1993; Park & Hopkins, 1992), and others argue that animation includes change such as zooming, dissolving, fading, coloration, shading, and other transition and alteration effects (Magnenat-Thalmann & Thalmann, 1985). For some, animation is simply another way of displaying images (Palmiter, Elkerton, & Baggett, 1991; Rieber, Boyce, & Assad, 1990); others contend that the user interface should be designed to support interactivity (Ginzberg & Stohr, 1982) so that the images of animation change in ways guided by user actions (Robertson et al., 1993).

It is clear that animation can engage and entertain. Its role in user interfaces designed for DSS, however, is only beginning to be considered, and the limited evidence is anecdotal. For the purposes of this study, animation in user interfaces designed for DSS is defined as images presented dynamically that change, guided by the user, in ways that improve decision quality. "Images presented dynamically that change" defines animation in user interfaces designed for DSS as consisting of different images presented in some series, one at a time. That these images are different in ways that "improve decision quality" defines the change as purposeful and consistent with the performance goal of DSS. That the "change" is also "guided by the user" highlights the directive role played by the user in DSS and the two-way exchange of symbols and actions that defines dialogue in human-computer interfaces. This definition combines the principal notions of animation, DSS, and human-computer dialogue design.

This chapter develops a research framework to evaluate the efficacy of animation in user interfaces designed for DSS and reports on a study that investigated the effectiveness of several of the components proposed in the framework. Specifically, the effects on decision quality of different animation symbols (image abstraction) and actions (transition and interactivity) were investigated in a laboratory study. The results indicate that the design of image abstraction, transition, and navigation interactivity affect decision quality.

Based on a review of selected background literature, properties affecting the efficacy of animation in user interfaces designed for DSS are developed below. Next, a study intended to compare the performance of subjects using different designs of animation in two different decision tasks is described. This is followed by a presentation of the data analysis and results. The results are then discussed. The chapter ends with a summary of the findings and concluding remarks.

Background

Even though we navigate daily through a perceptual world of three spatial dimensions and reason occasionally about higher dimensional arenas . . . *the world portrayed on our information displays is caught up in the two-dimensionality of the endless flatlands of paper and video screen. . . . Escaping this flatland is the essential task of envisioning information—for all the interesting worlds . . . that we seek to understand are inevitably and happily multivariate in nature.* (Tufte, 1990, p. 12)

Converting the four-dimensional reality of time and three-dimensional space into little marks on a two-dimensional screen is the essential dilemma of user interface design (Tufte, 1990). "One day this [conversion] will be accomplished using extremely high-resolution screens that combine *slightly abstracted, dynamic,* and *animated images*" (Tufte, 1990, p. 119, italics added). Effective animation depicts the four-dimensional reality of time and three-dimensional space in two dimensions by creating the illusions of depth and change over time.

Attempts to escape the flatland of paper and screen are chronicled by Tufte (1990) and include the pop-up models used in a 1570 edition of Euclid's book *Elements* to explain solid geometry. In a more recent example, two Connecticut teenagers, using software that allowed them to draw and redraw lines, solved the regular partitioning problem posited by Euclid some 2,300 years ago: Given a line of any length, devise a universal geometric method for subdividing it into any number of equal parts ("Teen Math Whizzes," 1996). Another example, and one that makes clear use of change, is the computer animation created by the Geometry Center at the University of Minnesota illustrating the 1957 mathematical discovery of how one can turn the surface of a sphere inside out without making a hole (*Outside In,* 1994). In terms of decision making, many management decisions require identifying and assessing change, and, in particular, change over time. Time is a dimension, and change is a characteristic that animation is especially well suited to depict. Because of this, animation seems well suited to supporting many management decisions. Animation provides the designer of user interfaces for DSS with a tool to reduce the four-dimensional reality of time and three-dimensional space into the two dimensions of the display screen.

The basic unit of animation is the image. Composed of elemental symbols and their spatial orientation (Johnson-Laird, 1981), an image can be designed to be overlooked and unnoticed or to capture and maintain an observer's attention (Hochberg & Brooks, 1978; Treisman & Souther, 1985; Wickens, 1992; Woods, 1984). Attributes of elemental symbols include abstraction, color, form, and texture; examples of spatial orientation attributes are spatial proximity, similarity, closure, continuation, and depth cues (Finkel & Sajda, 1994; Hochberg, 1986; Kosslyn, 1985; Marr, 1982; Treisman & Souther, 1985). Using these attributes, an image can inform by what it abstracts, highlights, and mutes, capturing attention and reducing information overload where appropriate.

In addition to an image's elemental symbols and their spatial orientation, equally important considerations in animation are the design of transition and alteration effects. Transition and alteration effects mark or mitigate change between and within segments of images, respectively, by either accentuating or making the change "transparent" to the viewer. Transition effects include dissolving and fading. Alteration effects include coloration, texturing, and morphing.

In summary, the basic unit of animation, the image, can be designed to inform by accentuating or muting its elemental symbols and their spatial orientation and through transition and alteration effects within and between collections of images, respectively. The power of animation in interfaces designed for DSS may lie in its potential to highlight informative change and to mute uninformative change within and between images.

The techniques of animation are divided into so-called classical and, more recently, real-time techniques (Magnenat-Thalmann & Thalmann, 1985). Classical techniques, founded on the methods developed to produce cartoons, are oriented toward the production of lifelike figures for the purpose of entertaining a passive viewer. Classical techniques focus on developing a set of images that is later presented in a given sequence and rate. Two issues are central to this purpose: smoothness and simplicity (Halas, 1990). Simplicity refers to the parsimonious nature of the images, the degree to which the image has abstracted the essentials of a situation. Smoothness refers to the transition and alteration effects that maintain the dynamics of continuous change.

Real-time techniques are intended to provide a level of interactivity needed to support a two-way exchange of images (symbols) and actions to sustain a human-computer dialogue. For this exchange to be directed by the user at a "natural" pace, the system must be responsive. To produce images dynamically and at rates that maintain responsiveness has meant that real-time animation has focused on designing hardware and software techniques that can deal effectively with the trade-off between response time and interactivity (Robertson et al., 1993).

Interactivity, the focus of real-time-based animation, is not found in systems developed using classical techniques. Moreover, neither classical nor real-time techniques consider decision quality to be a performance goal. The effects on decision quality of image simplicity (abstraction), the smoothness of images in action (transition and alteration), and the nature of human-computer interaction (interactivity) must be explicitly considered if animation in user interfaces designed for DSS is to be effective. Each of these is included in the framework developed below.

A Framework for Studying Animation in User Interfaces Designed for DSS

Before the effects of animation on decision quality can be considered, some framework is needed to guide the research. Models have been proposed for animation using either real-time or classical animation techniques (Palmiter, 1993;

Robertson, Card, & Mackinlay, 1989), but none of these considers the effects of animation on decision quality. Likewise, several models have been proposed to describe different aspects of human-computer interaction (Shneiderman, 1992). Perhaps the best known of these models is the goals, operators, methods, and selection rules (GOMS) model proposed by Card, Moran, and Newell (1983). GOMS postulates that users formulate goals that are achieved using methods, procedures, and technologies defined by the design of the system. Methods are, in turn, chosen using selection rules that are formulated based on the user's abilities, expertise, and experiences. Operators are elementary perceptual, motor, and cognitive actions. Other models of human-computer interaction propose various combinations of goals, perception, cognition, symbols, actions, technologies, task, and user characteristics (Shneiderman).

Design is prescriptive and goal oriented (Walls, Widmeyer, & El Sawy, 1992). It specifies the goal(s), properties (operators and methods), and (selection) rules and structures needed for these properties to achieve the goal. The goal, properties, and hypothesized selection rules for choosing among the properties of animation to achieve the goal of animation in user interfaces designed for DSS are introduced and developed below.

The Goal of Animation in User Interfaces Designed for DSS

The goal of animation in user interfaces designed for DSS is to improve decision quality. Achieving this goal requires combining the simplicity and smoothness of classical animation technology with the interactivity of real-time systems. Simplicity addresses the content of an image, its elemental symbols and their spatial orientation; smoothness is a result of transition and alteration effects; and interactivity adds the responsiveness and user controllability needed for DSS. Simplicity, smoothness, and interactivity define properties of animation in user interfaces designed for DSS and, through the process of design, can be specified so that decision quality is improved.

Properties of Animation in User Interfaces Designed for DSS

DSS integrates user, task, and information (in this case, animation) technologies into a synergistic unit to improve decision quality. The interplay among user, task, and information technologies is the foundation for DSS and is a well-known triad in the information systems literature (Mason & Mitroff, 1973; Newell & Simon, 1972). Based on this foundation and the literature discussed earlier, a research framework for investigating the interplay among user, task, and animation technologies in user interfaces designed for DSS is proposed in Figure 3.1.

Cognition

Perception

TASK	ANIMATION	USER
Type Structure	Image 　Abstraction 　　realistic-abstract Transition 　gradual-abrupt 　dissolving, fading, etc. Alteration 　gradual-abrupt 　texturing, coloration, etc. Interactivity 　Manipulation 　　direct/indirect 　Navigation 　　sequential/parallel	Visual & spatial abilities Experience

Design　　　*Action*

Decision Quality

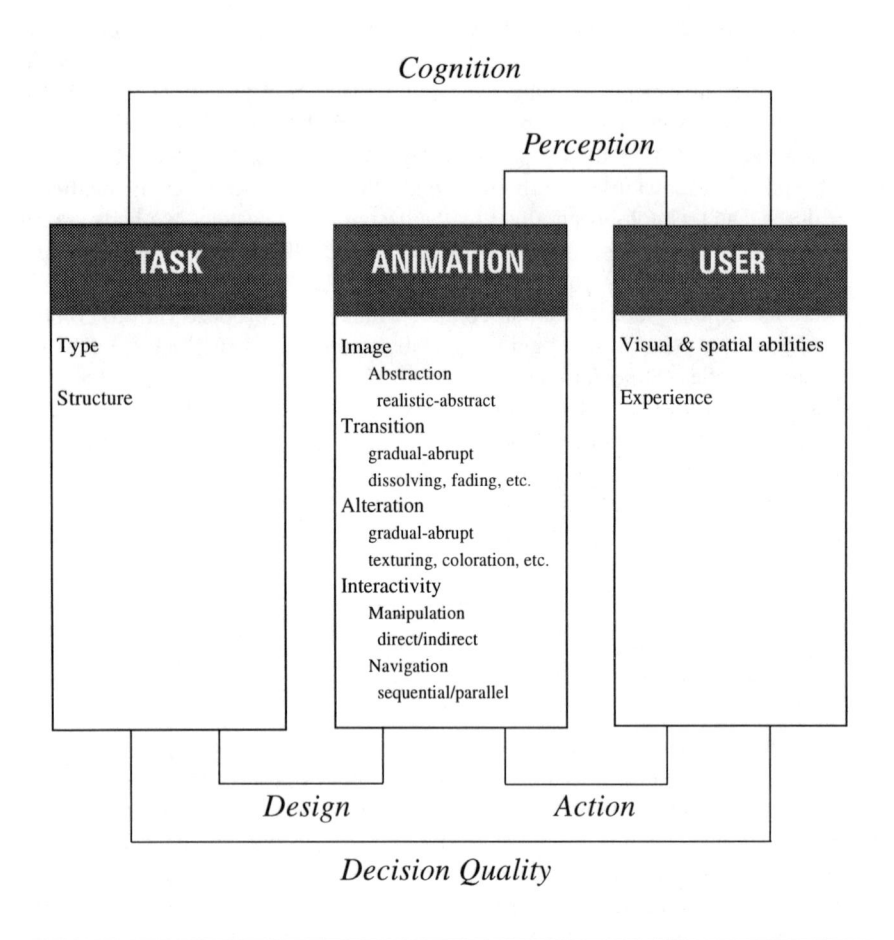

Figure 3.1. A Framework for Studying Animation in User Interfaces Designed for DSS

Selected instantiations of Task, User, and Animation believed to be particularly relevant to DSS are identified in Figure 3.1. The figure also suggests operators acting on Task, User, and/or Animation. Identifying (often empirically) the most effective combinations of these properties (i.e., the selection rules) is a key to effective design.

Animation

At the center of Figure 3.1 is Animation. The classical property of simplicity is instantiated as image abstraction. Image abstraction ranges from low, realistic images to high, abstract images, depending upon how closely the symbols in the image resemble real-world objects (Deregowski, 1990; Hochberg, 1986). Images near the realistic end of this continuum offer the eye the same pattern of light as that of the real-world scene. Conversely, images near the high end of the abstraction continuum bear little resemblance to reality or real-world objects (Krampen, 1990). Abstract images often appear as line drawings and geometric shapes, whereas photographs of real-world objects are considered realistic images (Deregowski, 1990; Espe, 1990; Paivio, 1971).

Conventional wisdom is that abstract images are parsimonious and therefore effective conveyors of information. Abstraction, however, always runs the risk of going too far, removing information and adversely affecting decision quality. Moreover, abstract images can be used to depict both real and imaginary worlds, whereas realistic images can depict only "real" objects and actions.

Animation in Figure 3.1 includes the classical notion of smoothness in the forms of Transition and Alteration. Transition and Alteration manipulate pictorial and spatial attributes of an image so as to optimize the user's attention level and reception to the information displayed. Theories of visual perception and cognition agree that gradual, progressive changes between visual patterns are needed to produce smooth, actively changing stimuli (Gibson, 1979; Hochberg & Brooks, 1978; Woods, 1984). Alteration defines differences in consecutive images within a series (i.e., changes such as coloration and texturing that instantiate consecutive images of the animation; Rieber & Hannafin, 1988; Stasko, 1993; Treisman & Souther, 1985). Transition specifies changes between major scenes (e.g., dissolving, fading, morphing, etc.; Baecker & Small, 1990; Chang & Ungar, 1993).

Another instantiation of animation in Figure 3.1 is Interactivity. Interactivity ranges from the one-way to the two-way exchange of images and actions (Ginzberg & Stohr, 1982). In one-way interactivity, the exchange of information is in only one direction. Animation based on classical techniques, typified by the motion picture, is an example of one-way interactivity. In one-way interactivity, the user takes the passive role of simply responding to the actions of the system (Keen, 1987). In contrast, the two-way interactivity of human-computer dialogue requires the exchange of information. In two-way interactivity, the user views and responds to the animation and the animation "views" and responds to the user's directives (Hollnagel & Woods, 1983). Because of this, two-way interactivity requires the responsiveness of real-time systems (Badler, Phillips, & Webber, 1993; Magnenat-Thalmann & Thalmann, 1985). Two-way interactivity requires systems that can respond by producing images at speeds such that they can be displayed at a rate approaching 24 frames per second, the current motion picture standard (Halas, 1990; Robertson et al., 1993).

It is generally believed that two-way interactivity engages the user and results in improved decision quality (Ginzberg & Stohr, 1982). Two-way interactivity, however, would be counterproductive if it reduced decision quality, perhaps by imposing an overhead that increased the user's cognitive workload (Benbasat & Todd, 1993; Davis & Bostrom, 1993; Hale & Kasper, 1989; Palmiter et al., 1991; Rieber & Hannafin, 1988; Robertson et al., 1989).

As identified in Figure 3.1, Interactivity for animation in user interfaces designed for DSS combines the properties of manipulation and navigation. Manipulation can be either direct or indirect. As the name implies, direct manipulation involves the direct control of a displayed symbol (i.e., grasping, moving, rotating, etc.; Gobbetti, Balaguer, & Thalmann, 1993; Isdale, 1993). In contrast, indirect manipulation utilizes some secondary means, such as commands, to apply actions to the elemental symbols of an image.

The second form of Interactivity identified in Figure 3.1 is navigation. Navigation is either parallel or sequential. In parallel navigation, images can be selected in any order, whereas in sequential navigation, images are displayed in a specific sequence (Ahlberg & Shneiderman, 1994; Thuring, Hannemann, & Haake, 1995). Sequential navigation allows the user to navigate forward and backward in a fixed order from one end of a series of images to the other. Parallel navigation allows the user to go either forward or backward as desired from any point in a series of images. Parallel navigation may be better for DSS because it imposes less of an order restriction than does sequential navigation. On the other hand, sequential navigation is easier to operate and may be less cognitively taxing.

User

The user is shown on the right side of Figure 3.1. The user's ability to generate an appropriate mental model depends upon the processes of perception and cognition. Visual perception is determined by experiential information and spatial and visual abilities (Anderson, 1990; Hochberg, 1978; Kaufmann, 1980, 1985). *Perception* is shown at the top of Figure 3.1 as connecting the properties (images, transition and alterations, and interactivity) of animation and the user's visual and spatial abilities and experiential information. The user's experience with both the task and the form of the presentation are considered major determinants of human performance and decision quality (Anderson, 1990; Jarvenpaa & Dickson, 1988; Kaufmann, 1980, 1985; Palmiter et al., 1991; Rouse & Morris, 1986; Wickens, 1987; Woods, 1984).

Users differ in their visual and visualizing abilities and therefore perceive and perform visual tasks differently (Anderson, 1990; MacLeod, Hunt, & Matthews, 1978). Users with high visual and spatial abilities develop more accurate visualizations when the information is depicted using images than do those with poor visual and spatial abilities (Kaufmann, 1980, 1985; Paivio, 1971; Rouse & Morris, 1986; Simon, 1975). Users with high visual abilities seem to perform better on tasks that involve spatial orientation than do users with poor visual ability (Just & Carpenter, 1985). This literature suggests that the user's visual and visualizing abilities may play important roles in determining the efficacy of animation in user interfaces designed for DSS.

In addition to perception, *Cognition* is a determinant of decision quality (Gillan & Cooke, 1994; Hochberg, 1978; Hochberg & Brooks, 1978; Treisman & Souther,

1985; Wickens, 1987, 1992; Woods, 1984). Experiences influence cognition, and experiences in the task domain and with animation technologies would be expected to influence the efficacy of animation in user interfaces designed for DSS. Collectively, the user's visual and visualizing abilities, and experiences in the task domain and animation technologies should all be considered when investigating the efficacy of animation in user interfaces designed for DSS.

As Figure 3.1 indicates, the processes of *Cognition* and *Action* link Task and User, and User and Animation, respectively. Shown near the bottom of Figure 3.1, the User interacts with Animation through Action. Because the user seeks to better understand the task through the animation, *Cognition* is shown as linking User and Task (at the top of Figure 3.1). Likewise, *Decision Quality* reflects the quality of the user's decisions in relation to the task, and therefore, *Decision Quality* is shown as a relationship between User and Task (at the bottom of Figure 3.1).

Task

The third property shown in Figure 3.1 is Task. The instantiation of Task includes type and structure. In terms of task type, some tasks are inherently visual and dynamic and may be more effectively depicted using animation than are tasks that are static and linguistic (Kaufmann, 1980, 1985). Likewise, problem structure is well known in the decision-making and DSS literature as a determinant of decision quality (Ginzberg & Stohr, 1982; Gorry & Scott Morton, 1971; Simon, 1960). Decisions are structured to the extent that they are repetitive and routine, to the extent that a definite procedure has been worked out for handling them so that they do not have to be treated *de novo* each time they occur (Simon, 1960). Decisions with little or no structure are novel and lack procedures to deal with the situation (Simon, 1960). In structured problems, much of the problem solving can be automated, whereas problems requiring a combination of judgment and automation are known as "semistructured" problems (Keen & Scott Morton, 1978). Unstructured problems rely on judgment alone.

Design is shown at the bottom of Figure 3.1 as linking Task and Animation. Good design produces useful artifacts. Design is the process of developing an architecture to build an artifact that satisfies requirements. Useful artifacts result from an understanding of requirements and a translation of requirements into an architecture that, when implemented and used, achieves the performance goal (Walls et al., 1992). Defining requirements is considered fundamental to all computer science (Newell & Simon, 1976) and is a well-known determinant of effective DSS design (Sprague & Carlson, 1982, p. 96). In the case of animation in user interfaces designed for DSS, the goal of improved decision quality dictates the design of the animation technologies used to build the artifact.

In summary, the goal of animation in user interfaces designed for DSS is to improve decision quality in the task domain. The user perceives (perception) and acts (action) on the animation artifact in an effort to understand (cognition) the task domain. Decision quality is a measure of the efficacy of the design of the animation artifact in relation to the user's abilities and experiences in the task requirements.

Hypotheses

If a model is to be useful as a scientific tool, it must be subject to refutation. The framework developed earlier and shown in Figure 3.1 suggests several research questions and hypotheses. Focusing on the effects of animation technologies on decision quality, three hypotheses are posited. Beginning with image abstraction, realistic images are believed to be cognitively and perceptually less demanding, making them simpler to comprehend, easier to use, and easier to interpret compared to abstract images (Anderson, 1990; Deregowski, 1990; Erickson, 1990; Espe, 1990; Gibson, 1979; Hochberg, 1978; Vaananen & Shmidt, 1994). The effect of image abstraction on decision quality, however, is unknown. Based on this, it is hypothesized that:

> H1: Animation using realistic images results in better decision quality than animation using abstract images.

The literature on classical animation techniques indicates that gradual transition effects focus attention, increasing the user's ability to locate important data, thereby decreasing the mental workload (Norman, 1986; Wickens, 1992; Woods, 1984). Whether this improves decision quality, however, is unclear. Based on this and Figure 3.1, it is hypothesized that:

> H2: Animation using gradual transitions results in better decision quality than animation using abrupt transitions.

The two common types of navigation interactivity identified earlier were parallel and sequential. Parallel navigation interactivity imposes less structure than sequential navigation interactivity, making it a more controllable decision support tool. On the other hand, sequential navigation interactivity may make decision making easier and less cognitively taxing precisely because it imposes more structure (Ginzberg & Stohr, 1982). A formal statement of this hypothesis is:

> H3: Animation using parallel navigation interactivity results in better decision quality than animation using sequential navigation interactivity.

These hypotheses are intended to be neither complete nor exhaustive. The universe of discourse on animation in user interfaces designed for DSS is very broad. These hypotheses simply give an indication of the questions suggested by the framework depicted in Figure 3.1. These hypotheses do, however, highlight improved decision quality as the goal of animation in user interfaces designed for DSS.

Experimental Design and Methodology

The hypotheses developed above were investigated in a laboratory experiment using a 2 (image abstraction) by 2 (transition) by 2 (navigation interactivity) experimental design. The three treatment factors resulted in eight treatment combinations. Responding to the hypotheses, the eight treatment combinations varied by type of image abstraction (realistic or abstract), type of transition (gradual or abrupt), and type of navigation interactivity (parallel or sequential). To increase the applicability of the results, this experimental design was applied to two different task domains in counterbalanced order. One task domain involved the relatively familiar, well-structured task of choosing the "best" place to live from a visually depicted set of attributes taken from a multiple-listing real estate guide. The second task placed the subject in the less familiar and less structured domain of fluid dynamics, judging the change in the level of water resulting from submerging an object in water. In both cases, decision quality was defined as the relationship between the choice made by the subject from among the available alternatives and the best alternative.

In addition to the direct control of variability in experimental error provided by the treatment conditions, indirect or statistical control was achieved by measuring the user's experiences and visualizing ability. Likewise, the user's decision time was recorded because of the potential trade-off between decision time and decision quality (Sperling & Dosher, 1986). These concomitant variates were used as covariates in the data analysis (Winer, 1971). In summary, the research model for this study was:

Decision quality$_{(Task)}$ = f (**Animation** [image abstraction, transition, navigation interactivity],
User [visualizing ability, experience $_{(Task)}$,
other relevant experiences, decision time $_{(Task)}$]),

where decision quality was measured for each of two tasks for each user, and the user's task experience and task decision time were recorded, as was the user's experiences with relevant technologies.

Task

Two different task domains were constructed for this study. One task, known as the Home Directory, or HomeD for short, involved the familiar problem of choosing the "best" place to rent from among a set of possible alternatives. The second task, known as the Bolt and Boat, or B&B for short, was a less well-known fluid dynamics problem. In selecting these tasks, several issues were considered. As suggested by Mennecke and Wheeler (1995), these included the appropriateness and attractiveness of the tasks to the subjects, the availability of procedures to represent and implement the tasks visually, the likelihood that the subjects would understand the objective of the tasks, and the means to measure and evaluate the subject's decision quality.

The HomeD task placed the subject in the hypothetical situation of finding a place to rent (houses or apartment) in a midsize city, well known to the subjects, in the southwestern United States. Evaluating 10 fixed, nonprioritized visual attributes used to describe each place to rent, subjects selected from among 20 alternatives the one that "most closely" matched the set of attributes defining the "best" place to live. Attributes for this best place were given to the subject at the beginning of the task. No single choice matched all of the attributes of this best place to live. The displayed image showed subjects a map of the city with icons indicating the location of the available properties. By directly pointing and clicking on a particular property, a picture of the property and a listing of its attributes were displayed in a window. Alternatives and their attributes were taken from the multiple-listing real estate guide for the city. The attributes were number of bedrooms, furnished, utilities, covered parking, fireplace, laundry facilities, pool, cable TV, location, and cost. The HomeD task was selected for this study because it is an application that has been touted as an exemplary use of computer visualization (Ahlberg & Shneiderman, 1994) and because it is similar to that used in other studies (e.g., Todd & Benbasat, 1994a, 1994b).

The B&B task required the subject to choose the alternative that best described the change in fluid level resulting from placing a bolt in a bucket of water. Subjects were shown the side view of a transparent bucket approximately three-quarters full of water. A boat was afloat on the water, and a bolt was suspended over the boat by a wire. The bolt was lowered into the boat, and the subject was shown an accurate representation of the resulting rise in the level of the water. The bolt was then lifted from the boat and the water level and boat returned to their starting points. The bolt was then moved so that it was suspended over the water, and it was dropped into the water, sinking to the bottom of the bucket. The subject was then instructed to select from among five alternatives the one that best described the level of the water with the bolt lying at the bottom of the bucket of water. Following the laws of fluid dynamics, only one alternative is correct, and the others vary in correctness as defined in Kaiser, Proffitt, Whelan, and Hecht (1992).

As in the HomeD task, the subject could consider a B&B alternative by pointing and clicking on it. The selected alternative was then displayed in a window on the screen. The window showed a picture of the level of the water and stated the specific displacement in millimeters and inches resulting from the alternative being considered by the subject. The subject could then choose the alternative just viewed or go on and consider another alternative. The B&B task domain was selected because it

Animation

According to the experimental design, eight different combinations of treatment factors (image abstraction, transition, and navigation interactivity) were constructed for each of the two task domains. These were built using Macromedia Director 4.0 on a PowerMac. The run-time version of each combination of manipulations was embedded in an application that controlled the execution of the task, computed and recorded the decision quality of the alternative selected by the subject, and recorded the subject's decision time (the elapsed time taken by the subject to select an alternative). Because it has been argued that sound improves user operation and understanding of interface animation (Clanton & Young, 1994), the same sound effects (e.g., mouse clicks and tones) were used in all manipulations. Finally, execution time was normed so that all HomeD and B&B manipulations took the same amount of time to execute, given identical user actions.

Following guidelines suggested by Hix and Hartson (1993), the screen layout for all manipulations was divided into three windows: the image window, the interactivity window, and the message window. The image window, approximately 80% of the screen, displayed either realistic or abstract images, as dictated by the experimental design, of either the HomeD or the B&B alternatives. The interactivity window, about 18% of the screen, displayed the navigational icons for the implementation of either sequential or parallel navigation interactivity. The balance of the screen, the message window, provided the user with instructions that were the same for all treatment combinations. By pointing and clicking on an alternative, a pop-up window allowed the user to view a specific choice. This provided a form of direct manipulation interactivity consistent with that found in Ahlberg and Shneiderman (1994).

According to Bertin (1983) and Dent (1985), a map is a realistic image of location information that is geographic in nature. Based on this, a city map was scanned and edited to form the basis for the HomeD realistic image. As the example in Figure 3.2a shows, somewhat embellished geometric shapes were superimposed on the scanned map to indicate the location of places to rent. These shapes, triangles for houses (not shown) and squares for apartments, varied in size to indicate the number of bedrooms (small = 1 bedroom, medium = 2 bedrooms, large = 3 bedrooms). In the abstract version of the HomeD task, Figure 3.2b, a starfield display, which is a two-dimensional scatterplot often used to display geographic information (Ahlberg & Shneiderman, 1994), was used to depict the city and to locate places to rent. Simple geometric shapes, again triangles for houses and squares for apartments, were used to indicate the location of places to rent. All other aspects of both the realistic and abstract images for the HomeD task were the same.

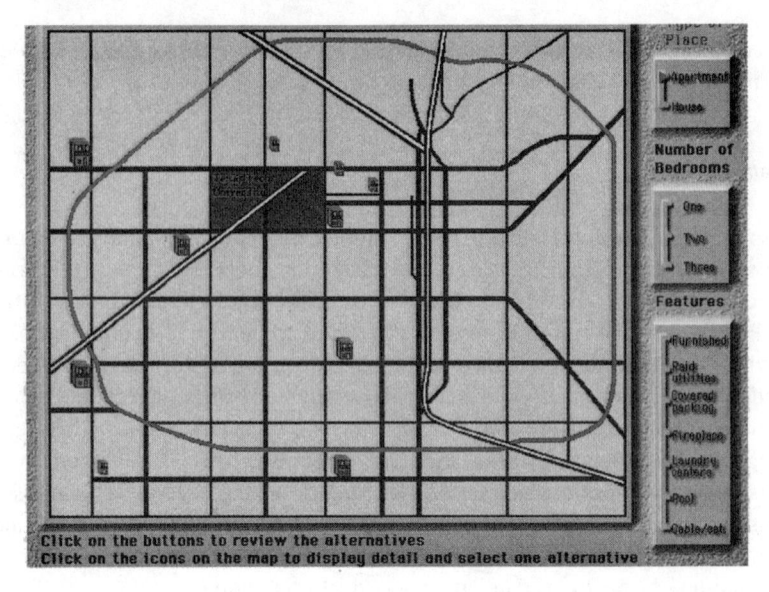

Figure 3.2a. Example of HomeD Task, Realistic Image, and Parallel Navigation Interactivity Treatment

The realistic image for the B&B task, shown in Figure 3.3a, was created by digitizing a picture taken of a model constructed for this purpose. The model was constructed using a transparent glass container and a toy boat. A picture of this model was taken with a digital camera and imported into Macromedia Director. Micromedia MacroModel was used to construct the bolt. For the abstract image, Figure 3.3b, a square represented the container, a trapezoid represented the boat, and a rectangle represented the bolt.

Transitions were either gradual or abrupt. Gradual transitions were implemented by making smooth transitions between consecutive frames and by providing transition effects between displayed alternatives. The dissolve (bits fast) effect initiated the fade-out of an image superimposed on the fade-in of the next image. In the gradual transition treatment level for the HomeD task, icons representing the alternative places to rent appeared one at a time; in the abrupt level, no transition effects were used with responses appearing all at once. For the B&B task, gradual transition was implemented by depicting small changes in the positioning of the boat, bolt, and water on consecutive images. In the abrupt transition, again, no transition effects were used, resulting in what appeared to be instantaneous changes between scenes. For example, in the B&B task, abrupt transition showed the bolt suspended out of the water; the next frame showed the bolt right above the water; and in the next frame, the bolt was shown at the bottom of the bucket.

Navigation interactivity was implemented as either parallel or sequential. These were designed based on those recommended by Ahlberg and Shneiderman (1994)

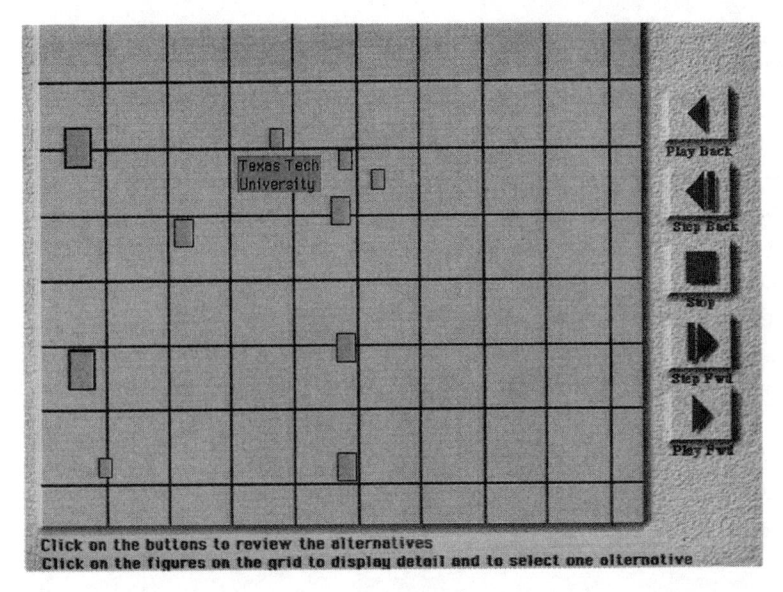

Figure 3.2b. Example of HomeD Task, Abstract Image, and Sequential Navigation Interactivity Treatment

and are shown in the interactivity windows of the displays in Figures 3.2a through 3.3b. Implementation of parallel navigation interactivity is shown in the interactivity windows in Figures 3.2a and 3.3b. Implementation of sequential navigation interactivity is shown in the interactivity windows in Figures 3.2b and 3.3a.

As shown, parallel navigation interactivity provided the user with control over the order in which the images in each series were presented. Buttons were used to run any segment of the animation in any order. For example, parallel navigation interactivity in the HomeD task (Figure 3.2a) allowed the user to choose the attribute and observe the alternatives or to choose the alternative and observe the attributes. Clicking on any button in the interactivity window at any time, the system would respond by showing the alternatives for the attribute or vice versa as directed by the user.

Sequential navigation interactivity, shown in Figures 3.2b and 3.3a, provided the user with buttons to navigate through the animation only in predefined sequences. The buttons were those normally found in any sequential navigation device: play forward, step forward, stop, step backward, and play backward. The user clicked on any one of these buttons at any time, playing the animation, stepping through the images either forward or backward, or stopping on one image.

As mentioned earlier, the user could select a specific alternative by pointing and clicking on it. This caused a pop-up window to appear on the screen that displayed the selected alternative. In the case of the HomeD task, a picture of the place to rent was displayed along with a listing of attributes and their values. For the B&B task,

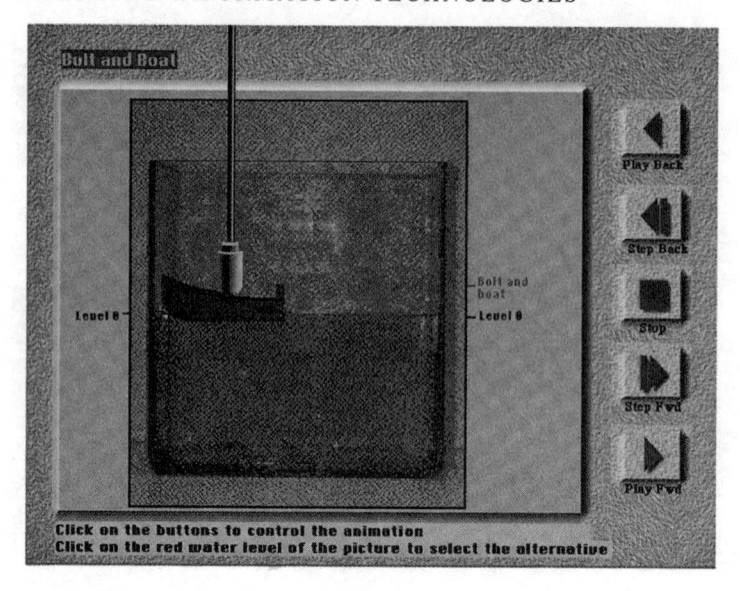

Figure 3.3a. Example of B&B Task, Realistic Image, and Sequential Navigation Interactivity Treatment

the window animated the scenario described by the selected alternative (e.g., one alternative animated the level of the fluid actually going down when the bolt was placed in the water). The user could then choose the displayed alternative or close the window and continue.

User Subjects

User subjects were recruited from undergraduate students in the College of Business Administration at Texas Tech University. Recruitment followed the guidelines of the American Psychological Association (1992). These guidelines require that all subjects participate voluntarily and receive course credit for their participation. Students were told that in order to participate, they could not be color blind and needed to have some experience using a personal computer and mouse. The study was briefly described to the students, and those willing and able to participate were asked to write their names and telephone numbers on a recruitment form. In total, 100 students volunteered to participate in the study. These subjects were later contacted and scheduled to take the experiment.

No specific hypotheses were proposed regarding user characteristics. Data on user subjects were collected to provide statistical control, increasing the precision of the experiment by reducing the experimental error (Winer, 1971). In accordance with the research model, measures of the subjects recorded in this study were task and technology experiences, visualizing ability, and decision time. The subject's

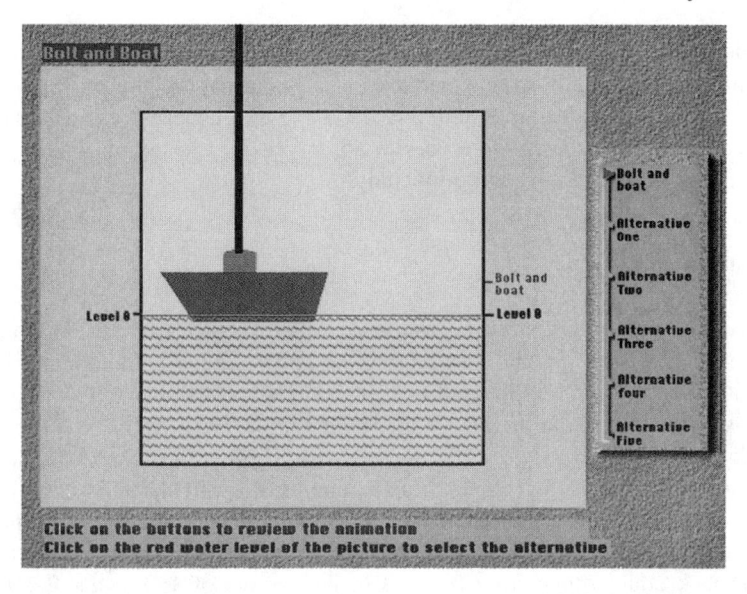

Figure 3.3b. Example of B&B Task, Abstract Image, and Parallel Navigation Interactivity Treatment

visualizing ability and experiences were gathered by two postexperiment questionnaires. Visualizing ability was measured by the Vividness of Visual Imagery Questionnaire (VVIQ), as formulated by Marks (1973). The VVIQ is a measure of the quality of one's ability to visualize an object. Each question on the VVIQ has a rating from 1 (*mental image is clear and vivid*) to 5 (*no mental image at all*). Consisting of 16 questions, the VVIQ requires about 10 minutes to complete. Used in more than 100 studies, reliability for the VVIQ is quite good, ranging from .85 to .94 (Marks, 1973, 1989; Richardson, 1994).

User experiences were measured using a questionnaire developed specifically for this study. Following Nielsen (1993), user experiences were measured along five dimensions: experience with computers in general, experience with each of the two tasks, and experiences with graphical interfaces and animation-type systems. Sixteen questions were developed to measure these dimensions. Factor analysis of the data collected from the subjects in this study resulted in five factors: user experience with computers in general, user experience in each of the two task domains of the study, and experiences using graphical interfaces and animation-type systems. Each of these factors had an eigenvalue greater than 1 and consisted of two or more questions. In total, these five factors explained 72% of the variance in the user-experiences data collected from the subjects in this study.

The final concomitant variate used in this study was decision time for each task. Decision time was recorded in seconds by the same software that presented the manipulations to the user and computed and recorded decision quality. Decision time was recorded because it has been suggested that the trade-off between decision time and decision quality be recognized in decision-making studies (Sperling & Dosher, 1986). Before being used in this study, the user-experiences questionnaire, treatments, and procedures were previewed and revised based on several evaluations, including the results of a pilot study.

Dependent Variables

The dependent variables for this study were decision quality for the HomeD and B&B tasks. Decision quality was determined and recorded automatically by the manipulation software. Following Kaiser et al. (1992), decision quality was defined based on how close the alternative selected by the subject was to the correct or "best" alternative. Recall that only one best answer existed for each of the two tasks used in this study. For the HomeD task, decision quality was calculated by counting the number of attributes of the alternative selected by the subject that matched those of the hypothetical place defined as the best place to live. Decision quality for the HomeD task could range from 0 to 10 in increments of 1. For the B&B task, decision quality was also defined based on how close the alternative selected by the subject was to the correct alternative. Using scoring defined in Kaiser et al., the selected alternative resulted in a decision quality score ranging from 1 to 5 in increments of 1.

Procedure

Subjects were scheduled to participate in the study in 1-hour time intervals. The experiment was administered to subjects in groups of eight over 5 consecutive days. Subjects took from 30 to 40 minutes to complete all aspects of the experiment.

Subjects gathered in a study area outside a computer laboratory. Instructions were delivered to the subjects in both written and videotaped form. For each of the tasks, the instructions specified the objective of the task and that decision quality would be used to evaluate performance. The written and videotaped instructions also discussed and demonstrated how each system would look and operate. After reading the instructions and viewing the 2-minute video, any questions the subjects had regarding the procedures and objectives of the study were answered. Next, subjects completed a consent form and started the laboratory work.

The computers used for the study were Power Macintoshes configured with a 13-inch color monitor and 8 MB of RAM. Subjects entered the laboratory and were free to select any one of the eight machines. Going to each machine, one of the researchers entered an identification number for each subject. This named the files on which the subject's data were to be recorded and assigned a treatment regimen according to the experimental design and the first of two tasks the subject was to consider. Based on the identification numbers, both treatment levels and task order were randomly assigned so that the task was counterbalanced and the number of observations in each treatment cell was expected to be balanced.

Subjects donned headphones and began the computer program and first task. The computer program began with a Welcome screen. As directed, the subject began the program by clicking on a button at the lower right-hand corner of the Welcome screen. Once the subject completed the first task, the program displayed a screen indicating that the subject should proceed to the next task. The subject began the second task just as the first by clicking on a button at the lower right-hand corner of the screen as directed. After choosing an answer to the second task, each subject completed the VVIQ and experience questionnaires. Each subject was then debriefed, thanked, and dismissed.

Data Analysis and Results

Of the 100 students who agreed to participate in the study, five failed to show up for the experiment, five did not follow the directions, and one declared himself to be colorblind. This resulted in a sample size of 89. Of these 89 subjects, 65% were undergraduate seniors, 27% were juniors, and 90% were business majors. Thirty-eight percent of the subjects were female, and four subjects (4.5%) reported that their native language was something other than English.

All 89 subjects completed both the HomeD and the B&B tasks in counterbalanced order but remained in the same treatment levels for both tasks. The counterbalancing of tasks provided a direct control for order, and the random assignment of subjects to order and treatment levels ensured that the expected differences between grouping (order and treatment levels) was zero at the time of the randomization (Cohen & Cohen, 1975). Forty-five subjects completed the HomeD and then the B&B task; the remaining 44 subjects completed the tasks in the reverse order. Table 3.1 shows the means, number of observations, and standard deviations for the dependent variable (decision quality) by animation treatment level (image abstraction, transition, and navigation interactivity) for each task. The data show that subjects exposed to realistic images had higher average decision quality for both tasks than did those exposed to abstract images. Likewise, subjects exposed to gradual transitions performed better on both tasks than did those who viewed abrupt transitions. Finally, the subjects using parallel navigation interactivity performed better on both tasks than did those using sequential navigation interactivity.

To assess the statistical significance of the differences in decision quality suggested by the means in Table 3.1, a two-step multivariate analysis of covariance was computed. The two-step procedure involved residualizing the decision quality data for each task by "removing" the effects of the covariates and then computing a multivariate analysis of variance (MANOVA) using these residuals as the dependent variables. This was done because two of the covariates, decision time and task

TABLE 3.1 Decision Quality Means, Standard Deviations, and Number of Observations by Treatment Levels for the HomeD and B&B Tasks

			\multicolumn{4}{c}{Task}
			HomeD (N = 89)		B&B (N = 89)	
Animation Treatment Levels			Mean	SD	Mean	SD
Image	abstract	(n = 44)	5.93	1.68	3.31	1.06
abstraction	realistic	(n = 45)	6.89	1.99	3.52	1.25
Transition and	abrupt	(n = 42)	6.26	1.93	3.05	1.25
alteration	gradual	(n = 47)	6.53	1.88	3.75	0.97
Direct manipulation	sequential	(n = 42)	5.74	1.74	3.12	1.11
interactivity	parallel	(n = 47)	7.00	1.84	3.68	1.14

experience, were task specific. Likewise, by design, the decision tasks differed, making repeated measures analysis inappropriate.

Multivariate analysis of covariance combines multiple regression analysis and MANOVA. Following Cohen and Cohen (1975, pp. 308-310), decision quality was residualized, and a MANOVA was computed on these residuals. This involved using multiple regression to "remove" the effects of the covariates from the dependent variable (decision quality) for each task. The residuals from these regressions were then used as the dependent variables in a MANOVA defined by the experimental design.

Regressing decision quality on the covariate measures (VVIQ, user experience with computers in general, experiences using graphical interfaces and animation-type systems, task experience, and decision time) for the HomeD task resulted in a significant reduction in the experimental error ($F_{(6,82)} = 2.65$, $p \leq .021$, $R^2 = .16$), but decision time was the only covariate significant at the $\alpha \leq .05$ level ($\beta = .261$, $t = 3.34$, $p \leq .002$). Removing the effects of the respective covariates from decision quality for the B&B task produced insignificant results ($F_{(6,82)} = 1.18$, $p \leq .324$, $R^2 = .08$). That the measures of the user (i.e., VVIQ, experience with computers in general, task experience, and experiences using graphical interfaces and animation-type systems) were not significant is consistent with the results reviewed in Huber (1983). The regression results of this study are not reported in more detail here because no specific hypotheses were proposed regarding these covariates and because, with the exception of decision time in the HomeD task, the results were insignificant.

Although very little of the experimental error was accounted for by the covariates, because decision time and task experience were task specific, a MANOVA was computed using the respective residuals of decision quality for each task following Cohen and Cohen (1975). Using this data, a MANOVA test criteria and exact F

TABLE 3.2 MANOVA Test Criteria and Exact F Statistics for the Hypotheses of No Overall Effect

Hypotheses	Wilks's Lambda	$F_{(2,84)}$	p Value
H1 (image)	.882	5.63	.005*
H2 (transition)	.884	5.49	.006*
H3 (navigation interactivity)	.851	7.38	.001*

*$p \leq .05$.

statistic were computed for each hypothesis of no overall effect. Results of the Wilks's Lambda test for each hypothesis are presented in Table 3.2.

Based on the results shown in Table 3.2, the hypothesis of an overall image abstraction effect (H1) cannot be rejected; overall, animation using realistic images did result in better decision quality than did animation using abstract images. These results also fail to reject H2; overall, subjects who viewed gradual transitions did have significantly higher decision quality than did those who viewed abrupt transitions. Likewise, the MANOVA test criteria and exact F statistic of the hypothesis for the overall navigation interactivity effect, H3, cannot be rejected, and it can be concluded that parallel navigation interactivity did result in better decision quality than did sequential navigation interactivity.

To clarify the MANOVA results, analysis of variance (ANOVA) was computed for the HomeD and the B&B residualized data separately. Presented in Table 3.3, these results clarify those of the MANOVA overall analysis. The ANOVA results show that decision quality for the HomeD task was affected significantly by both image abstraction and navigation interactivity, but transition did not affect decision quality. Subjects using realistic images had significantly higher decision quality than did those using abstract images. Again, H1 cannot be rejected; animation using realistic images did result in better decision quality than did animation using abstract images for the HomeD task. Likewise, the results fail to reject H3; parallel navigation interactivity resulted in better decision quality than did sequential navigation interactivity for the HomeD task. The HomeD results for H2, however, vary from the MANOVA overall results; there was no significant difference in the decision quality of subjects who viewed gradual transitions compared with those who viewed abrupt transitions.

Similarly, the ANOVA results for the B&B task vary from those of the HomeD task and the overall MANOVA. The data in Table 3.3 for the B&B task show that both transition and navigation interactivity had significant effects on decision quality. Consistent with the MANOVA overall results and the HomeD findings, the data again fail to reject H3; subjects using parallel navigation interactivity had higher decision quality than did those using sequential navigation interactivity. Consistent with the overall MANOVA results, but unlike the HomeD findings,

TABLE 3.3 Analysis of Variance of Decision Quality (Residuals) for the HomeD and B&B Tasks

a. ANOVA Results of Decision Quality (Residuals) for the Home Directory (HomeD) Task

Source	df	Sum of Squares	F Value	p Value
Model	3	52.61	7.05	.0003*
Error	85	211.36		
Corrected total	88	263.96		

$R^2 = .20$.

Source	df	Type III SS	F Value	p Value
Image	1	27.66	11.12	.0013*
Transition	1	1.48	0.60	.4424
Navigation interactivity	1	24.56	9.88	.0023*

*$p \leq .05$.

b. ANOVA Results of Decision Quality (Residuals) for the Bolt and Boat (B&B) Task

Source	df	Sum of Squares	F Value	p Value
Model	3	17.20	5.35	.0020*
Error	85	91.06		
Corrected total	88	108.26		

$R^2 = .16$.

Source	df	Type III SS	F Value	p Value
Image	1	.46	0.42	.5167
Transition	1	11.44	10.69	.0016*
Navigation interactivity	1	5.97	5.57	.0205*

*$p \leq .05$.

H2 cannot be rejected; gradual transitions did result in better decision quality compared with abrupt transitions in the B&B task. However, unlike both the HomeD and the MANOVA results, the B&B data rejected H1; the decision quality of subjects viewing realistic images was no higher than for those viewing the abstract images.

Collectively, H3 cannot be rejected; the results regarding interactivity are consistent. When employing animation in decision support systems, parallel navigation interactivity results in better decision quality than does sequential navigation interactivity. The results for H1 and H2, however, are inconsistent. In the HomeD task, decision quality varied by image abstraction but not transition levels. In the B&B task, the results were the opposite; decision quality varied by transition but not image abstraction levels.

Discussion of the Results

The effective use of animation in user interfaces designed for DSS is just emerging as a topic of research and practice. The results of this study indicate that the efficacy of animation in user interfaces designed for DSS is in part dependent upon the design of the navigation interactivity. Specifically, the decision quality of subjects exposed to parallel navigation interactivity was greater than that of those exposed to sequential navigation interactivity for both tasks considered here. One reason for this result might be that parallel navigation interactivity provides the user with greater control over the presentation of information than does sequential navigation interactivity. This reasoning is consistent with Ginzberg and Stohr's (1982) contention that "controllability," the degree to which the user directs the DSS, is central to the design of effective user interfaces for DSS. Moreover, previous research has demonstrated the importance of interactivity in human-computer interaction (Badler et al., 1993; Gobbetti et al., 1993; Jacob, Sibert, McFarlane, & Mullen, 1994) and DSS (Ginzberg & Stohr, 1982; Hale & Kasper, 1989; Kasper, 1996), and the results of this study add to the generalizability of this overall finding by showing that interactivity is also important for effective animation in user interfaces designed for DSS. Finally, the significance of parallel interactivity justifies highlighting the directive role of the user in the definition posited earlier for animation in user interfaces designed for DSS: images presented dynamically that change, guided by the user, in ways that improve decision quality.

In terms of image abstraction, the findings varied by task. In the HomeD task, subjects who used realistic images had significantly higher decision quality than did those who viewed the abstract images; but in the B&B task, no significant difference in decision quality was found between users of the abstract and realistic images. Recall that construction of the realistic and abstract images followed that suggested in the literature; that is, abstract images were constructed using geometric shapes, and realistic images were photographs of real-world objects.

An examination of the objects depicted in the images seems to suggest an apparent explanation for these conflicting results. In the B&B task, the objects (boat, bolt, bucket, water level, wire) are naturally geometric shapes. In this way, both the realistic and abstract images for the B&B task (Figures 3.3a and 3.3b) are fundamentally geometric shapes, perhaps accounting for the result of no difference in decision quality. Unfortunately, the same argument can also be made for the HomeD images; but in this case, the realistic images resulted in better decision quality than did the abstract images. The actual layout of the city depicted in the HomeD image is a geometric grid, making the realistic image of the city (Figure 3.2a) inherently the same as the abstract image (Figure 3.2b). Nevertheless, subjects using the HomeD realistic images did outperform (had significantly higher decision quality) those viewing the abstract image, even though the presentation of specific alternatives was the same for both levels of abstraction.

One implication of these results is that image abstraction is a much more complex issue than whether geometric shapes or photographs are used to construct the images. The degree to which symbols abstract reality probably depends upon the reality being depicted. Comparing Figures 3.2a with 3.2b and 3.3a with 3.3b suggests that the difference between the two B&B images (Figures 3.3a and 3.3b) may be greater than the two HomeD images (Figures 3.2a and 3.2b). However, in terms of decision quality, the statistical differences were the opposite: The difference in decision quality between the B&B images was not significant, whereas the HomeD images produced a statistically significant difference. The abstract version of the B&B (Figure 3.3b), appears easier to view than the realistic version (Figure 3.3a), but there was no significant difference in decision quality. Likewise, a map such as the one photographed as the realistic image in the HomeD (Figure 3.2a) is an abstraction of reality and not an aerial photograph of the actual street layout of a locale. From the perspective of improving decision quality, perhaps image abstraction needs to be considered more along the lines of that used in abstracting text; that is, indicative, informative, and explicative abstracts (Cremmins, 1982). To the extent that this distinction is somewhat akin to that made between information and data, information systems researchers would seem particularly well suited to developing the notion of image abstraction from the perspective of improving decision quality.

Transition also produced somewhat mixed results. Gradual transition resulted in better decision quality in the B&B task, but there was no statistically significant difference in decision quality between abrupt and gradual transition in the HomeD task. One possible explanation might be related to the dynamics of the situation. Animation such as that used in the HomeD task has been termed "stationary animation," as compared to animation that primarily involves change in the position of the objects (Harrison, 1993). In the HomeD task, transition primarily involved changing the appearance of the objects. In the B&B task, however, transition involved changing the position of objects. Perhaps when change is integral to making a decision, gradual transition is more important than when change is incidental to selecting a decision. In the B&B task, viewing the change in the water level was integral to choosing from among the available alternatives. In the HomeD task, however, change may have been incidental to selecting the best place to rent.

These results and the framework summarized in Figure 3.1 suggest a number of questions for future research. Questions regarding alterations were not considered in this study. The effects on decision quality of coloration and texturing, for example, remain to be investigated. Likewise, indirect manipulation was not a treatment level in this study. Other forms of image, transition, and interactivity also remain to be investigated. Based on the results of the study, image abstraction requires much greater attention than was given here. The results also suggest that the effects on decision quality of the relationship between the mix of animation technologies and the requirements of the task need much more investigation. For example, it was suggested that when change is integral to making a decision, transition may be more important than when change is incidental to selecting a decision. It is expected that consideration of these and related questions would constitute a program of research.

Summary and Conclusions

It is clear that animation is becoming an increasingly popular feature in user interfaces. This chapter developed the notion of animation in user interfaces designed for DSS, proposed a research framework for studying the effects of animation in user interfaces designed for DSS, and empirically tested three hypotheses derived from the framework.

Combining notions key to animation, human-computer interface, and DSS, animation in user interfaces designed for DSS was defined as images presented dynamically that change, guided by the user, in ways that improve decision quality. Animation was cited as providing the interface designer with a tool well suited to reducing the four-dimensional reality of time and three-dimensional space into the two-dimensions of the display screen. Moreover, it was suggested that the ability to depict change effectively might make animation particularly well suited to improving the decision quality of managers because so many of the decisions that managers make require identifying and assessing change, and change over time.

Based on a review of the animation literature, simplicity, smoothness, and interactivity were defined as properties of animation in user interfaces designed for DSS. It was suggested that through the process of design, properties of image simplicity, transition and alteration smoothness, and navigation and manipulation interactivity can be specified to improve decision quality. Integrating these properties of Animation with those of User and Task, a research framework for investigating the efficacy of animation in user interfaces designed for DSS was proposed.

Testing three hypotheses derived from the proposed research framework, the effects on decision quality of different designs of image abstraction, transition, and navigation interactivity were investigated in a laboratory experiment involving two different task domains. The results indicate that animation is more than just a creative way to display a decision situation. The design of animation can affect decision quality. The results are consistent with regard to interactivity: When using animation in decision support systems, parallel navigation interactivity results in better decision quality than does sequential navigation interactivity. The results regarding image abstraction and transition are not as clear. Based on the data in this study, transition effects appear to be significant when depicting dynamic, visual tasks, but they may not be as important for static, linguistic tasks. The results regarding realistic and abstract images suggest that from the perspective of improving decision quality, image abstraction is a very complex issue that perhaps needs to be considered somewhat akin to abstracting text and distinguishing information from data.

Many issues need to be investigated regarding the effective application of animation in user interfaces designed for DSS. Because so little is currently known about how to apply animation effectively in user interfaces, it is premature to make specific recommendations to the practitioner. The most robust finding of this study, however, is that the decision quality of subjects exposed to parallel navigation interactivity was greater than that of those exposed to sequential navigation interactivity. Recommendations regarding the use of image abstraction and transition effects require even more caution. Subjects using realistic images outperformed those using abstract images in one task; but in the other task, there was no difference in decision quality. Likewise, subjects exposed to gradual transition outperformed those using abrupt transition in one task; but in the other task, there was no difference in decision quality. These results might suggest that in terms of improving decision quality, realistic images should be preferred to abstract images, and gradual transitions should be preferred to abrupt transitions for animation in user interfaces designed for DSS. Again, these results need to be replicated in other task domains and investigated in much more detail before specific recommendations to practitioners can be made. Nevertheless, it is clear that animation in user interfaces designed for DSS can affect decision quality. This must be recognized when designing and using DSS that employ animation in the user interface.

The results of this study raise numerous research questions. Chief among these is development and validation of the notion of image abstraction as it relates to DSS in general and decision quality in particular. Investigations of alteration effects and manipulation interactivity are also indicated. The universe of discourse for interactive animation and animation in user interface design is just emerging, and there is a plethora of issues to be considered. The research reported here suggests that animation may provide designers of user interfaces for DSS with a tool to convert the four-dimensional reality of time and three-dimensional space into little marks on a two-dimensional screen in a way that improves decision quality. Making this conversion is a major challenge for both practitioners and researchers alike.

References

Ahlberg, C., & Shneiderman, B. (1994). Visual information seeking: Tight coupling of dynamic query filters with starfield displays. In *Proceedings of CHI '94* (pp. 313-317). New York: ACM Press.

American Psychological Association. (1992). Ethical principles of psychologists and code of conduct. *American Psychologist, 47,* 1597-1611.

Anderson, J. R. (1990). *Cognitive psychology and its implications.* New York: W. H. Freeman.

Badler, N. I., Phillips, C. B., & Webber, B. L. (1993). *Simulating humans: Computer graphics animation and control.* New York: Oxford University Press.

Baecker, R. M., & Small, I. (1990). Animation at the interface. In B. Laurel (Ed.), *The art of human-computer interface design.* Reading, MA: Addison-Wesley.

Benbasat, I., & Todd, P. (1993). An experimental investigation of interface design alternatives: Icon versus text and direct manipulation versus menus. *International Journal of Man-Machine Studies, 38,* 369-402.

Bertin, J. (1983). *Semiology of graphics.* Madison: University of Wisconsin Press.

Card, S. K., Moran, T. P., & Newell, A. (1983). *The psychology of human-computer interaction.* Hillsdale, NJ: Lawrence Erlbaum.

Chang, B., & Ungar, D. (1993). Animation: From cartoons to the user interface. In *Proceedings of UIST '93* (pp. 45-55). New York: ACM Press.

Clanton, C., & Young, E. (1994). Film craft in user interface design. In *Tutorial Notes of CHI '94.* New York: ACM Press.

Cohen, J., & Cohen, P. C. (1975). *Applied multiple regression/correlation analysis for the behavioral sciences.* Hillsdale, NJ: Lawrence Erlbaum.

Cremmins, E. T. (1982). *The art of abstracting.* Philadelphia: ISI Press.

Daft, R. L. (1991). *Management* (2nd ed.). New York: Dryden.

Davis, S. A., & Bostrom, R. P. (1993). Training end users: An experimental investigation of the roles of the computer interface and training methods. *MIS Quarterly, 17*(1), 61-85.

Dent, B. D. (1985). *Principles of thematic map design.* Reading, MA: Addison-Wesley.

Deregowski, J. B. (1990). On two distinct and quintessential kinds of pictorial representation. In K. Landwehr (Ed.), *Ecological perception research, visual communication, and aesthetics.* New York: Springer-Verlag.

DeSanctis, G., & Gallupe, R. B. (1987). A foundation for the study of group decision support systems. *Management Science, 33*(5), 589-609.

Erickson, D. T. (1990). Working with interface metaphors. In B. Laurel (Ed.), *The art of human-computer interface design.* Reading, MA: Addison-Wesley.

Espe, H. (1990). The communicative potential of pictures: Eleven theses. In K. Landwehr (Ed.), *Ecological perception research, visual communication, and aesthetics.* New York: Springer-Verlag.

Finkel, L. H., & Sajda, P. (1994, May-June). Constructing visual perception. *American Scientist, 82,* 224-237.

Gibson, J. J. (1979). *The ecological approach to visual perception.* New York: Houghton Mifflin.

Gillan, D., & Cooke, N. (1994). Methods of perceptual and cognitive research applied to interface design and testing. In *Tutorial Notes of CHI '94.* New York: ACM Press.

Ginzberg, M. J., & Stohr, E. A. (1982). Decision support systems: Issues and perspectives. In M. J. Ginzberg, W. Reitman, & E. A. Stohr (Eds.), *Decision support systems.* Amsterdam: North-Holland.

Gobbetti, E., Balaguer, J., & Thalmann, D. (1993). An architecture for interaction in synthetic worlds. In *Proceedings of UIST '93* (pp. 167-178). New York: ACM Press.

Goldstein, B. E. (1989). *Sensation and perception* (3rd ed.). Belmont, CA: Wadsworth.

Gorry, G. A., & Scott Morton, M. S. (1971). A framework for management information systems. *Sloan Management Review, 13*(1), 55-70.

Halas, J. (1990). *The contemporary animator.* Stoneham, MA: Focal Press, Butterworth-Heinemann.

Hale, D. P., & Kasper, G. M. (1989). The effect of human-computer interchange protocol on decision performance. *Journal of Management Information Systems, 6*(1), 5-20.

Harrison, S. (1993). *Still, animated, or nonillustrated on-line help with written or spoken instructions for performance of computer-based procedures.* Unpublished doctoral dissertation, University of Minnesota, Minneapolis.

Hartson, R. H., & Hix, D. (1989). Human-computer interface development: Concepts and systems for its management. *ACM Computing Survey, 21*(1), 5-92.

Henderson, J. C. (1987). Finding synergy between decision support systems and expert systems research. *Decision Sciences, 18*(3), 333-349.

Hix, D., & Hartson, R. H. (1993). *Developing user interfaces: Ensuring usability through product and process.* New York: John Wiley.

Hochberg, J. E. (1978). *Perception* (2nd ed.). Englewood Cliffs, NJ: Prentice Hall.
Hochberg, J. E. (1986). Visual perception of real and represented objects and events. In D. R. Gerstein & N. J. Smelser (Eds.), *Behavioral and social science: Fifty years of discovery.* Washington, DC: National Academy Press.
Hochberg, J. E., & Brooks, V. (1978). Film cutting and visual momentum. In J. W. Senders, D. F. Fisher, & R. A. Monty (Eds.), *Eye movements and the higher psychological functions.* Hillsdale, NJ: Lawrence Erlbaum.
Hollnagel, E., & Woods, D. D. (1983). Cognitive systems engineering: New wine in new bottles. *International Journal of Man-Machine Studies, 18,* 583-600.
Huber, G. P. (1983). Cognitive style as a basis for MIS and DSS design: Much ado about nothing. *Management Science, 29*(5), 567-579.
Humphreys, P. (1986). Intelligence in decision support. In B. Brehmer, H. Jungermann, P. Lourens, & G. Sevon (Eds.), *New directions in research on decision making.* Amsterdam: Elsevier Science, B.V. North-Holland.
Isdale, J. (1993). *What is virtual reality? A homebrew introduction and information resource list* [on-line]. October 8, Version 2.1. From ftp site ftp.u.washington.edu in public/virtual-worlds/papers as whatisvr.txt.
Jacob, R. J. K., Sibert, L. E., McFarlane, D. C., & Mullen, M. P. (1994). Integrality and separability of input devices. *ACM Transactions on Computer-Human Interaction, 1*(1), 3-26.
Jarvenpaa, S. L., & Dickson, G. W. (1988). Graphics and managerial decision making: Research-based guidelines. *Communications of the ACM, 31*(6), 764-774.
Johnson-Laird, P. N. (1981). Mental models in cognitive science. In D. A. Norman (Ed.), *Perspectives on cognitive science.* Norwood, NJ: Ablex.
Just, M. A., & Carpenter, P. (1985). Cognitive coordinate systems: Accounts of mental rotation and individual differences in spatial ability. *Psychological Review, 92*(2), 137-172.
Kaiser, M. K., Proffitt, D. R., Whelan, S. M., & Hecht, H. (1992). Influence of animation on dynamical judgments. *Journal of Experimental Psychology: Human Perception and Performance, 18*(3), 669-690.
Kasper, G. M. (1996). A theory of decision support system design for user calibration. *Information Systems Research, 7*(2), 215-232.
Kaufmann, G. A. (1980). *Imagery, language and cognition: Toward a theory of symbolic activity in human problem solving.* Norway: Reklametrykk A.S. Universitetsforlaget (printed in North America by Columbia University Press, NY).
Kaufmann, G. A. (1985). Theory of symbolic representation in problem solving. *Journal of Mental Imagery, 9*(2), 51-70.
Keen, P. G. W. (1987). Decision support systems: The next decade. *Decision Support Systems, 3,* 253-265.
Keen, P. G. W., & Scott Morton, M. S. (1978). *Decision support systems: An organizational perspective.* Reading, MA: Addison-Wesley.
Keller, P. R., & Keller, M. M. (1993). *Visual cues.* Los Alamitos, CA: IEEE Computer Society Press and IEEE Press.
Kosslyn, S. M. (1985). Graphics and human information processing. *Journal of the American Statistical Association, 80*(391), 499-512.
Krampen, M. (1990). Functional versus dysfunctional aspects of information surfaces. In K. Landwehr (Ed.), *Ecological perception research, visual communication, and aesthetics.* New York: Springer-Verlag.
Luconi, F. L., Malone, T. W., & Scott Morton, M. S. (1986). Expert systems: The next challenge for managers. *Sloan Management Review, 27*(4), 3-14.
MacLeod, C. M., Hunt, E. B., & Matthews, N. N. (1978). Individual differences in the verification of sentence-picture relationships. *Journal of Verbal Learning and Verbal Behavior, 17,* 493-507.
Magnenat-Thalmann, N., & Thalmann, D. (1985). *Computer animation: Theory and practice.* New York: Springer-Verlag.

Marks, D. F. (1973). Visual imagery differences in the recall of pictures. *British Journal of Psychology, 64*(1), 17-24.
Marks, D. F. (1989). Bibliography of research utilizing the Vividness of Visual Imagery Questionnaire. *Perception and Motor Skills, 69,* 707-718.
Marr, D. (1982). *Vision: A computational investigation into the human representation and processing of visual information.* San Francisco: W. H. Freeman.
Mason, R. O., & Mitroff, I. A. (1973). A program for research on management information systems. *Management Science, 19*(5), 475-487.
Mennecke, B. E., & Wheeler, B. C. (1995). *An essay and resource guide for dyadic and group task selection and usage* [on-line]. http://www.bmgt.umd.edu/business/academicdepts/IS/tasks/essay.html.
Newell, A., & Simon, H. A. (1972). *Human problem solving.* Englewood Cliffs, NJ: Prentice Hall.
Newell, A., & Simon, H. A. (1976). Computer science as empirical inquiry: Symbols and search. *Communications of the ACM, 19*(3), 113-126.
Nielsen, J. (1993). *Usability engineering.* San Diego, CA: Academic Press.
Norman, D. A. (1986). Cognitive engineering. In D. A. Norman & S. W. Draper (Eds.), *User-centered system design: New perspectives on human-computer interaction.* Hillsdale, NJ: Laurence Erlbaum.
Olson, G. M., & Olson, J. S. (1991). User-centered design of collaborative technology. *Organizational Computing, 1*(1), 61-83.
Outside In. (1994). Geometry Center, University of Minnesota. In *SIGGRAPH 94: Electronic theater.* ACM SIGGRAPH Video Review, Issue 101, ACM, New York.
Paivio, A. (1971). *Imagery and verbal processes.* New York: Holt, Rinehart & Winston.
Palmiter, S. (1993). The effectiveness of animated demonstrations for computer-based tasks: A summary, model and future research. *Journal of Visual Languages and Computing, 4,* 71-89.
Palmiter, S., Elkerton, J., & Baggett, P. (1991). Animated demonstrations vs. written instructions for learning procedural tasks: A preliminary investigation. *International Journal of Man-Machine Studies, 34,* 687-701.
Park, O., & Hopkins, R. (1992). Instructional conditions for using dynamic visual displays: A review. *Instructional Science, 21*(6), 427-449.
Payne, J. W. (1982). Contingent decision behavior. *Psychological Bulletin, 92*(2), 382-402.
Remus, W. E., & Kotteman, J. (1986). Toward intelligent decision support systems: An artificially intelligent statistician. *MIS Quarterly, 10*(4), 403-418.
Richardson, A. (1994). *Individual differences in imaging: Their measurement, origins, and consequences.* Amityville, NY: Baywood.
Rieber, L. P., Boyce, M. J., & Assad, C. (1990). The effects of computer animation on adult learning and retrieval tasks. *Journal of Computer-Based Instruction, 17*(2), 46-52.
Rieber, L. P., & Hannafin, M. J. (1988). Effects of textual and animated orienting activities and practice on learning from computer-based instruction. *Computers in the Schools, 5*(1&2), 77-89.
Robertson, G. G., Card, S. K., & Mackinlay, J. D. (1989). The cognitive coprocessor architecture for interactive user interfaces. In *Proceedings of UIST '89* (pp. 10-18). New York: ACM Press.
Robertson, G. G., Card, S. K., & Mackinlay, J. D. (1993). Information visualization using 3D interactive animation. *Communications of the ACM, 36*(4), 57-71.
Rouse, W. B., & Morris, N. M. (1986). On looking into the black box: Prospects and limits in the search for mental models. *Psychological Bulletin, 100*(3), 349-363.
Scott Morton, M. S. (1984). The state of the art of research. In F. W. McFarlan (Ed.), *The information systems research challenge.* Cambridge, MA: Harvard Business School Press.
Shneiderman, B. (1992). *Designing the user interface: Strategies for effective human-computer interaction* (2nd ed.). Reading, MA: Addison-Wesley.
SIGGRAPH 94: Electronic theater. (1994). ACM SIGGRAPH Video Review, Issue 101, ACM, New York.
Simon, H. A. (1960). *The new science of management decision.* New York: Harper & Row.

Simon, H. A. (1975). The functional equivalence of problem solving skills. *Cognitive Psychology, 36*(7), 268-289.
Solomon, C. (1983). *The computer Kodak animation book.* Rochester, NY: Eastman Kodak.
Sperling, G., & Dosher, B. (1986). Strategy and optimization in human information processing. In K. R. Boff, L. Kaufman, & J. P. Thomas (Eds.), *Handbook of perception and human performance.* San Diego, CA: Academic Press.
Sprague, R. H., & Carlson, E. D. (1982). *Building effective decision support systems.* Englewood Cliffs, NJ: Prentice Hall.
Stasko, J. T. (1993). Animation in user interfaces: Principles and techniques. In L. Bass & D. Prasun (Eds.), *User interface software.* New York: John Wiley.
Teen math whizzes go Euclid one better. (1996, December 9). *The Wall Street Journal,* p. B1.
Thuring, M., Hannemann, J., & Haake, J. M. (1995). Hypermedia and cognition: Designing for comprehension. *Communications of the ACM, 38*(8), 57-66.
Todd, P. A., & Benbasat, I. (1994a). The influence of decision aids on choice strategies: An experimental analysis of the role of cognitive effort. *Organizational Behavior and Human Decision Processes, 60,* 36-74.
Todd, P. A., & Benbasat, I. (1994b). The influence of decision aids on choice strategies under conditions of high cognitive load. *IEEE Transactions on Systems, Man, and Cybernetics, 24*(4), 537-547.
Treisman, A., & Souther, J. (1985). Search asymmetry: A diagnostic for preattentive processing of separable features. *Journal of Experimental Psychology, 114*(3), 285-310.
Tufte, E. R. (1990). *Envisioning information.* Cheshire, CT: Graphic Press.
Vaananen, K., & Shmidt, J. (1994). User interfaces for hypermedia: How to find good metaphors? In *Proceedings of CHI '94* (pp. 263-264). New York: ACM Press.
Walls, J. G., Widmeyer, G. R., & El Sawy, O. A. (1992). Building an information design theory for vigilant EIS. *Information Systems Research, 3*(1), 36-59.
Wickens, C. D. (1987). Information processing, decision making, and cognition. In *The handbook of human factors* (pp. 73-101). New York: John Wiley.
Wickens, C. D. (1992). *Engineering psychology and human performance.* New York: HarperCollins.
Winer, B. J. (1971). *Statistical principles in experimental design.* New York: McGraw-Hill.
Woods, D. D. (1984). Visual momentum: A concept to improve the cognitive coupling of person and computer. *International Journal of Man-Machine Studies, 21,* 229-244.

CHAPTER FOUR

The Emergence of Hypertext and Problem Solving

An Experimental Investigation of Accessing and Using Information From Linear Versus Nonlinear Systems

NARENDER K. RAMARAPU
MARK N. FROLICK
RONALD B. WILKES
JAMES C. WETHERBE

Many of the everyday decisions individuals make in today's world involve using computer hardware and software technologies that offer alternative ways to access and display information. One such alternative is to offer individuals a nonlinear system—a system that has nonlinear data structures in a manner similar to human cognition (Bush, 1945; Shneiderman, 1989). A nonlinear system, also referred to as "hypertext," allows information to be accessed in a nonsequential order. It refers to a computerized system that shares the common goal of encouraging more flexible exploration, presentation, search, and manipulation of information and ideas (Conklin, 1987). Thus, a nonlinear system frees users from the constraint of following predefined, hierarchical paths. For example, the now popular World Wide Web on the Internet is based on hypertext technology.

The traditional linear arrangement of text has dominated computer-based system design since the first use of computers. In this approach, text is organized and designed to be accessed and used in a fixed, sequential order, as in printed materials. The studies conducted on the computer-based linear systems, also referred to as "sequential," suggested that linear access of information aided human understanding of knowledge presentation (Nelson, 1986; Rich, 1983; Schank & Abelson, 1977) and the conventional way of learning (Anderson, 1981). A good understanding of a problem means improved problem solving or decision making. On the other hand, researchers contend that nonlinear links approximate the way human memory operates in associations (Bush, 1945; Shneiderman, 1989) and, thus, will lead to better information access and use. This, in turn, should have a positive influence on problem solving. Past research also suggests that problem-solving and/or decision behavior can be altered and improved by changes in the way

---

Reprinted by permission from *Decision Sciences*, Volume 28, Number 4, Fall 1997.

information is accessed and displayed (Russo, 1977). Decision makers have been found to use different problem-solving strategies when presented with information organized in alternative formats (Bettman & Kakkar, 1977). This research study investigates the impact of accessing and using (or displaying) information from two different formats (linear and nonlinear systems).

Further, the usefulness of accessing and displaying information appears to depend upon the characteristics of the problem task. Several studies in the "graphs versus tables" research have discussed and shown evidence that the impact of information representation on performance seemed to depend directly on the characteristics of the problem task (Benbasat & Dexter, 1985, 1986; Dickson, DeSanctis, & McBride, 1986; Jarvenpaa & Dickson, 1988; Powers, Lashley, Sanchez, & Shneiderman, 1984; Todd & Benbasat, 1991). Also, according to literature, matching the information representation directly to the problem task has significant effects on problem-solving performance (Bettman & Zins, 1979; Wright, 1975). Cognitive fit theory further extends this concept by suggesting that for the most effective and efficient problem solving to occur, the problem representation (i.e., the format used to present the data) and any tools or aids employed should all support the processes required to perform that task (Vessey, 1991). In fact, Goodhue and Thompson (1995) have highlighted the importance of "fit" between information technologies and users' tasks for individual performance improvement. Based on these arguments, the present research used different combinations of problem tasks to determine whether linear or nonlinear systems (in this case, accessing and displaying information from linear and nonlinear links) will lead to more accurate and quicker problem solving, and higher levels of user satisfaction.

Literature Review and Theoretical Foundation

This section describes the evolution, various levels, and research advances in the area of hypertext (nonlinear systems). Then, the theoretical foundation for this study is developed.

Emergence of Hypertext

Although hypertext has a rich history, most people have not heard of it until recent years. Vannevar Bush is considered the "grandfather" of hypertext. He first proposed a system in 1945 that we would now describe as a hypertext system. This system, the Memex ("memory extender"), was only described in theory and never implemented. Bush described his Memex as a device that individually stores books, records, and communications, and this procedure is mechanized so that it may be consulted with exceeding speed and flexibility. It was an enlarged, intimate supplement to human memory.

Engelbart (1963) and Nelson (1967) carried Bush's (1945) inspiring idea from the realm of theory to the useful world of technology. Douglas Engelbart (1963) envisioned the potential of a computer performing all the tasks of a Memex. His

NLS (later called AUGMENT) system put his vision into practice. NLS/AUGMENT was one of the earliest hypertext systems focusing on the group work environment (Engelbart, 1984). This system concentrated on three areas: first, a database of nonlinear text; second, view filters that selected information from the database; and lastly, views that structured the display of this information onto the screen (Conklin, 1987). The system also possessed some basic features, such as links, nodes, and network branching.

It was not until 1967 that the term "hypertext" was coined by Nelson. Nelson (1967) referred to the hypertext as nonlinear presentation and writing. His Xanadu project, one of the seminal hypertext systems, was one of the first technological applications in using machine-supported interdocument links for large online libraries. He defined hypertext as "a combination of natural language text which utilizes computer capabilities for interactive branching, or dynamic display . . . of a nonlinear text . . . which cannot be printed conveniently on a conventional page" (Nelson, 1967, p. 194). His thinking and writing were considered the most extravagant of the early nonlinear text design workers.

The term "hypertext" has been used quite loosely in the literature. Its definition and understanding varies based on the author's background and the different collection of system features. Also, hypertext webs, whether read on stand-alone systems or networks, can have two fundamentally different structures. The first (stand-alone system) relies closely upon the basic informational level similar to a linear book. The second (network) relates the dispersed, multiple-centered network organization inherent in electronic linking. From the viewpoint of information presentation and organization of information, and in this research, hypertext may be defined as an approach to information management in which data are stored as a network of nodes connected by links and from which data are presented in a nonsequential order.

Levels of Hypertext

Kendall and Kerola (1994) have proposed a three-level pyramid structure for conceptualizing the various levels of hypertext: beginning with the basic level, which is informational; going to the next level, which is experiential (includes informational); and further to the highest level, which is collaborative (includes the prior two levels). In the informational level, the capability for nonlinear access to information emerges at the most basic step. Here, "users query the system, asking for help. Hypertext responds by organizing text and linking multiple nodes of information together" (Kendall & Kerola, p. 5). These nodes of information can very well reside on a stand-alone system instead of a network. Another way to look at the informational level is in terms of offering an elaborate help menu. Here, "users make their desired selections among pieces of stored information, whether they are text or graphics" (Kendall & Kerola, p. 5). At the informational level, other characteristics the users can utilize include browsing through material; getting online reference help; getting illustrations of queried material, etc. Hypertext applications written for the informational level promote the goals of flexible organization of information and efficient access to information.

At the next two levels of hypertext (experiential and collaborative), more capabilities are engaged. The experiential level enables "users to step into a new set of circumstances and experience it interactively" (Kendall & Kerola, 1994, p. 5). The activities at this level can include learning and analysis, training and education, and applying theoretical concepts (Barnes, Baskerville, Kendall, & Kendall, 1992; Kendall & Kendall, 1992). In this level, users engage in an experience for themselves, guided by hypertext links, but take an active part to freely explore the paths at their own pace and in their own way. Here, "users not only query the system as to meanings, but make different meanings from the hypertext linked information by freely making associations, taking alternative pathways through the system" (Kendall & Kerola, p. 6). This, in turn, can promote alternative ways of arriving at the answers in an efficient way, or it can actually hinder an efficient way of accessing the information for the user.

The third, collaborative level, goes beyond "read-only" and permits users to write as well. This level empowers users to become contributors to the hypertext application. It enables users to build upon what each person contributes, sharing each others' experiences and putting them together in a common, easily manageable manner (Kendall & Kerola, 1994).

Most research in the area of hypertext has so far focused only on the informational level. In this particular research, the efforts are focused on a hypertext (nonlinear) system that is developed and tested at the experiential level, which also includes the informational level. At this level, a hypertext system permits the individual reader to choose his or her own center of investigation and navigate through an experiential application. What this principle means in practice is that the reader is not locked into any particular predefined path or hierarchy. This allows users to play an active part in discovery and enables them to make their own associations for effectively and efficiently arriving at problem solutions.

Research Related to Hypertext

Earlier applications of hypertext often focused on providing flexible access to a wide variety of information types (Bieber & Kimbrough, 1992; Conklin, 1987, 1991; Halasz, 1988; Minch, 1989; Nelson, 1967; Shneiderman & Kearsley, 1989). Some educational technology-related research attempted to structure knowledge-rich learning environments (Jacobson & Spiro, 1991a; Jonassen, 1986; Spiro, Feltovich, Jacobson, & Coulson, 1996). Also, in recent years, researchers have started to describe and show the hypertext application design environments, methods, and process (Fraisse, 1997; Garzotto, Paolini, & Schwabe, 1993; Nanard & Nanard, 1995; Schwabe, Rossi, & Barbosa, 1996).

Although many hypertext systems and projects have been developed, only a small number of observational and experimental studies have been reported. These studies cover three areas:

- *The effectiveness of hypertext systems.* Two studies at the University of Maryland investigated the effectiveness of hypertext versus paper form in scanning large textual databases. A hypertext browsing system called Hyperties (Shneiderman, 1987) was used for the hypertext application (Conklin, 1987; Marchionini & Shneiderman, 1988). Studies have been done at Brown University to test poetry-teaching effectiveness when using the Intermedia System (Yankelovich, Haan, Meyrowitz, & Drucker, 1988) as an electronic instructional system versus conventional classroom instruction. The Intermedia System is a highly integrated hypertext environment developed at Brown University (Yankelovich et al., 1988).
- *Interface design issues.* These studies tested certain interface design alternatives at the University of Maryland using the Hyperties System. One study compared the use of arrow keys to the use of a mouse for cursor movement on a display (Ewing, Mehrabanzad, Sheck, Ostroff, & Shneiderman, 1986). Several other studies were devoted to research on an embedded menu approach in Hyperties and also to comparing versions of Hyperties with and without embedded menus (Marchionini & Shneiderman, 1988).
- *Hypertext learning styles or strategies.* Several studies investigated different learning styles and information-seeking strategies of hypertext users. One study examined the information-seeking strategies of elementary school students (Marchionini & Shneiderman, 1988). In another study, Jacobson and Spiro (1991b) investigated instructional prescriptions for hypertext learning systems by using multiple representations of knowledge in multiple contexts.

Findings from all of these studies mainly related hypertext systems to instructional design, interface design, and learning strategies. Only one study, called HyperSolver, was developed using Hypercard 2.1 on a Macintosh to help in defining and solving problems effectively (Esichaikul, Madey, & Smith, 1994). But this application was never tested in measuring the user's effectiveness in problem-solving situations. No research to date has compared the problem-solving effects that develop when accessing and using a nonlinear (hypertext) system versus a linear system.

Theoretical Foundation

The theoretical foundation for this study is derived from the work on linear and nonlinear research. In linear research, investigators argue that humans arrange things in a sequence to facilitate memory and learning. Also, they contend that a computer-based linear approach has aided human understanding of knowledge presentation and learning well (Rich, 1983; Schank & Abelson, 1977). According to Schank and Abelson, a connected, causal chain of events is useful for representing any sequential flow of events. Because certain sequences of events frequently occur in a specific order, people have developed special mechanisms to deal with them. They call this mechanism a script, and define a script to be a structure that describes an appropriate sequence of events in a particular context. Scripts also exhibit a hierarchical structure in that they are composed of subscripts or scenes (Abelson,

1981). For example, a restaurant script generally includes entering, ordering, eating, and paying scenes, each of which has a script structure of its own. [Note, sequencing information is certainly a part of scripts, but scripts can also contain information that is not strictly sequenced. Here, we are only focusing on the ability to represent everyday situations occurring in linear or sequential fashion that are generally governed by specific procedures and rules of business conduct.]

Human understanding is viewed by Schank and Abelson (1977) as being heavily script based. Understanding is a process by which people match what they see and hear to prestored sequential groupings of actions previously experienced. New information is understood in terms of old information. Based on this script theory, many researchers have made strong claims that organizing information in a sequential or linear form leads to a good understanding process (Nelson, 1986; Zacarias, 1986).

On the other hand, a linear approach to organizing information has also raised problems in studies of human information processing. As Landauer, Dumais, Gomez, and Furnas (1982) pointed out, with linear text, the arrangement of data in a database and in a user's mind is often mismatched, with the user having no model of the way data are organized. Landauer et al. argued that "Typically, the data in a database are logically arranged for efficient system processing. Unfortunately, there is no guarantee that the partitioning or connections of data objects in the system will correspond to partitioning or connections in the user's mind" (p. 2489).

In nonlinear research, some cognitive psychology literature argues that nonlinear links to information overcome the problems raised in linear research caused by this mismatch. In theory, researchers argue that nonlinear links more closely resemble the way human memory operates (Bush, 1945; Motley, 1987; Shneiderman, 1989).

Over 50 years ago, Bush (1945) proposed the idea of nonlinear links and argued that nonlinear links approximate the way humans think more closely than linear indexing. Based on Bush's idea, Shneiderman (1989) described nonlinear data structures in a manner similar to human cognition. Specifically, he emphasized that the association provided by links in a hypertext (nonlinear) database should facilitate remembering, concept formulation, and understanding. Motley (1987) also offered a versatile explanation based on a theory known as "spreading activation." He explained that the association of words in human memory is interconnected in a manner similar to a nonlinear system. Thus, increased problem-solving efficiency and effectiveness should result because nonlinear links allow users to access information similar to the way they use memory (i.e., create their own links, not merely follow someone else's predefined paths).

Based on the arguments of linear and nonlinear research, it seems reasonable that some learning and understanding can be enhanced with sequential or linear data arrangement, while other learning and understanding may be better served with nonlinear systems (see Anderson, 1981, for an excellent review of some of the thinking in this area). The effectiveness of linear versus nonlinear structures on problem solving or decision making is still unknown, though, due to a lack of empirical verification.

Independent Variables   *Dependent Variables*

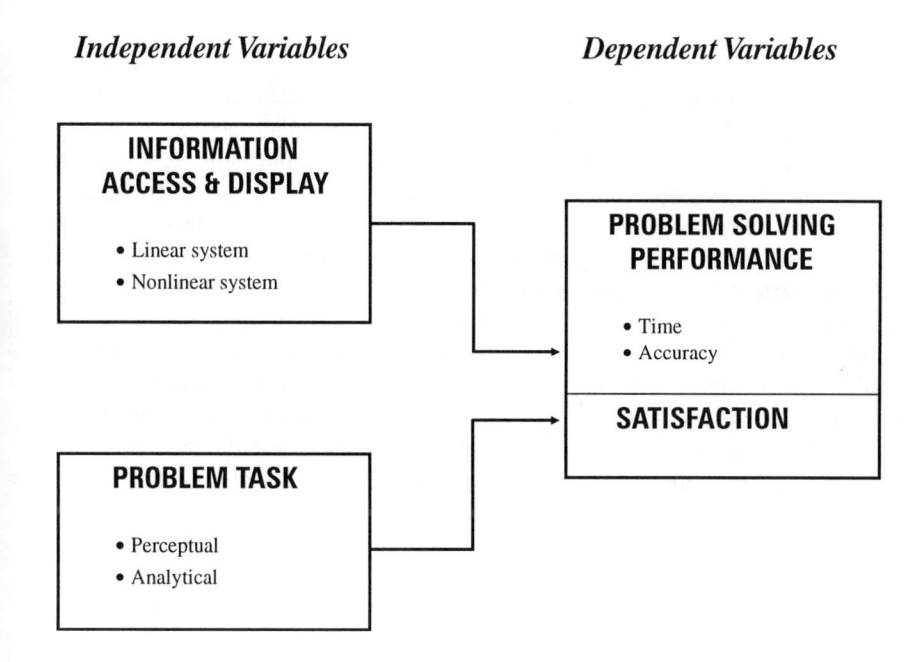

```
┌─────────────────────┐
│  INFORMATION        │
│  ACCESS & DISPLAY   │        ┌──────────────────────┐
│                     │───────▶│  PROBLEM SOLVING     │
│  • Linear system    │        │  PERFORMANCE         │
│  • Nonlinear system │        │                      │
└─────────────────────┘        │  • Time              │
                               │  • Accuracy          │
                               │                      │
                               │  SATISFACTION        │
┌─────────────────────┐        │                      │
│  PROBLEM TASK       │───────▶│                      │
│                     │        └──────────────────────┘
│  • Perceptual       │
│  • Analytical       │
│                     │
└─────────────────────┘
```

Figure 4.1. Research Model

Research Model and Hypotheses

The research model shown in Figure 4.1 depicts the effects of accessing and using information from linear and nonlinear systems on problem solving for specific types of problem tasks. The research model is composed of four main components: information access and display (linear versus nonlinear), problem task, problem-solving performance, and satisfaction. The figure also shows the major independent and dependent variables of the study.

Information Access and Display

The information in a linear system is organized to be accessed in a fixed hierarchical fashion and displayed in a fixed sequential order. Users must always progress through levels (or screens) in a predetermined order. By contrast, the nonlinear system is based on hypertext technology, in which information can be accessed and presented in a nonsequential order with no constraints requiring the user to follow any predefined paths. Nonlinear links allow branching to any cross-referenced screen (node) at any time. That is, users can navigate from one screen to another without going to previous or subsequent levels (or screens).

Problem Task

The type of problem tasks used in prior graphs/tables research were adapted in this study to investigate whether specific tasks might be better facilitated by linear or nonlinear systems. As with the majority of studies in graphs/tables research, this research also focuses on information acquisition and fairly simple evaluation tasks. Several researchers have identified and classified two basic types of tasks. Umanath and Scamell (1988), and Umanath, Scamell, and Das (1990) referred to these two tasks as "intraset pattern" and "point value recall" tasks. Vessey (1991, 1994) and Vessey and Galletta (1991) referred to them as "spatial" and "symbolic" tasks.

The first type of task assesses the entire problem area as a single whole unit rather than discrete components (see Vessey, 1991). These tasks require making associations or perceiving relationships in data such as trend detection, comparison, pattern recognition, integration of information, and interpolation. For the purpose of this analysis, such tasks are referred to as "perceptual tasks." Examples cited by Vessey (1991, p. 226) include:

"Between the year 1100 and 1438, whose earnings increased most rapidly, those of the wool, silk, or Calimala merchants?" (Washburne's (1927) study [as cited in Vessey])

"Who earned the most in the year 1100, the wool, silk, or Calimala merchants?" (Washburne's (1927) study [as cited in Vessey])

"Did sales exceed the cost of goods sold?" (Dickson et al.'s study [as cited in Vessey])

The second type of task involves extracting discrete and precise data values (see Umanath & Scamell, 1988; Umanath et al., 1990; Vessey, 1991, 1994). These tasks require specific fact retrieval as the response. Thus, the solution is achieved directly via the information acquisition process. For the purpose of this analysis, such tasks are referred to as "analytical tasks." Examples include (Vessey, 1991, p. 226):

"How much did the wool merchants earn in the year 1100?" (Washburne's (1927) study [as cited in Vessey])

"What was the company's net income for the past year?" (Dickson et al.'s study [as cited in Vessey])

The two above-mentioned examples are analytical in nature since both require a specific amount as the response. Note that in some situations, the perceptual problem task can be restated as an analytical problem task. For example, as Vessey (1991) stated, the perceptual example above could be reworded as the analytical problem task: "By what amount did sales exceed the cost of goods sold?" (pp. 226-227).

Problem-Solving Performance and Satisfaction

Problem-solving performance is measured in terms of efficiency (time) and effectiveness (solution accuracy). User satisfaction was also examined as another dependent variable to determine whether differences in satisfaction existed when linear and nonlinear systems were employed to solve varying types of tasks. The following describe the measures of time, accuracy, and user satisfaction used as dependent variables in this study:

> *Time* is measured from the time the task was first assigned until the user found a solution. The total time was measured to the 1/100th of a second.
> *Accuracy* is the extent to which the problem solvers' final solution for the task was correct or incorrect (i.e., "1" [*correct*] and "0" [*incorrect*]). Previously documented solutions served as the criteria for judging accuracy.
> *Satisfaction* is the users' self-reported feelings of satisfaction in using the two types of systems. Responses were recorded on a 7-point Likert scale ranging from "1" (*very satisfied*) to "7" (*very dissatisfied*).

In problem solving, two approaches are possible when accessing and using information. One approach is to consider the cognitive process experienced by an individual as information is displayed. The other is to examine those problem-solving outcomes that result from accessing and using information from different systems. The latter perspective is, perhaps, a more useful starting point and was considered in this research.

Hypotheses

The research model leads to the following three sets of hypotheses:

H1a: Faster and more accurate problem solving results from the nonlinear system as compared to the linear system.
H1b: Greater user satisfaction results from the nonlinear system as compared to the linear system.
H2a: When performing an analytical task, faster and more accurate problem solving results from the nonlinear system as compared to the linear system.
H2b: When performing an analytical task, greater user satisfaction results from the nonlinear system as compared to the linear system.
H3a: When performing a perceptual task, faster and more accurate problem solving results from the nonlinear system as compared to the linear system.
H3b: When performing a perceptual task, greater user satisfaction results from the nonlinear system as compared to the linear system.

Research Methodology

Sixty-four students were selected from various graduate business classes as subjects in this study. To motivate students to participate, the project was assigned as part of their class requirements. As a performance incentive, subjects were informed that prize money of $30, $20, and $10 would be awarded to the top three performers. Prizes were awarded based on the sum of the participants' normalized scores for time and accuracy in completing the tasks.

Tasks

The experimental task involved a bookkeeper responding to problems with bank accounts under his or her control. All experimental tasks were taken from the prior work of Vessey (1991) and Vessey and Galletta (1991) (used with the permission of the authors). Participants responded to problems regarding deposits and withdrawals on four bank accounts over a 12-month period. Perceptual and analytical tasks were used for each of the bank accounts.

Both types of problem tasks (perceptual and analytical) derive information from linear and nonlinear systems. Table 4.1 presents a few examples of the perceptual and analytical tasks used. For analytical tasks, the months for which participants extracted data were determined using random numbers, as was done by Vessey and Galletta (1991).

Laboratory Setting and Data Collection

Network computer-based systems were developed to facilitate both accessing and using information from linear and nonlinear modes. The linear method for accessing data was accomplished by using a software package called RediMaster. The nonlinear method was accomplished by using a hypertext software package called Guide. RediMaster has a facility called "External Program Call," which allows for adding external software that can be accessed from the same application (or screen). This facility gives the problem solver flexibility to access either the nonlinear system or the linear system from the single main (or starting) screen.

The linear system organizes information in a fixed, hierarchical structure in which information about various banks is arranged in different levels. Users start at the main screen (level 1) that lists the banks' names. At this level, the user chooses a particular bank to find information relating to it. For example, after choosing Bank "A," the next level (level 2) has information about the bank (e.g., deposits and withdrawals). Icons for different months go to the next level (level 3) for further details. To find information for Bank "B," users have to go back to the main screen (level 1), choose that particular bank, and repeat the level-to-level process. Here, the advantage is that at all times, the user knows where he or she started or at what level of the hierarchical path he or she is. On the negative side, users have to go back

TABLE 4.1 Examples of Tasks Used

Tasks	Directive
Perceptual	What is the longest period of consecutive decreases in deposits over the 12-month period? (Give first and last month.)
	In which month is the difference between deposits and withdrawals greatest?
	In which months do deposits exceed withdrawals?
	Do deposits exceed withdrawals more frequently, or do withdrawals exceed deposits more frequently?

Analytical	Please provide the following amounts:
	    withdrawals in October
	    deposits in July
	    withdrawals in January
	    withdrawals in June

	Please provide the following amounts:
	    deposits in September
	    withdrawals in November
	    deposits in April
	    withdrawals in May

	Please provide the following amounts:
	    withdrawals in April
	    deposits in February
	    withdrawals in January
	    withdrawals in November

to the main screen every time to find information for a new bank and follow that particular predefined path to the desired information.

The nonlinear system is similar to the concept of the World Wide Web, where one can click on hypertext-linked words or "buttons" enabling users to jump from one screen to another. There were no constraints in following any predefined path. Here, information was organized over a network of nodes, each having information relating to a particular bank, as well as links to other nodes on the network. Windows on the screen are associated with nodes in the database. Based on the hypertext technology, all nodes are interconnected so that one can navigate from one node to another without going through previous levels. To navigate from one screen to another, users simply click on the buttons or highlighted words listed on every screen that represent a particular link in the hyperdocument. The advantage with nonlinear links is that users do not have to go back and forth following a predefined path to arrive at another node. Users simply can navigate in their own sequence, or even take diversions and come back to the information they are looking for. On the negative side, users have no idea where the first bank and last bank's information is located, or what path to take to arrive at a particular node. Both linear and nonlinear systems were plain-colored, text-embedded data with no pictures or other graphic images.

Data Collection

As mentioned earlier, each subject was required to respond to the problems of a bookkeeper who had a number of bank accounts to control. The subjects performed one task at a time. Each task required the following steps: (1) read a task from the questionnaire, (2) find information relating to the task on the screen utilizing linear or nonlinear links, and (3) enter the solution to the task on the questionnaire. (Note that the total time to complete each task was measured from the time the task was first assigned until the final solution was entered on the questionnaire. Therefore, a stopwatch was used instead of computerized timing on the system.)

Four perceptual and four analytical tasks were presented to each subject. Two perceptual and two analytical tasks utilized a linear system, and the other two perceptual and two analytical tasks used a nonlinear system. User satisfaction was measured after answering each set of tasks (two perceptual or two analytical) under linear and nonlinear systems.

The experiment required approximately 20 minutes of each subject's time and was administered to one subject at a time in order to avoid the effects of peer pressure on performance. Each participant was given individual instructions in the experimental procedure, a demonstration exercise, and a practice exercise of the same type as the experimental task. Subjects were told about the objective of the research, and also how their problem-solving performance was measured in terms of time and accuracy. No time limit was imposed to complete the task, but subjects were encouraged to complete the tasks as soon as possible because their efficiency in solving problems was important. Data were collected over a four-week period.

Also, prior to the actual experiment, a pilot test was conducted to identify any deficiencies in the experimental materials and to provide practice for the researchers in administering the experiment. However, these data were not used for data analysis to avoid any bias.

Participants completed the experimental tasks in the order in which the tasks were presented to them. This procedure forced participants to examine only one task and one bank account at a time. To ensure that the order of task presentation did not affect the outcome, task sequence was mixed, as shown in Table 4.2. There was a total of four sets of 16 different task sequences. Four different subjects performed each sequence shown in Table 4.2. Subjects were randomly assigned to sequences.

After all eight tasks were performed, subjects provided demographic information. Approximately three-fourths of the participants were full-time students, and about 60% of them were employed full-time. (Note that there is a large amount of overlap between full-time students and full-time employees since the majority of the students were enrolled in evening MBA classes.) More than 90% of the

TABLE 4.2 Order of Task Presentation

	Linear				Nonlinear			
Sequences	Perceptual		Analytical		Perceptual		Analytical	
S-1	Tp-1	Tp-2	Ta-5	Ta-6	Tp-3	Tp-4	Ta-7	Ta-8
S-2	Tp-3	Tp-4	Ta-7	Ta-8	Tp-1	Tp-2	Ta-5	Ta-6
S-3	Tp-2	Tp-1	Ta-6	Ta-5	Tp-4	Tp-3	Ta-8	Ta-7
S-4	Tp-4	Tp-3	Ta-8	Ta-7	Tp-2	Tp-1	Ta-6	Ta-5

	Linear				Nonlinear			
Sequences	Analytical		Perceptual		Analytical		Perceptual	
S-5	Ta-5	Ta-6	Tp-1	Tp-2	Ta-7	Ta-8	Tp-3	Tp-4
S-6	Ta-7	Ta-8	Tp-3	Tp-4	Ta-5	Ta-6	Tp-1	Tp-2
S-7	Ta-6	Ta-5	Tp-2	Tp-1	Ta-8	Ta-7	Tp-4	Tp-3
S-8	Ta-8	Ta-7	Tp-4	Tp-3	Ta-6	Ta-5	Tp-2	Tp-1

	Nonlinear				Linear			
Sequences	Perceptual		Analytical		Perceptual		Analytical	
S-9	Tp-1	Tp-2	Ta-5	Ta-6	Tp-3	Tp-4	Ta-7	Ta-8
S-10	Tp-3	Tp-4	Ta-7	Ta-8	Tp-1	Tp-2	Ta-5	Ta-6
S-11	Tp-2	Tp-1	Ta-6	Ta-5	Tp-4	Tp-3	Ta-8	Ta-7
S-12	Tp-4	Tp-3	Ta-8	Ta-7	Tp-2	Tp-1	Ta-6	Ta-5

	Nonlinear				Linear			
Sequences	Analytical		Perceptual		Analytical		Perceptual	
S-13	Ta-5	Ta-6	Tp-1	Tp-2	Ta-7	Ta-8	Tp-3	Tp-4
S-14	Ta-7	Ta-8	Tp-3	Tp-4	Ta-5	Ta-6	Tp-1	Tp-2
S-15	Ta-6	Ta-5	Tp-2	Tp-1	Ta-8	Ta-7	Tp-4	Tp-3
S-16	Ta-8	Ta-7	Tp-4	Tp-3	Ta-6	Ta-5	Tp-2	Tp-1

NOTE: "Tp" represents perceptual tasks and "Ta" represents analytical tasks.

participants used a computer on a regular basis. Table 4.3 summarizes the participants' demographic and other characteristics, including student status (full-/part-time), employment status, and computer usage experience.

Experimental Design

The study used a two-factor, repeated-measures design employing multivariate analysis of variance (MANOVA) to analyze the data. Within-subjects repeated

TABLE 4.3 Demographic and Other Characteristics of Participants

Description	Value Label	Frequency	Percentage
Student status	Full-time	47	73.4
	Part-time	17	26.6
Employment status	Full-time	39	60.9
	Part-time	25	39.1
Computer usage	Regular	58	90.6
	Occasional	6	9.4

NOTE: $N = 64$.

measures were conducted to analyze each treatment factor (linear and nonlinear systems, perceptual and analytical problem tasks).

As shown in Figure 4.2, within the MANOVA, three planned contrasts were used to test the hypotheses about particular combinations of means. The first contrast compared the difference between all nonlinear and all linear tasks to test H1a. The second and third contrasts compared the difference between nonlinear analytical versus linear analytical, and nonlinear perceptual versus linear perceptual, respectively, to test H2a and H3a. Similarly, three planned contrasts were also used to test hypotheses about the particular combination of means relating to user satisfaction (H1b, H2b, and H3b). This planned contrast approach was used because it helps to clearly display and interpret all of the parameter estimates and univariate F-ratios for each hypothesis.

Because the same type of task had to be measured for each subject under two different treatments (linear and nonlinear), a repeated measures design was chosen. The advantages of repeated measures are well known (Kerlinger, 1986). Besides requiring fewer experimental subjects, this design provides a control on the differences among various subjects. That is, variability due to differences between subjects can be eliminated from the experimental error.

Research Results

Table 4.4 presents descriptive statistics for all three measures (accuracy, time, and satisfaction). For the dependent measure of accuracy, a higher average corresponds to better or more accurate performance. Time was measured in hundredths of a second, so a lower average corresponds to less time taken to complete the task. User satisfaction was measured on a 7-point Likert scale, ranging from "1" (*very satisfied*) to "7" (*very dissatisfied*). Therefore, lower scores correspond to higher user satisfaction. The results are based on the following interpretation of the hypotheses.

	L-Perceptual	NL-Perceptual	L-Analytical	NL-Analytical	
⎡	1	−1	1	−1	⎤
	0	0	1	−1	
⎣	1	−1	0	0	⎦

Figure 4.2. Planned Contrast Coefficient Matrix

Effect of Nonlinear Versus Linear System

H1a examines whether problem solving is superior in terms of time and accuracy when information is gathered from the nonlinear system as compared to the linear system. H1b considers whether user satisfaction is greater when information is gathered from a nonlinear as compared to the linear system. Table 4.5 summarizes the multivariate and univariate analysis of variance across nonlinear and linear systems. The multivariate analyses of variance indicated significant effects ($F = 38.06; p \leq .001$). Of the three univariate ANOVA analyses performed by the planned contrast approach, all three analyses showed a significant difference: (a) accuracy ($F_{(1,63)} = 9.16; p \leq .004$), (b) time ($F_{(1,63)} = 66.43; p \leq .001$), and (c) satisfaction ($F_{(1,63)} = 85.04; p \leq .001$). The findings support H1a and H1b that the nonlinear system resulted in superior problem solving and higher levels of user satisfaction than the linear system.

Effect of Nonlinear Analytical Versus Linear Analytical

H2a examines whether problem solving is superior in terms of time and accuracy for analytical problem tasks when information is gathered from the nonlinear

TABLE 4.4 Means and Standard Deviations for Each Dependent Measure

Dependent Measure	Statistics	Linear Perceptual Tasks	Linear Analytical Tasks	Nonlinear Perceptual Tasks	Nonlinear Analytical Tasks
Accuracy	Mean	.727	.984	.852	.973
	SD	.281	.061	.230	.079
Time	Mean	2563.094	1829.531	1990.125	1552.641
	SD	893.631	438.526	675.235	379.278
Satisfaction	Mean	3.750	2.844	2.688	2.094
	SD	1.491	1.493	1.139	1.123

TABLE 4.5 Results From MANOVA Test on the Effects of Nonlinear Versus Linear Systems

Multivariate Test of Significance
Wilks's Lambda = 0.23291; Hypothesis $df = 3$; Error $df = 61$; Exact $F = 38.06$; $p < .001$

Univariate ANOVA Analysis for Accuracy

Source	df	SS	MS	F	ProbF
L vs. NL	1	.205	.205	9.16	.004
Within cells	63	1.411	0.022		

Univariate ANOVA Analysis for Time

Source	df	SS	MS	F	ProbF
L vs. NL	1	11556175.3	11556175.3	66.43	.001
Within cells	63	10959972.9	173967.8		

Univariate ANOVA Analysis for Satisfaction

Source	df	SS	MS	F	ProbF
L vs. NL	1	52.562	52.562	85.04	.001
Within cells	63	38.937	.618		

system as compared to the linear system. H2b considers whether user satisfaction is greater when information is derived from a nonlinear system for analytical problem tasks. Table 4.6 summarizes the multivariate and univariate analysis of variance across nonlinear analytical and linear analytical tasks. For analytical tasks, the nonlinear approach significantly affected the outcome. The multivariate analysis of variance indicated a significant effect ($F_{(1,63)} = 38.06$; $p \leq .001$). The univariate ANOVA analysis performed by the planned contrast approach shows that subjects using the nonlinear system for analytical tasks performed faster ($F_{(1,63)} = 52.06$; $p \leq .001$) and were more satisfied ($F_{(1,63)} = 36.58$; $p \leq .001$) than with the linear approach. H2a was partially supported, and H2b was fully supported for nonlinear analytical versus linear analytical tasks.

Effect of Nonlinear Perceptual Versus Linear Perceptual

H3a examines whether problem solving is superior in terms of time and accuracy for perceptual problem tasks when information is gathered from the nonlinear system as compared to the linear system. H3b considers whether user satisfaction is greater when information is gathered from the nonlinear system for perceptual problem tasks. Table 4.7 summarizes the multivariate and univariate analysis of variance across nonlinear perceptual and linear perceptual tasks. For perceptual

TABLE 4.6 Results From MANOVA Test for Nonlinear Analytical Versus Linear Analytical

Multivariate Test of Significance
Wilks's Lambda = 0.13835; Hypothesis df = 9; Error df = 55; Exact F = 38.06; $p < .001$

Univariate ANOVA Analysis for Accuracy

Source	df	SS	MS	F	ProbF
NLA vs. LA	1	.004	.004	1.20	.277
Within cells	63	.229	.003		

Univariate ANOVA Analysis for Time

Source	df	SS	MS	F	ProbF
NLA vs. LA	1	2453389.3	2453389.3	52.06	.001
Within cells	63	2968694.1	47122.1		

Univariate ANOVA Analysis for Satisfaction

Source	df	SS	MS	F	ProbF
NLA vs. LA	1	18.000	18.000	36.58	.001
Within cells	63	31.000	.492		

tasks, the nonlinear approach significantly affected the performance. The multivariate analysis of variance indicated significant effect (F = 38.06; $p \leq .001$). The nonlinear system resulted in both faster ($F_{(1,63)}$ = 33.21; $p \leq .001$) and more accurate ($F_{(1,63)}$ = 11.45; $p \leq .001$) problem solving on perceptual tasks than did the linear system. Also, the subjects were more satisfied with the nonlinear approach ($F_{(1,63)}$ = 65.26; $p \leq .001$) than the linear approach. Thus, all three univariate analyses for the dependent measures showed a significant difference. H3a and H3b were fully supported for nonlinear perceptual versus linear perceptual tasks.

Discussion and Concluding Comments

This research investigated the impact of accessing and using information from linear and nonlinear systems on problem-solving outcomes. Specifically, the study tried to provide some empirical insights into the effectiveness of a nonlinear approach over a linear approach. The results support the proposition that problem-solving performance and user satisfaction are significantly higher for nonlinear systems.

The study also investigated different combinations of problem tasks (perceptual and analytical) to see whether linear or nonlinear systems lead to more accurate and quicker problem solving, and higher levels of user satisfaction. The results support

TABLE 4.7 Results From MANOVA Test for Nonlinear Perceptual Versus Linear Perceptual

Multivariate Test of Significance
Wilks's Lambda = 0.13835; Hypothesis $df = 9$; Error $df = 55$; Exact $F = 38.06$; $p < .001$

Univariate ANOVA Analysis for Accuracy

Source	df	SS	MS	F	ProbF
NLP vs. LP	1	.50	.500	11.45	.001
Within cells	63	2.75	.044		

Univariate ANOVA Analysis for Time

Source	df	SS	MS	F	ProbF
NLP vs. LP	1	10505382.1	10505382.1	33.21	.001
Within cells	63	19924465.9	316261.4		

Univariate ANOVA Analysis for Satisfaction

Source	df	SS	MS	F	ProbF
NLP vs. LP	1	36.13	52.562	65.26	.001
Within cells	63	34.88	.554		

the proposition that the nonlinear system resulted in better problem solving and increased user satisfaction for both perceptual and analytical problem tasks. Subjects solved perceptual problems faster and more accurately with a nonlinear system than with a linear system. However, for analytical tasks, although subjects performed faster in nonlinear than linear systems, there was no significant difference in accuracy. Satisfaction was higher for the nonlinear system for both perceptual and analytical tasks.

The results from the study confirm what has long been suspected but not substantiated empirically; problem solving using nonlinear links provides better results than does using linear links. In addition, individuals (users) are more satisfied using nonlinear links than linear links. Thus, for simple information acquisition and well-defined evaluation or extrapolation tasks performed in the context of a highly structured experiment, nonlinear links are better than linear ones.

The limitations of the study center on the types of tasks examined, the use of the pretested instrument and tasks, the use of student subjects, and the types of information used for solving the problems. First, the problem tasks used were quite simple in this study. The experiment should be replicated with complex perceptual tasks that embody stronger perceptual characteristics, such as determining a trend or determining other types of patterns in the data.

Second, the study used a pretested instrument and tasks from the prior work of Vessey (1991) and Vessey and Galletta (1991) to assess perceptual and analytical problem-solving skills. Instead, the study could have developed its own tasks to test the effects. However, these established tasks were used in the experiment to ensure the validity of the instrument and also to overcome the possibility of biasing the experimental results. Contrarily, future research can develop new tasks to add to the body of knowledge and generalizability of results.

Third, this study used student subjects. Therefore, the generalizability of the results to the population of real-world managers can be questioned. Note, however, that the focus of this study was on the impact of linear and nonlinear systems. Student subjects, as novices, may be more appropriate than other types of subjects to demonstrate the effects on problem solving.

Finally, the type of information used for solving the analytical and perceptual task could have included other types of qualitative information, such as metaphors, stories, examples, organizational objectives, case research strategies, etc. For example, metaphors are the cognitive lenses that can expand the understanding of the problem solver, reshape our thoughts, and influence our behavior to see the problem differently (see Kendall & Kendall, 1993, 1994; and Walsham, 1991 for an excellent review of using metaphors in systems research). There is also a rising enthusiasm for stories, examples, and organizational objectives to be used in determining the impact of information systems (Rao, 1995; Senn, 1989). According to Benbasat, Goldstein, and Mead (1987), the use of case research strategy in IS research has shown that case research can study system impact in a natural setting and help understand the nature and complexity of the problem differently. The new qualitative research in the IS literature now provides paradigms that hold some promise in developing these other types of information (Lacity & Janson, 1994; Kendall & Kendall, 1994). Therefore, the study could be extended to incorporate these types of information.

From the viewpoint of research contributions and implications, the study empirically tested problem-solving performance using linear and nonlinear links for fairly simple information acquisition and extrapolation tasks (analytical and perceptual). Even though the results were statistically significant, the research should be extended to encompass more complex problem-solving tasks. An important avenue to consider would be to extend the theory of cognitive fit into this research to investigate how linear or nonlinear links support the methods or processes required to perform the problem task. According to the theory of cognitive fit, the problem solver makes a mental representation of the problem solution using the characteristics of both the problem representation and the problem task (Umanath & Vessey, 1994; Vessey, 1991). Vessey (1991) further observed (based partially on Bettman & Zins, 1979, and Vessey & Weber, 1986) that cognitive fit reduces complexity in the task environment, thus yielding more effective problem solving, and, conversely, that mismatches (between problem representation and task) will lead to poor performance due to the need to transform the data to fit the problem or the problem to fit the data. It seems clear that nonlinear links might facilitate cognitive fit for a wider range of tasks, and hence improve problem-solving performance for a wider range of problem tasks than linear links. Correspondingly, for some tasks, the linear links could be an impediment to cognitive fit and to problem solving. Therefore, the next logical extension seems to incorporate the theory of cognitive fit into this research.

As noted by Vessey and Galletta (1991), another possible avenue is the cost-benefit theory (see Beach & Mitchell, 1978; Payne, 1982; Payne, Bettman, & Johnson, 1993). In general, cost-benefit theory views problem solving as a trade-off between effort and accuracy as a result of strategy shifts. Research into behavioral decision making, for example, has shown that strategies vary widely based on small changes in the task and task environment. In particular, decision makers have been shown to trade small losses in accuracy for large savings in effort (Russo & Dosher, 1983). Future research might apply the concepts of cognitive cost-benefit theory to problem solving using linear and nonlinear approaches in more complex tasks and in problem-solving environments that constrain the amount of time and, therefore, the extent of processing required for task solution.

This study examined only the problem-solving outcomes that result from linear and nonlinear systems. We consider these outcomes as a useful starting point. Perhaps a further test is needed to consider the cognitive process of an individual as information is derived from linear and nonlinear systems. This could be done by using a process tracing methodology such as protocol analysis (see Ericsson & Simon, 1984; Russo, Johnson, & Stephens, 1989). Also, for the design of display formats for DSS areas, this research can be extended to focus on the constructs of cognitive effort and the relationship between the display format and changes in decision processes that occur when different display formats are introduced (see Jarvenpaa, 1989).

Finally, for the information representation approaches and interface design, this research provides some insights into the superiority of nonlinear links to linear links. This will become even more important with the growth of HTML-based home pages. Particularly given the interest explosion in the WWW, along with the extensions to the HTML (e.g., Java, HTML Basic) that will allow procedural activities to be incorporated into such interfaces, this research provides some insights about the superiority of nonlinear systems over different types of tasks. Also, today's help systems often include tables of contents and indexes, which can be linear and nonlinear, respectively. This can be extended to include only nonlinear links. The concept of encouraging all users to use only nonlinear links can be approached either by training the users or by designing systems that have only nonlinear links.

References

Abelson, R. P. (1981). Psychological status of the script concept. *American Psychologist, 36*(7), 715-729.

Anderson, J. R. (1981). *Cognitive skills and their applications.* Hillsdale, NJ: Lawrence Erlbaum Associates.

Barnes, R. J., Baskerville, R. L., Kendall, J. E., & Kendall, K. E. (1992). HyperCase instructor's guide appendix. In A. Schmidt (Ed.), *Instructor's manual to accompany systems analysis and design* (2nd ed.). Englewood Cliffs, NJ: Prentice Hall.
Beach, L. R., & Mitchell, T. R. (1978). A contingency model for the selection of decision strategies. *Academy of Management Review, 3,* 439-449.
Benbasat, I., & Dexter, A. S. (1985). An experimental evaluation of graphical and color-enhanced information presentation. *Management Science, 31*(11), 1348-1364.
Benbasat, I., & Dexter, A. S. (1986). An investigation of the effectiveness of color and graphical information presentation under varying time constraints. *MIS Quarterly, 10*(1), 59-83.
Benbasat, I., Goldstein, D. K., & Mead, M. (1987). The case research strategy in studies of information systems. *MIS Quarterly, 11*(3), 369-386.
Bettman, J. R., & Kakkar, P. (1977). Effects of information presentation format on consumer information strategies. *Journal of Consumer Research, 3,* 233-240.
Bettman, J. R., & Zins, M. A. (1979). Information format and choice task effects in decision making. *Journal of Consumer Research, 6,* 141-153.
Bieber, M. P., & Kimbrough, S. O. (1992). On generalizing the concept of hypertext. *Management Information Systems Quarterly, 16*(1), 77-93.
Bush, V. (1945, July). As we may think. *Atlantic Monthly,* pp. 101-108.
Conklin, J. (1987). Hypertext: An introduction and survey. *IEEE Computer, 20*(9), 17-41.
Conklin, J. (1991). Geographic information system to hypertext. In A. Kent & J. Williams (Eds.), *Encyclopedia of microcomputers* (pp. 377-431). New York: Marcel Dekker.
Dickson, G. W., DeSanctis, G., & McBride, D. J. (1986). Understanding the effectiveness of computer graphics for decision support: A cumulative experimental approach. *Communications of the ACM, 29*(1), 40-47.
Engelbart, D. (1963). A conceptual framework for the augmentation of man's intellect. In P. W. Howerton & D. C. Weeks (Eds.), *Vistas in information handling.* London: Spartan.
Engelbart, D. (1984). Authorship provisions in AUGMENT. In *Proceedings of the 28th IEEE Computer Society International Conference* (pp. 9-21). Arlington, VA: AFIPS Press.
Ericsson, H. J., & Simon, H. A. (1984). *Protocol analysis: Verbal reports as data.* Cambridge, MA: MIT Press.
Esichaikul, V., Madey, G. R., & Smith, R. D. (1994). Problem-solving support for TQM: A hypertext approach. *Information Systems Management, 11*(1), 47-52.
Ewing, J., Mehrabanzad, S., Sheck, S., Ostroff, D., & Shneiderman, B. (1986). An experimental comparison of a mouse and arrow-jump keys for an interactive encyclopedia. *International Journal of Man-Machine Studies, 24,* 29-45.
Fraisse, S. (1997). A task driven design method and its associated tool for automatically generating hypertexts. In *Proceedings of HYPERTEXT'97* (pp. 234-235). Southampton, UK.
Garzotto, F., Paolini, P., & Schwabe, D. (1993). HDM: A model-based approach to hypertext application design. *ACM Transaction on Information Systems, 11*(1), 1-26.
Goodhue, D. L., & Thompson, R. L. (1995). Task-technology fit and individual performance. *MIS Quarterly, 19*(2), 213-236.
Halasz, F. (1988). Reflections on NoteCards: Seven issues for the next generation of hypermedia systems. *Communications of the ACM, 31*(7), 836-852.
Jacobson, M. J., & Spiro, R. J. (1991a). A framework for the contextual analysis of computer-based learning environments. *Journal of Computing & Higher Education, 5*(2), 3-32.
Jacobson, M. J., & Spiro, R. J. (1991b). Hypertext learning environments, cognitive flexibility and transfer of complex knowledge: An empirical investigation. *Journal of Educational Computing Research, 12*(4), 301-313.
Jarvenpaa, S. (1989). The effect of task and graphical format on information processing strategies. *Management Science, 35*(3), 285-303.
Jarvenpaa, S. L., & Dickson, G. W. (1988). Graphics and managerial decision making: Research-based guide lines. *Communications of the ACM, 31*(6), 764-774.

Jonassen, D. H. (1986). Hypertext principles for text and courseware design. *Educational Psychologist, 21*(4), 269-292.

Kendall, J. E., & Kendall, K. E. (1993). Metaphors and methodologies: Living beyond the systems machine. *MIS Quarterly, 17*(2), 149-171.

Kendall, J. E., & Kendall, K. E. (1994). Metaphors and their meaning for information systems development. *European Journal of Information Systems, 3*(1), 37-47.

Kendall, J. E., & Kerola, P. (1994). A foundation for the use of hypertext-based documentation techniques. *Journal of End-User Computing, 6*(1), 4-14.

Kendall, K. E., & Kendall, J. E. (1992). *Systems analysis and design.* Englewood Cliffs, NJ: Prentice Hall.

Kerlinger, F. N. (1986). *Foundation of behavioral research.* Fort Worth, TX: Holt, Rinehart & Winston.

Lacity, M. C., & Janson, M. A. (1994). Understanding qualitative data: A framework of text analysis methods. *Journal of Management Information Systems, 11*(2), 137-155.

Landauer, T. K., Dumais, S. T., Gomez, L. M., & Furnas, G. W. (1982). Human factors in data access. *The Bell System Technical Journal, 61,* 2487-2509.

Marchionini, G., & Shneiderman, B. (1988). Finding facts vs. browsing knowledge in hypertext systems. *IEEE Computer, 21*(1), 70-80.

Minch, R. P. (1989). Application and research areas for hypertext in decision support systems. *Journal of Management Information Systems, 6*(3), 119-138.

Motley, M. T. (1987, February). What I meant to say. *Psychology Today,* pp. 24-28.

Nanard, J., & Nanard, M. (1995). Hypertext design environments and the hypertext design process. *Communications of the ACM, 38*(8), 49-56.

Nelson, K. (1986). Event knowledge and cognitive development. In K. Nelson (Ed.), *Event knowledge: Structure and function in development* (pp. 1-10). Hillsdale, NJ: Erlbaum.

Nelson, T. H. (1967). Getting it out of our system. In G. Schecter (Ed.), *Information retrieval: A critical review.* Washington, DC: Thompson.

Payne, J. (1982). Contingent decision behavior. *Psychological Bulletin, 92*(2), 382-402.

Payne, J. W., Bettman, J. R., & Johnson, E. J. (1993). *The adaptive decision maker.* Cambridge, UK: Cambridge University Press.

Powers, M., Lashley, L., Sanchez, P., & Shneiderman, B. (1984). An experimental investigation of tabular and graphic data presentation. *International Journal of Man-Machine Studies, 20,* 545-566.

Rao, S. S. (1995). Putting fun back into learning. *Training, 32*(8), 44-48.

Rich, E. (1983). *Artificial intelligence.* New York: McGraw-Hill.

Russo, J. E. (1977). The value of unit price information. *Journal of Marketing Research, 14,* 193-201.

Russo, J. E., & Dosher, B. A. (1983). Strategies for multiattribute binary choice. *Journal of Experimental Psychology: Learning, Memory, and Cognition, 9*(4), 676-696.

Russo, J. E., Johnson, E. J., & Stephens, D. L. (1989). The validity of verbal protocols. *Cognitive Psychology, 17*(6), 759-769.

Schank, R. C., & Abelson, R. P. (1977). *Scripts, plans, goals, and understanding.* Hillsdale, NJ: Erlbaum.

Schwabe, D., Rossi, G., & Barbosa, S. (1996). Systematic hypermedia application design with OOHDM. In *Proceedings of Hypertext'96* (pp. 116-128). Washington, DC.

Senn, J. A. (1989). Debunking the myths of strategic information systems. *Business, 39*(4), 43-47.

Shneiderman, B. (1987). User interface design for the Hyperties electronic encyclopedia. In *Proceedings of Hypertext'87* (pp. 189-194). Chapel Hill, NC.

Shneiderman, B. (1989). Reflections on authoring, editing and managing hypertext. In E. Barrett (Ed.), *The society of text: Hypertext, hypermedia, and the social construction of information.* Cambridge, MA: MIT Press.

Shneiderman, B., & Kearsley, G. (1989). *Hypertext hands-on: An introduction to a new way of organizing and accessing information.* New York: Addison-Wesley.

Spiro, R. J., Feltovich, P. J., Jacobson, M. J., & Coulson, R. L. (1996). Cognitive flexibility, constructivism, and hypertext: Random access instruction for advanced knowledge acquisition in ill-structured domains. *Educational Technology, 11*(5), 24-33.

Todd, P., & Benbasat, I. (1991). An experimental investigation of the impact of computer-based decision aids on decision making. *Information Systems Research, 2*(2), 87-115.

Umanath, N. S., & Scamell, R. W. (1988). An experimental evaluation of the impact of data display format on recall performance. *Communications of the ACM, 31*(5), 562-570.

Umanath, N. S., Scamell, R. W., & Das, S. R. (1990). An examination of two screen/report design variables in an information recall context. *Decision Sciences, 21*(1), 216-240.

Umanath, N. S., & Vessey, I. (1994). Multiattribute data presentation and human judgment: A cognitive fit perspective. *Decision Sciences, 25*(5/6), 795-824.

Vessey, I. (1991). Cognitive fit: A theory-based analysis of the graph versus tables literature. *Decision Sciences, 22*, 219-239.

Vessey, I. (1994). The effect of information presentation on decision making: A cost-benefit analysis. *Information and Management, 27*, 103-119.

Vessey, I., & Galletta, D. (1991). Cognitive fit: An empirical study of information acquisition. *Information Systems Research, 2*(1), 63-86.

Vessey, I., & Weber, R. (1986). Structured tools and conditional logic: An experimental investigation. *Communications of the ACM, 29*(1), 48-57.

Walsham, G. (1991). Organizational metaphors and information systems research. *European Journal of Information Systems, 1*(2), 83-94.

Washburne, J. N. (1927). An experimental study of various graphic, tabular and textural methods of presenting quantitative material. *Journal of Educational Psychology, 18*(6), 361-376.

Wright, P. L. (1975). Consumer choice strategies: Simplifying vs. optimizing. *Journal of Marketing Research, 11*, 60-67.

Yankelovich, N., Haan, B., Meyrowitz, N., & Drucker, S. (1988). Intermedia: The concept and the construction of a seamless information environment. *IEEE Computer, 21*(10), 81-96.

Zacarias, P. T. (1986). *A script-based knowledge representation for intelligent office information systems.* Unpublished doctoral dissertation, Purdue University.

CHAPTER
FIVE

Data Warehousing

Three Major Applications and Their Significance

PAUL GRAY

Data warehousing is a major computer development of the 1990s that has changed the way information is obtained for decision support and other business functions performed in industry. Data warehouses are databases that provide decision makers with clean, consistent, and relevant data. Clean refers to the idea that the data are correct. Consistency results in there being only one version of the data. Relevant implies that data are organized so that they can be used to answer questions at the tactical and strategic level at which managers work, rather than at the transaction level used for operational and accounting purposes.

The invention of the data warehouse made it possible to create a set of interrelated applications that includes on-line analytical processing (OLAP), data mining, and database marketing. Although names such as data warehousing and data mining may seem out of keeping with the very white-collar worlds of computing and executive decision making, these developments are important advances in information systems.

This chapter is divided into several parts. After discussing the origins of data warehousing (Part 1), the characteristics of the warehouse and variants of it are described (Part 2). Then, the data warehousing industry is discussed briefly (Part 3). The chapter concludes with an analysis of the three major applications (Part 4) and the managerial perspective (Part 5).

Part 1: Origins of Data Warehousing

Data Warehousing and the DSS Legacy

Decision Support Systems (DSSs) was the name given in the 1970s to information systems designed to help managers in making choices. These systems used models and data to solve managerial problems ranging in complexity from simple spreadsheets to optimal site location using integer programming. The original concept was that managers would be able to create and operate such systems on their own. This assumption proved false. Most managers did not have the sophistication, skills, or time needed to do so. Therefore, starting in the early 1980s, a number of organizations and vendors offered simplified information systems called Executive Information Systems (EISs).

The basic assumption in an EIS was that managers wanted standard information about their firms and about the outside environment. This information included the time history of processes and outputs in the organization as well as prediction of their future state. The idea was that a manager could turn to his or her EIS and know instantly what was going on. The EISs included information on financials; production history, status, and plans; personnel; external events such as information on competitors; electronic mail; and more. The EIS did not have the computational capabilities of a DSS. As Rockart and DeLong (1988) indicate, an EIS is used by senior managers to find problems; the DSS is used by the staff people to study them and offer alternatives.

Although extremely useful, the EISs and DSSs lacked a strong database component. As is almost always the case, information gathered for one purpose cannot be used directly for another. Specifically, most organizational information gathering was (and is) directed to maintaining current (preferably on-line) information about individual transactions and customers. Managerial decision making, however, requires consideration of the past and the future, not just the present. As a result, most DSS and EIS builders had to create their own databases, an area that was not their prime expertise.

Data Warehousing and the Database Legacy

Database developers long understood that their software was required for both transactional and analytic processing. However, their principal developments were directed to ever-larger transactional databases at the expense of informational databases. This process occurred even though operational and analytical data are separate, with different requirements and different user communities.

However, as is the case for most new technology solutions, once everyone had one, databases became a steady replacement market rather than a growth market. At this point, the database developers began looking at new directions for using the knowledge they had acquired. They hit upon the idea of storing not just current data but historical data as well. They also knew that the data in their systems were often not as accurate or as consistent as they could be. Perhaps even more important, the developers saw that when complex analytical queries were posed to existing databases, the time required to respond was much too long and often tied up the relational systems so that they could not perform their intended transaction functions.

Once these differences were understood, new databases were created specifically for analytical use. These databases are called data warehouses because they store huge amounts of data, far beyond what had been the case previously, and the data are to be kept and used for long periods of time.

The data warehouse concept was originally developed to improve the data underlying DSSs and hence the decisions being made using DSSs and EISs. It has done so admirably. In addition, it has found other applications, particularly in data mining and database marketing.

Part 2: Characteristics of Data Warehouses

What Is a Data Warehouse?

A data warehouse is typically a dedicated database system that is separate from the production database systems used to support ongoing data processing operations on transaction data. It differs from these production systems in that

- It covers a much longer time horizon than transaction systems
- It includes multiple databases that have been processed so that the warehouse's data are defined uniformly (i.e., "clean data")
- It usually includes data for (or from) outside sources (such as the company's SEC filing or competitor stock prices) as well as data generated for internal use
- It is optimized for answering complex queries from managers and analysts

Definition of the Data Warehouse

The most commonly used definition comes from Inmon (1992):

A data warehouse is a:
– subject oriented
– integrated
– time-variant
– nonvolatile
collection of data in support of management decision processes. (p. 29)

This definition of the characteristics of a data warehouse implicitly assumes that a data warehouse is physically separated from operational systems and that it holds both aggregated data and transaction (atomic) data for management separate from the databases used for On Line Transaction Processing (OLTP).

The characteristics of data warehouses are implemented in three ways. The largest is the conventional *data warehouse,* which provides data on and supports the entire enterprise. Small data warehouses, designed to support particular business units or departments, are called *data marts.* When data warehousing principles are applied to transaction systems, the result is called an *operational data store.*

Characteristics

Table 5.1 summarizes the characteristics of a data warehouse. These characteristics are now discussed in detail.

Subject Orientation

In a data warehouse, data are organized around major subjects of the enterprise rather than individual transactions. That is, the organization is by subject areas across the enterprise rather than on an application-by-application basis. The reason for this difference is that applications are typically designed around processes and functions, each of which has its specific data needs, but many of the data elements are local to that function. These operational data requirements relate to the immediate needs of the application and are based on current business rules. A data warehouse, on the other hand, contains data oriented to decision making. The data spans time and allows for more complex relations.

Data Integration

In the data warehouse, the information should be *clean, validated,* and properly *aggregated.* By clean, we mean that the same piece of information is referred to in only one way. Unfortunately, legacy systems have many ways of referring to the same piece of data. Thus, gender may be referred to as "M, F" in one system, "Male, Female" in a second system, and "0, 1" in a third. Similarly, some systems use two digits for calendar year, whereas others use four digits.

When data are brought into the data warehouse, they are integrated so that they are referred to in only one way, and have the same format and the same units for measuring attributes. Thus, in a data warehouse, the data are stored in a single, globally acceptable fashion, even though their sources may differ.

Similarly, the data have to be correct. Errors slip into databases and, once there, tend to remain there forever unless some external event occurs. Some information may be left out. Specific steps are needed to make sure that the data that are in the data warehouse have been validated. Some data in the warehouse are aggregated. Care has to be taken to make certain that the aggregation is correct. If these operations are performed correctly, users can focus on the data, not the data's credibility or consistency.

Time

In an operational environment where decisions are made on-line (e.g., do I grant the customer on the phone credit?), data must be accurate at the moment of access. This level of timeliness is not needed for a data warehouse. Therefore, similar to a batch system, the data are accurate at the time they are loaded, but they decay between successive loadings. Time of loading is part of the metadata.

Data Warehousing   **103**

TABLE 5.1 Characteristics of a Data Warehouse

Characteristic	Description of Characteristic
Subject oriented	Data are organized by how users refer to them.
Integrated	Inconsistencies are removed in both nomenclature and conflicting information. That is, the data are clean.
Nonvolatile	Read-only data. Data do not change over time.
Time series	Data are time series, not current status.
Summarized	Operational data are mapped into decision-usable form.
Larger	Keeping time series implies that many more data are retained.
Not normalized	DSS data can be redundant.
Metadata	Metadata = data about the data.
Input	This is an unintegrated operational environment ("legacy systems").

The data warehouse typically has a 5- to 10-year horizon on the data that it contains. Operational data, on the other hand, typically cover 60 to 90 days.

In a data warehouse, the data are organized so that the key always contains the unit of time (day, week, etc.). Furthermore, correctly recorded warehouse data *cannot* be updated.

Nonvolatility

In an operational environment, updates (e.g., inserts, deletes, changes) are made regularly on a record-by-record basis as they occur. A data warehouse has a much simpler environment because it involves only data loading and data access.

When new data are loaded into the warehouse, they are filtered and transformed. Only data needed for decision making are stored. In addition, some calculations are performed to create summary data not found in operational data. Thus, for example, weekly sales figures may be obtained from aggregating daily sales to create summary data not found in operational data.

Structure of a Data Warehouse

A data warehouse contains five types of data:

- Current detail data
- Older detail data
- Lightly summarized data
- Highly summarized data
- Metadata

These data are not necessarily stored in the same medium. However, the software is such that access can be obtained to each. A key issue to be decided in the design of the data warehouse is the *granularity* of the data. Granularity refers to the amount of detail. Raw data, as kept in the organization's transaction processing system, are usually the most detailed. In the warehouse, the most detailed data may aggregate some information. Thus, for example, a warehouse used for decision support may contain daily sales by store of every stock item rather than keeping track of individual transactions by customers. The selection of levels of summarization is a design trade-off and more art than science at this time.

Current Detail Data

Current detail data reflect the most recent happenings. These data can become very voluminous if stored at the lowest level of granularity. Often, they are simply a replication of the current transaction data, which have been cleaned and then loaded. However, not all fields kept in the transaction systems may be moved to the warehouse. Note that although referred to as current, these data are up to date only to the time they were removed from the transaction system.

Many decision support questions involve using data that can be obtained directly from the detail records on transactions. For example, how many units did we sell today? What is the week-to-week trend in hardware sales? In returns? The reason the detail data are replicated in the warehouse is to make it possible to query them without bringing the transaction system down or stopping the transaction system for extensive periods of time while such legitimate queries are answered.

Older Detail Data

Most warehouses have rules that state that when detail information reaches a certain age, it is moved from disk to a mass storage medium. Although still retrievable in detail form, the access time is a little longer because the warehouse has to work with a slower medium.

Lightly Summarized Data

Experience shows that by summarizing the data in a form that anticipates requests for standard quantities, the responsiveness and use of the warehouse are improved. From the point of view of the designer, two decisions are required:

1. Selecting the attributes to summarize
2. Selecting the unit of time for summarization

Both of these decisions involve tradeoffs in that computations do not have to be performed over and over, but more storage space is needed. Clearly, attributes and combinations of attributes that are often queried should be summarized, and those that are rarely queried should not. Once the attributes are selected, the next decision is how frequently each particular attribute should be summarized.

Highly Summarized Data

Some information, particularly that required by very senior managers, should be available in compact and easily accessible form. This information typically includes information that is consulted repeatedly. This information goes beyond summarizing the transaction data being kept. It includes the ability to keep summary data over long time periods so that trends can be established. By storing highly summarized data, the amount of data to be searched in answering many queries is reduced, thereby improving the response times observed by senior managers.

Metadata

Metadata are defined as data about the data. It is information kept about the warehouse rather than information provided by the warehouse. Metadata turn out to be essential for a data warehouse. Metadata include the following:

1. A directory of what is in the warehouse; the directory indicates where data are being stored and is an index that is used when a query is posed to find the right information
2. A guide to mapping data from operational to warehouse form
3. The rules used for summarization

Form of Data

The concept of normalizing data in a transaction system, long popularized in relational databases, is not applicable to data warehouses. In transaction systems, it is considered desirable to eliminate redundancy so that, for example, all data about a given transaction are in the same place. The idea is to organize data fields into a group of tables that is easy to use and makes sense. There is also a sense that storage space is expensive and that it should not be wasted. The philosophy in the data warehouse is to arrange data so that it is useful and can be retrieved quickly. Redundancies are perfectly all right.

Flow of Data

As shown in Figure 5.1, almost all data enter the warehouse from the operational environment. The data are then cleaned and moved into the warehouse.

The data continue to reside unchanged in the warehouse until they are purged or archived or combined with other information and summarized. An aging process inside the warehouse moves current data into old detail data. The summarization process uses detailed data to calculate summarizations of data.

106 EMERGING INFORMATION TECHNOLOGIES

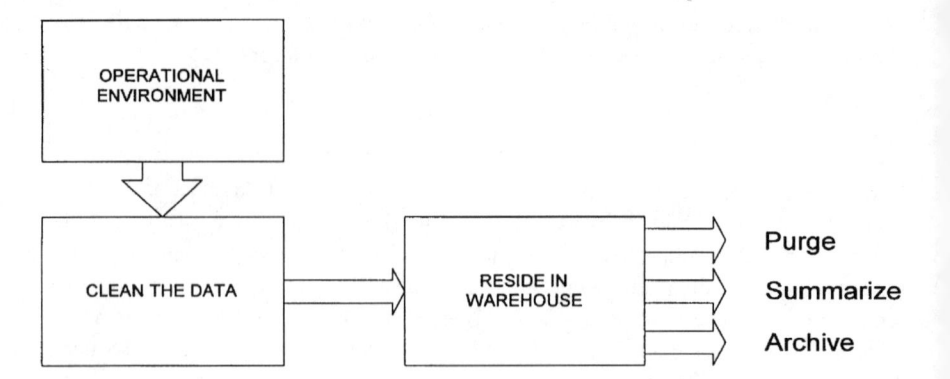

Figure 5.1. Data Flow

Warehouse Architecture

Typically, the data warehouse software architecture has three components (see Figure 5.2).

1. Data acquisition software (back end), which extracts data from legacy systems and external sources, consolidates and summarizes the data, and loads them into the data warehouse
2. The data warehouse itself, which contains the data, metadata, and associated software
3. The client (front-end) software, which allows DSS and EIS users to access and analyze data in the warehouse

In terms of hardware, the three components of a warehouse may be physically separate or, for smaller warehouses, may be combined into one or two platforms. For example, the data acquisition software and the warehouse may be on the same platform.

Why a Separate Data Warehouse?

Throughout this chapter, it is tacitly assumed that the data warehouse is separate from the on-line transaction processing (OLTP) system. Such separation is, in fact, the case. There are four reasons for this separation:

1. *Performance:* The peaks and valleys of requests degrade performance of the OLTP system.

```
┌──────────────┐      ┌──────────────┐      ┌──────────────┐
│    DATA      │      │              │      │              │
│ ACQUISITION  │─────▶│    DATA      │─────▶│   CLIENT     │
│   SOFTWARE   │      │  WAREHOUSE   │      │   SOFTWARE   │
│              │      │              │      │              │
└──────────────┘      └──────────────┘      └──────────────┘
```

BACK END:
Extract data from
legacy systems,
external sources.
Consolidate and
summarize data
Load data into
warehouse

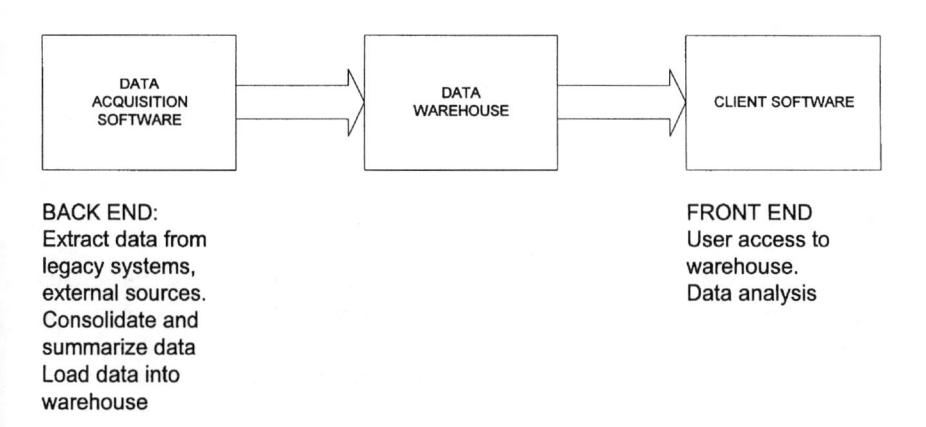

FRONT END
User access to
warehouse.
Data analysis

Figure 5.2. Data Warehouse Architecture

2. *Data access:* Organizations often maintain multiple databases that serve different OLTP functions. The data warehouse, being an integration of all of the enterprise's data, combines all these data sources and adds external data sources. The data for EIS and DSS use these multiple sources. The typical warehouse user does not care where the data are being stored. Users need and want access to data irrespective of which OLTP system has it.
3. *Data formats:* Because the data in the warehouse are integrated, information is kept in a single, standard format.
4. *Data quality:* The data in the warehouse are clean, validated, and properly aggregated. They have been inspected to make sure that only one value is stored in the warehouse for each data item. Thus, when people use the warehouse, they spend their time trying to understand what the data mean, not arguing about the correct value of the data.

Using the Warehouse—Summaries and Indexes

Like any software product, a data warehouse is of value to the organization only if it is used regularly. Experience with warehouses shows that the higher the level of summarization, the more the data are used and the quicker they are retrieved.

As a result, warehouses routinely create and store summaries of the data accessed most frequently. Prepositioning not only speeds up responses to queries that ask for summarized data, but it also speeds the response to other queries because it reduces the busy time of the warehouse.

Note that data at higher levels of summarization can be indexed and restructured for ease of use. However, data at lower levels are too voluminous to index or change structure.

Cost and Size

Data warehouses are not cheap. Multimillion-dollar costs are common. Their design and implementation is still an art, and they require considerable time to create.

Because they are designed for the enterprise so that everyone has access to a common data set, they are large and increase in size with time. Typical storage sizes run from 50 gigabytes to multiple terabytes.

Because of the large size, some firms use parallel computing to speed data retrieval. Parallel computers, although becoming affordable for business computers, are also not cheap. Furthermore, they require support from programmers who are skilled in parallel computing—a group that earns more than normal programmers. At present, approximately 90% of the parallel processors being used are SMP (Symmetric Multiprocessors). However, more powerful MPP (Massively Parallel Processor) and NUMA (Non-Uniform Memory Access) parallel computers are starting to be used and are expected to become more prevalent in future years as data warehouses become larger.

Not all data warehouse developments are successful. They are subject to the same problems as other large information systems projects. Failures are encountered because of poor requirements definitions, inadequate technical realizations, lack of project management and/or project budget, lack or loss of a champion, user resistance, and inadequate user training. Because companies typically report only their successes, estimates of failures vary widely, with numbers ranging from 20% to 80%.

Data Marts

The high cost of data warehouses limits them to large company operations. An alternative being used by many firms is to create a lower cost, scaled-down version of the data warehouse called the *data mart*. A data mart is a small warehouse designed for the strategic business unit (SBU) or department level. It is often a way to gain entry to the field and provide an opportunity to learn. The major problem encountered with data marts is that they often differ from department to department. Hence, integrating them enterprisewide can be difficult if this is tried after the fact.

Two approaches are used to overcome the integration problem. Some firms start with stand-alone data marts but have a plan in place for integrating them later. This is a step-by-step approach, with the goal of eventually creating an enterprisewide system. Other firms build a complete warehouse in the form of distributed data marts assigned to individual units. The advantage here is that the data marts are smaller and more tuned to local needs; the disadvantage is that obtaining enterprisewide solutions becomes more difficult.

Operational Data Stores

The operational data store (ODS) is a database for transaction processing systems that uses data warehouse concepts to provide clean data. It brings the concepts and benefits of the data warehouse to operational portions of the business. It is used for short-term, mission-critical decisions rather than the medium- and long-range decisions associated with decision support. An ODS differs from a data warehouse in that it deals with volatile data that are updated as they change, contains only current data, has a shorter time between data refreshing, and contains no summarized data. Metadata are not as central in an ODS as they are in a data warehouse.

Part 3: The Data Warehousing Industry

Size of Industry

Data warehouses are a major industry. Estimates vary, but it is clear that many more than half of the Fortune 500 have data warehouse projects under way or planned. The total world market is estimated to be in the $6- to $8-billion range in the late 1990s, and it is expected to continue growing. A partial list of major vendors[1] is shown in Table 5.2.

ROI

A 1996 International Data Corporation study of 62 organizations with data warehouses found the (very positive) results shown in Table 5.3 for these firms.

Clearly, data warehouses are significant investments being made by large firms. What are they using them for? In the next three sections, we describe three major applications of data warehouses: OLAP, data mining, and database marketing.

Part 4: Data Warehousing Applications

Application 1: OLAP (On-Line Analytic Processing)

The term OLAP was introduced by E. F. Codd in 1995 in a major article in *Computerworld* (Codd, 1995). Often credited with being the father of relational databases, Codd had concluded that relational databases for OLTP had reached their maximum capabilities in the views of the data they provided to the user. The problem stemmed principally from the massive computing required when relational databases were asked to answer relatively simple SQL queries.

He also concluded what DSS people had known for a long time—namely, that operational data are not adequate for answering managerial questions. Therefore,

TABLE 5.2 Partial List of Data Warehouse Vendors

Database Companies	Decision Support Vendors
IBM	Andyne
Informix	Brio
NCR	Business Objects
Oracle (plus subsidiary IRI)	Cognos
Sybase	Comshare
	Hyperion
	Pilot
	Platinum
	SAS
	Seagate

TABLE 5.3 Financial Impacts of Data Warehouses

Average 3 year ROI	401%
Median payback	1.67 years
Median ROI	167%
Average payback time	2.3 years
Average investment	$2.2 million

Codd advocated the use of multidimensional databases. Codd's conversion to the DSS viewpoint gave legitimacy to the data warehouse-based concepts.

The basic idea in OLAP is that managers should be able to manipulate enterprise data models across many dimensions to understand changes that are occurring. Codd assumed that the data used in OLAP would be in the form of a multidimensional cube (MOLAP). In practice, a relational database approach (called ROLAP) has also been developed. MOLAP proves to be preferable for databases of the order of 100 gigabytes. ROLAP is used for very large databases.

We now know enough about OLAP to be able to state the conditions under which OLAP should be used. These conditions are the following:

- Requests for data are analytic rather than transactional in nature.
- The information being analyzed is *not* at its first point of entry into the enterprise.

- Significant calculations and aggregations of transaction-level data are involved.
- The primary type of data element being analyzed is numeric.
- Cross-sectional views of data are often required across multiple dimensions and along multiple consolidation paths.
- Elements that identify data points remain relatively static over time.

Application 2: Data Mining

Data mining refers to finding answers in the information in the data warehouse to questions about an organization that an executive or an analyst had not thought to ask. Data mining, made easier by the very presence of the large, clean databases in the data warehouse, provides the techniques that allow managers to obtain managerial information from their legacy systems. Its objective is to identify valid, novel, potentially useful, and understandable patterns in data.[2]

Data mining is also known as Knowledge Data Discovery, or KDD. Those seeking to make a distinction between the terms *data mining* and *KDD* usually use KDD to mean the *process* of discovering useful knowledge from data, and use data mining to refer to the application of algorithms for extracting patterns from data. The difference lies in KDD's use of appropriate prior knowledge and proper interpretation of results rather than blind application of the data mining techniques. Thus, KDD is closer to an R&D process and data mining to an operational process.

KDD seeks to find patterns in data and to infer rules (i.e., to discover new information) that queries and reports do not reveal effectively. The techniques being used for knowledge discovery are listed in Table 5.4. The software associated with these approaches is called "siftware."

Every new field has its initial successes, which intrigue others to investigate it further. The following are some examples of early successes with KDD:

- People who buy scuba gear take Australian vacations
- Men who buy diapers buy beer
- Fraud detection, consumer loan analysis
- Optimization of manufacturing lines
- Play selection in the National Basketball Association
- Stock selection

In the case of loan analysis, for example, plots of data on repayment versus income and debt (as well as other variables) provide rules as to whether a requested loan should be granted or not. Although companies treat successful fraud detection techniques as proprietary, successes have been reported in such areas as detecting health care provider fraud in electronically submitted claims and using neural network tools for detecting credit card fraud.

Data mining can be bottom up (explore raw facts to find connections) or top down (search to test hypotheses). The process is iterative, with analysts asking questions

TABLE 5.4 Knowledge Discovery Techniques

Statistical analysis of data	Decision trees
Neural networks	Intelligent agents
Expert systems	Multidimensional analysis
Fuzzy logic	Data visualization

after each new output. Data mining, which is still in its early stages, deals with five kinds of data, as shown in the following table.

Associations	Things done together (buy groceries)
Sequences	Events over time (house, refrigerator)
Classifications	Pattern recognition (rules)
Clusters	Define new groups
Forecasting	Predictions from time series

The basic steps in the KDD process are shown in Figure 5.3.

Among the limits to data mining are the following:

- Dealing with very large (e.g., terabyte) databases
- Dealing with high dimensionality, which increases the size of the search space and may also create spurious patterns
- Overfitting available data
- Rapid changes in data (nonstationarity) that make previously discovered patterns invalid
- Missing and noisy data
- Lack of integration with other systems

Application 3: Database Marketing

Database marketing uses information in the large, clean databases available in the warehouse to market products and services customized to the individual. Several trends and opportunities led to the shift from "product push" mass marketing to "consumer pull" target marketing. Some of these changes are listed in Table 5.5.

The return to personalized service while maintaining economies of scale was made possible because the necessary data became available, the cost of data went down, the capabilities for storage and indexing went up, and data mining began to be applied to data warehouses. For example, for marketing to both existing and potential customers, the data warehouse lowers both marketing and direct mail costs. Sending a special offer to a general list typically results in a 2% response rate, but

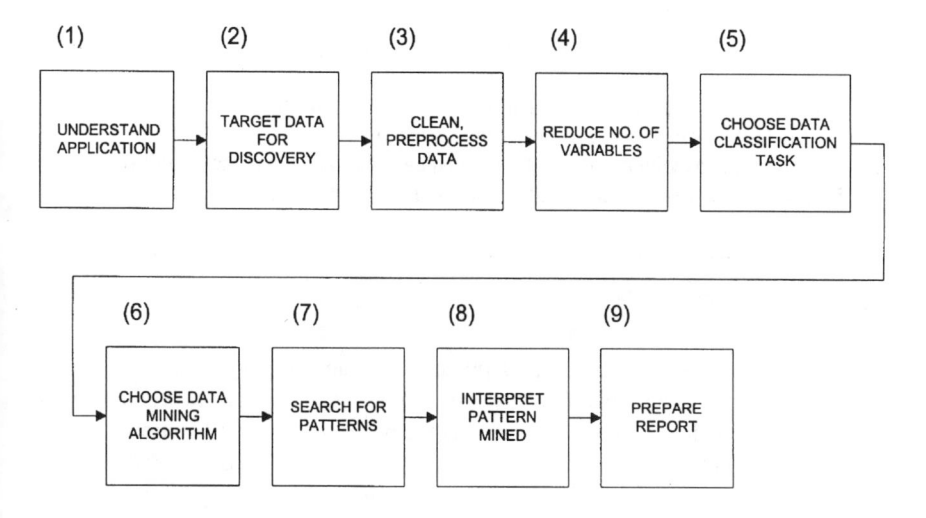

```
(1)              (2)              (3)              (4)              (5)
UNDERSTAND    TARGET DATA      CLEAN,         REDUCE NO. OF    CHOOSE DATA
APPLICATION   FOR DISCOVERY    PREPROCESS     VARIABLES        CLASSIFICATION
                               DATA                            TASK

(6)              (7)              (8)              (9)
CHOOSE DATA   SEARCH FOR       INTERPRET        PREPARE
MINING        PATTERNS         PATTERN MINED    REPORT
ALGORITHM
```

Figure 5.3. Steps in the Data Mining Process

TABLE 5.5 Some Trends and Opportunities in Marketing

Slowing growth	Increased time spent at work
Increased market diversity	More singles and single parents
Education and income gaps	Increased competition
Aging population	

with the information available in database marketing, response rates in the 15% to 25% range have been achieved. Thus, the data warehouse makes it possible to maintain a closer relationship with the customer.

Figure 5.4 shows the use of the data warehouse in relationship marketing. Note that in database marketing, it is important to keep detailed transaction data to run the needed analyses. Furthermore, among the tools used are geographic information systems (GIS) to visualize the spatial implications of the data.

Part 5: Managerial Perspective

Where Is Data Warehousing Going?

Data warehousing has undergone very rapid growth over the decade of the 1990s. However, it is plagued by a shortage of personnel that probably will not be resolved

Relationship marketing is successful when:

1. Periodic, repeat purchases make it possible to capture names at the point of sale (e.g., auto service, medical care, home services).
2. Affinity groups with common interests can be constructed (e.g., new babies)
3. Repeat buyer rewards can be developed (e.g., frequent flyers).

Figure 5.4. Relationship Marketing

for some time, because data warehousing and its related applications are not being studied or taught to any extent in the universities. Professional trade shows with accompanying technical programs serve as the prime source of education.

Data warehouses provided strategic advantage to many of the early adopters. That time is now past. The data warehouse is now a strategic necessity for many firms because their competitors use the technology.

Companies that began with an unintegrated set of data marts ran into serious difficulties. As a result, concepts such as "data mart in a box" have disappeared, and organizations introducing data marts are doing so as part of a deployment and integration strategy.

The web browser is the primary vehicle for access and the favored application development interface for the data warehouse. It is used routinely for distributing new warehouse software. Java, CORBA, Active-X, and other new software technologies are being used. On the other hand, the thin client, which had been discussed in early 1997, is not being widely adopted for warehouse applications.

A side consequence of the prevalence of the web as interface is that it has enabled new entrants into the field with low-end products.

As data warehouses grow in size, they are increasingly using mainframes as servers. Scalability, always a prime issue, is leading to increased use of parallel computing.

Data mining appears to be moving in two directions simultaneously. At one end, OLAP software is starting to incorporate generalized mining tools to allow decision support analysts to add these techniques to their arsenals. At the other end, application-specific mining tools are being created to solve specific problems, such as fraud detection.

Data warehouses, being databases, are primarily oriented to number and text fields. In future years, multimedia and knowledge management capabilities are expected to be added. Adding multimedia capabilities as more bandwidth becomes available implies that users will be able to retrieve video, audio, and text as well. Multimedia will contribute to the data warehouse as part of an organization's knowledge base, that is, its organizational memory of experience, values, contextual information, and insights.

Managerial Considerations

Data warehouses are being introduced into firms both as parts of specific initiatives (improved executive information, trying to capture the benefits of data mining, or as part of a database marketing thrust) and as new infrastructure. The former are championed and funded by line groups, and the latter by information systems departments (Watson & Haley, 1997). Being large investments, visible on the balance sheet, they require careful managerial control if they are to be successful.

The three applications of data warehousing described here are, individually and collectively, sufficient reasons for considering undertaking a data warehousing project. If carried out successfully, the data indicate significant returns on investment. However, such projects are risky because successful implementation is not guaranteed.

Data warehouses are a step along the road to knowledge management. Organizations want to be able to keep and use the information they have for both strategic and tactical purposes. In the long term, such disparate fields as organizational memory, document management, and data warehousing will coalesce with new integrating concepts to create a true knowledge management system.

In organizations implementing the data warehousing concept, both line and information systems managers are involved in making decisions that affect their warehousing capabilities. Among them is whether to build a single, centralized warehouse or to build a distribution warehouse consisting of multiple, integrated data marts. Experience thus far indicates that the choice of centralization vs. distribution should follow the degree of centralization of the organization as a whole.

The understanding of the technology of data warehouses, like that of other technologies, has outstripped the understanding of the related business issues such as sponsorship, identifying business needs, politics, and training. Users need to derive business value from the warehouse if it is to be successful. Simply solving the technology issues is not enough.

Notes

1. Readers who need more information about vendors and their products should consult *DM Review* magazine. This controlled circulation monthly can be found at URL: http:\\www.dmreview.com.
2. Data mining does not require a data warehouse but is made much easier by the organized, clean data available. As shown in Figure 5.3, data mining requires clean data as part of the process.

References

Codd, E. F. (1995, April 13). Twelve rules for on-line analytic processing. *Computerworld,* pp. 84-87.
Inmon, W. (1992). *Building the data warehouse.* New York: Wiley.

Rockart, J. F., & DeLong, D. W. (1988). *Executive support systems: The emergence of top management computer use.* Homewood, IL: Dow Jones Irwin.

Watson, H. J., & Haley, B. (1997). A framework for data warehousing. *Data Warehousing Journal, 2*(1), 10-17.

CHAPTER
SIX

Artificial Intelligence

A Short History and the Next 40 Years

PHILLIP EIN-DOR

A Short History of the Previous 40 Years of AI[1]

Empirical work on artificial intelligence began in the early to mid 1950s. That makes the field a little more than 40 years old now—a ripe enough age to assess what progress has been made and what lies ahead. In the space of a short chapter such as this, it is clearly impossible to cover the whole of a very diverse field; to attempt to do so would inevitably end in superficiality. The path we have chosen is to focus on a relatively small number of representative issues that we find to be of greatest interest and that we hope will also be of interest to readers of this volume.

Managerially oriented readers may note—correctly—that AI is essentially a technical specialty and a concentration area of computer science, and such readers may ask why this chapter should be of interest to them. The answer lies not in the details of the technology but in its application. Many AI applications have a business or managerial context. Consequently, many managers are called upon to decide whether to go ahead with AI applications for their organizations. This requires some understanding of the past and also of possible futures of the field in order to permit informed assessment of the opportunities and risks involved. The chapter was written with these considerations in mind. It does not dwell on technical considerations but does cite many business and management examples that should help the lay reader to draw balanced conclusions.

The History of Predictions

The history of artificial intelligence (AI) is replete with examples of overly optimistic predictions concerning the development of our capabilities to create intelligent artifacts. This tends to be true of any field of technology; the emergence of almost every new technology is accompanied by predictions of the rapidity with which it will obtain ubiquitous use. In fact, an examination of such cases indicates that the adoption cycle—from invention through early use to more widespread use and then general use—is usually about 25 years. In AI, it will be much, much longer. The principle reason is that AI is still being invented 50 years after the idea first germinated. Not only are the various technologies still being invented, but the conceptual underpinnings are still in a state of flux and continually evolving.[2] Thus, AI is still very much an emerging technology and will continue to be so for many years to come; the development and dissemination cycles will be far more extended than for most technologies.

Two examples will demonstrate this point. The first is the prediction in the mid 1950s by the Nobel Laureate and one of the founding fathers of the AI field, Herbert Simon, that within 10 years, a computer would be chess champion of the world. Forty years later, the IBM computer named Deep Blue defeated Gary Kasparov in one match. It remains to be proven whether this dominance can be maintained. Even assuming that this match was the turning point, and that from now on, computers will continue to retain the championship, the prediction was off by a factor of four[3]—and this for a well-defined, highly structured (albeit difficult) problem.

A second example is from the field of commonsense knowledge representation. Early in the work on natural language processing, it became evident that to understand human language, the processor must possess a vast store of the knowledge common to most of the speakers of the language. (More on this later.) John McCarthy (1960), another of the grand old men of the field, wrote an article in which he suggested that with sufficient effort, the problem of commonsense knowledge representation could be solved within a relatively short time. Almost 40 years have passed, and despite considerable effort as described below, the solution still seems extremely remote.

The Need for a Sense of History

The previous examples show that in addressing the question of where AI will be 40 years from now, prudence requires one to take a conservative point of view. Although progress has undoubtedly been made, much more remains to be achieved. Furthermore, the progress is basically restricted to specific and well-defined fields;[4] general intelligent machines are still well beyond the time horizon of this chapter. The achievement of general artificial intelligence remains, in my opinion, at least as far in the future as it was when the AI effort first began. I am not quite so pessimistic as to compare the future history of AI with that of the wheel; if that were the correct analogy, we would need to remember the several thousand years that elapsed between the invention of the wheel and its application in mechanically driven vehicles. I do expect several hundred years to elapse from the invention of the computer and the beginnings of artificial intelligence to their culmination in the construction of a general artificial intelligence. I am slightly more optimistic than those who believe such an achievement to be completely impossible.[5] However, I am not really *sure* that it will ever happen, and I would not be surprised to learn that it may take a millennium or two.

For more practically oriented readers, the question of interest may not be so much "When will a general artificial intelligence be available?" but rather "What snippets may become available for help in solving particular problems?" Expert systems are prime examples of such snippets, but even they have not been adopted with anything like the speed predicted when they first became available. It seems that even they exhibit considerable problems that inhibit widespread use; these are discussed later.

The Need for Humility

The previous discussion was intended to indicate the need for considerable humility in making predictions concerning AI. If the idea of a general artificial intelligence is still well over the horizon, what can we predict for the next 40 years? Certainly, progress will continue to be made in particular areas, and more and more artificial intelligence will be brought to bear on specific practical problems. It is the specific areas in which progress may be expected, as well as possible application areas, on which most of our discussion will focus, although this discussion will inevitably lead us back to more general questions.

As a famous wit once said, "It is difficult to make predictions, especially about the future." A fortiori, it is foolhardy to attempt to predict the future of a discipline so notorious for its surfeit of optimism. Nevertheless, the temptation is great to follow in the footsteps of those illustrious pioneers who were not afraid to go out on a limb. With that in mind, we have undertaken the task anyway. Making predictions for lengthy periods does have one advantage—some time must elapse before one can be taken to task for one's errors.

It is impossible to predict the future of AI, in all of its multiple facets, in a single short chapter. Therefore, we have chosen to focus on a number of specific issues, some of which are currently in the limelight and some of which may be more obscure but perhaps more significant. The topics to be covered are AI in general versus practical applications ("strong" vs. "weak" AI); some major roadblocks encountered in the development of artificial intelligence (knowledge acquisition, commonsense knowledge representation, and computing power); two currently popular techniques—neural nets and genetic algorithms; and finally, a number of specific application areas—human-machine interfaces, expert systems, autonomous intelligent machines (AIM), and data mining. Throughout, we will try to draw attention to some common issues pervading the field.

General AI Versus Business Applications: Cognitive Science Versus Engineering

Artificial intelligence is frequently categorized into two modalities—strong and weak. Strong AI refers to attempts to create general intelligent systems (i.e., simulacra of human intelligence, or at least some aspect of it; Searle, 1984). Strong

AI is often based on observations of the processes of human intelligence, and from this point of view, any successful attempt to build a strong AI becomes a theory of the way humans perform such activities.

Weak AI, on the other hand, has much more restricted goals and may be viewed as attempts to induce computers to behave at the level of intelligent humans on *specific, predefined tasks*. Chess programs are one example. Medical diagnostic systems, scheduling programs, credit evaluation systems, production robots, extraterrestrial rovers, and expert configuration systems are all additional examples of weak AI. The question of simulating human behavior is of no real interest in weak AI; the only real question is whether the system performs as well as, or better than, the alternative human operator in the same (limited) activity. It is weak AI that mainly interests us in the context of this chapter. This being the case, we are generally absolved from having to deal with the many fascinating philosophical issues associated with strong AI, but they may crop up from time to time. Furthermore, because this chapter is intended primarily for those who are not generally involved in the creation or use of artificial intelligence, an attempt has been made to keep the references as nontechnical as possible so that they may be accessible to lay readers.

In this context, two additional points should be mentioned. The first is that the more advanced weak AI systems become, the more they take on the attributes of, or at least adopt approaches from, strong AI. Thus, attempts to build mobile vision systems may be based on current understanding of the human optical system; similarly, attempts to build better chess programs use knowledge about the behavior of expert chess players. The second point is that theories of the human cognitive system have, in recent years, begun to adopt something of the viewpoint of weak AI—not necessarily consciously, but from the psychological data. In psychology, this view is that of multiple intelligences—that the human intelligence is not monolithic and the result of a single, central mechanism, but rather that there are many specialized mechanisms, each responsible for a different facet of behavior. Some are at a higher level, such as musical intelligence, mathematical intelligence, interpersonal intelligence, and linguistic intelligence, whereas others posited are even more specialized, such as recognizing human faces and identifying word breaks in continuous speech.[6]

Roadblocks in the Development of AI

Looking back over the history of AI, it becomes apparent that a number of roadblocks have hindered progress in the field. We will briefly describe three of those that we consider the most important. Obviously, if the field is to make substantial advances, these roadblocks must be removed, or at least substantially mitigated. The roadblocks we have in mind are knowledge acquisition and representation in general, commonsense knowledge in particular, and search and processing speed.

Knowledge Acquisition

At the heart of intelligence is knowledge. Knowledge consists of facts about the world and rules for manipulating them. In expert systems, this view is very clear-cut; the system developer first learns the relevant facts in the field. In medical expert systems, for example, the relevant facts are the symptoms associated with the illnesses that constitute the system's area of expertise. The rules define the conclusions that should be drawn from the different combinations of symptoms. To drive home an earlier point, note that medical diagnostic systems are restricted to specific parts of the body or to specific types of disease; this is domain constraint with a vengeance! One of the most important debates in AI today is how the necessary knowledge should be acquired—by registration or by learning.

Facts: Two Basic Paradigms

Two basic paradigms have served as bases for knowledge acquisition to date—the representational and the emergent.

Representational knowledge. The initial AI paradigm was representational. The assumption was that one could program into a machine representations of the domain or universe in which it was to function. Given such a representation and a set of rules for manipulating states in that universe, the machine would be able to move from any valid state in the universe of states to a goal state. This was the underlying philosophy of the General Problem Solver of Newell and Simon (1963) and many other successful AI programs. It is also the basis for arguably the most successful AI application to date—Expert Systems—which contain rules representing an expert's knowledge of how to function in his or her area of expertise.

Emergent knowledge. At the same time, experiments were carried out on an alternative paradigm, now commonly known as emergent AI. This approach argued that the best way to impart intelligence to a machine was to provide it with a learning capability, turn it loose in the world, and let it learn from its experiences in that world. Such learning mechanisms were generally modeled on the human central nervous system—a network of neurons, each with very limited functionality but extremely powerful when connected in large numbers. This approach fell into disregard for some 20 years but is now very much in vogue again. Thus, the two approaches are frequently viewed as being in competition with each other.

However, a more thoughtful analysis of work in the field indicates that each has its place, each being more effective in particular areas. This is not surprising; just as humans learn certain facts in packaged form by rote and others by induction from experience, so computers can best be programmed for different tasks by one means or the other. Looking into the future, it seems reasonable to assume that various knowledge representation methods will be combined with learning algorithms to produce more effective machines. Until such learning methods are perfected, representing and acquiring knowledge will remain serious impediments to building intelligent systems.

Common Sense: The Perennial Stopper

As already noted, a general problem in the development of intelligent systems is that of commonsense knowledge. Commonsense knowledge is that knowledge that we expect every person we meet to know, even if we have never before met him or her. This includes general knowledge of the physical world, expected behaviors and the ability to detect deviant behavior, and the ability to identify contexts in which events or conversations take place. This knowledge is essential for interpreting the information acquired by the senses and in understanding natural language, which itself consists basically of descriptions of real-world phenomena, sensory stimuli, and behaviors. The use of common sense is what distinguishes general intelligence from expert knowledge; in expert systems, the universe of discourse is strictly circumscribed to a particular domain—internal medicine, rock chemistry, or computer system structure, to name a few well-known examples.[7]

But now consider the simple prosaic statement,

"John broke his piggy bank to buy Mary a Barbie doll for her birthday."

When I make such a statement, I expect the hearer to understand that John needed money to buy the doll; that John kept his money in the piggy bank; and that some piggy banks must be broken to extract the money from them. I also expect the hearer to know that it is common to buy gifts for people who are celebrating birthdays, and that is the reason John bought the doll. Even further, I expect the speaker to infer that John and Mary are both young children, because dolls are appropriate gifts for girls but not generally for grown women, and that money is generally kept in piggy banks by children, not adults. In some cultures, we even expect people to know what a Barbie doll is! At an even deeper level, it is assumed that the listener knows the basic principles of trading—bargaining, buying, selling, and so on.[8] Thus, a simple sentence can contain a wealth of implicit information, which is what we mean by common sense.

Why is commonsense knowledge so difficult? There are many reasons. First and foremost, there is so much of it! The CYC project began in 1984 with the intention of formalizing all of the commonsense knowledge necessary for understanding an encyclopedia. By 1995, "a person-century of effort had gone into building CYC, a universal schema of roughly 10^5 general concepts spanning human reality" (Lenat, 1995, p. 33); about 10^6 facts had been encoded, but the work was not yet complete.[9] Thus, it really is a heroic task to formalize all of the knowledge that most humans have probably acquired by the age of about 15. The good news is that commonsense knowledge does not change very rapidly over time, but rather evolves as the world changes and as our perceptions of the world change. Thus, once the task has been completed, maintenance may not be overly difficult. Even this, however, may be wishful thinking; one should note that a major problem with expert systems is maintaining their knowledge bases, even though only a minuscule subset of total human knowledge is involved in each.

A second problem with commonsense knowledge representation is that common sense consists largely of defaults. As an example, consider the assertion "birds fly." This is a good first approximation to knowledge about birds; unfortunately, there are many specific cases in which it does not hold true; examples of these are if the bird happens to be an emu, an ostrich, or a penguin; if the bird is dead; if the bird has a broken wing; if the bird has its feet encased in concrete; and so on. For a corpus of knowledge to be complete, it must be able to deal with exceptions, not just the rule. Much of the work on commonsense knowledge has focused on formulating logics capable of dealing with just this problem. These generally fall under the heading of nonmonotonic logic.[10] A related problem is that most particular exemplars are variants of the "ideal" concept. For example, consider the definition of a canary (*Webster's*, 1983):

> **canary**: a small finch (*Serinus canarius*) of the Canary Islands that is usually greenish to yellow and is kept as a cage bird and singer.

This definition contains many sources of uncertainty or variation. How small is "small," and how much can the size vary? How often is "usually"? What is the spectral range of "greenish to yellow"? Is every canary kept as a "cage bird and singer"? Fuzzy logic (Zadeh, 1983) is a well-known attempt to deal with this problem.

This discussion of commonsense inference has so far begged the whole question of whether formal logics are the best tool for this. Herbert Simon (1991), for example, believes that they are not: "An influential coterie of contemporary artificial intelligence researchers . . . believe that formal logic provides the appropriate language for A.I. programs, and that problem solving is a process of proving theorems. They are horribly wrong on both counts" (p. 192). We will not pursue this debate beyond noting its existence and the further difficulty this entails for the whole commonsense knowledge representation effort.

A third problem involves the cultural or contextual specificity of commonsense knowledge. Thus, the common sense of the Eskimo is considerably different from that of the nomadic tribes of the Sahara. Bargaining processes and etiquette differ between cultures. Or, more locally, the concept that money is given in exchange for goods or services does not hold in the context of gifts or charitable donations.

For these and other reasons, I do not see any near-term solution to the commonsense knowledge problem in the sense of ready availability of programmed corpora of such knowledge. However, the problem is so central to the whole AI endeavor that I have no doubt that effort will continue to be expended on it and that at some point in the (rather distant) future, the goal will be realized.

Search

It frequently transpires that solving a problem intelligently requires search of a state space representing different possible states of the system. Obvious examples of this are games such as chess, checkers, and bridge. The player "looks ahead" to evaluate where different moves might lead; in other words, the player considers various potential states of the game. In more practical applications, a doctor considers the states of the patient that may have generated the symptoms observed. In trying to develop a production or classroom schedule, the scheduler examines various possible schedules until satisfied that a good solution has been found. State spaces of this kind may be thought of as trees, the roots of which are the initial state considered, and the nodes or branch points of which represent additional states. It is hoped that at least one of the nodes is the goal or solution sought.

Many search methods have been developed to navigate the trees representing search spaces. These include pattern matching, generate and test, hill climbing, and, most recently, genetic algorithms that are essentially a variant of hill climbing and proceed by random mutation rather than deterministic choice.

Speed of Search

As noted earlier, many AI programs can be stated as search problems. But search spaces tend to have the nasty quality of expanding very rapidly. A good example of this is chess programs; the more powerful computers became, the bigger the space they could search in the allotted time—that is, the more plies they could examine— and this raised their level of performance until the defeat of Gary Kasparov was achieved. Thus, hardware speed is a necessary condition for achieving advanced levels of intelligence, especially for systems that must function in real time. Current, visually directed mobile robots are seriously constrained by the limits on processing speed, impressive as these are. Hans Moravec, Director of the Mobile Robot Laboratory at Carnegie-Mellon University, has calculated that the human optic nerve conveys the results of about one billion computations per second (Moravec, 1988). He puts the power required to simulate the complete human brain at 10^{13} computations per second—well beyond the capabilities of any current machine.

The development of ever-faster computers continues rapidly; methods of applying large numbers of the faster machines to a single problem are also under way in the form of parallel and distributed computing. The faster machines become, the more problems they will be able to solve in a reasonable time and the larger the problems they will be able to address.

AI Techniques

Much work is currently devoted to developing and applying two AI techniques currently in vogue—neural networks and genetic algorithms. These seem to be enjoying considerable practical success and so are discussed briefly here.

Neural Nets

Neural nets are the quintessential example of the emergent AI approach and also demonstrate some interesting links between cognitive science and artificial intelligence. Historically, their beginnings are in the McCulloch-Pitts (1943) model of the human nervous system, and their application to learning is in the perceptron model of the 1950s and 1960s (Rosenblatt, 1962). These models aroused much early interest but then fell into limbo for two decades after Minsky and Pappert (1969) demonstrated their limitations. As the more recent neural network model, this approach to creating intelligence has now enjoyed a decade-long revival, arousing considerable interest and not inconsiderable success. The essence of neural nets consists of two elements—sets of interconnected nodes that simulate biological neural systems, and a training regime in which the net "learns" the parameters of the domain in which it is to operate.

There are at least two sets of nodes—input nodes and output nodes—and, frequently, one or more intermediate sets or hidden layers. Each node is initially linked to every node one level above it; that is, assuming one hidden layer, every input node is linked to every node in the hidden layer, and every node in the hidden layer is linked to every output node. The content of the nodes is a set of weights indicating the strength of the relationship between a given input and the next level nodes. Initially, the weights are all equal. A net is trained by giving it examples in accordance with which it adjusts the weights according to some weighting function. Training continues until the desired level of performance is achieved.

Some examples of areas in which neural nets have been applied successfully are data mining (see below); firm bankruptcy predictions (Tam & Kiang, 1992; Wilson & Sharda, 1994); loan application approval (Gallant, 1988); investment decisions (Cheng, McClain, & Kelly, 1997); fraud prevention (Rochester, 1990); and solving optimization problems (Nygard, Juell, & Kaddaba, 1990). At least one study found the prediction capability of neural nets to be better than that of classical linear discriminant analysis for classification problems (Leshno & Spector, 1996), whereas another found them superior to linear discriminant analysis and classification trees (Pompe & Feelders, 1996). However, results similar to, but no better than, those of statistical methods were found when using neural nets in a data mining problem, but the effort involved was considerably greater (Zahavi & Levin, 1995, 1997). For a bibliography of business applications of neural networks, see Sharda (1994).

Interestingly, nearly all of the examples in the literature are from the financial area. It is not clear whether this is the result of more frequent experimentation in finance or whether neural nets are inherently more suitable for some areas than for others. Clearly, much more experimentation is required to determine in which applications neural nets are most effective and appropriate when developing algorithms and training regimes. In general, though, it is fairly safe to predict the increasing use of neural nets as they and their application are better understood. It is also safe to say that they are not a universal solution and that their use will continue to be restricted to particular areas of AI application.

Genetic Algorithms

Genetic algorithms, based on the concept of biological mutation and evolution, begin, as do neural nets, with random solutions. However, instead of training toward a directed view of the problem space with right and wrong answers, genetic algorithms are essentially a hill-climbing technique. Given a criterion, the algorithm mutates solution parameter values (regarded as genes). The evolution is either random or on the basis of some simulation of biological evolution, with "father," "mother," "son," and "daughter" solutions; the offspring are composed of combinations of the parents' genes. Better solutions are maintained for further mating and mutation, and less successful adaptations are rejected.

One application of genetic algorithms in citrus harvest optimization has led, in a formal test, to better results than a straightforward linear program, and to results only 1.3% below those of a manually improved and unconstrained linear program (Levin & Zahavi, 1996).

We may expect continuing experimentation with genetic algorithms, both to develop new algorithms and to identify those problems to which they are best suited.

Applications

Having briefly discussed two AI techniques currently drawing attention, we next turn to a discussion of leading-edge applications. Again, because of the breadth of the fields, we will examine only a small number of examples rather than attempting anything like a complete enumeration. The general areas on which we will touch are computer interface systems—input and output modalities, expert systems, and various forms of autonomous intelligent machines.

Interfaces

Under this heading, we will first discuss human-computer interfaces, followed by some input and output modes relevant to such interfaces.

Human-Computer Interfaces

An area in which artificial intelligence is slowly being deployed and to great benefit is the human-computer interface. People vary tremendously in their knowledge of computers and their ability to operate them. The same is true of any specific computer application. At present, however, most operating and application systems assume a single prototypical user (one size fits all). As a result, the novice and the expert are both served by the same interface, which frequently is annoyingly verbose and simplistic for the expert, yet frustratingly complex and uninformative for the novice. The level of service could be improved greatly for both types of users (and those in between the extremes) if systems adapted themselves to the user's level of expertise. Furthermore, modern systems tend to offer a much broader range of functions and different ways of performing them than any one user can fully utilize. Thus, it would be extremely beneficial if systems adapted themselves so that the functions and options most frequently employed by each user were most easily accessible (i.e., the user would not have to burrow through levels of menus to access frequently employed capabilities). This implies an ability of systems to learn their users' characteristics and behaviors and to adapt accordingly, just as humans adapt their style to different people with whom they come into contact. Some beginnings along these lines are already appearing, and it is likely that highly developed system adaptation facilities will become available well within the time span of this forecast.

An added bonus would derive from providing speech input command systems in which the user could tell the system what to do (e.g., "Put a comma and space between the first two words of the second paragraph on the screen."). This would require the perfection of speech input—a capability that is developing quickly because of its obvious advantages in help desks, call-in systems, and so on—and machine understanding of the context in which the commands are delivered. Because this would be restricted to the application with which the user is working at the time (i.e., it would be part of the application), this should provide no insurmountable barriers and should be available within the decade. For a video preview, see Kai-Fu Lee (1993).

Humans spend a great deal of their time, in fact, all of their time when not asleep, interfacing with the physical world and with other humans by means of the senses and bodily effectors. This being the case, we should expect that intelligent artifacts should also have a rich portfolio of interfaces and effectors. Thus, it is not surprising that the history of AI, and of computing in general, contains a rich subtext dealing with interfaces and effectors.

A constant trend over the years has been the attempt to make computers amenable to a broader range of inputs and outputs. Beginning with punched cards and punched paper tape, input media developed first to magnetic tape and disks, and then to keyboards, magnetic character recognition, and optical character recognition. All of these are now standard except for the punched paper media, which have since disappeared.

In parallel, research proceeded on more human-oriented inputs such as speech recognition, speech production, visual image processing, and reading handwriting. We shall examine the potential uses and developments in each of these.

Speech Recognition and Production

Speech processing is an interesting example of the dichotomies that can develop between input and output capabilities in a single sensory medium. Whereas speech synthesis—the production of speech outputs—is relatively well developed and in widespread use, speech recognition is a much more difficult problem. The first main problem is that in continuous speech, there are no natural word boundaries—locution is indeed continuous. Thus, a string of phonemes frequently may be interpreted in different ways, each of which yields different words. Resolving such conflicts frequently requires an understanding of the speech context; once again, commonsense knowledge is required.

A second major problem is that the differences in characteristics between the voices of individuals are greater than those between the phonemes of any particular voice. Thus, the interpersonal differences still prevent the construction of robust, speaker-independent systems for general speech recognition that do not require a training period in which the system learns the characteristics of each user's voice. Having said that, there are already rudimentary systems for general speech recognition in use that require no training (e.g., those systems more and more widely used for telephone answering systems). These are, however, also severely constrained in the vocabularies they recognize. Furthermore, the system dictates which words are to be used and when; in a sense, the system trains the user rather than the other way around. Additional problems that will not be discussed here in any detail are the lack of robustness of such systems in noisy backgrounds and their limited vocabularies.

There are many obvious practical applications for speech recognition systems—applications, furthermore, that could considerably enhance productivity, reduce costs, and facilitate use of computers and, indeed, of virtually every type of machine. An in-depth discussion of speech recognition problems and techniques together with an interesting demonstration of the state of the art is available on video (Lee, 1993). I expect general purpose speech systems that do not require training but are restricted to specific domains to be available within two decades.

Vision

Vision systems must be divided into several categories. Optical character recognition (OCR) was a very early success in this field. However, OCR systems are constrained to recognizing digits and the characters of an alphabet, so the number of possibilities is quite limited. Furthermore, to render the problem even simpler, such systems were constrained to particular kinds of characters. This is not to deny the great practical importance of such systems, but the AI aspects of this type of vision system are not particularly interesting. Of greater interest is the problem of recognizing handwriting; here, the domain is still constrained to characters, but the permissible variation is much greater than that in the earlier systems. Systems of this kind are, of course, already available in personal digital assistants.

The real problem with vision systems arises when the system is required to recognize the general scenes that it acquires, and not a narrow range of images from some predetermined context. Even assuming that the image has been decomposed successfully into component outlines, occlusions have been correctly identified and filled in, light and shade have been correctly interpreted, and textures have been correctly identified, the question still remains: "What are the objects, and what does the image represent?" This question is easily answered by humans (in their natural habitat) but requires much commonsense knowledge. Once again, the specter of common sense is aroused, and good systems await its successful representation and application to recognizing visual scenes—at least as difficult a problem as acquiring the common sense necessary to understand text.

Vision systems will continue to improve and to permit new applications in controlled domains. However, as with many other problems in AI, high levels of performance are dependent on commonsense knowledge, and so application will continue to be restricted to specific domains for the foreseeable future.

Other Sensory Inputs and Outputs

We have concentrated on vision and speech input systems. However, the other senses are also candidates for application of artificial intelligence, and I will touch on these very briefly.

Touch: Touch inputs are already applied in robot effectors designed to lift or move objects. Clearly, the more delicate the task to be performed, the more developed the touch system needs to be. Much of the work in this field is also directed to touch outputs in the context of virtual reality systems. To date, this has been mainly for entertainment purposes, but it could become of great importance in human-machine systems requiring remote touch; one can think of a surgeon performing an operation from afar by means of virtual reality link requiring, among the other sensory outputs, a delicate sense of touch. The same would apply to robots performing operations—a topic in the experimental stage, with such operations already having been performed on animals. It has also been dealt with in science fiction (Ellison, 1979), and science fiction scenarios have a tendency to become true!

Smell: Applications of olfactory inputs already exist in machines that sniff out drugs, explosives, and other proscribed substances, and one can think of other applications, such as personal pollution detectors or smelling burning food in the oven. I am not aware of any efforts to produce olfactory outputs, but it would seem natural to incorporate such outputs in virtual reality systems, movies, and other forms of entertainment. It may also be possible to conceive of practical applications in order to attract attention to specific situations. A very rudimentary form of such an application is the addition of a smelly agent to odorless natural gas in order to alert people to gas leaks.

Taste: I am not aware of work on taste systems either for input or output, but just as with the other senses, there are sure to be practical applications that will encourage their development. After all, a robot chef will have to be able to taste its productions!

To summarize future developments in sensory systems, we can safely assume continuing effort on those sensory inputs and outputs that are already in use and the certain appearance of new forms of such interfaces. If some of the critics of AI who base their criticism on the fact that artifacts cannot participate in human experiences have a point, then the provision of the full range of such human experiences may be critical for achieving the goal of strong AI.

Expert Systems

Expert systems are of special interest in our context because they are, ostensibly, the earliest widespread type of knowledge-based system. They should also be the easiest kind of knowledge-based system because they are restricted to particular domains, are relatively well defined, and rely only minimally on commonsense knowledge. In spite of all these apparent advantages, and in spite of a considerable number of impressive successes, the diffusion of expert systems has been much slower than originally expected. Edward Feigenbaum, one of the pioneers of the field and a longtime practitioner, has listed the reasons for this state of affairs (Feigenbaum, 1993):

1. Knowledge is the prime factor in intelligence. However, most expert system companies sold expert system shells rather than application systems or application knowledge (i.e., they sold inference engines rather than knowledge).
2. Knowledge acquisition turned out to be extremely difficult. Feigenbaum quotes S. Sato, Director of Fujitsu Laboratories as saying that "It has been too difficult to get the knowledge."
3. Successful expert systems have focused on very narrow niches of knowledge. If they focus on broad domains, they tend to be not powerful enough; if focused on suitably narrow domains, the user group tends to be too small to warrant the investment involved.
4. They have been designed, frequently by academics, with the problem rather than the user in mind. This has led to systems that are complex, slow, and quirky, which deters users.
5. The wrong applications were generally chosen—complex or esoteric systems with narrow use rather than more routine, widespread applications, such as those required to fill government forms.
6. There is a serious maintenance problem. Knowledge changes over time and must be maintained. But maintenance has not been institutionalized, and many systems become outdated and are abandoned.[11]
7. No standards were developed to facilitate accessibility; the proliferation of small, overly competitive firms confused users. Nor was a standard testing methodology developed to permit comparison and validation of products. One need only consider the effects of the de facto standards developed for PC operating systems or the role of the TCP/IP communications protocol in development of the Internet to appreciate the galvanizing effect of standards and the debilitating effect of their absence.
8. Some of the technological infrastructure necessary for successful expert system deployment has become available only recently or is just becoming so. The infrastructure elements mentioned by Feigenbaum are desktop workstations with large memory, graphic user interfaces, object-oriented programming, communications networks, and rapid prototyping methodology.
9. There is a normal time lag before the acceptance of new technology; see the discussion in the section on the history of predictions.
10. Expectations were geared to notions of general artificial intelligence—strong AI—that did not materialize and so led to disappointment and disillusionment.

One of the most interesting features of this list of problems is the extent to which it replicates some of the problems discussed in the context of roadblocks to strong AI. If the problems are so severe in the small, that is, at the level of much more focused expert systems, one can begin to appreciate how much more difficult they must be in the context of strong AI. Particularly compelling is the centrality of knowledge to every aspect of the AI endeavor.

Autonomous Intelligent Machines, or Robots, Immobots, and Softbots: A Bot by Any Other Name

Robots, immobots, and softbots are all variations on the theme of autonomous intelligent machines (AIM). Autonomy implies the ability to function independently in some domain without direct control and the ability to adapt to changes in the domain as circumstances dictate.

Robots

The idea of mechanical men, or artificial beings, is as old as human mythology. Humanity, it seems, has long had the dream of creating creatures in its own image who would relieve it of unpleasant chores, perform humanly impossible deeds, or solve otherwise unsolvable problems. This dream culminated in the invention of the word *robot* to denote such creatures, the current application of industrial robots, and efforts to build ever more sophisticated artifacts of this kind. The ultimate goal is machines that will navigate the physical world, operate in it in real time, and adapt to changes in it. Thus, autonomous intelligent machines, to use the less loaded term, may be evaluated in terms of mobility, effector functionality, reaction time, and intelligence in executing tasks and solving problems. Just as chess has given rise to competitions between humans and chess-playing machines in the field of pure cognition, robotics has given rise to an annual competition between robots; the annual competitions are reported in *AI Magazine*.[12] However, at present, the goal of autonomous intelligent machines is still remote and, again, for reasons already enumerated with respect to other types of systems—processing speed and knowledge representation.

In practical terms, a classical robot consists of mechanisms for locomotion in the physical world and for manipulating objects in that world under the control of an intelligent computational component. As is natural in a field of endeavor requiring the fruition of research in many different disciplines—in particular, the combination of mechanics and AI—many partial solutions arise en route. Thus, industrial robots generally have mechanical effectors but lack locomotion, and the control mechanism is constrained to reasoning about the limited domain of the production process in which it is employed. Particularly interesting variations on the theme of autonomous intelligent machines are immobots and softbots.[13]

Immobots

The idea of the autonomous robot is that the machine should move to wherever it is required. The immobot takes a diametrically opposite approach. As the name implies, an immobot is immobile; on the other hand, it is widely distributed and interconnected.

> Structurally, immobots are massively distributed, physically embedded, autonomous systems with a large array of simple, fixed-location sensors and actuators. Functionally, an immobot's primary task is to control its massive regulatory, immune and nervous systems through a coupling of high-level reasoning and adaptive autonomous processes. (Williams & Nayak, 1996, p. 21)

An example of an immobot is a system spanning a campus of buildings in which the role of the immobot is environmental control. With multiple sensors and actuators, possibly in each room of the campus, as well as in hallways and external areas, such a system would be extremely complex simply because of its magnitude and possible diversity of conditions, even though each sensor or actuator might, of itself, be quite simple.

Such systems, equipped with initial models of their environments, would be expected to acquire additional knowledge from observing that environment over time. An immobot would have to be self-configuring, that is, be able to engage and disengage components and change its operating policies in response to changes in its goals, its internal structure, and the external environment. This would be the embodiment of control of the "massive regulatory, immune and nervous systems" mentioned in the quote.

AI and the Internet—Softbots

As the amount and variety of information on the Internet increases, more and more help will be required to navigate it and to find relevant items. This task is already being assigned to intelligent agents (also known as crawlers, spiders, softbots, robots, or just plain bots), and their role will surely increase. The tasks assigned to them will be as varied as putting together reference lists, making travel reservations, finding databases, or making a purchase as cheaply as possible. Going a step further, software agents could look over our shoulders as we handle our email or do our electronic shopping, and they could learn to behave as we do in order to perform tasks for us.[14] The main role of agents at present is to assemble the metaknowledge maintained by the various search engines, such as Alta Vista,[15] Lycos,[16] and Excite,[17] to name some of the better known ones. They do this by attaching themselves to web sites and mining the content and address information in them. However, the number of search engines is already so large that a higher level of help is convenient; this is provided by "metacrawlers," which are essentially parasites on the basic search engines. When a query is put to a metacrawler, it passes it on to a battery of search engines and compiles the answers received. Some of the better known of these are Metacrawler,[18] Mamma[19] (the mother of all search engines), and Highway 61.[20]

Anyone who has had the common experience of querying the Web for information only to receive tens, or even hundreds, of thousands of hits realizes how useful it would be to have an agent that *understood* the contexts of queries and information sources. To acquire such understanding, the system would have to have the necessary commonsense knowledge—that old bugbear again! Systems have already been built that have the knowledge to understand natural language queries, but these are always restricted to particular, limited domains so that the context is preordained and the commonsense problem is much less critical. As stated earlier, the prognosis for real commonsense understanding by machines is not bright; it will probably take many decades to solve the commonsense knowledge problem. Until then, there will be marginal improvements in keyword or otherwise lexically oriented systems, but the breakthrough probably will not occur within the time span of this forecast.

The difference between robots and software agents, on one hand, and other intelligent software on the other, is that intelligent software is locked inside a box and has no interaction with the outside world.[21] Robots, however, operate in, affect, and may some day roam the physical world; softbots roam cyberspace and take up different temporary abodes in it. Immobots, as their name suggests, are immobile, but because of their scope, they take on some of the characteristics of mobile artifacts, such as the ability to monitor a broad, if constrained, domain. Thus, immobots replace the mobility of the robot by multifarious sensors and centralized control.

A World Wide Intelligent Immobot?

Few prospects can be more exciting than that of a worldwide network of computer systems equipped with sensors. The possibilities, for good and evil, boggle the imagination. The beginnings of such a symbiosis are already available in network systems to input and transmit voice and images. But perhaps even more important is the application of sensory processing systems to the retrieval of information from the World Wide Web. At present, one can retrieve textual information on the basis of keywords; data from databases are also retrievable on the basis of relation and column names and data values (Ein-Dor & Spiegler, 1995). However, attempts to retrieve image or sound information usually fail miserably because the names of the content files (e.g. R125.gif) in no way hint at the content (e.g., a painting by Rembrandt). If search engines could analyze and understand the content of images and sounds, a whole new range of possibilities for information retrieval would open up. Currently, the only way to permit retrieval of sensory data is by manually cataloging them—an arduous and expensive process that is essentially a throwback to the era of library card catalogs. The retrieval of texts could also be improved immeasurably by agents that could understand the contents of the texts being scanned.

Data Mining

Organizations have collected, and are continuing to collect, vast amounts of raw data from their transaction processing systems. Obviously, there may be valuable information implicit in the data—the question is how to extract it. At present, the main method of harvesting the knowledge implicit in databases has been On-Line Analytic Processing (OLAP), in which the researcher formulates intuitive hypotheses about relationships within the data and then tests them with the help of the computer. More recent concepts are those of data mining, also called, and perhaps more accurately, Knowledge Discovery in Databases (KDD). The basic concept is that the system should find relationships and present them to the analyst for evaluation. Thus, this field combines artificial intelligence in formulating the hypotheses and statistical methods in testing them. Because the system has to formulate the hypotheses, considerable intelligence is required. Data mining is an area in which there has been a recent spate of activity in applying AI to organizational problems. Some examples of areas in which these techniques have been applied or are being developed are insurance (Galford, 1997); health care management (Borok, 1997); competitive intelligence (Mena, 1996); scientific data (Fayyad, Hausler, & Stolorz, 1996); and economic data (Kaufman & Michalski, 1996). A general treatment of data mining in a number of business contexts is to be found in Brachman, Khabaza, Kloesgen, Piatetsky-Shapiro, and Simoudis (1996).

The main goal of KDD systems should be to find relationships that surprise the analyst, that is, relationships whose existence he or she did not suspect or whose strength he or she did not anticipate. If the analyst is not surprised, the implication is that the system has provided information that was intuitively obvious or known from previous analysis, and therefore of little additional value. A role of the intelligent component of KDD systems, in addition to formulating hypotheses, should be the ability to distinguish interesting from uninteresting findings and so help to winnow the chaff from the wheat. This, in turn, requires systems to possess knowledge about the domain of discourse of the database; again, the knowledge representation problem raises its head! However, because the domain of discourse of databases is invariably restricted to the concepts composing the database schema—say, insurance, banking, manufacturing, or organic chemistry—this problem should be relatively tractable compared to the commonsense knowledge representation problem. The question still remains as to whether such knowledge should be built into the system or whether the system should learn it over time.

A serious issue in data mining is that the data mined can be no better than the data in the warehouse. Thus, a serious question arises: What should be stored in the warehouse, and what should be discarded? This is exacerbated by the very problem that data mining is intended to solve. We are not aware of all of the relevant connections in the data, so we will mine them; but can we know which data to retain if we are not aware of the relevant connections? A possible solution is to retain *all* of the data generated by the organization, but that is likely to be very costly. An interesting question is whether it is possible to apply AI techniques to deciding which data to maintain.

In spite of the problems mentioned, the prognosis for the role of AI in data mining is bright; competition between firms will strengthen the already existing demand, the ability of intelligent systems to manipulate statistical methods will improve, and the problems are relatively circumscribed.

Conclusions

1. *Weak and strong AI.* The more sophisticated weak AI systems become, the more they will begin to acquire the aspects of generality inherent in the idea of strong AI. Thus, we will begin to see a convergence between the two streams of research. The connection has never been as weak as some of the arguments in the field would seem to imply. After all, expert systems arose from basic research in the tradition of strong AI; they succeeded because the researchers had chosen relatively constrained and structured domains. Successes of this type in any science tend to spin off engineering applications. A highly visible example of this is basic research in physics spinning off nuclear weapons and then nuclear power plants. The prototype atomic pile was run by scientists; the bombs and power plants were built by engineers armed with the scientific findings. The same obviously happens in AI. People start out trying to understand basic phenomena, and when the level of understanding is sufficient, the techniques are spun off as engineering disciplines. The engineering, on the other hand, validates and enhances the understanding. Speech recognition, natural language processing, and expert systems are all examples of this dynamic.
2. *Merging of techniques.* At a lower but more immediate and more specific level of integration, we will see increasing use of combinations of techniques for solving problems rather than the current general reliance on single techniques. Some examples have been given above. Thus, the integration of neural nets or genetic algorithms with rule-based expert systems would be natural developments.
3. *Continuing development of techniques.* New and as yet unforeseen techniques will continue to emerge. The appearance of neural networks was presaged by much earlier work on perceptrons. However, genetic algorithms appeared with little forewarning that biological concepts could be applied usefully to problem solving. There is every reason to suppose that new techniques will continue to be adopted and adapted from other fields and that new techniques will arise within the AI community itself. Thus, one can envision, for example, the application of quantum mechanics or binary firing of neurons in neural networks.
4. *New technologies.* It has been pointed out above that advances in at least some areas of AI depend on the processing power available. Although Moore's Law[22] still seems to be in effect, the current silicon-based technology is approaching its limits. Its life can be extended somewhat by the maturation of parallel processing systems, but these have proven notoriously difficult to program effectively for any applications but those dependent on convoluting large matrices; good examples are basic image processing at the level of pixels and thermodynamic computations. Thus, no doubt we will continue to see improvements in the currently available technologies, but processing power of the order required to permit human-equivalent, general artificial intelligence will require a breakthrough—perhaps biological computers, perhaps some as yet undreamed of technology, but such a breakthrough is essential.

5. *Predictions.* We now turn to some predictions concerning specific applications of AI. I have listed them in what I think is more or less the order of difficulty in achieving high levels of performance from where the technology now stands. The order is important, because some developments depend on the accomplishment of previous milestones.
   a. Speech recognition is already sufficiently advanced that one can assume the advent of general speech recognition, at least for specific languages, within a decade. This will presage a quantum improvement in human-computer interfaces whereby it will be possible to control computers, and all other machines, in the most natural mode possible (i.e., by talking to them).
   b. The more people are connected to the Internet and the more information is available on it, the more important softbots will become, and greater efforts will be expended in improving them. The major problem is imparting them with sufficient knowledge to understand what it is the user wants them to do. However, even before the advent of general commonsense knowledge representation, it is clear that softbots will be able to perform multiple tasks, but perhaps not at quite the level we would like.

   With immobots, the problems are complexity and adaptivity. The larger the number of sensors and the greater the functionality required, the more difficult it will be to provide the algorithms necessary for performing the functions and adapting to changing environments.

   I see the most exciting challenge as turning the Internet into one gigantic immobot with sensors distributed throughout the world. This is a daunting challenge and one not likely to be realized within the time span of this forecast, but one that I believe will be realized.
   c. Vision systems will continue to improve, and their performance will be boosted by more powerful hardware. However, a solution to the general vision problem (i.e., general image recognition in any context) is dependent on a solution to the commonsense knowledge problem, and this seems to me to be quite far off. However, real-time vision systems for specific contexts, such as manufacturing facilities, road transportation, and so on, are well on the way to general availability.
   d. There are many obvious applications of good natural language processing systems; these include natural language query systems for databases and for the World Wide Web and translation systems. The combination of adequate natural language systems with robust speech recognition would be especially powerful, providing, for example, real-time translation of conversations between people with no common language. Such systems for restricted domains, such as electrical engineering or commerce, will probably become available within two to three decades. The emergence of general purpose systems for processing natural language requires a solution to the commonsense knowledge problem; I doubt that this problem will be adequately solved within the time span of this forecast. However, even the provision of domain-dependent language systems (e.g., in medicine or engineering) would be extremely valuable and is probably within reach.
   e. Research on autonomous robots or autonomous intelligent machines continues apace. However, mechanical and locomotional issues aside, the development of such machines is contingent on development in a number of more specific areas,

such as speech, vision, and commonsense knowledge representation. As a result, it will be quite some time before general purpose autonomous robots become available. However, progress will doubtless continue apace for machines adapted to specific environments. I do not expect to see general purpose AIMs within the time frame of this forecast.

f. It transpires that whenever one begins to discuss the possibility of general-purpose artificial intelligence, the commonsense knowledge problem raises its head. As Hamlet said, "Therein lies the rub." The encouraging thing about commonsense knowledge is that once it is acquired, it does not need to change very rapidly, so that keeping it up-to-date should not be too much of a problem. The real issue is to reach a level of commonsense knowledge representation at which one could buy common sense off the shelf for installation in any machine designed to function in any context, with a high level of confidence that it will be adequate. This would then absolve system developers from laboriously encoding snippets of context-dependent common sense anew in each system developed. It is my belief that such a representation is possible; it is also my belief that it is well off beyond the horizon of this chapter. A solution to the commonsense knowledge problem is, in my opinion, the essence of a solution to the construction of general artificial intelligence.

The conclusions so far have all been continuing development of techniques and understanding. It seems to me that most of the specific applications listed above will come to fruition, or close to it, well within the time horizon of this forecast; I am not so foolhardy as to venture more exact predictions than that. We will not see general purpose AI (i.e., human-equivalent mechanical intelligence) within the next 40 years. There are many very difficult problems remaining to be solved; the complexity, current lack of understanding, and slow rate of progress in defining the essence of intelligence and of human cognition make for slow progress.[23] Looking back on the first 40 years of AI, great progress has been made, but much, much more remains to be accomplished.

Notes

1. The term *artificial intelligence* is generally believed to have been coined at the Dartmouth Conference in the summer of 1956 (see McCorduck, 1979, Chapter 5). Work on some of the basic ideas began shortly before that time (see, especially, the famous paper by Turing, 1950). If we take Turing's paper as the starting point, AI will be 50 years old in 2000.

2. For an intellectually stimulating analysis of the development of AI paradigms, see Kendall (1996).

3. In later years, Simon maintained that his prediction was correct—only his timing was off!

4. It is by no chance that probably the greatest achievements of AI to date have been in chess and that chess-playing programs arouse so much interest. On one hand, this is a well-defined field par excellence; the rules are perfectly clear. On the other hand, these well-defined rules produce an environment sufficiently complex so that the majority of people can lay no claim to proficiency; to play well requires a high level of intelligence.

5. For example, and to summarize complex and not easily dismissible arguments in a sentence: The Dreyfus brothers hold that strong AI is impossible because computers cannot experience the emotions and

consciousness of humans (Dreyfus & Dreyfus, 1986, 1988). John Searle (1984) believes artificial intelligence to be impossible because machines cannot be conscious, and consciousness is a precondition for intelligence. The physicist Roger Penrose (1989) believes that artificial intelligence is impossible because the mind is a quantum-physical phenomenon. To demonstrate the complexity of the arguments, another physicist, Nick Herbert (1993), believes AI to be inevitable for the same reasons!

6. For these examples, see Gardner (1983) and Fodor (1983).

7. For a comprehensive list of early examples, see Hunt (1986).

8. See, for example, Ein-Dor and Ginzberg (1989).

9. The book by Lenat and Guha (1990) reports on the first five years of the project. For the more recent report quoted here, see Lenat (1995).

10. Examples of work on nonmonotonic logic include Lucaszewicz (1983), McCarthy (1980), and McDermott and Doyle (1980).

11. For one attempt to address this problem, see Lee (1996).

12. For details of the most recent competition, see several articles in *AI Magazine*, Vol. 18, No. 1 (1997).

13. As the reader is probably aware, the word "robot" first appeared in the play "R.U.R.: Rossum's Universal Robots" (1923) by the Czech playwright Karel Capek. The word itself is derived from the Slavic *robota*, or work. The adoption of the meaningless syllable "bot" to denote variations on the theme of robotics seems to me particularly inelegant. However, experience has taught me that once a linguistic artifact has been widely adopted, no matter how mistaken, it is pointless to fight it; see, for example, the widespread use of the plurals "data" and "criteria" to denote the singular "datum" and "criterion." I have noticed that dictionaries also consider discretion the better part of valor, and now they, too, accept these usages.

14. For a number of articles on intelligent agents, see the 1994 special issue of *Communications of the ACM, 37*(7), which was devoted to that topic. Two articles especially relevant to our discussion are Maes (1994) and Etzion and Weld (1994).

15. Home page at http://altavista.digital.com/.

16. Home page at http://lycos.cs.cmu.edu/.

17. Home page at http://www.excite.com/.

18. Home page at http://www.metacrawler.com/.

19. Home page at http://www.mamma.com/.

20. Home page at http://www.highway61.com/.

21. For an extremely interesting fictional account of what it must feel like for a superior intelligence to be immobilized within a box, I recommend *Imaginary Magnitude* by Stanislaw Lem (1973/1984). For scientists' views of the coming emergence of artificial intelligences superior to the human kind, see Fredkin (1983) and Moravec (1988).

22. Moore's Law, formulated in 1965, states that the density of transistors on a chip doubles every 18 to 24 months. In other words, the density increases by about 60% annually. The significance of this is that the higher the chip density, the faster and the cheaper the circuits. In 1997, Moore predicted that in about a decade, the rate of density doubling would slow considerably (Leyden, 1997).

23. For an additional concise view of directions in AI research, see Doyle, Dean et al. (1996).

References

Borok, L. S. (1997). Data mining: Sophisticated forms of managed care modeling through artificial intelligence. *Journal of Health Care Finance, 23*(3), 20-36.

Brachman, R. J., Khabaza, T., Kloesgen, W., Piatetsky-Shapiro, G., & Simoudis, E. (1996). Mining business databases. *Communications of the ACM, 39*(11), 42-48.

Cheng, W., McClain, B. W., & Kelly, C. (1997). Artificial neural networks make their mark as a powerful tool for investors. *Review of Business, 18*(4), 4-9.

Doyle, J., Dean, T. et al. (1996). Strategic directions in artificial intelligence. *Computing Surveys, 28,* 653-670.
Dreyfus, H. L., & Dreyfus, S. E. (1986). *Mind over machine: The power of human intuition and expertise in the era of the computer.* New York: Free Press.
Dreyfus, H. L., & Dreyfus, S. E. (1988). Making a mind versus modeling the brain: Artificial intelligence back at a branchpoint. In S. R. Grabaud (Ed.), *The artificial intelligence debate: False starts, real foundations* (pp. 15-43). Cambridge: MIT Press.
Ein-Dor, P., & Ginzberg, Y. (1989). Representing commonsense business knowledge: An initial implementation. In L. F. Pau, J. Motiwalla, Y. H. Pao, & H. H. Teh (Eds.), *Expert systems in economics, banking, and management* (pp. 417-426). Amsterdam: North-Holland.
Ein-Dor, P., & Spiegler, I. (1995). Natural language access to multiple databases: A model and a prototype. *Journal of Management Information Systems, 12*(1), 171-197.
Ellison, H. (1979). Wanted in surgery. In *The fantasies of Harlan Ellison* (pp. 121-152). Boston: Gregg Press.
Etzion, O., & Weld, D. (1994). A softbot-based interface to the Internet. *Communications of the ACM, 37*(7), 72-76.
Fayyad, U., Hausler, D., & Stolorz, P. (1996). Mining scientific data. *Communications of the ACM, 39*(11), 51-57.
Feigenbaum, E. A. (1993). *Tiger in a cage: Applications of knowledge-based systems.* Stanford, CA: University Video Communications.
Fodor, J. A. (1983). *Modularity of mind: A monograph on faculty psychology.* Cambridge: MIT Press.
Fredkin, E. (1983). *Better mind the computer* (BBC-TV). Willamette, IL: Films Incorporated.
Galford, G. (1997). Data mining creates advantages. *National Underwriter, 101*(23), 27ff.
Gallant S. (1988). Connectionist expert system. *Communications of the ACM, 31*(2), 152-169.
Gardner, H. (1983). *Frames of mind: The theory of multiple intelligences.* New York: Basic Books.
Herbert, N. (1993). *Elemental mind: Human consciousness and the new physics.* New York: Penguin-Plume.
Hunt, D. V. (1986). *Artificial intelligence and expert systems sourcebook.* New York: Chapman & Hall.
Kaufman, K. A., & Michalski, R. (1996). A multistrategy conceptual analysis of economic data. In P. Ein-Dor (Ed.), *Artificial intelligence in economics and management* (pp. 193-203). Boston: Kluwer Academic.
Kendall, K. (1996). Artificial intelligence and *Götterdämmerung:* The evolutionary paradigm of the future. *Data Base, 27*(4), 99-115.
Lee, K.-F. (1993). *Automatic speech recognition.* Stanford, CA: University Video Communications.
Lee, O. (1996). *Knowledge based system maintenance tools.* Unpublished doctoral dissertation, Claremont Graduate School, Claremont, CA.
Lem, S. (1984). *Imaginary magnitude* (M. E. Heine, Trans.). San Diego: Harcourt Brace Jovanovich. (Original work published 1973)
Lenat, D. B. (1995). CYC: A large-scale investment in knowledge infrastructure. *Communications of the ACM, 38*(11), 33-38.
Lenat, D. B., & Guha, R. V. (1990). *Building large knowledge-based systems: Reference and inference in the CYC project.* Reading, MA: Addison-Wesley.
Leshno, M., & Spector, Y. (1996). The effect of training data set size and complexity of the separation function on neural network classification capability: The two-group case. In P. Ein-Dor (Ed.), *Artificial intelligence in economics and management* (pp. 33-50). Boston: Kluwer Academic.
Levin, N., & Zahavi, J. (1996). Harvest optimization of citrus crop using genetic algorithms. In P. Ein-Dor (Ed.), *Artificial intelligence in economics and management* (pp. 129-138). Boston: Kluwer Academic.
Leyden, P. (1997). Moore's Law repealed, sort of. *Wired, 5*(5),
Lucaszewicz, W. (1983). General approach to nonmonotonic logics. *Proceedings of the Eighth International Joint Conference on Artificial Intelligence, 1,* 352-354.

Maes, P. (1994). Agents that reduce work and information overload. *Communications of the ACM, 37*(7), 30-40.
McCarthy, J. (1960). Programs with common sense. In *Proceedings of the Teddington Conference on the Mechanization of Thought Processes*. London: Her Majesty's Stationery Office.
McCarthy, J. (1980). Circumscription: A form of non-monotonic logic. *Artificial Intelligence, 13*, 27-39.
McCorduck, P. (1979). *Machines who think*. San Francisco: Freeman.
McCulloch, W. S., & Pitts, W. (1943). A logical calculus of the ideas immanent in nervous activity. *Bulletin of Mathematical Biophysics, 5*, 115-137.
McDermott, D., & Doyle, J. (1980). Non-monotonic logic I. *Artificial Intelligence, 13*(1-2), 41-72.
Mena, J. (1996). Machine-learning the business: Using data mining for competitive intelligence. *Competitive Intelligence Review, 7*(4), 18-25.
Minsky, M., & Pappert, S. (1969). *Perceptrons*. Cambridge: MIT Press.
Moravec, H. (1988). *Mind children: The future of robot and human intelligence*. Cambridge, MA: Harvard University Press.
Newell, A., & Simon, H. A. (1963). GPS: A program that simulates human thought. In E. A. Feigenbaum & J. Feldman (Eds.), *Computers and thought* (pp. 279-293). New York: McGraw-Hill.
Nygard, K., Juell, P., & Kaddaba, N. (1990). Neural networks for selecting vehicle routing heuristics. *ORSA Journal of Computing, 2*, 353-364.
Penrose, R. (1989). *The emperor's new mind: Concerning computers, minds, and the laws of physics*. New York: Penguin.
Pompe, P. P. M., & Feelders, A. J. (1996). Using machine learning, neural networks, and statistics to predict corporate bankruptcy: A comparative study. In P. Ein-Dor (Ed.), *Artificial intelligence in economics and management* (pp. 3-19). Boston: Kluwer Academic.
Rochester, J. B. (1990). New business uses for neurocomputing. *I/S Analyzer, 28*(2), 1-12.
Rosenblatt, F. (1962). *Principles of neurodynamics*. London: Spartan.
Searle, J. (1984). *Minds, brains and science*. Cambridge, MA: Harvard University Press.
Sharda, R. (1994). Neural networks for the MS/OR analyst: An application bibliography. *Interfaces, 24*(2), 116-130.
Simon, H. A. (1991). *Models of my life*. New York: Basic Books.
Tam, K. Y., & Kiang, M. Y. (1992). Managerial applications of neural networks: The case of bank failure predictions. *Management Science, 38*, 926-947.
Turing, A. M. (1950). Computing machinery and intelligence. *Mind, 59*, 433-460.
Webster's Ninth New Collegiate Dictionary. (1983). Springfield, MA: Merriam-Webster.
Williams, B. C., & Nayak, P. P. (1996). Immobile robots: AI in the new millennium. *AI Magazine, 17*(3), 17-35.
Wilson, R. I., & Sharda, R. (1994). Bankruptcy prediction using neural networks. *Decision Support Systems, 11*, 545-557.
Zadeh, L. A. (1983). Commonsense knowledge representation based on fuzzy logic. *Computer, 16*(10), 61-65.
Zahavi, J., & Levin, N. (1995). Issues and problems in applying neural computing to target marketing. *Journal of Direct Marketing, 9*(3), 33-44.
Zahavi, J., & Levin, N. (1997). Applying neural computing to direct marketing. *Journal of Direct Marketing, 11*(1), 5-22.

PART TWO

COOPERATION-FACILITATING TECHNOLOGIES

CHAPTER
SEVEN

Media Appropriateness

Effects of Experience on Communication Media Choice

RUTH C. KING
WEIDONG XIA

A wide range of emerging information technologies, such as groupware, electronic mail (email), and electronic meeting systems (EMS), has expanded organizational and managerial decision making and communication choices (Orlikowski, Yates, Okamura, & Fujimoto, 1995). Although the claimed benefits of these new technologies can be tremendous, many managers are more perplexed than overjoyed with the myriad of technology choices they are facing. Frequently, organizations have no choice but to simultaneously adopt similar emerging technologies, such as email, voice mail (Vmail), and fax, merely to stay competitive. The decision about when and which emerging technologies to adopt can be crucial. However, far more essential are the management practices that change employees' prior perceptions or misperceptions of certain information technology to a more informed understanding of the intricacies and functionalities of the adopted technologies. Organizations can benefit the most when employees recognize and become familiar with the purpose of each technology and further establish the appropriateness of each technology within the context of task environment.

The objective of this chapter is to demonstrate that an individual's perception toward the appropriateness of different communication media can be deliberately managed when learning opportunities are presented. More specifically, this study investigates the effects of the individual's experiences on one's evaluations of a spectrum of media that are concurrently available and used by most organizations, including both traditional media (such as face-to-face meeting, telephone, and written letters) and those emerging computer-based communication media (such as email and EMS). Although it may seem fundamental, understanding the relationship between technology experience and technology appropriateness examined in this study can be significant to effective management of emerging information technologies. With such an understanding, management can improve the effectiveness of new

---

Reprinted by permission from *Decision Sciences,* Volume 28, Number 4, Fall 1997.

technology adoption by linking the technology's purpose with task requirements, and by providing an environment for employees to learn.

Previous research on media appropriateness/choice and communication effectiveness has been primarily stimulated by and centered on two predominant theories: social presence theory (Short, Williams, & Christie, 1976) and media richness theory (Daft & Lengel, 1984, 1986; Daft, Lengel, & Trevino, 1987; Trevino, Lengel, & Daft, 1987). Both theories focus on the determinants of media choice or media appropriateness and posit that the match between the medium and the task results in effective communication. The underlying tenet of these theories is that media choice is dependent upon the characteristics of media, and each communication medium is unique in its ability to convey certain information contents. For instance, some media, such as face-to-face communication, can convey a broader range of information, and others, such as facsimile (fax) and handwritten notes, can convey only limited information. Therefore, these theories stipulate that media choice/appropriateness and communication effectiveness depend on properly matching the inherent characteristics of media to task requirements. Although social presence theory and media richness theory have provided an appealing conceptual framework and have stimulated a stream of research, the subsequent empirical tests have failed to produce consistent results (Lee, 1994; Markus, 1994; Rice, 1990; Rice & Shook, 1990).

In this chapter, we argue that experience with communication media will have a determining effect on the perceived appropriateness of media. We further argue that an individual's perception of media appropriateness does not remain static and should be examined from a dynamic or longitudinal perspective. Individuals construct their own unique understanding of each technology as they learn to use the medium, and this understanding can change and be redefined as their experience with the medium increases (Carlson & Zmud, 1994; Rogers, 1986). Investigating users' experiences with communication media may provide additional explanations and empirical evidence for the inconsistent research findings, and expand the existing media choice theories. Using a longitudinal quasi-experimental design, this chapter examines the effects of individual experiences with nine commonly used organizational communication media on the perceived media appropriateness over time. Organizational members normally have an array of media readily available to choose from; examining multiple coexisting communication media provides many more convincing explanations for the communicator's behavior than examining certain media alone.

The chapter is organized as follows. First, we review the literature about the media-task view of media choice, including the social presence theory, media richness theory, and related empirical findings. Second, we develop a set of hypotheses regarding the effect of experience on evaluations of media appropriateness over an ample period of time for sufficient learning and use of the studied media. Third, we present research methods and results of data analysis. The chapter concludes with a discussion of the research and practical implications of the study.

Media-Task Views of Media Choice

Considerable research attention has been focused on the choice, use, and consequences of communication media (Hiltz & Turoff, 1981; Rice, 1984, 1987; Rogers, 1986; Short et al., 1976). Although various factors have been proposed to be influential in predicting an individual's media choice (Culnan & Markus, 1987; Markus, 1994; Rice, 1992, 1993), the research has been dominated by a rational choice perspective that focuses on media-task interaction. According to this perspective, media choice is objectively determined by the congruence between the inherent characteristics of the media and the requirements of the tasks. Individuals make a rational choice of the media that best fulfill task requirements. This rational choice perspective is represented by two of the most widely cited media choice theories: social presence theory and media richness theory.

Social Presence Theory

Social presence refers to the degree to which a medium permits communicators to experience others as being psychologically present (Fulk, Steinfield, Schmitz, & Power, 1987; Short et al., 1976), or the degree to which a medium is perceived to convey the actual presence of the communicating participants (Short et al., 1976). Short et al. stated that "communication media differ in their capacity to transmit information about facial expression, direction of looking, posture, dress and nonverbal, vocal cues" (p. 65). Accordingly, communication media such as face-to-face and group meetings that have the capability to convey nonverbal cues and social-context cues are perceived as rating high in social presence. In contrast, media such as computer-based communication technologies and written documents are considered to rate low in social presence due to their paucity of nonverbal elements and feedback cues.

According to the social presence theory, communication tasks differ in their requirements for social presence. The appropriateness of a medium for performing certain communication tasks is determined by the degree to which the medium's characteristics of social presence fit the requirements of the tasks (Short et al., 1976). Tasks that involve interpersonal skills, such as resolving disagreements or negotiation, demand high social presence, whereas tasks such as exchanging routine information are low in their social presence requirements. Therefore, media like face-to-face and group meetings are more appropriate for performing tasks that require high social presence, whereas media such as email and written letters are more appropriate for tasks with low social presence requirements.

Media Richness Theory

Media richness theory (Daft & Lengel, 1984, 1986; Trevino et al., 1987), an alternative to social presence theory (Rice, 1992), takes a similar rational stand in that media choice depends on the matching of media richness to the characteristics of task analyzability. Media richness refers to a medium's material capability to convey certain types of information. Media differ in the extent to which they are able to bridge different frames of reference, to make issues less ambiguous, or to provide opportunities for learning in a given time interval (Daft & Lengel, 1986). Media richness is also determined by the medium's capacity for immediate feedback, multiple cues, language variety, and personal focus of sources (Daft & Lengel, 1984). Along these dimensions, media are ranked from richest to leanest: face-to-face being the richest medium, followed by telephone, email, written addressed documents and, finally, unaddressed documents (Daft et al., 1987; Rice, 1992; Steinfield, 1986).

Media richness theory postulates that communication tasks vary with respect to their analyzability (Perrow, 1967). Task analyzability refers to the degree to which tasks involve the application of objective, well-understood procedures that do not require novel solutions. Thus, unanalyzable tasks involve the process of equivocal information that often requires interpersonal negotiations to share various referent frames and to interpret cognitively conflicting situations. As a result, unanalyzable tasks require rich media that can convey multiple cues, construct collaborative meaning, and establish immediate feedback. Media choice is then determined by the fit between media richness and task analyzability. In other words, richer media such as face-to-face and group meetings are more appropriate for unanalyzable tasks, whereas leaner media such as email and written documents are more appropriate for analyzable tasks.

Related Empirical Findings

The empirical research testing media richness and social presence theories has so far failed to provide consistent and convincing support (Fulk et al., 1987; Fulk, Schmitz, & Steinfield, 1990; Johansen, 1977; Markus, 1988, 1994; Reid, 1977; Rice, 1984, 1992; Steinfield, 1986; Walther, 1995). In some cases, studies have shown some support for the social presence theory (e.g., Holland, Stead, & Leibroch, 1976; Ochsman & Chapanis, 1974; Trevino et al., 1987) and the media richness theory (Hiltz & Turoff, 1981; Rice, 1984; Rice & Case, 1983; Trevino et al., 1987; Zack, 1993). In other cases, communicators have chosen different media than the social presence and media richness theories would have predicted (e.g., El-Shinnawy & Markus, 1992; Markus, 1988, 1992; Markus, Bikson, El-Shinnawy, & Soe, 1992; Rice & Shook, 1990; Steinfield & Fulk, 1986). These inconsistent findings became more significant when the media under consideration involved new computer-based communication technologies such as email and electronic conferencing systems. For example, Lee (1994) found that email was often chosen for rich communications. Rice and Shook (1990), Markus (1994), and Rice, Hughes, and Love (1989) found that top management used certain lean media more often than did lower level managers, which contradicts the theories, because top management tends to spend more time dealing with equivocal tasks. Steinfield (1986) found that a considerable number of electronic messages in a large organization dealt with socioemotional topics, which also require richer media based on these two theories.

The inconsistent empirical findings suggest that media choice cannot be adequately explained or predicted by considering only the inherent richness or social presence of the medium and the characteristics of the task (Markus, 1988; Rice & Shook, 1990; Trevino & Webster, 1992; Yates & Orlikowski, 1992; Zmud, Lind, & Young, 1990). Furthermore, the theories' underlying assumptions about the media, task, and users may have impeded the predictive validity of the theories (Markus, 1994). Fulk and her colleagues (1987, 1990) pointed out that these theories are constrained by their assumptions about the objectivity of media and the rationality of user choice. Individuals are assumed to be aware of the intrinsic properties of media, to be able to objectively evaluate the characteristics of tasks and media, and to rationally choose media that best fit the requirements of tasks. Such an assumption has been challenged by the social influence model of technology use, which suggests that individuals' perceptions regarding media richness are affected by social context and user experience with the channel (Fulk et al., 1990, 1987; Schmitz & Fulk, 1991). Walther and Burgoon (1992) argued that only after examining users' postadoption activities can we understand the patterns of communication technology use and consequent changes.

As suggested by several researchers (e.g., Fulk et al., 1987, 1990; Markus, 1988, 1994), a complementary important research issue that has received minimal attention is the role that users' media experience plays in media choice. In particular, examining the effects of users' experience with media on their perception of media appropriateness may provide a better explanation of communication media behavior and may help resolve some of the inconsistencies in the literature (Carlson & Zmud, 1994).

Experience-Based Media Appropriateness

In this study, we argue that media properties such as richness are posited to be subjective and are influenced to some degree by individual experiences with different media over time. In other words, an individual's perceptions and appreciations about certain media may not be stable over time, particularly when the media involved are new. An individual's media experience not only influences one's rational evaluation and expectations about the fit between media and tasks, but also affects perception of media appropriateness. Since the media we investigated in this study include the individual's evaluation of a range of communication media (traditional and new media), three theories become pertinent in supporting our arguments: social cognitive theory, the theory of planned behavior, and the technology acceptance model.

Social Cognitive Theory

Bandura (1977, 1982) postulated two sets of expectations as major cognitive forces that guide behavior choices: outcome expectations and efficacy expectations. Outcome expectancy is defined as a person's estimate that a given behavior will lead to certain outcomes. An efficacy expectation is a belief about one's ability to perform the behavior required to produce the outcomes. Outcome expectations capture the rational or motivational aspect of behavioral choices, which is similar to the underpinning assumption of media richness and social presence theories. Individuals are more likely to undertake behaviors they believe will result in valued outcomes rather than those that are not expected to generate favorable consequences. Efficacy expectations capture the facilitating or control aspect of behavioral choices. Perceived self-efficacy influences choices of behavioral settings. Individuals fear and avoid threatening situations when they perceive they lack necessary coping skills, whereas they will engage in activities that they feel capable of handling—situations that would otherwise be intimidating.

While both outcome and efficacy expectations are important factors in determining behavioral choices, efficacy perceptions also influence an individual's outcome expectations (Bandura, 1978). Self-efficacy judgments are purported to influence outcome expectations since "the outcomes one expects derive largely from judgments as to how well one can execute the requisite behavior" (Bandura, 1978, p. 241). In the context of computer-based technologies, computer self-efficacy was found to exert a significant influence on individuals' expectations of the outcomes of using computers, their emotional reactions to computers (affect and anxiety), as well as their actual computer use (Compeau & Higgins, 1995a, 1995b). Individuals with high computer self-efficacy will demonstrate higher outcome expectations regarding computer use than individuals with low self-efficacy. Additionally, past experience is the most important source of information about self-efficacy (Bandura, 1986). Experienced mastery alters the level and strength of self-efficacy, which, in turn, influences choices of activities. Thus, individuals who have been successful and felt rewarded by their previous media experience are more likely to have positive expectations of media usage outcomes in the future and are more likely to choose those media.

Theory of Planned Behavior

The theory of planned behavior (Ajzen, 1985, 1991) posits that behavioral achievement depends jointly on behavioral intention and perceived behavioral control. As in the original theory of reasoned action (Fishbein & Ajzen, 1975), behavioral intentions are assumed to capture the motivational factors that influence a behavior. Perceived behavioral control, which captures such nonmotivational factors as availability of requisite opportunities and resources (e.g., skills and cooperation of others), can influence choice of activities, preparation for an activity, effort exerted during performance, as well as thought patterns and emotional reactions. Perceived behavioral control is assumed to reflect past experience as well as anticipated impediments and obstacles (Ajzen, 1991). Repeated performance of a behavior results in the establishment of a habit; behavioral choice at a later time then occurs, at least in part, habitually. To put this theory in the context of media choice, intentions (media choice) would be expected to influence performance (media use) to the extent that the person has behavioral control (past experience), and performance (media use) should increase behavioral control (experience).

Technology Acceptance Model

The technology acceptance model (Davis, 1989; Davis, Bagozzi, & Warshaw, 1989), specifically tailored for modeling user acceptance of information technologies, is an adaptation of the theory of reasoned action (Fishbein & Ajzen, 1975), which is the earlier version of the theory of planned behavior (Ajzen, 1985, 1991). The model posits that two particular beliefs, perceived usefulness and perceived ease of use, are primary determinants of computer acceptance. Perceived usefulness is defined as the prospective user's subjective assessment that using a specific computer application will increase his or her job performance within an organizational context. Perceived ease of use, which is similar to Bandura's (1977) self-efficacy and Ajzen's perceived behavioral control, refers to the degree to which the prospective user expects the target system to be free of effort.

A number of empirical studies have found that perceived ease of use not only directly affects acceptance of computer technologies but also indirectly affects acceptance through influencing perceived usefulness of the technologies (Adam, Nelson, & Todd, 1992; Davis et al., 1989; Mathieson, 1991; Taylor & Todd, 1995). Howard and Mendelow (1991) found that computer self-efficacy was related to an individual's attitude toward computers. Howard and Smith (1986) found that computer-anxious managers are more negative about the usefulness of computers in management tasks. Igbaria, Guimaraes, and Davis (1995) found that perceived usefulness and ease of use directly impact usage of information technologies.

Prior computer experience, representing individual use, skills, and comfort with the technologies, plays a very important role in influencing user beliefs (perceived usefulness and perceived ease of use) toward computer technologies (Davis & Bostrum, 1993). Increased experience is likely to enhance users' confidence in their ability to master and use computers in performing their tasks (DeLone, 1988; Kraemer, Danziger, Dunkle, & King, 1993). In addition, opportunities to gain experience using computers are found to influence users' beliefs about the technologies (Rivard & Huff, 1988). The acceptance of computer technology depends on the technology itself and the level of use, comfort, skill, or expertise of the individual using the technology (Nelson, 1990).

Effects of Experience on Media Appropriateness

Social cognitive, planned behavior, and technology acceptance theories provide a foundation for proposing our hypotheses regarding the effects of experience on media appropriateness. The rational choice, based on a match between media and task characteristics, is reflected by the concepts of outcome expectations (Bandura, 1977, 1982), behavioral intentions (Ajzen, 1985, 1991), and perceived usefulness (Davis et al., 1989). Our argument for the role of an individual's media experience (prior use, skills, and comfort) is reflected in the concept of efficacy expectations (Badura, 1977, 1982), perceived behavioral control (Ajzen, 1985, 1991), and perceived ease of use (Davis et al., 1989). A central premise derived from the above discussion is that prior experience influences outcome expectations or perceived usefulness of media in performing certain tasks, and thus plays an equal or even more important role in determining media appropriateness than the rational choice-based theories.

Human behavior is more self-interest, efficiency oriented than rationality motivated (Williams, Phillips, & Lum, 1985). Use of a rich medium, such as a meeting, to deliver a straightforward message to a large group is inefficient; most time-cautious individuals avoid doing this. But human behavior is also experience based. If individuals are uncomfortable or unfamiliar with using an email system to distribute a message, and view learning to send an email as more time consuming and inefficient than having a group meeting, they would choose a richer rather than a rationally efficient medium. This behavior outcome, though irrational, is certainly a reflection upon the previously established experience. In this instance, most individuals have tremendous experience with face-to-face, group meetings, or telephone communications in dealing with various types of tasks. Using these traditional media has become more instinctive or habitual than using new media, such as email or EMS.

Carlson and Zmud (1994) suggested that media choice is determined by the fit of the perceived media richness and perceived information richness. These perceptions are built upon previous experience with the media in addition to the objective view of media characteristics. Experience with media will increase the user's skill, comfort, and use of the media, which in turn, enables users to facilitate appropriate media choice. Following this logic of experienced-based media choice, face-to-face and telephone communications should be viewed as the richest media because individuals have extensive experience with them long before they are even exposed to handwriting and typing. Experience enables the development of familiarity, expertise, and comfort with the media. Because individuals have high levels of expertise and familiarity with face-to-face and telephone communication, they would naturally and instinctively prefer these media over other unfamiliar ones. This argument is consistent with the prior research, which has found face-to-face communication to be the richest and most appropriate medium for communicating both ambiguous and simple tasks.

Due to learning and habitual effects, individuals will perceive traditional media such as face-to-face, group meetings, and telephone as rich media, and this perception will remain more stable than the perception toward new media. For example, Rice (1993) and Rice and Case (1983) have found that people's perceptions about the appropriateness of face-to-face and group meetings for most tasks were ranked high and did not change over time, whereas perceptions about text and new media did. Rice and Case also found that managers' perceptions of email for different tasks changed over time. Therefore, we have the following hypotheses regarding the effects of experience on media appropriateness.

H1: An individual's perceived appropriate choices between traditional and new media will be associated with one's media experience. Specifically,

H1a: Traditionally rich media such as face-to-face, group meetings, and telephone will be perceived as more appropriate for most organizational tasks than new communication media.

H1b: Even after gaining experience with all media, individuals will perceive traditionally rich media as more appropriate than new media.

H1c: With experience, perceptions of new media appropriateness will change more than perceptions of traditionally rich media appropriateness.

An individual's experience with a medium also affects the degree to which he or she is aware of the capability of the medium. Individuals who have frequently used a medium or are comfortable and skillful with a certain medium should have a better understanding of the capability and appropriateness of the medium than those who have barely known or rarely used the medium. Schmitz and Fulk (1991) posited that expertise in using new communication technologies facilitates choice and use. Lack of media-related skills inhibits use; objectively defined rich or lean media may be perceived as irrelevant if the user does not have the skill to learn and use them. Individuals with little experience will have difficulty making judgments of the media's richness (Johansen, 1977; Kerr & Hiltz, 1982). Rice and Case (1983) found that manager judgments of an email system's overall appropriateness are significantly associated with the duration of usage. Schmitz and Fulk (1991) found that perceived email richness varied across individuals and covaried with social influences and media experience factors. Trevino and Webster (1992) reported that an individual's computer skill affected email and Vmail evaluation. Therefore, based on the above discussions, we suggest:

H2: An individual's perceptions of media appropriateness will be associated with one's media experiences. Specifically,

H2a: Increase in the perceived appropriateness of a medium will be associated with increase in frequency of use of that medium;

H2b: Increase in the perceived appropriateness of a medium will be associated with increase in comfort with the medium;

H2c: Increase in the perceived appropriateness of a medium will be associated with increase in the skill of using the medium.

Method

Subjects

Subjects included 295 MBA students who were recruited from an introductory computer information systems course. The course required students to be involved in several team projects during a seven-week period. Students were also taught to use new media to communicate with team members in addition to the use of familiar media. The average age of the subjects was 27 years old with an average of four years' work experience. Thirty-one percent of the subjects were women and 30% were international students. One hundred and ninety-three students owned personal computers and 113 students had modems that allowed them to communicate electronically with their peers from remote sites. Students' computer experiences ranged from novice users (10%), occasional users (36%), frequent users (33%), to professional users (21%).

An issue of using student subjects is the difference in their social backgrounds and contexts from those of business managers. However, there are two rationales on which the MBA students were considered as being appropriate subjects for this study. First, it has been demonstrated that, in studying managers' reaction and evaluation of new information technologies, MBA students may be used as samples that are representative to business managers. For example, Briggs, Balthazard, and Dennis (1996) reported a study that compares the reactions and evaluations of MBA students and working executives to an electronic meeting system. Their study revealed no significant differences in technology evaluation between the graduate business students and senior executives. The presumed social differences between MBA students and executives did not cause them to evaluate the technologies differently. Briggs et al. suggested that one can obtain a conservative estimate of the evaluations of executives to new technology by testing it with graduate business students. The focus of our study is on individual choice or appropriation of communication media, which include computer-based new media. Thus, we believe that the MBA student sample was an appropriate approximation of real-world managers.

Second, most of the MBA students in the sample had worked or were working as managers in business organizations (an average of four years of work experience). Although they were MBA students, subjects had sufficient business experiences or were themselves business managers at the time of our study. In addition, upon starting their program, these MBA students were organized into long-term working groups to simulate real business teams and contexts. Given this student profile and the nature of the task (evaluating communication media), we believe that this sample was appropriate for the research.

Longitudinal Quasi-Experimental Design and Procedures

The research involved a longitudinal quasi-experimental design to study the effect of experience on the perception of multiple coexisting communication technologies, specifically the perception of the appropriateness of each medium for various tasks. Longitudinal research provides important opportunities to investigate the media perception changes over time, which is largely lacking but greatly needed in communication research (Rogers, 1986). Additionally, a quasi-experimental design relaxes the rigorous control of all possible variables and provides a more natural communication setting for the purpose of this study (Emory, 1980). The essential nature of the design involved the following four steps:

1. *Pretest questionnaire.* At the beginning of the study, a pretest questionnaire was distributed among the subjects to collect measures such as background information, computer experience, and the subject's current experience with various communication technologies and his or her judgment of the appropriateness of nine communication media for 11 tasks. Two hundred and ninety-five subjects returned the measurements.
2. *Group formation and assignments.* Sixty groups were formed with five members in each group. Groups were formed based on the individual's area of expertise in order to approximate the cross-functional teams used in workplaces. Teams were given two projects with which to collaborate. The two projects entailed the analysis of two extensive business cases. Groups were required to write up their analysis and recommendations for each case based on the questions given. To ensure that group members were involved in collaborative team efforts, and thereby engaged in the use of various media to communicate, groups were instructed to (1) independently read the cases and draft their answers for each question prior to any meeting; (2) arrange group meeting(s) to discuss answers; (3) reach agreement for each question during the group meeting(s); (4) assign one to two members to write up the group results for each question on their own time and space; (5) electronically transmit the write-ups to one individual who will then edit, integrate, and format the final report; (6) electronically transmit the final report to all members for final approval; and (7) gather together for final preparation for the class and decide the order of authorship that will appear on the cover of the case report (the first two authors will get extra points for being the major contributors).
3. *Instructions in the use of new communication media.* Of the nine communication media examined in this study, only email and EMS showed uneven familiarity and prior experience. Most students were comfortable and familiar with the use of face-to-face meetings (one-to-one or group), telephone, Vmail/answering machine, fax, formal letter, and handwritten note. Thus, to equalize their skills with email and EMS, all subjects were taught to use both media. Several email functions, such as send, reply, copy, attch a file, and construct a distribution list, were taught. Subjects were also required to turn in copies of at least 10 email messages at the end of the seventh week. In terms of the EMS, VisionQuest, designed by Intellect Corporation to support group meetings, was adopted and taught for this study. All groups were taught to resolve a business dilemma case using VisionQuest in a computer lab that lasted one and a half hours. Groups used most of the features supported by the system. Groups were also encouraged to use VisionQuest on their own to conduct electronic brainstorming or idea generation in the computer lab. In fact, several students brought in their former colleagues to use the VisionQuest system.
4. *Post-experiment questionnaire.* A post-experiment questionnaire was collected from the subjects at the end of the seventh week. The measures collected were the

same as the pretest measurements to evaluate the differences before and after the study. In addition, one open-ended question asking the subjects to elaborate on the major changes of their perception was included in the final questionnaire. Two hundred and seventy-one subjects returned their questionnaires.

Communication Environment of the Study

This study was conducted in an environment where there were many common communication media available to the students. For example, every student had a mailbox located next to the school's cafeteria. They also had access to pay phones and fax machines in close proximity. There were two computer labs located on the second floor and several small meeting rooms scattered around the three-story building. Classrooms and library were both located on the first floor. Students thus had many communication choices conveniently located in the same building. Most MBA students in this environment were taking five to six classes concurrently in order to obtain their MBA degree in the 11-month period, thus spending most of their time in the same three-story building. There were many opportunities for subjects to engage in communications due to the common core courses they had to take at the time of this study. The availability of individual mailboxes to collect notes and letters, meeting rooms for face-to-face meetings, computer labs for email and the EMS, fax machines for quick transmission of documents, and pay phones for voice communication and messaging allowed students access to multiple media in a natural, business-like communication environment. Poststudy analysis of self-report found that groups, on average, were engaged in seven group meetings, conducted electronic meeting systems 2.7 times, composed 14 emails, initiated 11.4 phone calls and nine voice messages, wrote 3.2 notes/letters, transmitted two fax messages, and were involved in 10.5 face-to-face individual meetings during the seven-week period.

The MBA students and the testing environment were appropriate for this study to evaluate media appropriateness with different tasks since the nature of the projects entailed many activities that were examined in this study. Students had to exchange routine, urgent, sensitive, and important information; generate ideas; and clarify viewpoints to complete the projects based on the specific work procedures given by the instructor. In addition, the division of labor, ordering of authorship, and the coordination of work naturally involves negotiation and conflict resolution, which were tasks examined in the study. The instructor provided specific comments and marks on each answer so that team members could easily identify contributions from their peers.

Measures

Judgments of media appropriateness and self-report of media experience were collected from 295 MBA students during the seven-week period. The same measures on these two variables were collected twice: once before and once after the study.

Media Appropriateness

Social Presence Activities

Eleven tasks were used to evaluate how appropriate various communication technologies are for each of the activities. These tasks are adapted from a set of commonly recurring office activities developed by Short et al. (1976). Based on extensive validation using different methods, Short et al. concluded that these activities are likely to be affected differently by various communication media. These activities have been used in several recent studies (e.g., Rice, 1992, 1993). The 10 tasks originally developed by Short et al. are exchanging information, negotiating or bargaining, getting to know someone, asking questions, staying in touch, exchanging time-sensitive information, generating ideas, resolving disagreements, making decisions, and exchanging confidential information.

Among the existing 10 tasks/activities, this study modified the original "exchanging information" into two specific tasks: exchanging routine information and exchanging important information. The purpose of this modification was to complement the existing two other information exchanges that were added in recent research (urgent/timely and confidential/sensitive information) (Rice, 1993; Rice & Case, 1983; Steinfield, 1986). Although the characteristics of each individual medium in terms of its richness or social presence can be evaluated from a set of semantic differential ratings such as (im)personable, (in)sensitive, and cold/warm, the use of specific tasks allows better comparison and evaluation between a task and a medium (Rice, 1993).

Communication Media

Nine communication media were evaluated in this study. With the exception of EMS, the remaining eight communication media used in this study are commonly used in most organizations: face-to-face (one-to-one), group meetings, telephone, Vmail (answering machine), handwritten note, formal letter, email, and fax. The answering machine, though not equivalent to the Vmail system, is grouped with Vmail due to the characteristics of the subjects used in this study. Not all students own expensive Vmail systems like those installed in many corporations, but most have answering machines attached to their telephones. However, it is not uncommon for corporate workers to use their Vmail systems as merely an answering machine to leave and track messages. In addition, faculty members who taught these MBA students all have Vmail systems in their offices, and students had many opportunities to use Vmail when communicating with their instructors.

Media Experience

Media experience was captured by asking participants to evaluate their frequency, competency/skill, and comfort of using nine communication media in three questions: (1) How frequently do you use these media? (2) How good are you in using these media? and (3) How comfortable are you when using these media? Likert-like 7-point scales were used (1 [least] to 7 [most]) to evaluate media experience across 11 media at the beginning and at the seventh week of the study. Measurements were taken twice.

Results

Test-Retest Reliability of the Instrument

To assess the reliability of the instruments, a follow-up independent sample was collected that consisted of 68 MBA students whose demographic characteristics were similar to those in our original sample. The test-retest data were collected respectively with a three-hour interval, which is similar to the time interval used in Galletta and Lederer's test-retest study (1989). The scales and wording of items in the test-retest instruments were exactly the same as used in our initial data gathering.

Test-retest statistics for the measures of respondents' frequency of use, skill, and comfort with different media show that all test-retest correlations were significant at $p < .01$. There were no significant differences in mean scores between test and retest. All test-retest correlations for the measures of respondents' media evaluations and choices were significant at $p < .01$. Except for "exchange urgent information," there were no significant differences in mean scores between test and retest. All test-retest correlations for overall task scales and media scales were significant at $p < .01$, and there were no significant differences in mean scores between test and retest.

The above results indicate that our instrument is internally consistent and stable over the test-retest time period, which further suggests that the instrument is not likely to elicit a substantial reactivity effect. The test-retest results certainly help establish reliability and enhance confidence in the results of the study.

Individual Characteristics

To examine the effect of individual characteristics such as gender, computer ownership, and general computer experience, regression analysis was used to test whether these individual differences have any significant impact on subjects' perception of appropriateness with each medium. Except for one case in which gender had a significant effect on appropriateness of face-to-face meetings, an individual's general computer experience, gender, and computer ownership did not have significant effects on media choices. Additional tests were done to examine if the inclusion of these three variables to the existing research model would alter the pattern, and the addition of these variables did not significantly change the research model. This indifference supports the research tenet that states that immediately related experience with media will affect an individual's perception of media appropriateness.

TABLE 7.1 Factors and Loading of Media Across All Activities

Medium	Factor 1	Factor 2	Factor 3
Letter	.8114		
Written notes	.7930		
Vmail	.6825		
Fax	.5710	.5537	
Electronic meeting systems		.8867	
Email		.8255	
Group meeting			.8488
Face-to-face			.8282
Telephone	.4840		.5296
Eigenvalue	3.51	1.57	1.03
Percentage variance explained	39.00	17.40	11.50
Cronbach's alpha	.77	.78	.74
Overall alpha	.80		

Dimensionality of Communication Media

To evaluate the dimensionality of the communication media, the overall mean for each medium across 11 communication activities was entered into a principal component analysis with varimax rotation. Table 7.1 presents the results of the factor loading of the nine communication media. Letters, written notes, Vmail/answering machine, and fax loaded on the first factor (39% variance explained). Electronic meeting system and email, which are usually referred to as new media in recent communication research, loaded on the second dimension and explain 17% of the variance. Group meetings, face-to-face, and telephone communications, which are generally viewed as having high social presence and being the traditionally rich media, loaded on the third factor (12% variance explained). All eigenvalues from the three factors were greater than 1.0. The results suggest that communication media can be a multidimensional construct. The Cronbach's alphas for the three factors were .77, .78, and .74, respectively. The overall Cronbach's alpha for the nine communication media was .80.

Social Presence Activities as Multidimensional

Table 7.2 shows the results of the factor loadings of the 11 social presence activities using a principal component analysis. Six communication activities, such as "resolve disagreements," "make important decision," and "get to know someone," which are generally categorized as requiring high social presence (Rice, 1993), loaded on the first dimension and explained 45% of the variance. The

TABLE 7.2 Factors and Loadings of Activity Evaluations Across All Media

Activity Evaluation	Factor 1	Factor 2
Resolve disagreement	.8750	
Make important decisions	.7932	
Generate ideas/brainstorm	.6993	
Negotiation or bargain	.6496	
Get to know someone	.6400	
Exchange confidential/sensitive information	.6319	
Stay in touch		.7639
Exchange routine information		.7407
Exchange urgent/timely information		.7073
Clarify confusing viewpoint	.4463	.6446
Exchange important information		.6125
Eigenvalue	4.98	1.38
Percentage variance explained	45.30	12.60
Cronbach's alpha	.86	.80
Overall alpha	.88	

remaining five social presence activities, such as "exchange routine information" and "stay in touch," loaded on the second dimension and explained 13% of the variance. Since the variances of the two dimensions are not extremely divergent (45% versus 13%), which is distinctively different from Rice's 74% versus 10% (1993, p. 467), it can be argued that these 11 social presence activities are a two-dimensional construct. The Cronbach's alphas for the two factors were .86 and .80, respectively. The overall Cronbach's alpha for the 11 tasks was .88.

Hare (1960) proposed social presence as involving two dimensions: task and social behavior; Steinfield (1986) also labeled media use as involving social and task purposes. In addition, Tsuneki (1988) found emotionality and transmission of meaning as two major components of media. Although the five activities loaded into the second factor in this study were viewed as low social presence activities (Rice, 1993), these five activities (e.g., clarifying confusing viewpoints, exchanging important information, or staying in touch) can also be argued to be high social presence activities based on the media richness definition (Daft & Lengel, 1986).

Upon further evaluation of the underlying assumptions of the 11 activities and the analysis of subjects' open-ended comments on the questionnaires, two categories seem to emerge to better describe these communication activities: reciprocal communications (first factor) and nonreciprocal communications (second factor). Reciprocal communication activities require high personal presence or attention from both the communication sender and the recipient during the communication act.

Activities such as "exchange confidential or sensitive information" or "get to know someone" require that both communication parties be involved to be effective; thus, the media choices are different than for those activities not requiring reciprocated interactions. Nonreciprocal communication activities such as clarifying confusing viewpoints, though, may be categorized as rating high in social presence from the social presence and media richness literature, requiring less personal presence from both communication parties during the communication. This nonreciprocal communication activity can be effectively accomplished by having one party engaged in the process at a time or via the use of other media or support staff without distorting the original meaning or purpose of the communication tasks.

To further illustrate the concept of reciprocal and nonreciprocal communications, a former production manager commented on this study's project requirement to electronically transmit an individual case analysis write-up to the case integrator: "Why should 'I' use email to transmit my report to my partner? When I was a manager, I just gave it to my secretary. That's what secretary and staff are for—delegate! I should spend my time and attention dealing with things that absolutely need 'me' there." Exchanging information, though the message can be important or urgent, does not require both parties to be involved and can also be delegated so that neither party needs to be present to complete the task of exchanging information. Some tasks, such as "stay in touch with old friends," that were traditionally considered as requiring rich media or high social presence can also be communicated via the "lean" email medium. One subject was impressed with the versatility of email and exclaimed, "I used to spend hours calling my friends in Jersey just to stay in touch. Now, I compose one email and send it to 10 friends that I usually called and I get 10 wonderful emails back without spending 10 times my valuable time. . . . That is cool!" It is evident that social presence activities were evaluated not by the social/emotional and task dimensions but by whether the tasks demand personal involvement/attention/time during the process of communication. This catogorization of tasks is certainly a "time-based" orientation toward communication and media, which is usually ignored in the traditional communication research. One possible explanation of this lack of focus on time as a variable may be due in large part to the one-shot data-gathering approach used previously (Rogers, 1986). The longitudinal nature of this study enabled subjects to function in a realistic environment for a good period of time, thus enabling them to provide a more realistic and reliable evaluation than can be provided in a one-shot experimental study.

Hypothesis 1: Appropriateness of Traditional Versus New Communication Media

Table 7.3 shows the mean score results of media-task appropriateness at two different times. Tables 7.4a and 7.4b present the individual and overall rankings of media under each task at Time 1 and Time 2. The overall means of each medium at two different times are illustrated below. According to the means across all communication tasks, the traditionally rich media, such as face-to-face (6.26 vs. 6.41),

(Text continued on p. 163)

TABLE 7.3 T-Test Comparison of Media Appropriateness Over Time

Activities Communication Medium		1. Exchange Routine Information	2. Negotiate or Bargain	3. Get to Know Someone	4. Clarify Confusing Viewpoints	5. Stay in Touch	6. Exchange Urgent/Timely Information	7. Generate Ideas/ Brainstorm	8. Resolve Disagreements	9. Make Important Decisions	10. Exchange Confidential/ Sensitive Information	11. Exchange Important Information
Face-to-face (one-to-one)	T₁	6.08	6.65	6.81	6.49	5.54	5.38	6.11	6.65	6.38	6.56	6.36
					(*)	(*)	(**)			(*)	(*)	(**)
	T₂	6.21	6.66	6.81	6.64	5.77	5.71	6.25	6.62	6.53	6.71	6.56
Face-to-face (group)	T₁	5.51	6.00	5.71	5.98	4.78	5.17	6.69	5.88	6.16	4.18	5.87
			(*)		(*)						(*)	
	T₂	5.64	6.14	5.62	6.14	4.78	5.00	6.60	6.02	6.18	5.51	5.89
Telephone	T₁	6.19	4.79	4.50	5.26	6.45	6.50	6.67	5.22	4.95	4.90	5.51
				(*)							(+)	
	T₂	6.18	4.71	4.73	5.42	6.53	6.41	6.61	5.15	4.80	4.68	5.70
Voice mail answering machine	T₁	5.44	2.23	2.11	3.10	4.56	4.60	4.42	2.48	2.39	2.48	3.68
									(*)			
	T₂	5.37	2.24	2.26	3.23	4.72	4.44	4.45	2.70	2.52	2.38	3.61
Handwritten note	T₁	5.26	2.74	3.05	4.12	5.35	4.11	2.90	3.20	2.82	3.55	4.00
						(**)					(**)	
	T₂	5.03	2.72	3.03	4.06	5.06	4.06	2.77	3.20	2.86	3.17	4.05
Formal letter	T₁	3.56	4.08	2.72	4.49	3.86	3.35	2.64	3.58	4.08	4.50	5.29
											(*)	(*)
	T₂	3.59	4.09	2.77	4.48	3.89	3.48	2.65	3.75	3.95	4.26	5.05

TABLE 7.3 Continued

Activities Communication Medium		1. Exchange Routine Information	2. Negotiate or Bargain	3. Get to Know Someone	4. Clarify Confusing Viewpoints	5. Stay in Touch	6. Exchange Urgent/Timely Information	7. Generate Ideas/ Brainstorm	8. Resolve Disagreements	9. Make Important Decisions	10. Exchange Confidential/ Sensitive Information	11. Exchange Important Information
Computer email	T_1	5.82	3.23	3.17	4.55	5.31	5.60	3.98	3.50	3.51	3.27	4.90
		(***)		(***)		(**)	(***)		(*)	(*)		
	T_2	5.76	3.23	3.80	4.67	5.64	5.05	4.12	3.70	3.75	3.42	4.77
Electronic meeting systems	T_1	4.24	4.08	3.05	4.49	3.77	4.86	4.89	4.14	4.35	3.05	4.71
		(***)				(*)	(***)	(***)	(***)	(***)		(*)
	T_2	3.74	4.11	3.10	4.51	3.54	4.24	5.55	4.60	4.74	2.85	4.42
Fax	T_1	5.04	3.49	2.29	4.18	3.82	6.06	3.24	3.18	3.44	2.53	4.89
			(*)	(*)		(+)	(**)					
	T_2	5.00	3.28	2.52	4.10	4.08	5.74	3.22	3.34	3.37	2.73	4.84

NOTE: $+p < .10$; $*p < .05$; $**p < .01$; $***p < .005$; T_1 = Time 1, T_2 = Time 2; the asterisk(s) in the parentheses indicate the significance of difference between T_1 and T_2.

TABLE 7.4 Ranking of Media by Full Mean Scales (evaluations of appropriateness of medium for communication activities)

Ranking of Nine Media for Each Full Mean Scale and Overall Mean Scale

Rank	RSLV	DESN	IDEA	NEGO	GETK	CNFX	STAY	RTNX	TIMX	CLFY	IMPX	SCALE1	SCALE2	Overall
a. Ranking of mean scales by medium at Time 1
1	Face	Face	Group	Face	Face	Face	Phone	Phone	Phone	Face	Face	Face	Phone	Face
2	Group	Group	Face	Group	Group	Phone	Face	Face	Fax	Group	Group	Group	Face	Group
3	Phone	Phone	EMS	Phone	Phone	Letter	Note	Email	Email	Phone	Phone	Phone	Group	Phone
4	EMS	EMS	Phone	Letter	Email	Group	Email	Group	Face	Letter	Letter	EMS	Email	Email
5	Letter	Letter	Email	EMS	Note	Note	Group	Vmail	Group	Email	Email	Letter	Fax	EMS
6	Email	Email	Fax	Fax	EMS	Email	Vmail	Note	EMS	EMS	EMS	Email	Note	Fax
7	Note	Fax	Note	Email	Letter	EMS	Fax	Fax	Vmail	Fax	Fax	Note	EMS	Letter
8	Fax	Note	Letter	Note	Fax	Fax	EMS	EMS	Note	Note	Note	Fax	Vmail	Note
9	Vmail	Vmail	Vmail	Vmail	Vmail	Vmail	Letter	Letter	Letter	Vmail	Vmail	Vmail	Letter	Vmail
b. Ranking of mean scales by medium at Time 2
1	Face	Face	Group	Face	Face	Face	Phone	Phone	Phone	Face	Face	Face	Phone	Face
2	Group	Group	Face	Group	Group	Phone	Face	Face	Fax	Group	Group	Group	Phone	Group
3	Phone	EMS	EMS	Phone	Phone	Group	Email	Email	Face	Phone	Phone	Phone	Group	Phone
4	EMS	Phone	Phone	EMS	Email	Letter	Note	Group	Email	Email	Letter	EMS	Email	Email
5	Email	Letter	Email	Letter	EMS	Email	Group	Vmail	Group	EMS	Fax	Email	Fax	EMS
6	Letter	Email	Fax	Email	Note	Note	Vmail	Fax	Vmail	Letter	Email	Letter	Note	Fax
7	Fax	Fax	Note	Fax	Letter	EMS	Fax	Note	EMS	Note	EMS	Fax	Vmail	Letter
8	Note	Note	Letter	Note	Fax	Fax	Letter	EMS	Note	Fax	Note	Note	Letter	Note
9	Vmail	Vmail	Vmail	Vmail	Vmail	Vmail	EMS	Letter	Letter	Vmail	Vmail	Vmail	EMS	Vmail

NOTE: RSLV = Resolve disagreement; DESN = Make important decision; IDEA = Generate ideas/brainstorm; NEGO = Negotiate a bargain; GETK = Get to know someone; CNFX = Exchange confidential/sensitive information; STAY = Stay in touch; RTNX = Exchange routine information; TIMX = Exchange urgent/timely information; CLFY = Clarify confusing viewpoint; IMPX = Exchange important information.

group meetings (5.62 vs. 5.70), and telephone (5.38 vs. 5.35), were ranked higher and as more appropriate media than email (4.28 vs. 4.41), EMS (4.15 vs. 4.26), fax (3.84 vs. 3.85), letter (3.84 vs. 3.81), note (3.77 vs. 3.62), and voice mail/answering machine (3.26 vs. 3.25) at both times. This pattern of media perception supports H1a and H1b. H1a states that traditionally rich media will be perceived as more appropriate when compared with new media. Face-to-face, group meetings, and telephone were ranked as the most appropriate media even after seven weeks of experience in the study. This finding supports H1b, which suggests that the traditionally rich media will be perceived as more appropriate even when an individual has gained experience with the new media. However, some of the traditional media such as letter and handwritten note were ranked lower than new communication media at both time intervals. These rankings are similar to many studies in which email ranks higher than many traditional communications media, such as letters or handwritten notes (Rice & Love, 1987; Trevino, Lengel, Gerloff, & Muir, 1990). Interestingly, EMS, which was ranked just below email, was considered more appropriate than many other traditional media. Voice mail, which was ranked higher in many other comparisons (El-Shinnawy & Markus, 1992; Rice, 1993), ranked lowest among all nine communication media at both times in this study. This ranking might be the result of the wide use of email and group meetings among the participants.

T-test results (Table 7.3) comparing an individual's evaluation from Time 1 to Time 2 revealed the effect of experience on perceptual changes in the appropriateness of each medium for each task. Significant changes in perceived appropriateness between Time 1 and Time 2 included the following: Face-to-face communication was perceived as more appropriate in dealing with clarifying confusing viewpoints (6.49 vs. 6.64; $p < .05$), staying in touch (5.54 vs. 5.77; $p < .05$), exchanging urgent information (5.38 vs. 5.71; $p < .01$), making important decisions (6.38 vs. 6.53; $p < .05$), exchanging confidential information (6.56 vs. 6.71; $p < .05$), and exchanging important information (6.36 vs. 6.56; $p < .01$). Group meetings were perceived as more appropriate for negotiating (6.00 vs. 6.14; $p < .05$), clarifying confusing viewpoints (5.98 vs. 6.14; $p < .05$), and exchanging sensitive information (4.18 vs. 5.51; $p < .05$). Telephone communication was viewed as more appropriate for getting to know someone (4.50 vs. 4.73; $p < .05$); and voice mail was considered more appropriate to resolve disagreements (2.48 vs. 2.70; $p < .05$).

The appropriateness of using handwritten notes and formal letters to deal with certain tasks demonstrated some significant but reverse changes. Using handwritten notes to stay in touch (5.35 vs. 5.06; $p < .01$) and to exchange sensitive information (3.55 vs. 3.17; $p < .01$) was perceived at Time 2 as less appropriate than it was at Time 1. Similarly, using formal letters to exchange sensitive information (4.50 vs. 4.26; $p < .05$) and important information (5.29 vs. 5.05; $p < .05$) was also considered less appropriate at Time 2.

Among the new communication media, email was judged as more appropriate for several tasks, such as getting to know someone (3.17 vs. 3.80; $p < .005$), staying in touch (5.31 vs. 5.64; $p < .01$), resolving disagreements (3.50 vs. 3.70; $p < .05$), and making important decisions (3.51 vs. 3.75; $p < .05$). EMS, on the other hand, received mixed evaluations, but the most changes (7 out of 11 tasks) in perceived medium appropriateness. EMS was considered more appropriate in dealing with idea generation (4.89 vs. 5.55; $p < .005$), disagreement resolution (4.14 vs. 4.60; $p < .005$), and important decision making (4.35 vs. 4.74; $p < .005$). EMS was also considered as less appropriate in dealing with exchanging routine (4.24 vs. 3.74; $p < .005$), urgent, and timely information (4.86 vs. 4.24; $p < .005$), as well as staying in touch (3.77 vs. 3.54; $p < .05$). Fax was also perceived as less appropriate for negotiating (3.49 vs. 3.28; $p < .05$) and exchanging timely information (6.06 vs. 5.74; $p < .01$), and more appropriate for getting to know someone (2.29 vs. 2.52; $p < .05$).

The above results indicate that appropriateness perceptions changed more for new media than for traditionally rich media (12 significant changes among email and EMS between Time 1 and Time 2, compared with 10 significant changes among face-to-face, group meetings, and telephone media). Even if all traditional media were grouped together to compare with new media, the average perception change of new media is still higher than all traditional media (6 vs. 2.57). Therefore, H1c is supported. Although not to the extent of new media, perceptions of the appropriateness of traditionally rich media such as face-to-face and group meetings did change over time. These findings demonstrate that individuals can obtain new insights even when using the most familiar communication media.

Hypothesis 2: Effects of Experience on Media Appropriateness

Table 7.5 shows t-test comparisons of user experience changes in terms of frequency, skill, and comfort with nine communication media. The results from this table help demonstrate the subjects' experience changes during the seven-week period. These findings were then used to calculate the correlation between experience changes with a specific communication medium and perception on media appropriateness, which serves as the basis to support H2. The results show that frequency of use with group meetings (4.97 vs. 5.81; $p < .005$), email (2.11 vs. 4.33; $p < .005$), and EMS (1.17 vs. 1.66; $p < .005$) increased significantly, whereas the reported use of telephones (6.25 vs. 5.88; $p < .005$), letters (3.55 vs. 3.03; $p < .005$), and faxes (3.74 vs. 3.03; $p < .005$) decreased significantly. Face-to-face, note, and Vmail did not present significant changes in terms of usage during the seven-week period.

Results also indicate that communication media skill increased significantly with six communication media: face-to-face (6.15 vs. 6.34; $p < .05$), group meeting (5.18 vs. 5.86; $p < .005$), voice mail (5.30 vs. 5.56; $p < .05$), note (5.17 vs. 5.50; $p < .005$), email (2.63 vs. 5.13; $p < .005$), and EMS (1.40 vs. 2.95; $p < .005$). The level of comfort using communication media also increased significantly by the end of the seventh week. In particular, individuals reported a higher comfort level with face-to-face communication (6.32 vs. 6.55; $p < .005$), group meetings (5.18 vs. 5.94; $p < .005$), email (3.06 vs. 5.39; $p < .005$), EMS (1.65 vs. 3.23; $p < .005$), voice mail

TABLE 7.5 *t*-Test Comparison of User Experience Over Time With Nine Media

		Face	Group	Vmail	Phone	Note	Letter	Email	EMS	Fax
	T₁	6.52	4.97	4.74	6.25	4.15	3.55	2.11	1.17	3.74
			(***)		(***)		(***)	(***)	(***)	(***)
Frequent	T₂	6.56	5.81	4.70	5.88	4.03	3.03	4.33	1.66	3.03
	T₁	6.15	5.18	5.30	6.15	5.17	4.80	2.63	1.40	5.09
		(*)	(***)	(*)		(***)		(***)	(***)	
Skillful	T₂	6.34	5.86	5.56	6.16	5.50	4.94	5.13	2.95	5.05
	T₁	6.32	5.18	5.19	6.19	5.48	4.82	3.06	1.65	5.30
		(***)	(***)	(*)		(*)		(***)	(***)	
Comfortable	T₂	6.55	5.94	5.47	6.24	5.67	4.95	5.39	3.23	5.23

NOTE: +$p < .10$; *$p < .05$; **$p < .01$; ***$p < .005$; T₁ = Time 1, T₂ = Time 2; the asterisk(s) in the parentheses indicate the significance of difference between T₁ and T₂.

(5.19 vs. 5.47; $p < .05$), and note writing (5.48 vs. 5.67; $p < .05$). Interestingly, among the three aspects of media experience, the results reveal that increased frequency of use is consistently correlated with increased skill and comfort.

Stepwise regressions were used to examine the associations between media experience and perceptions of media appropriateness. To enrich and broaden the understanding of effects of experience with media appropriateness and various tasks, two factors (reciprocal vs. nonreciprocal communications) that emerged from the earlier factor analysis of social presence communications (Table 7.2) were also included in the data analysis. All three scales of social presence activities (i.e., full scale—all activities; reciprocal—six activities; nonreciprocal—five activities) were regressed on the three experience measures. Table 7.6 presents standardized coefficients that are significant.

The results indicate that increased frequency of use with group meetings ($p < .005$; .005; .005), note writing ($p < .005$; .005; .005), letter writing ($p < .005$; .005; .005), email ($p < .005$; .005; .005), and fax ($p < .005$; .005; .05) were related significantly with the full scale, reciprocal, and nonreciprocal scales. For face-to-face communication, increased frequency of use was associated with the full scale ($p < .005$) and nonreciprocal scale ($p < .005$), but not with reciprocal scale. For telephone, voice mail, and EMS, increased frequency of use did not demonstrate significant relations with full scale, reciprocal, or nonreciprocal scales. This finding is relatively consistent with the changes in frequency of use found earlier (Table 7.5) in that subjects had shown significantly increased experience with group meetings, letter, email, and fax. Therefore, H2a was supported for face-to-face, group meetings, notes, letters, email, and fax, but not for telephone, voice mail, and EMS.

Table 7.6 shows that for EMS ($p < .005$; .05; .05) and phone ($p < .01$; .005; .005), increased skills were associated with appropriateness perceptions regarding all three scales. For voice mail ($p < .05$; $p < .005$) and note ($p < .05$; .005), increased skills

TABLE 7.6 Stepwise Regression of Nine Media—Full Scale and Subscales of Media Appropriateness on Experience Measures

	Scales		
Media and Experience	Full	Reciprocal	Nonreciprocal
Face-to-face (1-to-1)			
Frequency	.21***	—	.34***
Skill	—	—	—
Comfort	.26***	.33***	.13*
F	25.55***	32.66***	29.00***
Adjusted R^2	.1543	.1053	.1723
Face-to-face (group)			
Frequency	.24***	.17**	.25***
Skill	—	—	.16*
Comfort	.22***	.26***	—
F	23.64***	20.02***	19.68**
Adjusted R^2	.1450	.1247	.1227
Telephone			
Frequency	—	—	—
Skill	.22**	.17***	.23***
Comfort	—	—	—
F	13.94***	8.30***	14.77**
Adjusted R^2	.0462	.0266	.0490
Voice mail			
Frequency	—	—	—
Skill	.14*	—	.17***
Comfort	—	—	—
F	5.34*	—	8.22***
Adjusted R^2	.016	—	.0263
Note			
Frequency	.23***	.23***	.21***
Skill	.16*	—	.25***
Comfort	—	—	—
F	16.94***	15.02***	25.15***
Adjusted R^2	.1070	.0501	.1537
Letter			
Frequency	.30***	.27***	.30***
Skill	—	—	.15*
Comfort	.19***	—	.17*
F	27.36***	20.91***	29.67***
Adjusted R^2	.1654	.0696	.2443
Email			
Frequency	.31***	.36***	.17*
Skill	—	—	—
Comfort	.18*	—	.33***
F	31.22***	8.31***	34.92
Adjusted R^2	.1851	.1263	.2032

TABLE 7.6 Continued

	Scales		
Media and Experience	Full	Reciprocal	Nonreciprocal
EMS			
Frequency	—	—	—
Skill	.18***	.17*	.17*
Comfort	—	—	—
F	8.11***	6.54*	6.57*
Adjusted R^2	.0295	.0232	.0233
Fax			
Frequency	.32***	.28***	.31***
Skill	—	—	—
Comfort	—	—	—
F	27.03***	19.77***	25.12
Adjusted R^2	.1005	.0746	.0938

NOTE: Only significant independent variables are retained in the final stepwise equations (PIN = 0.05) and reported here. Values shown are standardized beta coefficients.
*$p < .05$; **$p < .01$; ***$p < .005$.

were related to both full scale and nonreciprocal scales. Increased skills with group meetings ($p < .05$) and letters ($p < .05$) were associated with the nonreciprocal scale only. However, skills with face-to-face, email, and fax were not associated with any of the activities' scales. This is consistent with the skill changes found in Table 7.5, where subjects reported significant changes in their skills with group meetings, voice mail, notes, and EMS. Therefore, H2b was supported for Vmail, note, EMS, and phone, but not supported for face-to-face, email, and fax.

Table 7.6 also shows that increased comfort with face-to-face communication ($p < .005$; .005; .05) was related to appropriateness perceptions regarding all three scales. Increased comfort with email ($p < .05$; .005) and letter writing ($p < .005$; .05) was associated with appropriateness perceptions of the full and nonreciprocal scales, whereas increased comfort with group meetings ($p < .005$; .005) was related to the full and reciprocal scales. However, for phone, Vmail, note, EMS, and fax communications, there were no significant associations between increased comfort and appropriateness perceptions. Although subjects reported a significant increased level of comfort with all media except phone, letter, and fax, only face-to-face, group, letter, and email were significantly correlated with the perception of media appropriateness. Therefore, H2c was supported for face-to-face communication, group meetings, email, and letter writing, but not for phone, Vmail, notes, EMS, and fax.

Discussion

Unlike the predictions of the media richness or social presence theories, this study found that individuals do not exclusively or rationally evaluate communication media appropriateness from the sole viewpoint of task nature or social presence. This study found that an individual's choice of media for a certain task is significantly correlated with one's experience with the media rather than the rationally evaluated fit between media and tasks. An individual's perceptions of media appropriateness vary widely according to one's skill, comfort, and use of the media. This phenomenon is particularly notable in dealing with new media. Our findings suggest that as individuals gain more experience with media over time, they may reform their perceptions of media appropriateness for performing certain tasks. Over time, an individual's media experience helps develop better understanding of the purposes and uses of new media and thus will allow the individual to make his or her media choice accordingly. An individual's perception of media appropriateness will not remain constant over time if opportunities exist for learning. Therefore, instead of taking a mere mechanistic view of media-task fit, we need to consider dynamically the individual differences in media experience as well as media richness and task analyzability.

Based on the factor analysis results, the 11 generic communication tasks used in this study clustered into two factors. The factor loading patterns in this study appear difficult to interpret using a task analyzability or social presence perspective because some tasks with low analyzability/social presence and some tasks with high analyzability/social presence loaded into the same factor. This result suggests that the categorization of communication tasks into reciprocal and nonreciprocal communication tasks may provide an alternative way for investigating media choice behavior. This time-based view on communication tasks is more appropriate for organizational members who are constantly dealing with multiple tasks at hand and face a myriad of communication media. Individuals, when faced with the need to communicate, tend to evaluate whether the communication tasks require personal attendance/attention/time or can be communicated via the use of delegation or media other than personal presence. Individuals appear to be more interested in completing the task at hand rather than consciously or intentionally choosing a "right" medium. In order to get the task done effectively, individuals may not always choose the most rational medium. This finding, though different from the current normative media-task thinking, provides an interesting and more relevant angle to examine an individual's communication behavior.

Another interesting finding from this study is that increased frequency of use of certain communication media appears to be related to the decreased frequency of use of other media. In this study, subjects reported significantly increased use of group meetings, email, and EMS, and reported significantly decreased use of phone, letter, and fax during the same seven-week period. If viewing the total usage of communication media to complete a task as a linear equation, these results suggest that the increased experience with and use of group meetings, email, and EMS expanded the users' media choices and allowed them to substitute other media with more suitable or appropriate media in a given time frame. This compensatory effect, tentatively labeled, seems contrary to some postulations in the literature. Huber (1990) stated that one of the mistaken impressions of advanced information technologies such as email and EMS was that they were often viewed "solely as substitutes for traditional technologies" (p. 51). However, he agreed that "people do substitute computer-assisted media for traditional media when it seems efficacious to do so" (p. 51). In this study, subjects were able to use multiple media and choose more appropriate media to compensate for the less appropriate media as their experience with media changed.

This study found that traditionally rich media were perceived as more appropriate for most of the communication tasks even after new media were introduced. This finding is not surprising given that the experience with these traditional media has been extensive and habitual. However, the encouraging findings from this study demonstrate that given proper experience with new media, individuals can develop new insight and perception toward new media, which can facilitate their habitual choice and use of the media, thus, successful implementation of new technologies.

While media-specific experiences as measured by frequency of use, skill, and comfort were found to affect perceived media appropriateness and choices, general individual characteristics such as computer experience, computer ownership, and gender did not have direct effect on perceptions of media appropriateness. This result is somewhat surprising given that one would expect computer experience to affect individual perception formation regarding the new computer-based media such as email and EMS. A plausible interpretation is that individual perceptions regarding appropriateness of email and EMS are more directly related to their specific experiences with email and EMS than to their generic computer experiences. Further research is needed to investigate the relationship between media-specific experience and generic computer experience, and how this relationship affects individual media appropriateness and choice.

Management can change employees' perceptions and choice of communication media by mediating their experiences with different communication media. Use of new communication media may be limited if employees are not given opportunities to develop skill and comfort with new media. This study found that gaining experience means more than increasing the frequency of use. Although increased use of media certainly affects user perception of media appropriateness, increased skill and comfort level can also have significant effect on an individual's perception. Companies need to formulate policies and provide means through which employees are encouraged to access and gain proper experience with the new communication media.

Limitations of the Study and Future Research

As with most studies of this type, the findings of the study should be interpreted with caution due to certain limitations discussed below. Media appropriateness was measured by abstract schemes of tasks rather than the specific communication incidents or scenarios used to investigate the media richness theory (Daft et al., 1987). However, as indicated by Rice (1993), little empirical validation has been done to test the media richness construct. The media-task appropriateness construct used in this study provides a more useful, meaningful, stable, and discriminating way to capture media (Rice, p. 481). This study further supports Rice's postulation.

In addition, self-report measures were used to capture individual experiences with the media. However, concerns about whether participants actually used the media should be alleviated by knowing that the two team projects in which the teams were involved during the period of this study naturally led to the need for frequent communications among participants. Even so, it may be interesting in future research to use computer-generated logs of emails or all communications occurring among team members.

This study did not link individual experience with task performance. However, since the main concern of this study is to investigate whether an individual's perception of media-task appropriateness remains stable over time as experience changes, the main focus and dependent variable of this study is not performance. Future research may take a step further to collect communication effectiveness as well as task performance to see if increased experience with media affects performance.

Finally, this study's use of MBA students as subjects circumscribes the extent to which our findings generalize. MBA students are not completely representative of the entire population of managers and professionals whose media evaluation and choices we would like to examine. These students are younger and, as a group, probably more computer literate than their counterparts in industry. Hence, computer experiences and skills may have been less an issue for this sample than it would have been for managers and professionals in general. However, the tests of individual gender, general computer experience, and computer ownership did not reveal any significant effect on media appropriateness; thus, these demographic differences between the MBA students and managers may not present an issue. These subjects were also probably more highly motivated to perform well than the general population, which may have caused perceived appropriateness of certain media to take on greater importance than it generally would. Management can assist employees to communicate effectively by mediating their media experience. Future research using real teams in an organizational setting will enhance our understanding and generalizability.

Conclusion

The proliferation of advanced computer-based technology has rapidly changed how organizations communicate. To increase the effectiveness of organizational communications and to develop appropriate investment strategies and training programs, it is critical for management to understand the nature and implications of the new communication media. This study simultaneously examined nine commonly used organizational communication technologies over a seven-week period with 295 MBA students who were actively engaged in two team projects. The contributions of this study can be demonstrated from three major areas.

First, the design of the study remedies some of the methodological problems of past research. It involved real teams who were engaged in performance-based projects in an environment where the availability of communication media is similar to modern corporations, and subjects were able to experience multiple communication media simultaneously over a seven-week period. This provides a more appropriate environment and research design for assessing media appropriateness and choice. It focuses on the over-time process nature of communication that was "almost entirely ignored" (Rogers, 1986) in the past communication research.

Second, this study used a large sample size to empirically demonstrate the effect of deliberately managed learning experience on media perception. The results can be applied by management to develop a "technology-use-mediation" organizational mechanism (Orlikowski et al., 1995) to help management provide ongoing attention and resources needed to effectively adopt computer-based communication technologies.

Third, researchers can build upon the results of this study to advance research in the areas of communication and management of advanced information technologies. Currently, theoretical developments on media choice or use mostly "presume" that organizational members learn to choose communication technologies wisely (Huber, 1986, p. 51). This study empirically demonstrates that a user's communication media experience will affect his or her perception of the fit between media and task.

Another contribution of this study is the understanding of how different media (new and old) can augment, complement, and substitute for one another even when the tasks at hand are qualitatively and quantitatively different. In fact, results indicate that increased use of some media (e.g., group meeting, email, and EMS) was associated with significantly decreased use of other media (e.g., phone, formal letter, and fax). This compensatory effect across new and old media suggests that organizations can strategically implement selected communication technologies if the implementation includes provisions for training experience.

The findings of this study have some important research and practical implications. One implication is that individual perceptions of media appropriateness are linked with prior media experience, regardless of the media and tasks. As an individual's use, comfort, and skill with media change, so will one's perceptions of media appropriateness change. This result suggests that, in addition to considering medium-task fit, researchers need to investigate the effect of individual media experience on media perception and choice. In other words, there is a need to expand the current theories of media richness and social presence to systematically investigate the joint effects of communication technologies, task characteristics, and individual experience.

From an organizational perspective, management can develop effective programs to encourage the use of new technologies, which in turn may affect employees' perceptions of the new technologies. Management should be aware that although an individual's perceptions of media can be manipulated, the traditional face-to-face communication may still be habitually viewed as the most appropriate medium. It should not be presumed that traditional communication media, such as face-to-face interactions, can be substituted with new media in all cases. Rather, traditional and new communication media complement each other. An individual's perceptions and choice of media depend on factors such as one's experience with the media as well as the characteristics of the media and the communication task. Therefore, management needs to take a balanced view when adopting and managing new communications technologies.

References

Adam, D. A., Nelson, R. R., & Todd, P. A. (1992). Perceived usefulness, ease of use and usage of information technology. *MIS Quarterly, 16*(2), 227-247.
Ajzen, I. (1985). From intentions to actions: A theory of planned behavior. In J. Kuhl & J. Beckmann (Eds.), *Action-control: From cognition to behavior* (pp. 11-39). Heidelberg: Springer.
Ajzen, I. (1991). The theory of planned behavior. *Organizational Behavior and Human Decision Processes, 50*(3), 179-211.
Bandura, A. (1977). Self-efficacy: Toward a unifying theory of behavioral change. *Psychological Review, 84*(2), 191-215.
Bandura, A. (1978). Reflections on self-efficacy. In S. Rachman (Ed.), *Advances in behavioral research and therapy* (Vol. 1, pp. 237-269). Oxford, UK: Pergamon.
Bandura, A. (1982). Self-efficacy mechanism in human agency. *American Psychologist, 37*(2), 122-147.
Bandura, A. (1986). *Social foundations of thought and action*. Englewood Cliffs, NJ: Prentice Hall.
Briggs, R. W., Balthazard, P. A., & Dennis, A. R. (1996). Graduate business students as surrogates for executives in the evaluation of technology. *Journal of End-User Computing, 8*(4), 11-17.
Carlson, J. R., & Zmud, R. W. (1994). Channel expansion theory: A dynamic view of media and information richness perceptions. In *Academy of Management Conference Proceedings* (pp. 280-284). Dallas, TX.
Compeau, D. R., & Higgins, C. A. (1995a). Application of social cognitive theory to training for computer skills. *Information Systems Research, 6*(2), 118-143.
Compeau, D. R., & Higgins, C. A. (1995b). Computer self-efficacy: Development of a measure and initial test. *MIS Quarterly, 19*(2), 189-211.
Culnan, M. J., & Markus, M. L. (1987). Information technology. In F. M. Jablin, L. L. Putnam, K. H. Robert, & L. W. Porter (Eds.), *Handbook of organizational communication: An interdisciplinary perspective* (pp. 420-443). Newbury Park, CA: Sage.
Daft, R. L., & Lengel, R. H. (1984). Information richness: A new approach to managerial behavior and organization design. *Research in Organizational Behavior, 6*(2), 191-233.
Daft, R. L., & Lengel, R. H. (1986). Organizational information requirements, media richness and structural design. *Management Science, 32*(5), 554-571.
Daft, R. L., Lengel, R. H., & Trevino, L. K. (1987). Message equivocality, media selection, and manager performance: Implications for information systems. *MIS Quarterly, 11*(3), 355-366.
Davis, F. D. (1989). Perceived usefulness, ease of use, and user acceptance of information technology. *MIS Quarterly, 13*(3), 319-339.

Davis, F. D., Bagozzi, R. P., & Warshaw, P. R. (1989). A comparison of two theoretical models. *Management Science, 35*(8), 982-1003.

Davis, S., & Bostrum, R. P. (1993). Training end users: An experimental investigation of the roles of computer interface and training methods. *MIS Quarterly, 17*(1), 61-85.

DeLone, W. H. (1988). Determinants of success for computer usage in small business. *MIS Quarterly, 12*(1), 51-61.

El-Shinnawy, M. M., & Markus, M. L. (1992). Media richness theory and new electronic communication media: A study of voice mail and electronic mail. In *Proceedings of the Thirteenth International Conference on Information Systems* (pp. 91-105). Dallas, TX.

Emory, C. W. (1980). *Business research methods.* Homewood, IL: Irwin.

Fishbein, M., & Ajzen, I. (1975). *Belief, attitude, intention, and behavior: An introduction to theory and research.* Reading, MA: Addison-Wesley.

Fulk, J., Schmitz, J., & Steinfeld, C. W. (1990). A social influence model of technology use. In J. Fulk & C. Steinfield (Eds.), *Organizations and communication technology* (pp. 117-140). Newbury Park, CA: Sage.

Fulk, J., Steinfield, C. W., Schmitz, J., & Power, J. G. (1987). A social information processing model of media use in organizations. *Communication Research, 14*(5), 529-552.

Galletta, D. F., & Lederer, A. L. (1989). Some cautions on the measurement of user involvement satisfaction. *Decision Sciences, 20*(3), 419-438.

Hare, A. P. (1960). The dimensions of social interaction. *Behavioral Science, 5,* 211-215.

Hiltz, S. R., & Turoff, M. (1981). The evolution of user behavior in a computerized conferencing system. *Communication of the ACM, 24*(11), 739-751.

Holland, W., Stead, B., & Leibrock, R. (1976). Information channel/source selection as a correlate of technical uncertainty in a research and development organization. *IEEE Transactions on Engineering Management, EM-23, 4*(2), 163-167.

Howard, G. S., & Mendelow, A. L. (1991). Discretionary use of computers: An empirically derived explanatory model. *Decision Sciences, 22*(2), 241-265.

Howard, G. S., & Smith, R. (1986). Computer anxiety in management: Myth or reality? *Communications of the ACM, 29*(7), 611-615.

Huber, G. P. (1990). A theory of the effects of advanced information technologies on organizational design, intelligence, and decision making. *Academy of Management Review, 15*(1), 47-71.

Igbaria, M., Guimaraes, T., & Davis, G. (1995). Testing the determinants of microcomputer usage via a structural equation model. *Journal of Management Information Systems, 11*(4), 87-144.

Johansen, R. (1977). Social evaluations of teleconferencing. *Telecommunications Policy, 1*(4), 395-419.

Kerr, E., & Hiltz, S. R. (1982). *Computer-mediated communication systems.* New York: Academic Press.

Kraemer, L., Danziger, J. N., Dunkle, D. E., & King, J. L. (1993). The usefulness of computer-based information to public managers. *MIS Quarterly, 17*(2), 129-148.

Lee, A. S. (1994). Electronic mail as a medium for rich communication: An empirical investigation using hermeneutic interpretation. *MIS Quarterly, 18*(2), 143-157.

Markus, M. L. (1988, August). *Information richness theory, managers, and electronic mail.* Paper presented at the Academy of Management National Meeting, Anaheim, CA.

Markus, M. L. (1992). Asynchronous technologies in small face-to-face groups. *Information Technology & People, 6*(1), 29-48.

Markus, M. L. (1994). Electronic mail as the medium of managerial choice. *Organization Science, 5*(4), 502-527.

Markus, M. L., Bikson, T. K., El-Shinnawy, M., & Soe, L. L. (1992). Fragments of your communication: Email, vmail, and fax. *The Information Society, 8*(4), 207-226.

Mathieson, K. (1991). Predicting use intentions: Comparing the technology acceptance model with the theory of planned behavior. *Information Systems Research, 2*(3), 173-191.

Nelson, R. R. (1990). Individual adjustment to information-driven technologies: A critical review. *MIS Quarterly, 14*(1), 87-98.

Ochsman, R., & Chapanis, A. (1974). The effects of 10 communication modes on the behavior of team during co-operative problem-solving. *International Journal of Man-Machine Studies, 6*(5), 579-619.

Orlikowski, W. J., Yates, J., Okamura, K., & Fujimoto, M. (1995). Shaping electronic communication: The metastructuring of technology in the context of use. *Organization Science, 4*(4), 423-444.

Perrow, C. (1967). A framework for the comparative analysis of organizations. *American Sociological Review, 32*(2), 194-208.

Reid, A. (1977). Comparing telephone with face-to-face contact. In I. de Sola Pool (Ed.), *The social impact of the telephone* (pp. 386-415). Cambridge: MIT Press.

Rice, R. E. (1984). Mediated group communication. In R. E. Rice & Associates, *The new media: Communication, research and technology* (pp. 129-154). Beverly Hills, CA: Sage.

Rice, R. E. (1987). Computer-mediated communication systems and organizational innovation. *Journal of Communication, 37*(4), 65-94.

Rice, R. E. (1990). Computer-mediated communication system network data: Theoretical concerns and empirical examples. *International Journal of Man-Machine Studies, 32*(6), 627-647.

Rice, R. E. (1992). Task analyzability, use of new media, and effectiveness: A multi-site exploration of media richness. *Organization Science, 3*(4), 475-500.

Rice, R. E. (1993). Media appropriateness: Using social presence theory to compare traditional and new organizational media. *Human Communication Research, 19*(4), 451-484.

Rice, R. E., & Case, D. (1983, Winter). Electronic message systems in the university: A decision of use and utility. *Journal of Communication*, pp. 131-152.

Rice, R. E., Hughes, D., & Love, G. (1989). Usage and outcomes of electronic messaging at an R&D organization: Situational constraints, job levels, and media awareness. *Office: Technology and People, 5*(2), 141-161.

Rice, R. E., & Love, G. (1987). Electronic emotion: Socioemotional content in a computer-mediated communication network. *Communication Research, 14*(1), 85-108.

Rice, R. E., & Shook, D. E. (1990). Relationships of job categories and organizational levels to use of communication channels, including electronic mail: A meta-analysis and extension. *Journal of Management Studies, 27*(2), 195-229.

Rivard, S., & Huff, S. (1988). Factors of success for end-user computing. *Communications of the ACM, 31*(5), 552-561.

Rogers, E. M. (1986). *Communication technology: The new media in society.* New York: Free Press.

Schmitz, J., & Fulk, J. (1991). Organizational colleagues, information richness and electronic mail: A test of the social influence model of technology use. *Communication Research, 18*(4), 487-523.

Short, J., Williams, E., & Christie, B. (1976). *The social psychology of telecommunications.* London: Wiley.

Steinfield, C. W. (1986). Computer-mediated communication in an organizational setting: Explaining task-related and socioemotional uses. In M. McLaughlin (Ed.), *Communication yearbook 9* (pp. 777-804). Beverly Hills, CA: Sage.

Steinfield, C. W., & Fulk, J. (1986). Task demands and managers' use of communication media: An information processing view. In *Proceedings of the Academy of Management Conference,* Chicago.

Taylor, S., & Todd, P. A. (1995). Understanding information technology usage: A test of competing models. *Information Systems Research, 6*(2), 144-176.

Trevino, L. K., Lengel, R. H., & Daft, R. L. (1987). Media symbolism, media richness, and media choice in organizations. *Communication Research, 14*(5), 553-574.

Trevino, L. K., Lengel, R. H., Gerloff, E. A., & Muir, N. K. (1990). The richness imperative and cognitive styles: The role of individual differences in media choice behavior. *Management Communication Quarterly, 4*(2), 176-197.

Trevino, L. K., & Webster, J. (1992). Flow in computer-mediated communication. *Communication Research, 19*(5), 539-573.

Tsuneki, T. (1988). An experimental study on the measurement of the amount of information. *KEIO Communication Review, 9*(1), 33-52.

Walther, J. B. (1995). Relational aspects of computer-mediated communication: Experimental observations over time. *Organizational Science, 6*(2), 168-185.

Walther, J. B., & Burgoon, J. K. (1992). Relational communication in computer-mediated interaction. *Human Communication Research, 19*(1), 50-88.

Williams, F., Phillips, A. F., & Lum, P. (1985). Gratifications associated with new communication technologies. In K. E. Rosengren, L. A. Wenner, & P. Palmgreen (Eds.), *Media gratifications research: Current perspectives* (pp. 241-252). Beverly Hills, CA: Sage.

Yates, J., & Orlikowski, W. J. (1992). Genres of organizational communication: A structural approach to studying communication and media. *Academy of Management Review, 17*(2), 299-326.

Zack, M. H. (1993). Interactivity and communication mode choice in ongoing management groups. *Information Systems Research, 4*(3), 207-239.

Zmud, R. W., Lind, M. R., & Young, F. W. (1990). An attribute space for organizational communication channels. *Information Systems Research, 1*(4), 440-457.

CHAPTER
EIGHT

Group Support Systems, Power, and Influence in an Organization

A Field Study

SUSAN REBSTOCK WILLIAMS
RICK L. WILSON

Group support systems have attracted attention from researchers and practitioners as potentially improving organizational effectiveness through their abilities to reduce communication barriers, increase productivity, and facilitate decision-making activities (Benbasat, DeSanctis, & Nault, 1991; Dennis, George, Jessup, Nunamaker, & Vogel, 1988; Pinsonneault & Kraemer, 1989; Gray, Vogel, & Beauclair, 1990). Research in this area has concentrated on one of two streams: (1) the design and evaluation of features of the technology; and (2) the effects of the technology on group decision outcomes and processes. The second of these categories has received a great amount of interest from IS researchers, and the number of variables addressed has been extensive. However, the focus of the research remains somewhat narrowly confined to the study of individual and group level outcomes. Thus, while our understanding of the relationships between decision variables and information technologies in the context of group decision making is maturing, our understanding of the impact of group technologies on the broader plane of organizational design and structure remains limited.

The development of insight into the interplay between these technologies and organizational design factors is important for both theoretical and practical reasons. From a theoretical standpoint, the failure to consider the interaction of new technologies with the social and structural dimensions of the firm (as suggested by systems theory) may cause problems that obscure the potential benefits of these systems when they are implemented within an organization. From a practical standpoint, group support systems are intended to enable improved workflows and communication patterns. As organizations adopt and utilize these technologies, it stands to reason that the manner in which work is accomplished and, therefore, the social and structural relationships necessary to support the work being done, are

---

Reprinted by permission from *Decision Sciences,* Volume 28, Number 4, Fall 1997.

likely to change. Thus, from an organizational perspective, the use of group technologies is viewed not only as technical change but also as social change affecting the behaviors of individuals and groups within the organization, and as structural change that alters information flows and the way that people work (Nelson, 1990). More specifically, when group technologies such as electronic mail, decision rooms, video teleconferencing, etc. are used, information may be redistributed, channels through which information can be obtained may be altered, and usual patterns of participation may be disrupted (DeSanctis & Gallupe, 1987). The relationships among the enabling technologies, information flows, and power/status issues, therefore, are likely to be affected. Although several studies have addressed the issues of participation and influence in controlled laboratory settings, the relationships among group support systems and power and influence in actual organizations remain largely unexplored.

By their nature, the social, structural, and political changes imposed by the use of group technologies requires analysis from within the organizational context. The need for this orientation has long been recognized. Organizational and IS researchers alike have argued that the effects of technology should not be considered in isolation, but rather viewed as part of the total organizational environment (Agervold, 1987; Buchanan & Boddy, 1982; DeSanctis & Gallupe, 1987; Huber, 1990; Kendall, Lyytinen, & Degross, 1992; Nelson, 1990; Pinsonneault & Kraemer, 1989; Poole & DeSanctis, 1990). Nonetheless, most contemporary empirical studies of group technologies have given organizational issues only cursory attention.

This chapter reports on a field study conducted at a major U.S. corporation to investigate users' perceptions of the impact of group support systems on power and influence. The next section presents a brief overview of the group support systems literature. The theoretical determinants of power and influence are then identified. This is followed by a description of the research methodology. The findings of the study are then presented and discussed, and the insights gained from the field are integrated with the conceptual framework drawn from the literature. The conclusion summarizes the contributions of this study, addresses the limitations, and identifies directions for future research.

Background

Group Support Systems

Group support systems, as originally envisioned by Huber (1984), extended the concepts of Decision Support Systems (DSS), which were intended for use by individual decision makers, to the group decision-making setting. Early research emphasized the support of group decision-making activities (particularly in face-to-face meetings), and thus these systems were labeled Group Decision Support Systems (GDSS). The seminal framework of DeSanctis and Gallupe (1987) extended the role of GDSS to include the support of planning, brainstorming, negotiating, problem solving, and creative tasks (as well as decision-making activities), utilizing a variety of technologies, including but not limited to the "decision room" setting. As a result of this broadened role and spectrum of underlying technologies, the "D" in "GDSS" is commonly dropped, and the term "GSS" (Group Support Systems) is used in its stead.

The term "GSS" remains difficult to define concisely. However, several common characteristics of group support technologies (which we will use interchangeably with GSS) can be identified. First, group support systems attempt to reduce barriers to communication that might otherwise be present and, in most cases, also attempt to structure group activities and processes in a positive way. Second, as mentioned above, group technologies support many different types of intellectual group activities (planning, problem solving, creative tasks, etc.). Third, group support systems are social technologies, and as such, the study of these technologies is complicated by the nature of social relationships and behaviors. Fourth, these systems are comprised of a combination of computer, decision, and communications technologies, but the mix of these technologies varies substantially from system to system. This means that systems labeled as "Group Support Systems" are often qualitatively different from one another. For example, some systems provide extensive decision support and only limited communication support, while other systems provide just the opposite mix. Some technologies link decision makers in geographically separate locations, while others support decision makers in a conference room or boardroom setting. Therefore, a GSS can mean anything from electronic mail (email) to sophisticated electronic decision rooms, and just about anything in between. In keeping with this broad view, we adopt (with slight modifications) the definition of GSS given by Dennis et al. (1988) and define Group Support Systems (GSS) as follows:

> GSS are social, information technology-based environments that support intellectual group activities either within or across geographical and temporal boundaries, where
>
> 1. information technology environments encompass communication, computing, and decision support technologies, and include, but are not limited to, distributed facilities, computer hardware and software, audio and video technology, procedures, methodologies, facilitation, and applicable group data, and
> 2. intellectual group activities include, but are not limited to, planning, idea generation, problem solving, decision making, issue discussion, negotiation, conflict resolution, and creative or collaborative group activities such as document preparation and sharing.

Overview of GSS Research

GSS research has typically involved the study of the relationships among the following factors: task type, group characteristics, features of the technology, decision outcomes (time to consensus, number of alternatives considered, etc.) and process outcomes (participation, satisfaction, etc.). Extensive reviews of empirical GSS studies have been provided by Pinsonneault and Kraemer (1990), Gray et al. (1990), Benbasat et al. (1991), and Rebstock (1995), and thus are not repeated here.

From these reviews, three shortcomings in the body of GSS research can be identified.

First, dependent variables in the majority of empirical studies have been limited to the decision outcome category and, to a lesser extent, the process outcome category. Although some researchers have begun to address issues relating to the process of adoption and use (e.g., Gopal, Bostrom, & Chin, 1992; Poole & DeSanctis, 1990), factors such as intentions, political behaviors, and organizational context are frequently glossed over. Thus, questions as to how changes in organizational factors such as power, influence, and political behaviors are related to the use of GSS have largely been ignored. Second, much of the research reported in the literature has utilized "decision room" or "same time, same place" technologies, which are often made available to organizations through universities or other external providers. Although decision rooms offer a number of desirable features, there are reasons to believe that distributed work group systems (of which electronic mail and products like LotusNotes are a major component) have become more widely adopted in organizations. For example, a study by Beauclair and Straub (1990) indicated that distributed forms of GSS (electronic mail, video teleconferencing, etc.) had a higher adoption rate than their decision room counterparts, and a review of the popular press suggests that distributed packages, which include email and shared database capabilities, may have wider organizational appeal. Third, most studies have utilized student groups (with little or no history) in controlled settings. Thus, an understanding of the interaction of group support technologies with the political behaviors that occur within an organizational context is missing.

Overall, there is little previous empirical work in the interdisciplinary area representing the "interaction" of GSS and power and influence. In the aforementioned literature reviews, only two studies could be identified that touch on these relationships. Zigurs, Poole, and DeSanctis (1988) conducted a laboratory study to investigate influence behavior in computer-mediated, decision-making groups, while Ho and Raman (1991) conducted a controlled laboratory study of the effects of GSS on leadership in small groups. Both of these studies utilized student groups and "same time, same place" technologies, and therefore provide little insight into the effects of GSS on power and influence in an organization.

Power and Influence

Although researchers in organizational behavior have studied power and politics for many years, measurement of these concepts in scientific terms remains somewhat elusive. Interestingly, despite the measurement difficulties faced by social scientists, most individuals in organizations have little or no difficulty recognizing who the powerful people in the workplace are (Salancik & Pfeffer, 1977). Furthermore, the model of organizational decision making in which power and influence play a key role is widely supported in the organizational behavior literature. In a review of nearly 50 case and field studies, Eisenhardt and Zbaracki (1992) found strong empirical evidence that "power wins battles of choice" (p. 17). To the extent that political maneuvers and influence attempts are successful, they may result in suboptimal and inefficient allocation of organizational resources. Power and influence thus represent an "irrational" but nonetheless very real component of organizational decision making and need to be considered when evaluating the effects of group support technologies.

Although power and influence represent slightly different concepts, the two terms are closely related and often used interchangeably (Tannenbaum, 1968). Many different definitions have appeared in the literature, and in some cases, power and influence have been used to define each other. For purposes of this study, we distinguish the two terms by defining power as the ability to influence *decision outcomes,* and influence as the ability to effect a change in *beliefs* (French & Raven, 1959).

The Components of Power and Influence

The pioneering theoretical work regarding the concepts of power and social influence in organizations was conducted by French and Raven (1959). French and Raven suggested that certain relationships among organizational subunits give rise to power. Their conceptualization, along with that of Perrow (1970), Emerson (1962), and Hickson, Hinings, Lee, Schneck, and Pennings (1971), suggests that power should be viewed as a property of social/structural relationships rather than simply as attributes of individuals, and that power is tied to the perceptions of those at whom influence attempts are directed. That is, power relates not just to the actual ability of an individual or subunit to bring about outcomes, but also to the perceived ability to do so.

Theoretical components of power have been set forth in the strategic contingencies models proposed by Hickson et al. (1971) and Salancik and Pfeffer (1977), and the resource dependence model proposed by Mechanic (1962). The components of power drawn from these models include the following:

Uncertainty. Uncertainty is a catalyst for the presence of power in an organization (Crozier, 1964; Lawrence & Lorsch, 1967; Perrow, 1970; Salancik & Pfeffer, 1977). Theoretically, in the absence of uncertainty, there would be no disagreement about what should be done and no rational reason to attempt to influence decision making. When uncertainty is present, disagreement as to what actions should be taken can be expected, as can the use of power to influence action in the desired direction. Lawrence and Lorsch also asserted that uncertainty is reflected by the amount, speed, and specificity with which feedback is provided within an organization, suggesting a potential impact of improved communication on power and influence.

Coping with uncertainty. While uncertainty is considered necessary for the development of power, it is the ability to cope with uncertainty, not the uncertainty itself, which actually gives rise to power (Crozier, 1964; Hinings, Hickson,

Pennings, & Schneck, 1974; Landsberger, 1961; Lawrence & Lorsch, 1967; Perrow, 1970). Coping with uncertainty is the extent to which the unpredictability of future events can be reduced or effectively dealt with. Those organizational subunits that are best able to cope with uncertainty, both on their own behalf and on the behalf of others, will tend to have the most power. Coping strategies include taking proactive interaction (coping by prevention), forecasting future outcomes (coping by information), and absorbing the consequences after the fact (coping by absorption) (Hickson et al., 1971; Hinings et al., 1974).

Substitutability. Substitutability is the ease with which the activities of one organizational subunit can be performed by other subunits. Essentially, the more difficult the activities of a subunit are to replace, the more dependent other subunits will be upon that subunit, and the more power that subunit will have (Blau, 1964; Dubin, 1963; Emerson, 1962; Mechanic, 1962).

Pervasiveness. Pervasiveness refers to the degree to which the activities of one organizational subunit are linked to the activities of other subunits. When the activities of a subunit are highly connected with many other activities in the organization, a greater amount of workflow interaction is required to accomplish organizational tasks, and a mutually dependent relationship is fostered. As the degree of dependence on another subunit increases, so does the potential power of the providing subunit.

Immediacy. Immediacy reflects the extent to which the activities of a subunit are essential to the primary workflow of the organization. An alternate term, *task criticality,* has been adopted by some researchers (Saunders & Scamell, 1986). Theoretically, the more critical the tasks performed by a subunit, the greater its power.

Criticality of resources. Salancik and Pfeffer (1977) and Mechanic (1962) have suggested that subunits that control critical resources will have a greater ability to influence decisions, and thus, greater power. Mechanic (1962) suggested that the ability to control access to information, persons, and instrumentalities (raw materials, equipment, etc.) creates the dependencies among subunits that ultimately give rise to power.

Scarcity of resources. Salancik and Pfeffer (1977) argued that the scarcity of the resources controlled by a subunit contributes to the amount of power that subunit can attain. To the extent that resources (such as funding, expertise, and information) are scarce, the control of such resources will enhance the power of the controlling subunit.

Physical centrality. Mechanic (1962) has argued that centrality in terms of physical location or social position within the firm is also an important factor. The argument is that physical proximity affords greater opportunity for interaction; leads to the establishment of better communication; improves access to persons, information, and instrumentalities; and thus provides increased opportunities to exert influence.

The Dimensions of Power and Influence

In addition to the above-mentioned components, organizational researchers have suggested that power has multiple dimensions that are observable in different ways. The most common of these are perceived power, participation power, and position power. Perceived power can be defined as the influence attributed to a subunit by members of the organization. As such, perceived power may or may not equate with actual power. However, it can be argued that subunits that are perceived as having power, at least to some extent, acquire or enhance power simply by virtue of the perception. Participation power is based on the involvement and scope of influence a given subunit has in decision making across the organization. Kaplan (1964) described three subdimensions of participation power: weight, scope, and domain. Weight is the extent or degree to which a subunit affects the decision process. Scope refers to the range of decision areas that are affected, while domain is the number of subunits whose behaviors are involved. Position power is based on the formal, legitimate position of the subunit within the organization. A primary indicator is the level the subunit occupies on a formal organization chart.

The previous discussion provides a theoretical basis for the study of the relationships among GSS and power and influence. To the extent that GSS reduce uncertainties; confer an ability to cope; create linkages and dependencies among subunits; enable access to information, persons, or other organizational resources; and alter communication and participation patterns, power and influence are likely to be affected.

A review of the literature has demonstrated that detailed investigations of the relationships among GSS use and power and influence in actual organizations are lacking. Although models of information technology implementation do exist (Ginzberg, 1981; Lucas, 1978; Markus, 1983), they primarily deal with user involvement in IS development. As such, these models fall short of addressing issues related to organizational change in general (Orlikowski, 1993), and to GSS adoption and use in particular.

The purpose of this study is to gain insight from the field into the dynamics among GSS and power and influence in organizations.

Research Methodology

Whyte (1984) suggested that the most complete understanding of behavior is gained by studying behavior in its context. Because organizational context is likely to interact with GSS in important ways in which issues related to power and influence are concerned, context needs to be considered explicitly in the analysis rather than simplified or assumed away. Yin (1994) defined a typology of qualitative research strategies that are appropriate when the purpose of an empirical inquiry is to investigate "a contemporary phenomenon within its real-life context, especially when the boundaries between phenomenon and context are not clearly evident" (p. 13). The nature of the inquiry being made in this study is in keeping with this description, and thus, a qualitative approach was employed. A single research site was favored in this instance because this study represents an initial attempt to describe the relationships of interest as they occur in the field. In such instances, Whyte (1984) suggested that studies focus on individuals within groups, before attempts are made to compare relationships among groups or among organizations.

In this chapter, a field study utilizing qualitative research methods was used to develop an understanding of changes in social and structural relationships within an organization. Kaplan and Maxwell (1994) argued that the goal of understanding a phenomenon from the insider perspective is all but lost when textual data are quantified. The qualitative method is aimed at explanation and understanding, rather than prediction and control. While the findings from such a study are particularistic, Eisenhardt (1989), Glaser and Strauss (1967), Yin (1989), and Orlikowski (1993) suggested that "analytic generalization" from the results of such a study to theoretical concepts and patterns, rather than "statistical generalization" from samples to populations, can be produced by combining insights generated inductively through the field study with those obtained from existing formal theory.

Qualitative research can be either positivist or interpretive. Positivist studies attempt to test theory and to increase the predictive understanding of phenomena (Myers, 1997). Orlikowski and Baroudi (1991, p. 5) classified IS research as positivist if there was evidence of formal propositions, quantifiable measures of variables, hypothesis testing, and the drawing of inferences about a phenomenon from the sample to a stated population. Interpretive studies attempt to understand phenomena through the meanings that people assign to them (Myers, 1997) and are "aimed at producing an understanding of the context of the information system, and the process whereby the information system influences and is influenced by the context" (Walsham, 1993, pp. 4-5). Interpretive research does not predefine dependent and independent variables, but focuses on the full complexity of human sense making as the situation emerges (Kaplan & Maxwell, 1994). As such, the current study (which seeks to generate an understanding of particular social and structural dynamics, rather than to test a set of hypotheses) can be classified as interpretive rather than positivist in nature.

Insights generated from qualitative studies provide a useful complement to quantitative IS research by enabling results to be understood and explained within the organizational context. This perspective is important, given that the primary distinction of our discipline is the study of information in organizations, and because "interest has shifted to organizational rather than technical issues" (Benbasat, Goldstein, & Mead, 1987). The qualitative method is well suited for the current study because it is appropriate as a "discovery" methodology. The qualitative approach supports the development of an understanding of relationships not previously considered (Eisenhardt, 1989; Orlikowski, 1993), such as those among GSS and power and influence. The field study design allows for the preservation of contextual and process variables, enabling social phenomena within the organization to be understood in terms of the interactions of the conditions and actions that exist within the organizational context (Orlikowski). Studies that rely solely on variance models and quantitative data typically omit such contextual and process factors from the analysis (Markus & Robey, 1988; Orlikowski; Orlikowski & Baroudi, 1991). By incorporating multiple sources of data (interviews, direct observation, documents, etc.), the research strategy selected for this study provides for triangulation of evidence while minimizing variance and preserving contextual factors.

Research Site

The organization selected for this study is a southeastern division of a major software company specializing in the development of business software tools for desktop PCs (such as word processors, spreadsheets, business graphics, database management systems, etc.). One of the offerings included in the product line is a "groupware" product. The company employs more than 5,500 people worldwide and has been in business for more than 13 years. The firm is considered a leader in its industry, grossing over one billion dollars in revenues during the last fiscal year. Market share for its products varies by product line, ranging from as low as 5% to as high as 90%. The firm's market share is relatively stable for most products, but is growing with respect to both the word processing product and a newly introduced product that integrates a set of five business software tools. Like many organizations, the firm is slowly reducing the number of employees in response to changes in organizational structure and competitive pressures to keep costs as low as possible.

The company is headquartered in the northeastern United States. Numerous offices and facilities are located across the U.S. and around the world. At the highest level, the company is organized around functional lines. That is, there is a worldwide sales and marketing division, a worldwide research and development division, and a worldwide finance division. Within each of these three major groups, there is segmentation by product line (word processing, spreadsheet, communication software, etc.). In order to ensure that each of the product offerings has a similar "look and feel," many activities require collaboration across and within divisions.

Decision making within the firm is highly distributed and is best characterized as following a matrix structure. Work groups are formed and dissolved as needed to deal with situations as they arise. Due to the constant state of flux created by this approach, formal organization charts are not maintained at either the corporate or the divisional level. Within the matrix framework, the company strives to maintain a relatively flat structure. The current goal is that "dotted lines" will be no more than five levels deep, with no more than eight people reporting to any one person at a given time.

The southeastern division (where this study was conducted) employs approximately 250 people and is responsible solely for the development, sales, and support of the company's word-processing product. The division is organized into six formal groups (Research and Development, Sales and Marketing, Customer Support, Quality Assurance, Documentation, and Human Resources). However, work groups are formed and dissolved across department lines as needed in response to the changing nature and fast pace of the software industry. The overall perception of the workplace expressed by the participants can be characterized as open and friendly. Direct observations made by the researchers during numerous site visits supported this positive view of the workplace.

The southeastern division utilizes three distinct group support technologies: voice mail, video teleconferencing, and a groupware product developed and marketed by a separate division of the firm. The voice mail system provides traditional voice mail technology features and is used throughout the organization. The video teleconferencing system is utilized primarily by the managers, enabling them to participate in meetings and executive briefings occurring at other sites. The groupware product includes a full-featured electronic mail system, but is distinguished as a groupware product by virtue of additional features that are not found in traditional electronic mail systems. Paramount among these are database features that enable the sharing of information across departments, across divisions, and across enterprises. This system supports communication across time and place dimensions. It is used for everything from simple information storage and retrieval, to collaborative work (such as joint authorship of documents), to group discussions and decision making. The groupware product is available to and used by every member of the southeastern division, and has been in place for a little more than four years.

The characteristics of the research site were considered advantageous for the following reasons. First, the level of adoption and experience using the groupware technology is high. Thus, spurious effects often associated with the adoption of new technologies and innovations, such as overcoming learning curves and unbridled enthusiasm for a new "toy," should be minimized. Second, within the framework of research designs suggested by Yin (1984), the site represents an "extreme" case, that is, one where an effect is considered likely to be found. If no relationships between power and the use of GSS technologies are perceived by organizational members in a company where the level of adoption and experience are high, and where there is a vested interest in the technology, then an argument can be made against the existence of such relationships.

Participants

Participants for this study were purposively recruited on the basis of their position within the company, their familiarity with the group technologies, and the length of time they had been employed at the organization. The goal was to obtain a representative cross-section of users from which meaningful data for the study could be derived. Both managers and nonmanagers representing various functional areas, genders, and ethnicities were sought to provide a variety of different perspectives regarding the use of the technologies as well as the perceived relationship of the technologies to power and influence in the decision-making process. To minimize learning effects, participants were sought who had a reasonable level of experience with at least two of the group technologies. Additionally, only those with a reasonable length of service were included, as it was believed that employees who had been with the organization for a short time might not have a complete understanding of the power relationships and decision-making processes within the organization.

Data Collection Methods

Data for this study were collected using a variety of methods, including personal interviews, documentation review, and on-site observation. Personal interviews, however, were the primary source of data. Interview questions were pretested first with academic colleagues and then in pilot interviews within another organization. Interviews for this study were semistructured, allowing for open-ended responses. Interviews were guided by a set of questions regarding participants' perceptions of the technology and its relationship to the determinants of power and influence. Data collection focused on the topics of context, technology, and the theoretical components and dimensions of power and influence. Information was sought on, among other things, perceptions of the organizational environment, size, structure, composition, and location; the nature and description of the group technologies, including how and when they are utilized; levels of uncertainty; coping strategies; communication patterns; availability of and accessibility to information and to persons; workflow interaction and dependencies; pervasiveness; substitutability; participation in decision making; and changes in these and other factors perceived to be associated with the use of GSS.

Interviews were conducted primarily in the company conference room. In some instances, participants asked to demonstrate ways in which they used the system, and in these cases, a portion of the interview took place in the participant's office or work area. Interviews were scheduled two hours apart, with an intended duration of one hour. Most interviews lasted 45 to 75 minutes. The time between interviews was used to record additional field notes and to write memos regarding insights and patterns that seemed to be emerging. In an attempt to put the participant at ease with the interview process, each participant was first asked to describe his or her job duties, work history, and experience with the firm. This was followed by a standard set of questions regarding the frequency and purposes of the participant's personal use of the group technologies. This led to a series of open-ended questions regarding the respondent's perceptions of whether and how these technologies affected factors related to power and influence; for example, accessibility to individuals and information, participation in decision-making activities, changes in decision-making roles, etc. An effort was made to follow up on ideas suggested by the respondents rather than to restrict questions or elicit responses based solely on a set of dimensions held by the researcher. The purpose of the interviews was to gain an emic view of the relationship of the technologies to power and influence factors through the respondents' perceptions and feelings. Thus, while the planned set of questions served as a guide to bound the interviews, each interview proceeded in a slightly different fashion from the others. That is, questions were not read verbatim, nor in exactly the same order, to each participant. This enabled a more natural flow of information and an ability to probe more deeply into the more striking responses given by the participants.

Rather than determining a set number of interviews a priori, the research design called for interviews to continue in "rounds" or "waves" until the data gathered offered little additional insight, consistent with the methodology prescribed by Yin (1984) and Eisenhardt (1989). The first round of interviews was conducted approximately one month after a preliminary site visit. A second round of interviews was conducted approximately one month after the first round. The pattern of responses at the conclusion of the second round of interviews appeared to be stable, and no new or emerging patterns could be identified. Thus, no further interviews were conducted. The participants ultimately included nine managers (the CEO, a product manager, three sales managers, the quality assurance manager, the documentation manager, the IS manager, and the HR manager) and six nonmanagers (a senior support specialist, an administrative assistant, an inside sales coordinator, a product sales specialist, a public relations specialist, and a financial analyst). Because (1) the participants spanned all functional areas, represented both genders, and were diverse in ethnicity and organizational levels; and (2) the last few interviews conducted resulted in no changes in the basic themes found, the interview data collected from these participants can be considered a good representation of the domain of possible responses.

Data Analysis Methods

Analysis of the verbal data in this study followed the iterative content analysis and open coding techniques prescribed by Glaser and Strauss (1967), Yin (1984, 1989), and Miles and Huberman (1994). This type of qualitative data analysis involves iterative movement between data and concepts, and begins early in the data collection process rather than at the end. The approach requires the data from multiple individuals to be continuously contextualized within the broader setting of the organization, as well as within the theoretical framework of the study, enabling new insights to be derived from each round of interviews before data collection from the next round is begun. The ability to incorporate new insights as they unfold from the data is one of the strengths of the approach, enabling researchers to "take advantage of the uniqueness of a specific case and the emergence of new themes to improve resultant theory" (Eisenhardt, 1989, p. 539; Orlikowski, 1993).

The open coding technique begins by repeatedly going through the verbal data and assigning labels to identifiable themes and recurrent patterns of responses. As suggested by Miles and Huberman (1994), the process of developing codes began with a line by line review of the data. Categories or labels were written in the margin next to the "chunk" captured by the label, and a list of these categories or codes was developed. For example, the following excerpt from one of the interview transcripts was assigned a code identifying the "chunk" as an indicator of the "Access to Persons" theme:

> I can get through to the CEO if I want to, and I know he will get my message. Without this technology, that would be very difficult.

(See the Appendix for additional examples of codes and portions of transcripts indicating them.) Codes were modified as each subsequent set of interview data was analyzed and new insights emerged. Throughout the code development and refinement process, an effort was made to group individual codes into more abstract categories, which could then be used to organize the content of the verbal data. The movement between specific and general-level codes continued iteratively as patterns previously unclassified emerged across respondents.

The final set of codes emerged from a lengthy refinement process. Following numerous passes through the entire data set, an initial set of codes identifying patterns of responses was established. A research assistant was asked to independently code several pages of interview data using this coding scheme as a guideline. The primary researcher provided the assistant with background material, explained the purpose of the study, and provided written descriptions of each of the codes. The research assistant was then asked to code a portion of the verbal data independently, and was invited to suggest additional codes if she encountered situations for which none of the codes provided seemed adequate. Upon the first attempt, interrater reliability, calculated as the number of "agreements" divided by the total number of "agreements and disagreements" (Miles & Huberman, 1994), was unacceptably low. The low rate of agreement (less than 30%) was attributable to two problems. First, the two coders interpreted some responses differently. Most of the "disagreements" stemmed from the fact that one coder had assigned codes (and in some instances, multiple codes) to individual words within the transcripts, while the other coder tended to assign codes to larger "chunks" of linguistic units (i.e., phrases). To resolve this problem, the two coders worked jointly to determine how big a "chunk" should be. It was agreed that while a "chunk" could be as small as an individual word, it would more likely consist of a group of words that expressed a complete thought and had a reasonably clear meaning within the context of the entire response to the interview question. Further, it was agreed that when multiple codes were possible, they should reflect different ideas expressed by the respondent, rather than all possible interpretations that could be read into the "chunk" by the coder.

In an iterative manner, the researcher and research assistant discussed indicators of various codes, revised the list of codes, and refined categories. At the end of the third round of code refinement, interrater reliability reached an acceptable level of 91% (greater than the 90% target level suggested by Miles & Huberman, 1994). The final list of codes was then used by the primary researcher to code the entire set of interview data. As an ongoing check of reliability, the research assistant was periodically asked to code additional interviews as the primary researcher progressed through the data set. In every case, interrater reliability remained at or above the 90% level.

Similarly, internal consistency was checked by examining intrarater reliabilities. This reliability measure was calculated in a similar manner, with "agreements" and "disagreements" arising from the codes initially assigned by the coder and those assigned to the same segment of the data by the same coder several weeks later. Intrarater reliabilities consistently met or exceeded the 90% acceptance level.

Results and Discussion

The content analysis revealed a number of common themes in the interview data. These responses suggest that the use of group technologies is perceived to affect several of the theoretical determinants of power and influence. Specifically, the pattern of responses suggests that GSS are perceived to (1) improve access to information, thus reducing uncertainty; (2) increase participation in the decision-making process; (3) provide increased opportunities to influence the opinions of others; and (4) improve access to persons, thereby reducing the perceived "power distance" (Hofstede, 1980) to key individuals within the organization. Additionally, participants perceived that GSS (1) altered communication patterns in a variety of interesting ways, (2) are utilized for a variety of purposes, and (3) are associated with changes in work practices.

The emergent themes and examples of the data that brought them forth are discussed below. Table 8.1 summarizes the relative frequency with which these themes were mentioned by the participants. It is interesting to note that no discernable pattern of differences between managers and nonmanagers emerged in the study.

Power and Influence Themes

Access to Information

Participants in this study perceived that group support systems provide them with improved access to information, both within and external to the organization. Users perceived that they have access not only to more information than before, but also to different information. Specifically, information available is perceived to be (1) more in-depth and detailed, and (2) more process oriented, enabling a course of events to be followed. Improved access to information was described as imparting a sense of being included, as well as a sense of well-being and comfort. Organizational members described feeling more in control as a result of being able to find

TABLE 8.1 Percentage of Times the Themes Were Identified in the Responses

Item	Percentage of Responses
Power and Influence Themes	
Access to information/reduced uncertainty	100
Participation in decision making	87
Opportunity to exert influence	73
Access to persons/reduced power distance	40
Communication Pattern Themes	
Increased volume of information	100
Preferred channel of communication	93
Increased sphere of communication	87
High level of dependence on the technology	87
Increased responsiveness from message recipients	47
Increased frequency of communication	20
Increased depth of information	20
Purpose for System Use Themes	
Sharing/disseminating information	100
Organizational memory	87
Collaborative projects and processes	73
Work Practice Themes	
Increased efficiency	87
Increased effectiveness/quality	80
Increased ability to exercise control	53
General changes in work practices	53

the information they need without having to rely as heavily on others. As noted by several of the participants:

> The depth of the information I would have otherwise, the details I would have gotten the old way, wouldn't really compare to the information I have [now].... You're kind of limited if you walk over and ask one question. That person is deciding how much information you are going to get. Are they going to answer your question and tell you more, or just answer your question? I feel like I know a lot more about our products now.

> [In groupware] you can see the chain of events, you can see the date that things happened, whereas with the phone you can't do that.

> It helps you feel tied in, in the loop. It helps you know what's going on with your company, an integral part.

Logically and theoretically, improved access to the right kinds of information increases one's ability to deal with uncertainty. Participants in this study felt better able to cope with uncertainty through the information provided in internal and external databases. They perceived that the groupware product enabled them to find the information needed to do their jobs, and to keep a finger on the pulse of the industry and their organization. As two participants noted:

> If you are uncertain about something you are doing, you can put your feelers out to people you know and ask for guidance or assistance. As far as uncertainty in the industry, I use [groupware] every day to log in to the industry newswire so that gives me the latest and greatest about what's going on. I always know corporate-wide what is happening. So in a sense... it's a communication tool that links you to the outside. So you're not in a box. You know what's going on.

> I feel like it does help you cope. It really becomes your lifeline to the company and the industry.

Organizational members in this study have equal access to most databases. Thus, with group technologies, access to information was perceived to be similar across the organization, rather than dependent upon organizational position. On the down side, some participants did express concern about the volume of information available. As noted by one participant:

> It's very hard because I'm addicted to the amount of information that's available to me over [groupware], but yet I know that, at the same time, I'm numbed by it.

Participation in Decision-Making Activities

The data in this study suggest that the use of group support systems are perceived to increase the opportunities for individuals throughout the organization to be heard and to participate in the decision-making process. This increase in participation is noteworthy in several aspects. First, group technologies are perceived to extend the sphere of communication, and thus the potential sphere of influence of individual users. The range, level, and frequency of communication are believed to increase when such systems are adopted. As noted by one participant:

> I do feel like I have a relationship with a lot of people that I wouldn't otherwise, that I would never even know, maybe never even talk to even though we work for the same company.

Participants felt that the GSS enabled them to communicate and establish working relationships with a wider range of organizational members, some of whom they would otherwise have little or no contact with due to physical distance or organizational position (across functional areas or managerial levels). The reason most often cited by the participants for this was that in the absence of the group technologies, it would be too time consuming to establish and maintain such communications.

Participants also perceived that with this increase in communication come opportunities to participate in decision-making activities at many levels across the organization. Users perceive that they are able to share ideas, provide input, negotiate, and discuss alternatives regardless of organizational status, physical location, or functional affiliation. Numerous participants characterized the system as "inclusionary," bringing "more people into the process," and establishing "the same sort of forum, regardless of your position." The breadth or scope of participation is perceived to increase as input from individuals in diverse departments is more easily sought and obtained. Similarly, those at lower levels of the organization perceive increased opportunities to participate as their opinions and input are solicited. Thus, participation in decision making is perceived as becoming less dependent on functional, positional, and geographical boundaries. As stated by the participants:

> If this were on paper, the chances of someone in marketing or R&D putting my name on it and having the secretary forward it to me as well as others is much less. There's much more effort involved in that. Here, you just add a name and that's it. It's in there.

> [Without groupware] I probably would not have any participation, little if any [with headquarters and overseas].

Relatedly, participants perceived that as the opportunities to participate increase, so too does the frequency of participation. In other words, participants reported that they were responsive to the opportunities afforded by the technology and capitalized on them. Reasons given by the participants for this phenomenon included the ease of use and convenience of the technology, the reliability of the system (i.e., reduced risks of "lost" messages), the quasi-anonymous or "removed" nature of the electronic medium, and the perception that electronic communication is more difficult to ignore than paper or voice messages.

The perception that email is more difficult to ignore than paper and voice equivalents is a very interesting finding. Several possible reasons for this were suggested by the participants. First, many users prefer email, like to use it, and as a result, check their email often. Participants in this study indicated that they check their email several times each day. Second, the convenience and reliability of the system may encourage a greater degree of responsiveness by reducing the need to play "phone tag" as well as reducing the risk of lost messages. Third, the groupware product utilized at the research site includes a feature, which when activated, notifies the sender of the date and time when recipients open their mail. This feature is perceived as making it more difficult for recipients to ignore messages, and virtually eliminating the excuse "I didn't get the message." A related finding is that users perceive that they get a better, faster response to email than to alternative forms of communication.

Increased participation is perceived to be most prevalent in the information gathering and alternative evaluation stages of the decision-making process, and to a lesser extent, in the implementation stage. The system was perceived to enable full and extensive input and exchange of in-depth ideas as well as free-flowing discussions regarding organizational matters particularly for discussions that span longer time frames. As one person stated:

> You want to take into account a lot of people in a conversation like that over a period of months. That's not something you can sit down and decide in a matter of a conference call in an hour.

The impact of group support systems upon the choice stage of the decision-making process was less obvious. Ultimately, the perception was that the important organizational decisions are made by an elite few. However, participants reported that group support systems enable those decisions to be made on the basis of knowledge drawn from the ideas of a much larger set of people, enabling a more participative style of management. Overall, increased participation and communication was perceived as an equalizing force. Because individuals have an opportunity to provide input and a mechanism through which they can attempt to influence decision outcomes, power and influence within the organization was perceived as becoming more equal.

Other evidence in the study suggests that the increase in participation and communication may be dependent on individual preferences for and skills in written communication. Nearly all of those interviewed expressed a personal preference for communicating (as both a sender and a receiver of information) in written rather than oral form, and 60% of the participants felt they were more skilled in the written media. The preference for written communication was consistent across managerial levels and functional areas. Interestingly, those who believed that they possess strong writing skills also perceived that email technologies provided them with increased opportunities to participate in and influence decision outcomes. It is clear that many important issues are brought up, defined, evaluated, and discussed through electronic channels. Those that communicate very well in written form may find that group technologies provide a vehicle for acquiring visibility and influence that they otherwise would not have had. However, those without strong written communication skills may be unable to capitalize on the opportunities provided by the technology. Thus, the equalizing effect of the technology may be mitigated when users possess poor writing skills.

Opportunities to Exert Influence

Respondents who believed that they possessed good written communication skills also felt that the group technologies provided them with improved opportunities to influence the opinions of others within the organization, including those at higher levels. Most study respondents perceived that they were able to make a stronger and more cohesive argument through written channels of communication than they could orally. Written communication was thought to be more clear, succinct, honest, and complete. As noted by one of the participants:

> I tend to get stuck on my words when I'm trying to sit there and present something, whereas if I'm writing it down it can be clear and concise and I can remember everything and get it all in there. . . . When you go face-to-face with someone you tend to not remember everything that you meant to say as to why this would be good. It helps. I think I do better in writing than in talking.

An interesting perception of several respondents was that their ability to influence others was enhanced by the groupware product because the technology allows them to express their opinions without being interrupted by others with conflicting viewpoints, enabling them to make a clear and complete statement of their position. For example, participants stated:

> It's easier to come across with your own opinion, because you know nobody's going to interrupt you, and you can get everything out at once, and then just kind of wait on a reply.

> Since you can't interrupt, you have full leeway to write however you want to to influence people.

Most participants stated that the groupware product not only encourages the contribution of ideas, but elicits higher levels of responsiveness from management. A number of respondents expressed a belief that the groupware product enables them to have more of a voice in decision making and a greater opportunity to influence outcomes than they would otherwise have. As suggested by one participant:

> You feel more a part of it. If you're included in a decision, you feel like the opportunity is there to put your two cents in, if you have a view about a certain topic.

However, most respondents also acknowledged that the ability to influence others and to be influenced by them again depends on the communication skills of the user. For those with strong written communication skills, the groupware product may provide a significant opportunity to exert influence. For those with weak writing skills, the technology may impose a barrier that limits the ability to influence others. The following comments illustrate this point:

> I know that for some people who have really strong written communication skills and are just really very eloquent on paper, [groupware] is a great way for them to get their point across.

> But some people can't write, and you read it, and you're not necessarily informed or influenced. It's a tool, but it's not always effective for everyone.

Access to Persons

Many of those interviewed perceived that access to persons was improved through the use of the groupware product. Participants cited a number of difficulties in reaching people that appear to be alleviated by the use of the group technologies. The use of group support systems was believed to encourage cross-level and cross-functional discourse, thus increasing "virtual" access to persons. Participants in this study perceived that accessibility to others in the organization, particularly to those at higher managerial levels, improved when the group support system was used. Decision makers appeared to be more accessible, and organizational members reported feeling more a part of the decision-making loop and more comfortable in approaching key players with their thoughts and ideas. Thus, the "power distance" from lower to upper levels (Hofstede, 1980) was perceived to be reduced. Participants felt that their messages not only got through to and were read by the recipient, but also received a higher degree of responsiveness. Consequently, they felt much more comfortable, willing, and likely to send electronic messages to higher level managers than to try to contact them in other ways. The following comments were typical:

> If there were an executive or someone higher up, if they were to see an email from me, see the chain of events, I think they would respond quicker if they were to see the importance of it versus if I were to leave a voice mail saying, "My name is _____, you don't know me, but I've got something very important to talk about, please call me." I think it does open up doors to higher levels, both ways. I think higher levels see the importance of some functions that they normally wouldn't be exposed to, via [groupware].

> There's so much more a sense of knowing who the players are in the company when you at least see their names on email several times a day—whether you've met them or not, you feel like you know them.

> My first response is to say [that access to persons is] better. I can reach anybody in this company that I want.... I have a feeling people tend to correspond better through email than they do through phone mail because it's just easier. It's easier to respond to my

email with a quick reply than it is for you to call me and answer my questions; so I think, better.

While this was the general pattern, there were exceptions. Several respondents felt that the increased reliance on electronic communication had made it more difficult to obtain physical access to organizational members, indicating that the change of communication forms from physical to "virtual" reduced the amount of face-to-face contact with other individuals. Additional concerns stemmed from problems related to information overload. Several participants perceived that the system was sometimes used inappropriately to indiscriminately copy messages to large numbers of people (dubbed "CYA" copying), resulting in an inordinate number of messages being received. It was suggested that this practice makes it difficult for recipients to distinguish between important and unimportant messages. One possible remedy to this problem is to develop filters for message screening. However, if users at lower levels of the organization begin to sense that their messages are not being read, they may begin to perceive the system as a hindering rather than an enabling technology. This suggests that it will be important for managers to evaluate their electronic accessibility and the effect that limiting this accessibility may have on others in the organization.

Other Themes

Communication Patterns

Many of the communication patterns identified in Table 8.1 have been discussed in the previous section. To summarize, participants perceived (1) that the volume, depth, and frequency of communication increased with the use of GSS, and (2) that electronic communication increased both the sphere of communication and the responsiveness of message recipients. In general, participants appeared to prefer electronic channels of communication to paper alternatives. An additional theme that emerged from the data is that participants perceived that the organization had a high level of dependence on the various group technologies. As one manager stated:

> I rely on [groupware] to be my communication. I always tell people I work with that, whether they are [at headquarters] or wherever, the easiest way to get in touch with me, or the most efficient, or the way to get the best response is to go through email, because I'm hardly ever at my phone.

Purpose of System Use

As would be expected, all participants perceived that the GSS was used to share and disseminate information. A majority also indicated that they use the system to work on collaborative projects. However, nearly all of the participants also stated that a primary reason for using the group support system is to provide a tracking mechanism. The prevalent use of GSS as an organizational memory is another interesting finding. The ability of GSS to provide an "audit trail" appears to be very important to most organizational members. The evidence in this study suggests that the ability of the system to track and organize correspondence, to follow a chain of events, and to demonstrate that particular directives were or were not issued is one of the key reasons that organizational members favor this form of communication. Among other things, the ability to track information in this manner provides users with a degree of control by establishing a clear, indisputable way to go back and check previous activities, correspondence, and decisions and directives. Comments such as the following were typical:

> A lot of times you want to document it and save it . . . and it's a paper trail, in the sense that it helps you manage it, and remembering exactly what you said, and going back to that point, getting detailed information.

> It allows you to review back. Like two months ago we had a meeting, and somebody put something in here, and I can scroll back through that discussion and find out—I just don't know how you would do that without [groupware].

Work Practice Themes

For many of the reasons noted above, group technologies were perceived as making the organization more effective and more efficient. As a result of improved communication, it was perceived that fewer things were able to "fall through the cracks," and in many instances, the technologies enabled the "right" person (rather than the most available one) to be included. Organizational members perceived that they were more informed, had a higher degree of control, and that they were more involved in organizational activities than they would have been without the technology. Additionally, users perceived that use of the technologies has increased both the pace and the nature of what they are able to accomplish.

Group technologies were perceived as enabling users to have increased control over the execution of some job duties. Participants reported that the groupware product enabled them to deal with problems, issues, and persons when they wanted and were ready to do so. This allows individuals to be more protective of their time, to avoid unnecessary interruptions, and to exercise control over when certain job duties would be carried out. A second aspect of control associated with the use of group technologies is the ability to escalate problems. The groupware product was perceived to impart a sense of having legitimate rights to expect a timely response, and to provide an effective and convenient way to escalate matters (with the complete sequence of events, if necessary) when such responses were not forthcoming. This was perceived as enabling individuals to take the initiative as well as to shift the responsibility when needed. The organizational memory capabilities of the groupware system supported this by providing the ability to track sequences of actions and illustrate a chain of events in such instances.

Individuals within virtually every subunit of the organization perceived that they were highly linked to other organizational subunits through the groupware technology. Linkages to other subunits appear to be more tightly interwoven in the respect that all subunits share information in organizational databases. Because information is centrally available and easily accessible, there is less dependence on someone from another subunit to provide the information needed. However, all subunits are dependent upon the information being in the databases. This codependence is perceived as an equalizing force, in that individual subunits are generally not in a position to control or limit access to organizational information.

Additionally, physical centrality appears to become less important when group technologies are adopted. Individuals and information are perceived to be easily and equally accessible regardless of their physical location or organizational position. Thus, "virtual" centrality is provided to every subunit by the technology.

Limitations and Conclusions

This study has several limitations. Because this study has been conducted within a single organization, generalization of the results to other organizations is limited. As discussed earlier, the purpose of this study has been to explore potential relationships and gain insight into social and structural changes associated with the use of group technologies. As such, our methodology supports analytic rather than statistical generalization. Nonetheless, additional field studies will be needed to validate, refine, and extend the findings of this study.

A second limitation stems from potential biases within the study site due to its vested interest in groupware products. However, as previously discussed, the benefits afforded by this particular site were thought to outweigh the limitations imposed by it. A finding of no relationship among group support systems and power and influence in this organization would have provided strong evidence that no such relationships exist. Because relationships were found in this study, they will need to be further explored, and confirmed or disconfirmed through additional studies at other organizations. It is possible that the patterns identified herein would have been present in the organization without the technology.

Another potential limitation is that biases and preconceptions of the researcher may have entered into the interpretation of the data. Explicit attempts were made in this study to avoid such biases through the a priori development of protocols and the use of multiple raters. Nonetheless, the effects of researcher biases on the interpretation of the data cannot be totally ruled out.

Similarly, this study is limited by the fact that the ability of the researcher to conduct interviews may have improved as the project progressed. Therefore, interviews conducted at the end of the project may have contained richer information than those conducted at the beginning of the project. Furthermore, the researcher was an outsider to the organization. Participants may have been unwilling to share thoughts and perceptions that could have been perceived by the researcher in a negative fashion.

The findings of this study suggest many directions for future research. First and foremost, additional field studies involving other organizations and other group technologies should be conducted to determine if the pattern of findings differs from that found in this study. Thus, specific organizational context issues related to power and influence and group support systems can be further fleshed out. Additionally, a number of fresh issues that can be evaluated quantitatively have been identified. For example, perceptions that (1) the lost message rate for electronic communications is lower than for paper and voice alternatives, and (2) that there are differences in responsiveness to electronic versus paper or voice messages need to be addressed. Additionally, future studies should address more fully the relationships among user preferences for written communication, actual writing skill levels, and the use of GSS.

In summary, this study has explored the relationships among group support systems and power and influence in an organization using a qualitative, field study approach. The evidence gathered suggests that group support systems are perceived to exert an equalizing force on a number of the theoretical determinants and dimensions of power and influence in organizations. The overall image depicted by the results suggests that these relationships are worthy of further investigation.

Appendix

This section provides examples of the coding manual used in the content analysis of the verbal data. The codes illustrated herein pertain to the purposes for which the system was used.

OM The system is used to provide an "organizational memory." This category includes using the technology to track, organize, and categorize information. Examples:

"I use it to track things."

"I categorize everything."

"I backlog everything for a year."

SHARE The system is used to share information. This includes disseminating information (FYI-type stuff), gathering information, soliciting ideas from others, and holding online discussions. Examples:

"I use it to inform—to say we're going to have a meeting at 2:00 pm Friday and here's the agenda."

"I use it to ensure that everybody gets the same information at the same time."

"It puts us all on the same page (information-wise)."

"I use it to say 'What are your ideas?'"

"I use it to look up information I need to do my job—to look up part numbers, for example."

"I use it to get information about the competition off the newswire."

"We have discussions online."

ATT The system is used to gain someone's attention, to become recognized or known to others, or to gain visibility. Examples:

"I use it to get in someone's face."

"I use it when I want to get someone's attention."

"I use it because I want them to know who I am."

INFL The system is used with an intent to influence decision outcomes or to persuade the opinions of others. This includes negotiating solutions when conflicting points of view are held. Examples:

"I use it to persuade others to see my point of view."

"We use it to hammer out solutions—to negotiate."

MOT The system is used to motivate, to get someone to take action. Examples:

"I use it to get someone to take action."

"I use it to motivate my people."

References

Agervold, M. (1987). New technology in the office: Attitudes and consequences. *Work and Stress, 1*(2), 143-153.
Beauclair, R. A., & Straub, D. W. (1990). Utilizing GDSS technology: Final report from a recent empirical study. *Information & Management, 18*(5), 213-220.
Benbasat, I., DeSanctis, G., & Nault, B. (1991). *Empirical research in managerial support systems: A review and assessment.* Working Paper. University of British Columbia.
Benbasat, I., Goldstein, D. K., & Mead, M. (1987). The case research strategy in studies of information systems. *MIS Quarterly, 11*(3), 369-386.
Blau, P. (1964). *Exchange and power in social life.* New York: Wiley.
Buchanan, D. A., & Boddy, D. (1982). Advanced technology and the quality of working life: The effects of computerized controls on biscuit-making operators. *Journal of Occupational Psychology, 56*(2), 109-119.
Crozier, M. (1964). *The bureaucratic phenomenon.* Chicago: University of Chicago Press.
Dennis, A. R., George, J. F., Jessup, L. M., Nunamaker, J. F., Jr., & Vogel, D. R. (1988). Information technology to support electronic meetings. *MIS Quarterly, 12*(4), 591-618.
DeSanctis, G., & Gallupe, R. B. (1987). A foundation for the study of group decision support systems. *Management Science, 33*(5), 589-609.
Dubin, R. (1963). Power function and the organization. *Pacific Sociological Review, 6*(1), 16-24.
Eisenhardt, K. M. (1989). Building theories from case study research. *Academy of Management Review, 14*(4), 432-450.
Eisenhardt, K. M., & Zbaracki, M. J. (1992). Strategic decision making. *Strategic Management Journal, 13*(Special Issue), 17-37.
Emerson, R. E. (1962). Power-dependence relations. *American Sociological Review, 27*(1), 31-41.
French, J., & Raven, B. (1959). The bases of social power. In D. Cartwright (Ed.), *Studies in social power.* Ann Arbor: University of Michigan Press.
Ginzberg, M. J. (1981). Early diagnosis of MIS implementation failure: Promising results and unanswered questions. *Management Science, 27*(4), 459-478.
Glaser, B. G., & Strauss, A. L. (1967). *The discovery of grounded theory: Strategies for qualitative research.* New York: Aldine.
Gopal, A., Bostrom, R. P., & Chin, W. W. (1992). Applying adaptive structuration theory to investigate the process of group support systems use. *Journal of Management Information Systems, 9*(3), 45-69.
Gray, P., Vogel, D., & Beauclair, R. (1990). Assessing GSS empirical research. *European Journal of Operational Research, 6*(2), 162-176.
Hickson, D. J., Hinings, C. R., Lee, C. A., Schneck, R. E., & Pennings, J. M. (1971). A strategic contingencies' theory of intraorganizational power. *Administrative Science Quarterly, 16*(2), 216-229.
Hinings, C. R., Hickson, D. J., Pennings, J. M., & Schneck, R. E. (1974). Structural conditions of intraorganizational power. *Administrative Science Quarterly, 19*(1), 22-44.
Ho, T. H., & Raman, K. S. (1991). The effect of GDSS and elected leadership on small group meetings. *Journal of MIS, 8*(2), 109-133.
Hofstede, G. (1980). Motivation leadership and organization: Do American theories apply abroad? *Organizational Dynamics, 9*(1), 46-49.
Huber, G. P. (1984). Issues in the design of group decision support systems. *MIS Quarterly, 8*(3), 195-204.
Huber, G. P. (1990). A theory of the effects of advanced information technologies on organizational design, intelligence, and decision making. *Academy of Management Review, 15*(1), 47-71.
Kaplan, A. (1964). Power in perspective. In R. L. Kahn & E. Boulding (Eds.), *Power and conflict in organizations.* London: Tavistock.

Kaplan, B., & Maxwell, J. A. (1994). Qualitative research methods for evaluating computer information systems. In J. G. Anderson, C. E. Aydin, & S. J. Jay (Eds.), *Evaluating health care information systems*. Thousand Oaks, CA: Sage.

Kendall, K. E., Lyytinen, K., & Degross, J. I. (Eds.). (1992). *The impact of computer supported technologies on information systems development*. Amsterdam: North-Holland.

Landsberger, H. (1961). The horizontal dimensions in a bureaucracy. *Administrative Science Quarterly, 6*(3), 299-332.

Lawrence, P. R., & Lorsch, J. W. (1967). *Organization and environment*. Boston: Division of Research, Harvard Business School.

Lucas, H. C., Jr. (1978). Empirical evidence for a descriptive model of implementation. *MIS Quarterly, 2*(2), 27-42.

Markus, M. L. (1983). Power, politics, and MIS implementation. *Communications of the ACM, 26*(6), 430-444.

Markus, M. L., & Robey, D. (1988). Information technology and organizational change: Causal structure in theory and research. *Management Science, 34*(5), 583-598.

Mechanic, D. (1962). Sources of power of lower participants in complex organizations. *Administrative Science Quarterly, 7*(3), 349-364.

Miles, M. B., & Huberman, A. M. (1994). *Qualitative data analysis: An expanded sourcebook*. Thousand Oaks, CA: Sage.

Myers, M. D. (1997). Qualitative research in information systems. *MIS Quarterly, 21*(2), 241-242.

Nelson, D. (1990). Individual adjustment to information-driven technologies: A critical review. *MIS Quarterly, 14*(1), 79-91.

Orlikowski, W. J. (1993). CASE tools as organizational change: Investigating incremental and radical changes in systems development. *MIS Quarterly, 17*(3), 309-340.

Orlikowski, W. J., & Baroudi, J. J. (1991). Studying information technology in organizations: Research approaches and assumptions. *Information Systems Research, 2*(1), 1-28.

Perrow, C. (1970). Departmental power and perspectives in industrial firms. In M. N. Zald (Ed.), *Power in organizations*. Nashville: Vanderbilt University Press.

Pinsonneault, A., & Kraemer, K. L. (1989). The impact of technological support on groups: An assessment of the empirical research. *Decision Support Systems, 5*(2), 197-216.

Pinsonneault, A., & Kraemer, K. L. (1990). The effects of electronic meetings on group processes and outcomes: An assessment of the empirical research. *European Journal of Operational Research, 46*(2), 143-161.

Poole, M. S., & DeSanctis, G. (1990). Understanding the use of group decision support systems: The theory of adaptive structuration. In J. Fulk & C. Steinfield (Eds.), *Organizations and communication technology*. Newbury Park, CA: Sage.

Rebstock, S. E. (1995). *Group support systems and power and influence: A case study*. Unpublished doctoral dissertation, Oklahoma State University, Stillwater, OK.

Salancik, G. R., & Pfeffer, J. (1977). Who gets power—And how they hold onto it: A strategic-contingency model of power. *Organizational Dynamics, 5*(3), 3-21.

Saunders, C. S., & Scamell, R. (1986). Organizational power and the information services department: A reexamination. *Communications of the ACM, 29*(2), 142-147.

Tannenbaum, A. S. (1968). *Control in organizations*. New York: McGraw-Hill.

Walsham, G. (1993). *Interpreting information systems in organizations*. Chichester, UK: Wiley.

Whyte, W. F. (1984). *Learning from the field: A guide from experience*. Beverly Hills, CA: Sage.

Yin, R. K. (1984). *Case study research: Design and methods*. Beverly Hills, CA: Sage.

Yin, R. K. (1989). Research design issues in using the case study method to study management information systems. In J. I. Cash, Jr. & P. R. Lawrence (Eds.), *The information systems research challenge: Qualitative research methods*. Boston: Harvard Business School Press.

Yin, R. K. (1994). *Case study research, design and methods* (2nd ed.). Thousand Oaks, CA: Sage.

Zigurs, I., Poole, M. S., & DeSanctis, G. L. (1988). A study of influence in computer-mediated group decision making. *MIS Quarterly, 12*(4), 625-644.

CHAPTER
NINE

An Empirical Investigation Into Factors Relating to the Adoption of Executive Information Systems

An Analysis of EIS for Collaboration and Decision Support

ARUN RAI
DEEPINDER S. BAJWA

Emergent Perspective of EIS

Advances in information technology provide organizations with an opportunity to redesign traditional, and often archaic, work processes. Executive Information Systems (EIS) are a product of these rapid developments in information technology. EIS can be defined as computer-based information systems designed to support the managerial work activities of executives (Elam & Leidner, 1995). In fact, the evolution of EIS has led to a shift in the attributes of these systems and in the support that these systems can potentially offer executives. Table 9.1 compares the traditional and emergent perspectives of EIS along four dimensions.

While traditional EIS supported only a few top executives, the emerging view is that EIS can spread horizontally across and vertically down to other organizational managers (Belcher & Watson, 1993). Thus, the emerging trend is to view EIS "as technology for information delivery to all business end users" (Volonino, Watson, & Robinson, 1995, p. 106). It was also believed that EIS were likely to be developed in the context of large firms (Rockart & DeLong, 1988; Watson, Rainer, & Koh, 1991). The underlying rationale was that EIS were expensive and predominantly resource-rich firms could afford them. Moreover, the complexities of operating larger organizations made them better candidates for EIS. However, EIS vendors now offer products such as Lightship and Paradigm, which are targeted specifically at small and midsized firms. Traditional EIS focused primarily on internal information sources to provide monitoring support through "drill down" applications for top-level executives. Today, EIS allow for convenient access to both internal and external data/information sources (Rainer & Watson, 1995; Volonino et al., 1995; Watson, Watson, Singh, & Holmes, 1995). As a result, while traditional EIS

Reprinted by permission from *Decision Sciences*, Volume 28, Number 4, Fall 1997.

TABLE 9.1 EIS—Traditional and Emergent Perspectives

EIS-Related Attributes	Traditional Perspective	Emergent Perspective
1. Users	Few top-level executives	Executives at all levels
2. Organization size	Large firms	Large and small firms
3. Data/information sources	Internal	Internal and external
4. Type of support	Control	Communication, coordination, control, and planning

provided limited support (typically in the form of control-oriented information for a handful of top executives), today's EIS incorporate technologies such as electronic mail, voice mail, computer conferencing, electronic calendaring, tickler files, data analysis tools, vertical and horizontal "drill-down," modeling/simulation capabilities, etc., to provide substantial support for executive work. Some researchers have also suggested that as EIS evolve, they are likely to have a significant impact on the organization's planning and control systems (Fried, 1991; Gulden & Ewers, 1989; Mitchell, 1988; Rockart & De Long, 1988; Shoebridge, 1988) and lead to higher levels of organizational effectiveness (Paller & Laska, 1990). Recent empirical evidence indicates that EIS can enhance mental models of executives (Vandenbosch & Higgins, 1995) and lead to faster responses in decision situations (Leidner & Elam, 1993).

Objectives and Motivation

Despite touted organizational benefits, few have been successful in developing EIS (Watson et al., 1991). Several explanations have been forwarded for this lack of EIS growth. First, substantial financial resources are needed to develop EIS. It was reported that the "cost of a typical private sector system varies between $1 million to $2 million for the hardware, software tools, and development effort" (Mohan, Holstein, & Adams, 1990, p. 435). However, a recent survey suggests that, on average, EIS can cost about $325,000 (Watson et al., 1995). Although the price of acquiring EIS has decreased over the years, the current tag may well be out of reach for some firms. Second, developers have often found it difficult to identify user requirements since the clientele they are dealing with (i.e., executives) often face uncertain environments (Watson & Frolick, 1993). While several strategies have been suggested to facilitate user information requirements determination for EIS (Wetherbe, 1991), there is little empirical work aimed at understanding EIS adoption patterns.

In lieu of the emerging role of EIS and its increasing penetration among executive and managerial ranks at all levels, it is imperative to understand why EIS are adopted and which attributes facilitate EIS adoption levels in organizations. Some researchers suggest that the decision to adopt an EIS may simply be an outcome of the decision maker's style, decision environment, and the time frame for decision making (Elam & Leidner, 1995). Managers with analytical or directive decision styles and facing greater time pressures are likely to adopt EIS to a greater extent than others. On the other hand, it has been suggested that internal and external pressures often force firms to adopt EIS (Watson et al., 1991). The importance of such internal and external contextual factors in promoting or inhibiting the adoption of information technology has been examined in past studies (Zmud, 1982, 1984a, 1984b; Rai & Patnayakuni, 1996). Thus, contextual factors may be important determinants of EIS adoption.

Our study focuses on the contextual factors that are likely to impact EIS adoption and does not examine EIS from an outcome perspective. Although some contextual attributes of EIS adoption have been explored in case studies (Armstrong, 1990; Cottrell & Rapley, 1991; Fireworker & Zirkel, 1990; Gunter & Frolick, 1991; Houdeshel & Watson, 1987; Joslow, 1991; Rees-Evans, 1989; Wallis, 1989), they represent isolated incidents of varying adoption levels in single firms. While such case studies capture the nuances and details of context, and improve understanding of the forces underlying the phenomenon, they have limited generalizability (Harrigan, 1983). Jenkins (1990) observed that the usefulness of these case studies can only be extended if researchers agree to share frameworks, constructs, variables, and relationships to facilitate comparisons across studies.

The emergent perspective of EIS incorporates two related, complementary, but distinct facets of information technology support. First, collaboration technology is directed at supporting managerial processes of communication and coordination. We refer to this as EIS for collaboration support (EIS_c). Second, decision support technology is targeted at supporting the informational needs for planning and control. We refer to this as EIS for decision support (EIS_d). This distinction between collaboration support technology and decision support technology has been made in the recent IS literature (Turban, McLean, & Wetherbe, 1996). A similar distinction has also been made in the context of computer-based support for executives (Rockart & DeLong, 1988). Making such a distinction in the case of EIS may result in interesting insights about differences in adoption-related issues pertaining to these two facets of EIS.

Furthermore, organizations may explore EIS and even decide to commit resources at some point in time; the benefits accrued are likely to be enhanced if EIS are adopted to support most executives. The organization innovation and IS adoption literature streams make an important distinction between defining and understanding the transition from a state of nonadoption to initial adoption, and the subsequent propagation of the innovation across the population of potential adopters within a given organization (Rai, 1995; Zmud, 1982). Accordingly, the objectives of this chapter are to:

- ⬥ Profile the current adoption of EIS_c and EIS_d in U.S. organizations,
- ⬥ Investigate contextual differences between adopters and nonadopters of EIS_c and EIS_d, and

⋄ Investigate the relationships between contextual factors and the adoption levels of EIS_c and EIS_d.

The remainder of our chapter is organized as follows. First, we present the theoretical foundations of the study and outline the conceptual framework. Second, the research model is presented along with the research hypotheses. Third, we provide the details of our empirical study and statistical analysis. Fourth, we interpret our results and discuss their implications. Finally, we conclude by suggesting some grounds for future research.

Theoretical Foundations

Dependent Variables: Adoption Status and Adoption Level

Innovation theory has been a popular theoretical basis for researchers investigating the adoption of information technology (IT) in organizations (Grover, 1993; Grover & Goslar, 1993; Huff & Munro, 1985; Rai, 1995; Zmud, 1982, 1984a, 1984b). The process of organization innovation can be defined as the adoption of an internally generated or purchased device, system, policy, program, process, product, or service that is new to the adopting organization (Daft, 1982; Damanpour & Evans, 1984). In general, adopters and nonadopters are differentiated using a binary measure that assesses whether or not any resource commitments have been made toward the innovation. We define an organization as having adopted EIS_c or EIS_d if these systems have been developed and installed for at least one executive. Nonadopters of EIS_c and EIS_d do not support any of their executives with these systems. The adoption status of EIS_c and EIS_d classifies an organization as either an adopter or a nonadopter.

Examining the discontinuity from nonadoption to adoption can provide useful insights about the factors that trigger initial adoption. It is necessary to complement this by understanding why adopter organizations differ in their levels of adoption. Some organizations may have one or a few executives supported by EIS_c and EIS_d capabilities, while other organizations may have a significant majority of their executives supported by these technologies. The level of adoption of EIS_c and EIS_d is defined as the proportion of executives supported by these systems.

Independent Variables: Selection of Contextual Variables

Several variable categories have been proposed to influence organizational adoption of innovations. Based on their synthesis of the past literature, Kwon and Zmud (1987) identified five variable categories that should influence IT innovations. These include user characteristics, environmental characteristics, organizational characteristics, technology characteristics, and task characteristics. We focus specifically on environmental characteristics and organizational characteristics, and include an additional factor called IS characteristics.

Past studies in organizational innovation (Kimberly & Evanisko, 1981; Utterback, 1974), strategic management (Miller & Friesen, 1982), information systems (Lederer & Mendelow, 1990), and diffusion of IT innovations (Grover & Goslar, 1993) emphasized the importance of studying the impact of the environment on key organizational capabilities. Organizations operating in different environments have to manage information of differing natures and complexity. It is conceivable that environmental characteristics create a "pull" for EIS, and we specifically examine the relationship between environmental uncertainty and EIS adoption. The underlying rationale is that uncertain environments are likely to require more effective and efficient management of information. Given the focus of EIS, it could be viewed as more useful by organizations operating in such contexts.

Organizational factors are believed to influence innovations in organizations. Popular variables in this category include centralization, formalization, specialization, information sources, leadership, and organization size. However, conclusive results were most likely obtained only when "researchers extended diffusion theory to account for new factors specific to the IT context under study" (Fichman, 1992, p. 195). We focus on top management support and organization size. Top management support may well be among the critical factors that influence the level of EIS adoption within organizations. Innovation studies have reported a positive association between top management support and innovation behavior observed in organizations (Kimberly & Evanisko, 1981; Meyer & Goes, 1988). Top management support may be important from a resource standpoint. Further, political support from top management can ameliorate resistance from vested interest groups. Similarly, a majority of past studies in innovation suggest that organizational size should positively influence the capability of organizations to adopt innovations. The common rationale provided is that larger organizations typically have "more" resources to absorb the costs associated with the adoption of innovations. The EIS literature also suggests that larger organizations are more likely to adopt EIS as compared to smaller organizations (Rockart & DeLong, 1988). Therefore, we also examine the relationship between organization size and the level of EIS adoption.

We include an additional category of IS factors that are likely to influence EIS adoption behavior. There is some empirical support that IS factors are critical for the propagation of IT innovations (Grover & Goslar, 1993). The two IS factors considered here include IS support and IS department (ISD) size. Appropriate support from internal sources, such as competent in-house IS staff, can accelerate learning processes and rapidly reduce knowledge barriers associated with the deployment of complex information technology innovations (Attewell, 1992). In the context of EIS, IS support can assist in the propagation of EIS (Watson et al., 1995). As in the case of organization size, ISD size may well determine the availability of technical resources that can create a momentum for EIS adoption in organizations.

Thus, we focus on five contextual variables in investigating organizational adoption of EIS. Three of these variables, namely, environmental uncertainty, organization size, and ISD size, are proposed to differ between adopters and nonadopters and promote the level of EIS adoption. The remaining two variables, top management support and IS support, are proposed to influence EIS adoption levels.

Research Model and Hypotheses

Based upon the above discussion, the research model is shown in Figure 9.1. The dependent variables are the adoption status and adoption levels of EIS_c and EIS_d. The contextual variables considered include environmental characteristics (uncertainty); organizational characteristics (top management support, organization size); and IS characteristics (IS support and ISD size).

Environmental Uncertainty

Environmental uncertainty exists due to forces in the firm's external environment. Miller and Friesen (1982) identified three external forces that contribute to environmental uncertainty: dynamism, heterogeneity, and hostility. Dynamism refers to the turbulence in an organization's external environment; heterogeneity refers to the complexities in the environment; and hostility refers to the competitive pressures faced by the organization. In one of the earlier efforts to study computer-based information systems for executives, Rockart and Treacy (1982) claimed that computer-based support for executives was increasing because "volatile competitive conditions heighten the desire among top executives for ever more timely information and analysis." Seven years later, Gulden and Ewers (1989) noted that EIS were

> becoming key tools in the executive arsenal. In this era of reorganization, mergers and acquisitions, turbulent markets and increasing competition, managers now more than ever need more effective ways to understand their markets and their competition and guide their operations and their people. (p. 91)

Watson et al. (1991) noted that competitive environments, rapidly changing external environments, and the need to be proactive in dealing with the external environment are among the main reasons for developing EIS. As the researchers suggest, the external pressures for EIS usually come from changing raw material costs, increased competition, and increased regulatory pressures from the government.

Accordingly, we hypothesize that:

> H1a: Firms that have adopted EIS_c face a higher level of environmental uncertainty than nonadopters.

Adopting Executive Information Systems 211

```
┌──────────────────┐                                    ┌──────────────────────┐
│ Organization Size│────────────────────┐               │ Top Management Support│
└──────────────────┘                    │               └──────────────────────┘
                       ┌────────────────┴──┐    ┌──────────────────────┐
          ┌──────────▶│ EIS Adoption Status│───▶│ EIS Adoption Level   │◀──┌─────────┐
┌────────┐│           │ for                │    │ for                  │   │ ISD Size│
│ISD Size│┘           │ • Collaboration    │    │ • Collaboration      │   └─────────┘
└────────┘            │   Support          │    │   Support            │
        │             │ • Decision Support │    │ • Decision Support   │
        │             └────────────────────┘    └──────────────────────┘
        │                       ▲                          ▲
        │                       │                          │        ┌──────────┐
┌──────────────────────┐        │                          │        │ IS Support│
│Environmental Uncertainty│─────┘──────────────────────────┘        └──────────┘
└──────────────────────┘
```

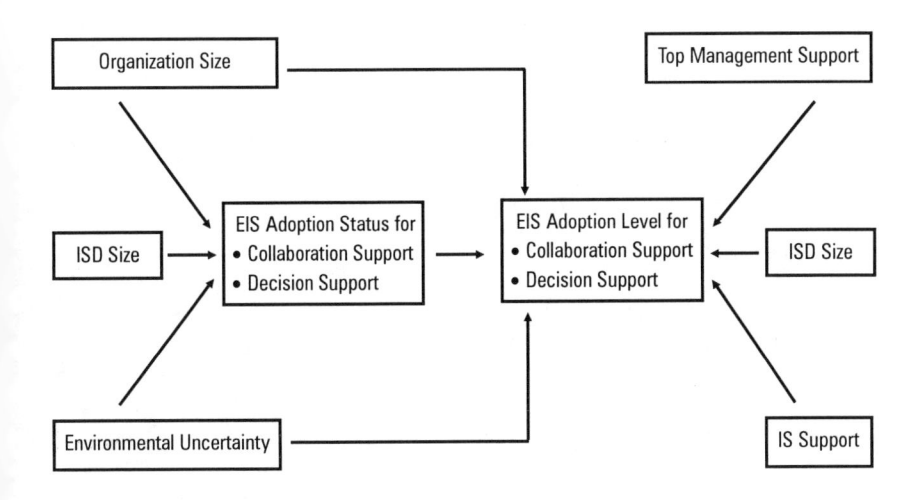

Figure 9.1. The research model

H1b: Firms that have adopted EIS_d face a higher level of environmental uncertainty than nonadopters.

H2a: There is a positive relationship between environmental uncertainty and the adoption level of EIS_c.

H2b: There is a positive relationship between environmental uncertainty and the adoption level of EIS_d.

Organizational Characteristics

Organization Size

The effect of organization size on the propagation of IT innovations has produced inconclusive results. Some researchers have suggested that organization size has a positive impact on IS success (Ein-Dor & Segev, 1978; Raymond, 1990). In other instances, no direct relationship has been found between organization size and IS success (Gremillion, 1984; Raymond, 1985). However, for the most part, the EIS literature seems to suggest a positive relationship between organization size and adoption of the technology (Paller & Laska, 1990; Rockart & De Long, 1988). The rationale provided include: (1) larger organizations have more executives, who are spatially dispersed, thereby leading to a greater need for a sophisticated information technology infrastructure for communication and coordination; (2) the complexity of larger organizations leads to a greater need for information infrastructures that can improve managerial control and planning systems; and (3) larger organizations are more likely to be able to afford the costs of innovation. Given the balance of literature and existing evidence, we hypothesize that:

H3a: Larger organizations are more likely to adopt EIS_c than smaller organizations.
H3b: Larger organizations are more likely to adopt EIS_d than smaller organizations.
H4a: There is a positive relationship between organization size and the adoption level of EIS_c.
H4b: There is a positive relationship between organization size and the adoption level of EIS_d.

Top Management Support

Top management support refers to the extent to which EIS efforts are promoted by the top/corporate management of the firm. The importance of top management support for MIS implementation is widely accepted in the literature. As Jarvenpaa and Ives (1991) stated: "Few nostrums have been prescribed so religiously and ignored as regularly as executive support in the development and implementation of management information systems (MIS)" (p. 205).

The importance of top management support for EIS adoption has been voiced by both practitioners and researchers. Major suggestions include locking in support from a politically secure senior executive in the early phases of development, involving senior executives in information requirements specification phases (Rinaldi & Jastrzembski, 1986a, 1986b), and obtaining commitment from a member of the top management who is willing to oversee development activities (Houdeshel & Watson, 1987; Rockart & De Long, 1988). McNamara, Danziger, and Barton (1990) also noted that top management must get involved in EIS efforts to avoid development of unrealistic applications. Thus, we hypothesize that:

H5a: There is a positive relationship between top management support and the adoption level of EIS_c.
H5b: There is a positive relationship between top management support and the adoption level of EIS_d.

IS Characteristics

ISD Size

The relationship between ISD size and adoption of IT innovations has not received much attention among IS researchers. Nevertheless, ISD size is likely to have a significant impact on the adoption of emerging IT innovations. For example, Rai (1995) found that ISD size had a significant impact on the propagation of CASE technology in U.S. organizations. Since large ISDs present more options for organizing innovation efforts by drawing upon their resources and technical skills (Fuller & Swanson, 1992), they are likely to better support EIS innovation efforts. Therefore, we hypothesize that:

H6a: Organizations with larger ISDs are more likely to adopt EIS_c than organizations with smaller ISDs.
H6b: Organizations with larger ISDs are more likely to adopt EIS_d than organizations with smaller ISDs.
H7a: There is a positive relationship between ISD size and the adoption level of EIS_c.
H7b: There is a positive relationship between ISD size and the adoption level of EIS_d.

IS Support

IS support refers to the extent of involvement of the IS function in an organization's EIS efforts. Rockart and De Long (1988) observed that appropriate IS staff can play an important role in facilitating EIS adoption and suggested that:

> If systems (EIS) are to be used by a broad range of executives and have wide impact on the organization, their chances for success are greater when developed by a mainstream IS team working with a strong operating sponsor. (p. 175)

However, Rockart and De Long also noted that all EIS need not be developed with high involvement from the mainstream IS function of the organization. Others have reported that an increasing number of ISDs are getting involved in the development of EIS by actively communicating the potential benefits of such systems to senior executives (Volonino & Drinkard, 1989). In some organizations, IS personnel are, in fact, taking a lead role in developing EIS for executives (Watson et al., 1991). Involvement of IS personnel in EIS efforts is also critical as important technical expertise is needed for applications development, integration of fragmented and heterogenous databases (Barrow, 1990), and application systems maintenance (Fried, 1991; Moad, 1988). This leads us to hypothesize that:

H8a: There is a positive relationship between IS support and the adoption level of EIS_c.
H8b: There is a positive relationship between IS support and the adoption level of EIS_d.

The Empirical Study

The Sample

A survey design was adopted for the study, and questionnaires were sent to the top computer executives in 1,423 randomly selected organizations (Directory of Top Computer Executives, 1992). A cover letter explained the purpose of the study, sought cooperation for participation, and requested that the questionnaire be completed by the person most knowledgeable about EIS efforts in the organization. A follow-up questionnaire along with a reminder letter was mailed two weeks after the initial mailing.

A total of 238 questionnaires were received from 13 key industries in 42 states of the U.S., resulting in a response rate of 16.7%. Of these, 28 were discarded due to insufficient data. Table 9.2 shows the EIS adoption profile across the industries represented in our sample, and Table 9.3 highlights the respondent position profile and reported status of EIS adoption. A majority of respondents (64%) held top management positions (both IS and corporate combined), 32% were middle managers (both IS and functional management combined), and 4% belonged to lower management levels (IS and functional combined).

Of the 210 usable responses, 140 organizations (66.7%) had not adopted EIS. These respondents were not required to answer questions relating to top management support, IS support, and organizational adoption level, but did provide information on demographic and environmental variables. Seventy organizations (33.3%) had adopted some EIS capabilities to support one or more of their executives.

Response Rate and Nonresponse Bias

A low response rate of 16.7% raises concerns of possible response bias. There can be several reasons for the low response rate in our study. First, the instrument was rather long, and some questions required factual responses. Second, EIS are still in the early stages of macro-adoption across the population of potential adopters. Organizations with little or no use for EIS may have found the questionnaire "early" in timing and disregarded it for this reason. Third, the questionnaire may not have been targeted directly to the executives most knowledgeable about EIS efforts, and our request for redirection to such individuals could have resulted in misplaced surveys. Finally, our national survey approach may have lowered the response rate.

To investigate this further, we decided to compare our response rate and sample profile with other EIS studies. Toward this end, six empirical studies were identified (Benard & Satir, 1993; Fitzgerald, 1992; Leidner & Elam, 1993; Watson & Frolick, 1993; Watson et al., 1991; Watson, Rainer, & Frolick, 1992). Even though a selective sampling methodology was adopted for each of these studies, the response rates and adoption profiles of our database are comparable with past studies with the added advantage of being obtained from a large-scale national survey. Furthermore, our sample includes both adopters and nonadopters of EIS.

We also checked for commonly suggested elements of nonresponse bias in our sample. A chi-square test suggested no significant differences between the proportionate makeup of the surveys sent out and those received by industry and regional classification ($\alpha = .05$). A comparison of responses was also conducted between

TABLE 9.2 Respondent Industry Profile

Industry	Total Mailed	Returned (%)		Nonadopters	Adopters: EIS_c or EIS_d
Banking	61	4	(1.9)	3	1
Diversified finance	43	7	(3.3)	3	4
Education	144	30	(14.3)	23	7
Government					
Federal	63	7	(3.3)	2	5
State	53	8	(3.8)	3	5
Local	95	15	(7.1)	10	5
Health services	84	14	(6.7)	10	4
Insurance	59	11	(5.2)	5	6
Manufacturing	680	90	(42.9)	66	24
Retail	62	8	(3.8)	6	2
Transport	21	2	(1.0)	1	1
Utilities	41	12	(5.7)	8	4
Others	17	1	(0.5)		1
		1	(0.5)*		1*
Totals	1,423	210	(100)	140	70

*One respondent from an EIS-adopting organization did not provide industry information.

TABLE 9.3 Respondent Position Profile

Respondent Position	N = 207	Nonadopters	Adopters: EIS_c or EIS_d
IS top management (VPs, directors)	114	78	36
IS middle management (managers)	60	36	24
IS lower management (programmers and analysts)	6	2	4
Corporate management (presidents, CEOs, VPs)	18	15	3
Functional middle management (managers)	7	5	2
Lower management (branch managers, etc.)	2	1	1

"early" and "late" respondents, and no significant differences in the mean values of the study variables were observed between the two groups.

Measurement

The lack of reliable and valid measures is a source of concern with MIS empirical research (Jarvenpaa, Dickson, & DeSanctis, 1984; Sethi & King, 1991; Straub,

TABLE 9.4 Relevant References for Research Model Constructs

Constructs	References
Environmental uncertainty	Miller and Friesen (1982); Sabherwal and King (1992); Grover and Goslar (1993)
Top management support	Garrity (1963); Bean, Neal, Radnor, and Tansik (1975); Vanlommel and De Brabander (1975); Kimberly and Evanisko (1981); Meador, Guyote, and Keen (1984); Sanders and Courtney (1985); Rinaldi and Jastrzembski (1986); Houdeshel and Watson (1987); Meyer and Goes (1988); DeLone (1988); Rockart and De Long (1988); McNamara et al. (1990); Reich and Benbasat (1990); Jarvenpaa and Ives (1991)
IS support	Rockart and De Long (1988); Moad (1988); Volonino and Drinkard (1989); Paller and Laska (1990); Barrow (1990); Watson et al. (1991); Fried (1991)
Organization size	Utterback (1974); Ein-Dor and Segev (1978); Kimberly and Evanisko (1981); Gremillion (1984); Raymond (1985, 1990); Rockart and De Long (1988); Meyer and Goes (1988); Paller and Laska (1990); Watson et al. (1991)
ISD size	Fuller and Swanson (1992); Rai (1995)

1989). Using guidelines suggested by Straub and Sethi and King, a three-phase instrument development process was undertaken. In the first phase, a thorough review of the innovation, IT implementation, and EIS literatures was conducted to identify studies in which similar variables had been theoretically dealt with or operationalized. Where existing measures were not available, a list of items characterizing the variable under investigation was generated using the literature reviewed. Table 9.4 shows the relevant references from the literature for each of our study variables.

In the second phase, a group interview was conducted with the executive sponsor at a leading computer leasing firm where EIS is used by several executives, and with faculty members actively involved in EIS research. The discussion was semistructured and focused on whether items formulated in the first phase appropriately measured the study variables. Based on the input received, some modifications were made to the instrument.

As part of the third phase, which can be characterized as the pilot study, key members of the EIS development team in six organizations were contacted and asked to participate in an interview. All six agreed, and interviews were conducted with these individuals at their respective organization sites. On average, each interview lasted for about an hour. Participants were asked to provide comments on the appropriateness and clarity of questionnaire items. Appropriate changes were made prior to the national mailing. The questionnaire items for each of the multi-item scales are included in the Appendix. We now describe each of the operational measures used, including a discussion of their reliability and validity.

Dependent Variables

Respondents were asked to indicate the proportion of key executives/managers for whom EIS applications had been developed and installed to support each of the four managerial functions of communication, coordination, control, and planning. The proportion of executives/managers were ordinally anchored on a 5-point scale as follows: 0 (*none*), 1 (*one*), 2 (*few*), 3 (*many*), and 4 (*most*). Popular applications that support each of these functions were included as illustrative examples. Responses to these questions (shown in the Appendix) were used as a basis to compute the scores for each of the dependent variables. Table 9.5a summarizes the measures for each of the dependent variables.

Adoption Status

Dichotomous measures were defined to classify organizations as adopters and non-adopters of EIS_c and EIS_d. Each organization was assigned scores to represent its adoption status for EIS_c (1 [*adopter*] and 0 [*nonadopter*]) and EIS_d (1 [*adopter*] and 0 [*nonadopter*]). An organization was classified as an adopter of EIS_c if it had installed applications to support communication or coordination functions for at least one of their executives. Similarly, organizations that had installed applications to support control and planning functions for one or more executives were classified as EIS_d adopters.

Adoption Level

Variations in the EIS adoption level among organizations was captured using two measures. The first measure assessed the adoption level for EIS_c, and the second gauged the adoption level for EIS_d. EIS_c adoption level was assessed as the sum of the indicated proportion of executives for whom EIS applications had been developed and installed to support communication and coordination. Similarly, EIS_d adoption level was measured by summing the indicated proportion of executives for whom EIS applications had been developed and installed to support control and planning.

A factor analysis of EIS adoption levels for each of the four managerial functions resulted in a two-factor solution (Table 9.5b). EIS adoption levels for managerial communication and coordination loaded on one factor, while EIS adoption levels for managerial control and planning loaded on the second factor. This two-factor solution corroborates our conceptual distinction between EIS for collaboration support (Factor 1) and EIS for decision support (Factor 2).

218 EMERGING INFORMATION TECHNOLOGIES

TABLE 9.5 Definition and Measures of EIS Adoption

a. Measures of EIS Adoption

	EIS for Collaboration Support	EIS for Decision Support
Adoption status	Dichotomous measure. Organizations that had developed and installed EIS applications to support communication or coordination for one or more executives classified as adopters. The others are classified as nonadopters.	Dichotomous measure. Organizations that had developed and installed EIS applications to support control or planning for one or more executives classified as adopters. The others are classified as nonadopters.
Adoption level	Ordinal measure with a range of 2-10. Sum of the indicated proportion of executives for whom EIS applications had been developed and installed to support communication and coordination.	Ordinal measure with a range of 2-10. Sum of the indicated proportion of executives for whom EIS applications had been developed and installed to support control and planning.

b. Factor Analysis Results of EIS Adoption Level

Factors and Items (N = 70)	Loadings
Factor 1: Adoption level of EIS for collaboration support (Eigenvalue = 1.71)	
1. Applications supporting communications	.85
2. Applications supporting coordination	.83
Factor 2: Adoption level of EIS for decision support (Eigenvalue = 1.14)	
1. Applications supporting control	.86
2. Applications supporting planning	.79

Independent Variables

Environmental Uncertainty

Miller and Friesen's (1982) view of an organization's external environment properties was adopted to measure environmental uncertainty. Specifically, dynamism, heterogeneity, and hostility of an organization's environment were assessed using a total of 14 items. As all respondents provided information on environmental uncertainty, 210 observations were used to validate the factor structure of these items. Nunnally (1978) suggested that items should be dropped if they exhibit low item-total correlations as these items reduce the internal consistency of the measurement scale. Three items had low item-total correlations and were accordingly dropped from further analysis. One item was part of the dynamism scale, while the other two items were part of the hostility scale.

Stewart (1981) suggested that Bartlett's test of sphericity and the Kaiser-Meyer-Olin measure of sampling adequacy (MSA) should be examined to assess whether or not a set of variables is appropriate for factor analysis. Bartlett's test assesses whether the correlation matrix comes from a population of variables that are independent. As expected, the null hypothesis of variable independence for the 11 items was rejected at a level of significance of .000. MSA provides a measure of the extent to which variables belong together. Kaiser and Rice (1974) provided a calibration of the MSA measure, and they classified a value of .90+ as "marvelous" and .80+ as "meritorious." Our MSA measure was .884 and suggested that the 11 items were appropriate for factor analysis.

A principal component factor analysis followed by a varimax rotation was conducted on the 11 items. This resulted in the expected three-factor structure (Table 9.6a) suggested by Miller and Friesen (1982) and recently validated by Sabherwal and King (1992) and Grover and Goslar (1993). A second-order factor analysis was conducted using the item means for the dynamism, hostility, and heterogeneity scales, and the expected one-factor solution representing environmental uncertainty was obtained (Table 9.6b). This factor captures approximately 70% of the total variance represented by the three items. The Cronbach's alpha measure for internal consistency was computed to be .78 for environmental uncertainty.

Top Management Support

The three-phase instrument development process yielded a six-item measure for top management support. A 7-point Likert type scale, ranging from *strongly disagree* to *strongly agree,* was used for each of these items. Bartlett's test for sphericity led to a rejection of the null hypothesis of variable independence at a level of significance of .000. The measure of sampling adequacy was computed to be .79 and suggested that the items were appropriate for factor analysis. Principal component factor analysis resulted in a one-factor solution that explained 61% of the total variance represented by the six items (see Table 9.7).

The item-total correlations indicated no sudden drops, providing evidence of homogeneity among the items, and a Cronbach's alpha value of .87 reveals a high level of internal consistency among the measurement items.

Organization Size

The number of employees was used as a measure of organization size. This measure has been used in other studies on organizational innovation (Kimberley & Evanisko, 1981; Meyer & Goes, 1988) and IS innovation (Rai, 1995; Zmud, 1982). Given large variations in organization size, and consistent with previous studies, the

TABLE 9.6 Factor Analysis Result of External Environment Uncertainty

a. First-Order Factor Analysis

Factors and Items (N = 199)	Loadings
Factor 1: Environment dynamism (eigenvalue = 5.02)	
1. Changes in marketing practices	.70
2. Rate of product/service obsolescence	.66
3. Prediction of competitor actions	.60
4. Prediction of demand and consumer tastes	.74
5. Changes in product/service technology	.71
Factor 2: Environment heterogeneity (eigenvalue = 1.07)	
Differences among product/services due to:	
1. Customer buying habits	.84
2. Nature of competition	.82
3. Market dynamism and uncertainty	.74
Factor 3: Environment hostility (eigenvalue = 1.01)	
Threat of survival due to:	
1. Tough price competition	.68
2. Competition in product quality	.76
3. Dwindling markets for products	.71

b. Second-Order Factor Analysis

Factors and Items (N = 199)	Loadings
Factor 1: Environmental uncertainty (eigenvalue = 2.12)	
1. Environment dynamism	.85
2. Environment heterogeneity	.85
3. Environment hostility	.82

z scores of the natural logarithm of organization size were computed and used in subsequent analysis.

ISD Size

One objective item was used to assess the number of full-time employees as a measure of ISD size. Similar measures have been used by Nilakanta and Scamell (1990), Fuller and Swanson (1992), and Rai (1995). As with organization size, the

TABLE 9.7 Factor Analysis of Top Management Support and IS Support Variables

Factor and Items	Loadings
Top management support (eigenvalue = 3.6645, N = 68)	
1. Executive sponsor(s) participation in EIS development	.7385
2. Top management contact with sponsor on EIS-related issues	.8019
3. Resource support for EIS	.7340
4. Top management perception of importance of EIS	.8209
5. Top management's constructive feedback on EIS application	.7881
6. EIS regarded as high priority by top management	.8015
IS management support (eigenvalue = 3.8696, N = 65)	
1. IS executive participation in EIS development	.7647
2. IS cooperation in identifying data sources	.8535
3. IS cooperation in resolving technical problems	.9203
4. IS accept accountability for EIS	.6621
5. Communication between IS and top management on role of EIS	.8154
6. High IS involved in development	.7786

z scores of the natural logarithm of ISD size were computed and used in subsequent analysis.

IS Support

The three-phase instrument development process yielded a six-item measure for IS support. As with top management support, a 7-point Likert-type scale that ranged from *strongly disagree* to *strongly agree* was used for each of the items. Bartlett's test for sphericity led to a rejection of the null hypothesis of variable independence at a level of significance of .000. The measure of sampling adequacy was computed to be .85 and suggested that the items were appropriate for factor analysis. Principal component factor analysis resulted in a one-factor solution that explained 64.5% of the total variance represented by the six items (see Table 9.7). There were no sudden drops in the item-total correlations, and a Cronbach's alpha value of .89 suggests a high level of internal consistency among measurement items.

Summary of Psychometric Properties

Venkatraman and Grant (1986) recommended that survey instruments used for research should use scales (1) with multiple, higher level items rather than single, nominal items; (2) that are internally consistent; and (3) that are valid. The measures for environmental characteristics were adopted from previous research, while the measures for top management support for EIS and IS support were developed for this study. Interviews with practicing senior managers and the subsequent pretest ensured the appropriateness of measurement items employed for each of the variables. Factor analysis of measurement items resulted in expected factor structures providing evidence of measurement validity. The intercorrelations between independent variables and their reliability values are summarized in Table 9.8.

Analysis and Results

Differences Between Adopters and Nonadopters

Table 9.9 presents some demographic data about respondents. Fifty-nine organizations had adopted EIS_c for one or more of their executives, while 54 organizations had adopted EIS_d. Analysis of variance was used to test hypothesized differences in the mean values for environmental uncertainty across adopter and nonadopter groups for both EIS_c and EIS_d. Given the low correlation between organization size and environmental uncertainty, and no significant correlation between ISD size and environmental uncertainty, it was appropriate to use ANOVA as opposed to MANOVA. The results of the ANOVA tests summarized in Table 9.10 provide strong support for differences in environmental uncertainty between adopters and nonadopters, suggesting that organizations that have adopted EIS_c or EIS_d face higher levels of environmental uncertainty than their nonadopting counterparts. The risk of a Type I error is .031 for differences in environmental uncertainty between adopters and nonadopters of EIS_c and .02 for EIS_d.

The bivariate correlation matrix (see Table 9.8) shows a moderate correlation between organization size and ISD size. We would have liked ideally to use MANOVA to examine differences in size-related variables between adopting and nonadopting organizations. However, missing data on one variable leads to a loss of the entire case. We did not consider it appropriate to use approaches such as mean substitution for missing data as these approaches are typically less conservative. While 53 and 40 organizations had missing values for organization size and ISD size, respectively, 80 organizations had missing data on at least one of these variables. Given the nature of this missing data, we would have faced significant sample attrition if we decided to proceed with the use of MANOVA. Accordingly, ANOVA was used to test size-related differences between adopters and nonadopters of EIS_c and EIS_d.

The mean differences in organization size and ISD size between adopters and nonadopters, as detected by ANOVA analysis and directional t tests, are also summarized in Table 9.10. Organization size was not found to significantly differ between adopters and nonadopters for either EIS_c or EIS_d. While ISD size was not found to significantly differ between adopters and nonadopters of EIS_c, significant differences were observed between adopters and nonadopters of EIS_d. Organizations adopting EIS_d were found to have significantly larger ISDs than nonadopting organizations.

TABLE 9.8 Descriptive Statistics and Intercorrelations

Independent Variables	n	Mean	SD	Standard Alpha	Environmental Uncertainty	Organization Size	ISD Size	Top Management Support	IS Support
Environmental uncertainty	201	15.17	4.16	.78	1.00				
Organization size (employees)	157	5482	172267		.21*	1.00			
Natural log of organization size	157	7.01	1.75						
ISD size (employees)	172	53.06	75.51						
Natural log of ISD size	170	3.26	1.22			.41**	1.00		
Top management support	65	27.17	8.84	.87				1.00	
IS support	65	32.65	8.01	.89			−.27*	.41**	1.00

Natural Logarithm

*$p < .10$ (two-tailed levels of significance); **$p < .05$.

TABLE 9.9 Sample Profile—Adopters and Nonadopters

	Applications Developed and Installed		
Type of EIS Support	No	Yes	Missing
EIS_c (collaboration support)	145	59	6
EIS_d (decision support)	151	54	5

TABLE 9.10 Mean Comparisons Between Adopters and Nonadopters

	Adopters vs. Nonadopters of EIS for Collaboration Support			Adopters vs. Nonadopters of EIS for Decision Support		
	F	p*	n	F	p	n
Environment uncertainty	3.52	.031	204	9.97	.002	205
Natural log of ISD size	1.85	.085	165	4.26	.020	165
Natural log of firm size	.05	.415	152	.24	.313	153

*As we have developed directional hypotheses, the reported significance values are for one-tailed, directional *t* tests.

Relationships Between Contextual Variables and Adoption Level

The measures of adoption level for EIS_c and EIS_d assess the proportion of executives who have been provided collaboration support and decision support capabilities. These measures are designed to assess the degree of propagation of these technologies within organizations classified as having "adopted" them. Table 9.11 shows that the mean adoption level for EIS_c is significantly higher than that for EIS_d, providing evidence that the propagation of EIS_d may be facing greater challenges, and possibly different challenges, than the propagation of EIS_c.

Table 9.12 summarizes the bivariate correlations between the adoption levels of EIS_c and EIS_d and each of the contextual variables. Three of the independent variables (environmental uncertainty, top management support, and IS organization support) correlated significantly with the adoption level of EIS_c. All five contextual variables correlated significantly with the adoption level of EIS_d.

Multiple regression analyses were used to test the hypotheses associating the contextual variables with the adoption levels of EIS_c and EIS_d. As discussed earlier, missing data constrained us from including organization size and ISD size as part of the regression models. For each of the two regression analyses, violations of linearity, normality, and homoscedasticity were carefully examined. Standardized residuals plots and case-wise outlier statistics (Mahalonobis distance, Cook's D, and leverage) suggested that some observations were leading to significant violations of

TABLE 9.11 Sample Profile: Level of Adoption

	Descriptive Statistics				
Type of EIS Support	Range	Mean	SD	Min	Max
EIS_c (collaboration support) [n = 59]	1-8	5.83	1.90	2	8
EIS_d (decision support) [n = 54]	1-8	4.13	1.83	1	8

TABLE 9.12 Zero-Order Correlations: Independent With Dependent Variables

	EIS Adoption Level			
Independent Variables	EIS_c (Collaboration support)		EIS_d (Decision support)	
Environment uncertainty	.19*	(59)	.27**	(54)
Natural log of organization size	n.s.	(46)	.28**	(43)
Natural log of ISD size	n.s.	(45)	.33**	(42)
Top management support	.29**	(58)	.22**	(53)
IS support	.25**	(58)	.17*	(53)

NOTE: n = Numbers in parentheses.
*$p \leq .10$; **$p \leq .05$.

these assumptions. Accordingly, problematic observations were deleted, and the remainder of the sample closely met the required assumptions for regression analysis. In the regression analyses for both EIS_c and EIS_d, there were adequate observations as both models have three independent variables.

Table 9.13a summarizes the results of the regression analysis between adoption level of EIS_c and environmental uncertainty, top management support, and IS support. The overall model is found to be significant with a low risk of a Type I error (p = .0003). An adjusted R-square of 29% suggests that variations in levels of adoption of EIS_c are substantially explained by the model. Interestingly, top management support is the only independent variable that emerges as significant. The regression results provide strong support for the importance of top management support in propagating the level of EIS_c adoption within an organization.

Table 9.13b summarizes the results of the regression analysis between adoption level of EIS_d and environmental uncertainty, top management support, and IS support. The overall model is again found to be significant with a low risk of a Type I error (p = .0004). The model has an adjusted R-square of 34%, suggesting that variations in levels of adoption of EIS_d are substantially explained by the three independent variables. All three independent variables emerge as highly significant.

The regression analyses support the hypotheses associating top management support with the adoption level of EIS_c and EIS_d. Our analyses also supported the

TABLE 9.13 Regression Analysis Results

a. **Adoption Level of EIS$_c$**

	df	Sum of Squares	Mean Square
Regression	3	39.12	13.04
Residual	46	78.10	1.70

$F = 7.68$ Significance of $F = 0.0003$

Independent Variables	Standardized Beta	T	$p <$
Environment uncertainty	.12	.93	.18
Top management support	.53	4.02	.00
IS support	.04	.32	.37

R-square: 0.33, Adjusted R-square = 0.29

b: **Adoption Level of EIS$_d$**

	df	Sum of Squares	Mean Square
Regression	3	40.79	13.60
Residual	37	63.99	1.73

$F = 7.86$, Significance of $F = 0.0004$

Independent Variables	Standardized Beta	T	$p <$
Environment uncertainty	.40	3.09	.002
Top management support	.28	2.04	.024
IS support	.29	2.14	.020

R-square: 0.39 Adjusted R-square = 0.34

hypotheses associating environmental uncertainty and IS support with the adoption level of EIS$_d$. However, the hypotheses associating environmental uncertainty and IS support with the adoption level of EIS$_c$ are not supported.

Although size-related hypotheses could not be included in the regression analyses due to reasons mentioned earlier, the bivariate correlations between the independent variables and adoption levels of EIS$_c$ and EIS$_d$ (see Table 9.12) indicate that both organization size and ISD size correlated significantly with level of adoption of EIS$_d$. Thus, there is support for hypotheses associating organization size and ISD size with level of adoption of EIS$_d$ and no support for hypotheses associating organization size and ISD size with level of adoption of EIS$_c$. As we did not include the size-related variables in the multiple regression analyses, we do not assess whether ISD size and organization size are significantly related to adoption level of EIS_d in the presence of other contextual variables.

Statistical Interpretation of Insignificant Results

Cohen (1988) noted a broadly prevalent problem in the application of classical statistical inference by researchers in many fields. The lack of significance is often interpreted as lack of any effect, and the researcher springs into a trap of de facto sustaining the null hypotheses. Baroudi and Orlikowski (1989) forcefully reiterated this in the context of MIS research and pointed out that most empirical studies in the field have made similar erroneous conclusions. In addition to the probability of a false positive (a Type I error), it is important to guard against false negatives, or the probability of a Type II error.

Given that statistical analysis for large effects is purely a process of "statistical sanctification" (Cohen, 1988), we examined the power of our insignificant results under assumptions of small and medium effects. The same standards of small and medium effect sizes suggested by Cohen and used by Baroudi and Orlikowski (1989) to evaluate the power of MIS empirical research were adopted.

Since we are dealing with unequal samples, the harmonic mean was used as the effective sample size in power computations for the insignificant ANOVA results. The level of significance was fixed at .10 for these directional tests. Our values for power, under assumptions of small or medium effects, compare favorably with those compiled and reported by Baroudi and Orlikowski (1989). The mean of organization size was insignificant between adopters and nonadopters of both EIS_c and EIS_d. ISD size was insignificant between adopters and nonadopters of EIS_c. These three tests have high power levels (.80) at the .4 and .5 effect size levels. While we cannot state that adopters and nonadopters do not differ in these aspects, we are in a position to state that if size differences do exist between these groups, they are, in fact, small.

Correlation analyses were used to assess the relationships between ISD size and organization size with the adoption levels of EIS_c and EIS_d. No significant correlations were detected between either of the size variables and the adoption level of EIS_c. The power of these two tests have high values ranging from .67 for a medium effect size (.3) to .98 for a large effect size (.5). Here again, we are in a position to state that if the two size-related variables correlate with the adoption level of EIS_c, the strength of these associations is, in fact, very small.

Only top management support was found to be significant in the regression model associating the contextual variables and adoption level of EIS_c. Accordingly, we assessed the power of the F test, which compared the variation in EIS_c explained uniquely by environmental uncertainty and IS support relative to top management support. Essentially, we partialed out the variance in the adoption level of EIS_c explained by top management support and then assessed the additional variance in adoption level of EIS_c explained by environmental uncertainty and IS support. The power of the test rejecting additional variance explanation by IS support and environmental uncertainty is greater than .95 when the risk of a Type I error is fixed at .05.

Discussion

Based on a review of the literature, we observed that there were two different facets of EIS support, and accordingly, it was considered useful to make a distinction between EIS applications targeted at providing collaboration support (EIS_c) and decision support (EIS_d). This section is organized to address the three objectives of the study. First, we focus on the current adoption profile of EIS_c and EIS_d in U.S. organizations. Second, we focus on the differences in environmental, organizational, and IS factors between adopters and nonadopters of EIS_c and EIS_d. Third, we discuss the relationships between environmental, organizational, and IS factors and the levels of adoption of EIS_c and EIS_d.

Adoption Profile

Our results suggest that EIS have not been widely adopted. Overall, only a third of our sample had adopted either EIS_C or EIS_d. Fifty-nine firms had adopted EIS_C, while 54 firms had adopted EIS_d to support at least one of their executives. Our analysis suggests that the adoption levels of EIS applications vary significantly, with EIS_C being more widely adopted than EIS_d. Determining the information requirements for managerial decision making is complex and difficult to identify. Rapley (1993) observed that current EIS efforts in organizations may not be based on an understanding of the complex information needs of executives. Developments in technology and development approaches should better align the capabilities of EIS_d systems with the information characteristics of managerial decision-making environments.

Differences Between Adopters and Nonadopters

Table 9.14 shows the summary of results and the hypotheses that were supported by our statistical analyses. Strong support was found for hypotheses (H1a and H2a) relating increases in environmental uncertainty with the transition from a state of nonadoption to one of adoption for both EIS_C and EIS_d. Environmental uncertainty increases the velocity, variety, and intensity of information that organizations, including executives, need to process. Thus, organizations in more uncertain environments are more likely to face a greater "pull" for EIS, because it could be viewed as a possible means to enhance the information-processing capabilities of their executives.

H3a and H3b were not supported as no significant differences in firm size were detected between adopters and nonadopters of either EIS_C or EIS_d. The traditional

TABLE 9.14 Summary of Statistical Analyses

	Mean Comparisons Between Adopters and Nonadopters		Correlation Analyses*** Level of Adoption		Regression Analyses Level of Adoption	
	EIS_c	EIS_d	EIS_c	EIS_d	EIS_c [Adj. R^2 = .29]	EIS_d [Adj. R^2 = .34]
Environment uncertainty	H1a**	H1b**	*	**	H2a (n.s.)	H2b**
Organization size	H3a (n.s.)	H3b (n.s.)	H4a (n.s.)	H4b**	Missing data—variables not included in regression analyses	
ISD size	H6a*	H6b**	H7a (n.s.)	H7b**		
Top management support	N/A		**	**	H5a**	H5b**
IS support	N/A		**	*	H8a (n.s.)	H8b**

NOTE: n.s. = not significant.
*$p \leq .10$; **$p \leq .05$; ***We use correlation analyses to assess the relationships between size-related variables and adoption levels of EIS_c and EIS_d. Due to the nature of missing data, these variables were not included in the multiple regression analyses.

229

notion that EIS were suitable for large firms seems to be waning. Clearly, the evolution of EIS from a control-oriented technology to one that encompasses collaboration and decision support capabilities makes the technology a viable option for large, mid-sized, and small organizations. The emergence of relatively inexpensive products has made EIS more accessible to smaller firms.

While no significant differences were detected in ISD size between adopters and nonadopters of EIS_c, adopters of EIS_d had larger ISD size than nonadopters. Thus, hypothesis H6a is not supported, while H6b is supported. Why is it that significant differences were detected between adopters and nonadopters of EIS_d but not between adopters and nonadopters of EIS_c? We suggest that EIS_d is likely to require intensive IS resources for requirements determination, data integration from disparate functional databases, systems development, enhancement, and maintenance. The technology for EIS_c is relatively standardized, and minimal in situ development of the technology needs to be undertaken.

Level of EIS Adoption

Our analysis suggests a significant relationship between environmental uncertainty and the level of adoption of EIS_d, but not with the adoption level of EIS_c, thereby providing support for H2b and no support for H2a. Thus, environmental uncertainty provides the impetus to shift from a state of nonadoption to adoption for both EIS_c and EIS_d, and promotes the propagation of EIS_d through the organization. It appears that organizations operating in uncertain environments will provide (or will be demanded by their executives to provide!) EIS_d capabilities to a larger number of their executives so as to improve their access to timely and accurate information. Information search tools incorporated in an EIS can alert executives to specific situations, and by identifying patterns of activities, executives can be better supported to respond to changing conditions in the environment.

Significant relationships between top management support and level of adoption of EIS_c and EIS_d were detected, thereby supporting H5a and H5b. The literature strongly supports the notion that top management support is critical for successful EIS efforts (Houdeshel & Watson, 1987; Rinaldi & Jastrzembski, 1986a, 1986b; Rockart & De Long, 1988). As noted by Rainer and Watson (1995): "The most important variables affecting the (EIS) development process are those that the executives provide through their leadership and continued involvement in the development process" (p. 97). EIS_c capabilities help executives to better communicate with stakeholders and coordinate their activities with others. EIS_d capabilities allow executives to aggregate and disaggregate information, explore relationships between different operational variables, and present information in meaningful formats. Such capabilities can assist executives to enhance their mental models of their organization's activities. It is not very surprising, therefore, that EIS efforts strongly supported by top management will lead to higher levels of organizational adoption.

Our regression analyses suggest that IS support is positively related to the adoption level of EIS_d but not EIS_c. Thus, H8b was supported, while H8a was not supported. The relative standardization of collaboration technologies may make it easier to spread across executives in comparison with applications targeted at supporting decision processes of executives. Decisional information needs vary significantly across an organization. This leads to significant variations in the data sources, internal and external, that need to be integrated, models that need to be developed, and user interface characteristics that need to be provided. Each application has to be tailored to a great extent to the executive and the decision at hand. This clearly calls for significant IS support to spread these systems across the cadre of executives at all levels.

Conclusions

Can executives actually receive effective support from EIS? The nature of their information-processing tasks marks one important structural aspect of higher levels of management (Rai, Stubbart, & Paper, 1994). As organizations get larger and more diversified, the complexity of information that managers need to deal with increases as well. Similarly, as an organization's environmental uncertainty increases, so does the variety, complexity, and ambiguity of executive information. Today, both large and small firms face increasing levels of environmental uncertainty. These factors clearly create a need for a technology that can be used to better manage executive information. This is prompting organizations, large and small, to explore EIS to support the informational needs of their executives.

The need for improvements in executive information management is further enhanced by one long-standing but often overlooked factor. The basic constraints of human cognition apply to executives as well. While the need for information-processing support seems apparent, the low level of EIS adoption suggests a lack of enthusiasm among organizations to invest in present technology. A significant majority of surveyed organizations have not installed EIS support for either collaboration or decision making for even one of their executives. Furthermore, those that have started the adoption process have not progressed very far in spreading the technology across their executives. However, the relative spread of EIS_c is greater than that of EIS_d in these organizations.

Enhancing collaboration support requires developing a technology infrastructure that increases the "reach" of executives. With such capability, executives can distribute information and interact with others, possibly in real time, even if they are geographically dispersed. It is evident that the need to establish such an information technology infrastructure is also driven by the uncertainties in the firm's external environment. Turbulent environments create a need to communicate more effectively and to better coordinate organizational activities. However, once initiated, the critical issue for the internal spread of such systems appears to be top management support. Providing resource support and designing and implementing corporate policies such as the use of electronic messaging systems, scheduling systems, and document management systems may propagate the internal spread of these systems. Furthermore, the advent of value-added networks and collaboration software environments is making the development of such infrastructures less of an "internal" IS development issue.

EIS applications targeted at providing decision support have been adopted to relatively lower levels than applications providing collaboration support. Traditional EIS applications have focused on monitoring critical business activities. The information delivered was typically internal and well structured. The dominant logical challenge is to identify and provide relevant information to support executive decisional roles. Information supporting executive decision making tends to be unstructured and includes information from both internal and external sources. The challenge rests not in merely providing access to these sources, but in actually integrating and transforming data, and presenting information in a suitable form for executive decision making. Providing decision support to executives requires a detailed understanding of their information requirements in specific problem situations. Questions such as "Have we identified information that will build, challenge, or reinforce executive mental models in specific problem-solving situations?" need to be posed during application development and evolution. Recent empirical evidence suggests that competitive advantage can be achieved if EIS can build the mental models of executives (Vandenbosch & Higgins, 1995).

The IS organization and its data administration function can face a formidable task in semantically and technologically integrating fragmented databases. It is incumbent on executives to provide necessary political and resource support. They can also significantly influence the quality of EIS by participating in requirements determination and providing feedback on the appropriateness of information content delivered and the form of delivery.

Given the current state of EIS adoption, can emerging technologies help promote the growth of EIS in U.S. organizations? The picture appears promising. Emerging information technologies have the capabilities to expand the "reach" of EIS applications providing collaborative support. The advent of wireless LANs, cellular technologies, multimedia, and notebook computers, coupled with dropping hardware prices, has enhanced the portability of EIS applications in the workplace (Volonino et al., 1995). The barriers of physical boundaries to accessing data, sharing information, and enhancing collaboration are being systematically ameliorated. As noted by these researchers: "Mobile technologies eliminate the common acceptance barrier that exists when information delivery is limited to the desktop from which executives are often trying to break away" (p. 112).

Similarly, advances in large-scale textual databases, data and information warehouses, data analysis and reporting tools (DARTs), knowledge-based systems, and group support systems individually, but even more so collectively, represent significant promise for EIS. For example, multiple expert systems can be integrated and interfaced with EIS to improve environmental scanning and provide intelligent support in problem identification and decision making (Chi & Turban, 1995). At the same time, group support system capabilities incorporated into EIS can promote greater collaboration between executives.

While EIS capabilities are likely to be greatly enhanced by emerging technologies, the organizational and IS context necessary to introduce and assimilate EIS applications is critical. Environmental factors do influence the introduction of EIS capabilities in organizations. More volatile information environments provide a catalyst for exploring EIS. Such environments also catalyze the spread of EIS among executives for decision support, all of whom are conceivably trying to make better decisions in complex information environments. It also appears that organizations of all sizes, small and large, will need to focus on improving information management for their executives.

A firm arguably has little control over its environment. However, there are factors that a firm has some control over. These include ISD size, IS support, and top management support. Given the relative standardization of collaboration support capabilities, it appears that internal IS resources are unlikely to play a critical role in determining whether or not they are explored. On the other hand, availability of internal IS resources is more likely to enable exploration of EIS for decision support. IS support is also critical in propagating the adoption level of such systems across executive and problem contexts. Furthermore, top management support is of paramount importance in internally propagating both types of EIS capabilities examined here.

Appendix

Instruction for Respondents

This questionnaire relates to your organization's environment and your Executive Information Systems (EIS) efforts. We refer to EIS as "computer-based applications that support communication, coordination, controlling, and planning functions of key executives/managers." EIS are believed to have the potential to improve executive productivity and organizational performance. As part of a major effort to understand more about EIS success, we need your cooperation by responding to this survey, which should take a maximum of 10 minutes. Your responses are extremely important and will be *strictly confidential*.

Environmental Characteristics

The following items relate to your primary industry that accounts for the largest percentage of your sales. Please circle the number in each scale that best approximates the actual conditions in it.

How rapid or intense is each of the following in your primary industry?

Our organization/division rarely changes its marketing practices to keep up with the market and competitors.	1 2 3 4 5 6 7	Our organization/division must change its marketing practices extremely frequently.
The rate at which products/services are getting obsolete in the primary industry is very slow.	1 2 3 4 5 6 7	The rate of product/service obsolescence is very high.
Actions of competitors are quite easy to predict in our primary industry.	1 2 3 4 5 6 7	Actions of competitors are unpredictable.
Demand and consumer tastes are fairly easy to forecast in our primary industry.	1 2 3 4 5 6 7	Demand and tastes are almost unpredictable.
The production/service technology is not subject to very much change.	1 2 3 4 5 6 7	The modes of production/service change often and in a major way.
The environment causes a great deal of threat to the survival of our organization/division.	1 2 3 4 5 6 7	Environment causes very little threat to the survival of our organization/division.

Are there great differences among the products/services you offer, with regard to:

About same for all our products	1 2 3 4 5 6 7	Varies a great deal from line to line

Customer buying habits	1	2	3	4	5	6	7
The nature of the competition	1	2	3	4	5	6	7
Market dynamism & uncertainty	1	2	3	4	5	6	7

How severe are the following challenges:

This is not a substantial threat	1	2	3	4	5	6	7	This is a very substantial threat
Tough price competition	1	2	3	4	5	6	7	
Competition in product quality	1	2	3	4	5	6	7	
Dwindling markets for products	1	2	3	4	5	6	7	
Scarce supply of labor/material	1	2	3	4	5	6	7	
Government interference	1	2	3	4	5	6	7	

Organizational EIS Efforts

Please circle the responses that indicate the proportion of key executives/managers for which EIS applications have been installed.

	1 none	2 one	3 few	4 many	5 most
Communication support like email, voice mail, etc.	1	2	3	4	5
Coordination support like electronic calendaring, file ticklers, computer conferencing, etc.	1	2	3	4	5
Controlling support like monitoring critical success factors, variance reporting, horizontal & vertical "drill-down," etc.	1	2	3	4	5
Planning support like Newswire & Dow Jones access, "what if" analysis, trend analysis, etc.	1	2	3	4	5

Organizational Support Factors

Please circle the appropriate response that best describes your EIS efforts.

SD Strongly Disagree	D Disagree	DS Disagree Slightly	N Neutral	AS Agree Slightly	A Agree	SA Strongly Agree

a. Executive Sponsor(s) personally participates in EIS development on a regular basis.	SD	D	DS	N	AS	A	SA
b. Top/corporate management's contact with the Executive Sponsor(s) on EIS-related issues has been frequent.	SD	D	DS	N	AS	A	SA
c. Top/corporate management provides sufficient resources for EIS.	SD	D	DS	N	AS	A	SA
d. Top/corporate management perceives EIS to be important.	SD	D	DS	N	AS	A	SA

e. Top/corporate management usually provided constructive feedback on the appropriateness of EIS applications. SD D DS N AS A SA

f. EIS is regarded as a high priority by top/corporate management. SD D DS N AS A SA

g. Information System (IS) executives participate in meetings concerning EIS development. SD D DS N AS A SA

h. IS personnel cooperate in identifying data sources for EIS applications. SD D DS N AS A SA

i. IS personnel cooperate to resolve technical problems encountered in EIS development. SD D DS N AS A SA

j. IS personnel accept accountability for EIS. SD D DS N AS A SA

k. There is active two-way communication between IS executives and top/corporate management on the role of EIS. SD D DS N AS A SA

l. IS function is highly involved in EIS development. SD D DS N AS A SA

References

Armstrong, D. A. (1990). How Rockwell launched its EIS. *Datamation, 36*(5), 69-72.

Attewell, P. (1992). Technology diffusion and organizational learning: The case of business computing. *Organization Science, 3*(1), 1-19.

Baroudi, J. J., & Orlikowski, W. (1989). The power of statistical power in MIS research. *MIS Quarterly, 13*(1), 87-106.

Barrow, C. (1990). Implementing an executive information system: Seven steps for success. *Journal of Information Systems Management, 7*(2), 41-46.

Bean, A. S., Neal, R. D., Radnor, M., & Tansik, D. A. (1975). Structural and behavioral correlates of implementation in U.S. business organizations. In R. L. Schultz & D. P. Slevin (Eds.), *Implementing operations research/management science* (pp. 77-132). New York: Elsevier North-Holland.

Belcher, L. W., & Watson, H. J. (1993). Assessing the value of Conoco's EIS. *MIS Quarterly, 17*(3), 239-253.

Benard, R., & Satir, A. (1993). User satisfaction with EISs: Meeting the needs of executive users. *Information Systems Management, 10*(4), 21-29.

Chi, R. T., & Turban, E. (1995). Distributed intelligent executive information systems. *Decision Support Systems, 14*(2), 117-130.

Cohen, J. (1988). *Statistical power for the behavioral sciences* (2nd ed.). Hillsdale, NJ: Lawrence Erlbaum.

Cottrell, N., & Rapley, K. (1991). Factors critical to the success of executive information systems in British Airways. *European Journal of Information Systems, 1*(1), 65-71.

Daft, R. L. (1982). Bureaucratic versus nonbureaucratic structure and the process of innovation and change. *Research in the Sociology of Organizations, 1.*

Damanpour, F., & Evans, W. M. (1984). Organizational innovation and performance: The problem of organizational lag. *Administrative Science Quarterly, 29*(3), 392-409.

DeLone, W. H. (1988). Determinants of success for computer usage in small business. *MIS Quarterly, 12*(1), 51-61.

Directory of top computer executives. (1992). Phoenix, AZ: Applied Computer Research, Inc.

Ein-Dor, P., & Segev, E. (1978). Organizational context and the success of management information systems. *Management Science, 24*(10), 1064-1077.

Elam, J. J., & Leidner, D. G. (1995). EIS adoption, use, and impact: The executive perspective. *Decision Support Systems, 14*(2), 89-103.

Fichman, G. R. (1992). Information technology diffusion: A review of empirical research. In *Proceedings of the Thirteenth International Conference on Information Systems* (pp. 195-206). Dallas, TX.

Fireworker, R. B., & Zirkel, W. (1990). Designing an EIS in a multidivisional environment. *Journal of Systems Management, 41*(2), 25-31.

Fitzgerald, G. (1992). Executive information systems and their development in the U.K.: A research study. *International Information Systems, 1*(2), 1-35.

Fried, L. (1991). Decision-making prowess. *Computerworld, 25*(9), 59-60.

Fuller, M. K., & Swanson, E. B. (1992). Information centers as organizational innovation: Exploring the correlates of implementation success. *Journal of Management Information Systems, 9*(1), 47-68.

Garrity, J. T. (1963). Top management and computer profits. *Harvard Business Review, 41*(4), 6-12, 172-174.

Gremillion, L. L. (1984). Organization size and information system use. *Journal of Management Information Systems, 1*(2), 4-7.

Grover, V. (1993). An empirically derived model for the adoption of customer-based interorganizational systems. *Decision Sciences, 24*(3), 603-640.

Grover, V., & Goslar, M. D. (1993). The initiation, adoption, and implementation of telecommunication technologies in the U.S. *Journal of Management Information Systems, 10*(1), 141-163.

Gulden, G. K., & Ewers, D. E. (1989). Is your ESS meeting the need? *Computerworld, 23*(28), 85-89.

Gunter, A., & Frolick, M. (1991). The evolution of EIS at Georgia Power Company. *Information Executive, 4*(4), 23-26.

Harrigan, K. R. (1983). Research methodologies for contingency approaches to business strategy. *Academy of Management Review, 8*(3), 398-405.

Houdeshel, G., & Watson, H. J. (1987). The management information and decision support (MIDS) system at Lockheed-Georgia. *MIS Quarterly, 11*(1), 127-140.

Huff, S. L., & Munro, M. C. (1985). Information technology assessment and adoption: A field study. *MIS Quarterly, 9*(4), 327-340.

Jarvenpaa, S. L., Dickson, G. W., & DeSanctis, G. L. (1984). Methodological issues in experimental IS research: Experiences and recommendations. In *Proceedings of the Fifth International Conference on Information Systems* (p. 1030). Tucson, AZ.

Jarvenpaa, S. L., & Ives, B. (1991). Executive involvement and participation in the management of information technology. *MIS Quarterly, 15*(2), 204-224.

Jenkins, A. M. (1990). Executive education and executive information systems: Problems, solutions and research. In *Research issues on information systems: An agenda for the 1990s* (pp. 153-172). Dubuque, IA: William C. Brown.

Joslow, S. (1991, Winter). Case study: Building an EIS. *Information Center Quarterly,* pp. 6-9.

Kaiser, H. F., & Rice, J. (1974). Little jiffy mark IV. *Educational and Psychological Measurement, 34*(2), 111-117.

Kimberley, J., & Evanisko, M. (1981). Organizational innovation: The influence of individual, organizational, and contextual factors on hospital adoption of technological and administrative innovations. *Academy of Management Journal, 24*(4), 689-713.

Kwon, T. H., & Zmud, R. W. (1987). Unifying the fragmented models of information systems implementation. In R. J. Boland & R. Hirschheim (Eds.), *Critical issues in information systems research*. New York: Wiley.

Lederer, A. L., & Mendelow, A. L. (1990). The impact of the environment on the management of information systems. *Information Systems Research, 1*(2), 205-222.

Leidner, D., & Elam, J. J. (1993). Executive information systems: Their impact on executive decision making. *Journal of Management Information Systems, 10*(3), 139-155.

McNamara, B., Danziger, G., & Barton, E. (1990). An appraisal of executive information and decision support systems. *Journal of Systems Management, 41*(5), 14-18.

Meador, C. L., Guyote, M. J., & Keen, P. G. W. (1984). Setting priorities for DSS development. *MIS Quarterly, 8*(2), 117-129.

Meyer, A. D., & Goes, J. B. (1988). Organization assimilation of innovations: A multilevel contextual analysis. *Academy of Management Journal, 31*(4), 897-923.

Miller, D., & Friesen, P. H. (1982). Innovation in conservative and entrepreneurial firms: Two models of strategic momentum. *Strategic Management Journal, 3*(1), 1-25.

Mitchell, R. (1988, June). How top brass is taking to the keyboard at Xerox. *Business Week*, p. 86.

Moad, J. (1988). The latest challenge for IS is in the executive suite. *Datamation, 34*(10), 43-52.

Mohan, L., Holstein, W. K., & Adams, R. B. (1990). EIS can work in the public sector. *MIS Quarterly, 14*(4), 435-448.

Nilakanta, S., & Scamell, R. (1990). The effect of information sources and communication channels on the diffusion of innovation in a data base environment. *Management Science, 36*(1), 24-40.

Nunnally, J. C. (1978). *Psychometric theory.* New York: McGraw-Hill.

Paller, A., & Laska, R. (1990). *The EIS book.* Homewood, IL: Dow Jones-Irwin.

Rai, A. (1995). External information source and channel effectiveness and the diffusion of CASE innovations: An empirical study. *European Journal of Information Systems, 4*, 93-102.

Rai, A., & Patnayakuni, R. (1996). A structural model for CASE adoption behavior. *Journal of Management Information Systems, 13*(2), 205-234.

Rai, A., Stubbart, C. S., & Paper, D. (1994). Can executive information systems reinforce biases? *Accounting, Management and Information Technologies, 4*(2), 87-106.

Rainer, R. K., & Watson, H. J. (1995). What does it take for successful executive information systems? *Decision Support Systems, 14*(2), 147-156.

Rapley, K. (1993). A plausible impossibility: Supporting top executives with information systems. In D. Avison & J. E. Kendall (Eds.), *Human, organization, and social dimensions of information systems development* (pp. 375-380). IFIP North Holland Proceedings.

Raymond, L. (1985). Organizational characteristics and MIS success in the context of small business. *MIS Quarterly, 9*(1), 37-52.

Raymond, L. (1990). Organizational context and information systems success: A contingency approach. *Journal of Management Information Systems, 6*(4), 5-20.

Rees-Evans, H. (1989). Top management transformed as EIS arrives. *Accountancy, 103*(1148), 143-144.

Reich, B. H., & Benbasat, I. (1990). An empirical investigation of factors influencing the success of customer-oriented strategic systems. *Information Systems Research, 1*(3), 325-347.

Rinaldi, D., & Jastrzembski, T. (1986a). Executive information systems put strategic data at your CEO's fingertips. *Computerworld, 20*(43), 37-50.

Rinaldi, D., & Jastrzembski, T. (1986b). Golden rules: EIS installation. *Computerworld, 20*(43), 51.

Rockart, J. F., & De Long, D. W. (1988). *Executive support systems.* Homewood, IL: Dow Jones-Irwin.

Rockart, J. F., & Treacy, M. E. (1982). The CEO goes on-line. *Harvard Business Review, 60*(1), 82-88.

Sabherwal, R., & King, W. R. (1992). Decision processes for developing strategic applications of information systems: A contingency approach. *Decision Sciences, 23*(4), 917-943.

Sanders, G. L., & Courtney, J. F. (1985). A field study of organizational factors influencing DSS success. *MIS Quarterly, 9*(1), 77-89.

Sethi, V., & King, W. R. (1991). Construct measurement in information systems research: An illustration in strategic systems. *Decision Sciences, 22*(3), 455-472.

Shoebridge, A. (1988). EIS: Friend or foe. *Accountancy, 102*(1142), 150-151.

Stewart, D. W. (1981). The application and misapplication of factor analysis in marketing research. *Journal of Marketing Research, 18*(1), 51-62.

Straub, D. W. (1989). Validating instruments in MIS research. *MIS Quarterly, 13*(2), 147-165.

Turban, E., McLean, E., & Wetherbe, J. (1996). *Information technology for management: Improving quality and productivity.* New York: Wiley.

Utterback, J. M. (1974). Innovation in industry and the diffusion of technology. *Science, 183*(2), 620-626.

Vandenbosch, B., & Higgins, C. A. (1995). Executive support systems and learning: A model and empirical test. *Journal of Management Information Systems, 12*(2), 99-130.

Vanlommel, E., & De Brabander, B. (1975). The organization of electronic data processing (EDP) activities and computer use. *Journal of Business, 48*(3), 391-410.

Venkatraman, N., & Grant, J. H. (1986). Construct measurement in organizational strategy research: A critique and proposal. *Academy of Management Review, 11*(1), 71-87.

Volonino, L., & Drinkard, G. (1989). Integrating EIS into the strategic plan: A case study of Fisher-Price. In *Transactions of the Ninth International Conference on Decision Support Systems* (pp. 37-45). Providence, RI.

Volonino, L., Watson, H. J., & Robinson, S. (1995). Using EIS to respond to dynamic business conditions. *Decision Support Systems, 14*(2), 105-116.

Wallis, L. (1989). Power computing at the top. *Across the Board, 26*(1-2), 42-51.

Watson, H. J., & Frolick, M. (1993). Determining information requirements of an EIS. *MIS Quarterly, 17*(3), 255-269.

Watson, H. J., Rainer, R. K., & Frolick, M. N. (1992). Executive information systems: An ongoing study of current practices. *International Information Systems, 1*(2), 37-56.

Watson, H. J., Rainer, R. K., Jr., & Koh, C. E. (1991). Executive information systems: A framework and a survey of current practices. *MIS Quarterly, 15*(1), 12-30.

Watson, H. J., Watson, R. T., Singh, S., & Holmes, D. (1995). Development practices for executive information systems: Findings of a field study. *Decision Support Systems, 14*(2), 171-184.

Wetherbe, J. C. (1991). Executive information requirements: Getting it right. *MIS Quarterly, 15*(1), 50-65.

Zmud, R. W. (1982). Diffusion of modern software practices: Influence of centralization and formalization. *Management Science, 28*(12), 1421-1431.

Zmud, R. W. (1984a). The effectiveness of external information channels in facilitating innovation within software groups. *MIS Quarterly, 7*(2), 43-58.

Zmud, R. W. (1984b). Examination of "push-pull" theory applied to process innovation in knowledge work. *Management Science, 30*(6), 727-738.

CHAPTER
TEN

Virtual Teams Versus Face-to-Face Teams

An Exploratory Study of a Web-Based Conference System

MERRILL WARKENTIN
LUTFUS SAYEED
ROSS HIGHTOWER

Do teams that collaborate online suffer from constraints in their ability to communicate? Can companies implement virtual teams with the same confidence they have when they assign workers to collaborate on group tasks through traditional face-to-face meetings? Questions like these are increasingly important for managers as virtual teams become more common. The findings of research in recent years are not encouraging. Much of this research suggests that groups using computer-mediated communication systems (CMCS) communicate less effectively in many circumstances than groups meeting face-to-face. For example, Hightower and Sayeed (1995, 1996) found that virtual teams exchange information less effectively than face-to-face groups.

However, many of these recent studies are limited in two important aspects. First, they used ad hoc groups or did not give their groups sufficient time to adapt to one another or the communication medium. Recent evidence suggests that when virtual teams are given sufficient time to develop strong intragroup relationships and to adapt to the communication medium, they may communicate as effectively as face-to-face groups (Chidambaram, 1996). A second limitation of the CMCS literature is the predominance of studies using synchronous (same time) rather than asynchronous (different time) technologies. Asynchronous technologies, which include email and discussion forums, are probably more common in the business world than synchronous technologies (Kinney & Panko, 1996). Further, asynchronous technologies offer certain advantages for groups exchanging information and may allow group members to concentrate on message content. For example, individuals can take time to reflect on the message they receive and to carefully consider their responses.

In this study, teams using an asynchronous system are compared to teams meeting face-to-face. All teams are engaged in a specific information exchange task. The

---

Reprinted by permission from *Decision Sciences*, Volume 28, Number 4, Fall 1997.

primary research question is whether teams using an asynchronous system develop social links or relationships (relational links) as strong as those in face-to-face groups. In the next section, computer-mediated communication systems are briefly described, focusing on the differences between synchronous and asynchronous systems. Next, the relevant literature on the effects of CMCS on groups is summarized, followed by the development of a set of hypotheses. The results of an experiment designed to test the hypotheses is described, and, finally, the implications of the results are discussed.

Computer-Mediated Communication Systems

Computer-mediated communication systems (CMCS) are sociotechnical systems that support and enhance the communication-related activities of team members engaged in computer-supported cooperative work. The communication and coordination activities of team members are facilitated by technologies that can be characterized along the three continua of time, space, and level of group support (Alavi & Keen, 1989; DeSanctis & Gallupe, 1987; Johansen, 1988). Teams can communicate synchronously or asynchronously; they may be located together or remotely; and the technology can provide task support primarily for the individual team member or for the group's activities. These computer-based communication technologies are utilized to overcome space and time constraints that burden face-to-face meetings; to increase the range and depth of information access; and to improve group task performance effectiveness, especially by overcoming "process losses" (McGrath & Hollingshead, 1993, 1994). Further, CMCS increase the range, capacity, and speed of managerial communications (Culnan & Markus, 1987). They can also "reduce or eliminate the expense and inconvenience associated with distributed work" (Galegher & Kraut, 1994, p. 111). One objective of using these technologies is to create comparable levels of communication speed and effectiveness as those achieved at traditional meetings.

CMCS provide support for either synchronous or asynchronous meetings. Synchronous meetings are spontaneous, where ideas are exchanged with little structure. Participants communicate with each other in such a way that it is sometimes difficult to attribute an idea to one participant or to establish the reason behind a particular decision. It is estimated that managers spend 60% of their communication time in synchronous meetings (Panko, 1992), which include face-to-face meetings, telephone calls, desktop conferencing, Web-based "chat rooms," and the Internet Relay Chat (IRC).

On the other hand, asynchronous meetings are more structured than synchronous meetings. These meetings rely more on documents exchanged among participants. Compared to synchronous meetings, asynchronous meeting participants have longer to compose their messages and, therefore, it is easy to attribute an idea to its originator and establish the reason behind a particular decision. However, asynchronous meetings require more time than synchronous meetings because information exchange takes longer. Asynchronous meetings are frequently used by groups in which at least one participant is in a remote location (Kinney & Panko, 1996). CMCS technologies that facilitate asynchronous meetings include electronic mail (email), Electronic Document Management, bulletin board systems, and Internet Usenet newsgroups. One study (Straub & Karahanna, 1990) indicated that email (the most popular medium of communication in the workplace) users who share pre-meeting information report more effective communication during the meeting.

Computer conferencing, which is a "structured form of electronic mail in which messages are organized by topic and dialogues are often mediated" (Baecker, 1993, p. 1; see also Hiltz & Turoff, 1978), can be asynchronous (such as bulletin board systems and Internet Usenet newsgroups) or synchronous (such as "chat rooms" and the IRC). The technology explored in this chapter (MeetingWeb™) is an asynchronous computer conference technology and is explained in detail below.

Virtual Versus Face-to-Face Teams: The Impact of CMCS on Groups

The effects of the reduced "communication modalities" on virtual team members and the circumstances in which these effects occur has been the focus of much of the CMCS research (McGrath & Hollingshead, 1994). Although not definitive in terms of specific effects, the research in this area suggests that CMCS groups communicate differently than face-to-face groups (Chidambaram, 1996; Hightower & Hagmann, 1995; Hightower & Sayeed, 1995; Hiltz, Johnson, & Turoff, 1986; Kiesler & Sproull, 1992; McGrath & Hollingshead, 1994; Siegal, Dubrovsky, Kiesler, & McGuire, 1986; Wiseband, Schneider, & Connolly, 1995). While there is a plethora of research describing various technologies for computer-mediated communications, there is a lack of studies examining "sustained, project-oriented teamwork of the sort that is important in most real-world organizations" (Galegher & Kraut, 1994, p. 111). An analysis of CMCS communication characteristics is warranted.

The present study explores the role of a CMCS in facilitating communication among members of virtual teams. CMCS impose constraints on communication that are likely to affect a group's performance. People rely on multiple modes of communication in face-to-face conversation, such as paraverbal (tone of voice, inflection, voice volume) and nonverbal (eye movement, facial expression, hand gestures, and other body language) cues. These cues help regulate the flow of conversation, facilitate turn taking, provide feedback, and convey subtle meanings. As a result, face-to-face conversation is a remarkably orderly process. In normal face-to-face conversation, there are few interruptions or long pauses and the distribution of participation is consistent, though skewed toward higher status members (McGrath, 1990). CMCS preclude these secondary communication modes, thus altering the orderliness and effectiveness of information exchange (Hightower,

Sayeed, Warkentin, & McHaney, 1997). Such communication modalities are constrained to a varying extent depending on the characteristics of the technological system. For example, electronic mail prevents both paraverbal and nonverbal cues, telephone conference calls allow the use of most paraverbal cues (but not nonverbal ones), while videoconferencing enables extensive use of both paraverbal and nonverbal cues.

Virtual teams are not able to duplicate the normal "give and take" of face-to-face discussion. For example, comments of group members using a synchronous CMCS sometimes appear to be out of context, or the conversation may appear to lack focus because multiple group members are "talking" at once. This is exacerbated by the inefficiency inherent in the use of a keyboard and the fact that people type and read at different rates (Siegal et al., 1986). Group members who type slowly or edit more thoroughly may find their comments are no longer relevant when they are ready to transmit them. Moreover, because everyone can transmit their comments simultaneously, group members may be required to process a large number of comments in a short period of time. For asynchronous CMCS, considerable delays typically occur between the time a message is sent and the time a reply is received. This may make it difficult to maintain a train of thought or a discussion theme.

The lack of nonverbal and paraverbal cues also reduces the richness of the information transmitted by virtual team members. Daft and Lengel (1986) defined media richness as "the ability of information to change understanding within a time interval" (p. 560). Rich media allow multiple information cues (the words spoken, tone of voice, body language, etc.) and feedback. It takes more time and effort by group members to achieve the same level of mutual understanding in a lean medium, such as CMCS, than in a rich one, such as face-to-face communication.

There is substantial evidence that virtual teams communicate less efficiently than face-to-face groups (Hightower & Sayeed, 1995, 1996; McGrath & Hollingshead, 1994). Because exchanging information is more difficult, virtual teams tend to be more task oriented and exchange less social-emotional information, slowing the development of relational links (Chidambaram, 1996). Development of relational links is important because researchers have associated strong relational links with many positive outcomes including enhanced creativity and motivation, increased morale, better decisions, and fewer process losses (Walther & Burgoon, 1992).

McGrath's TIP theory (Time-Interaction-Performance) offered a means for understanding the development of relational links in groups (McGrath, 1990). According to TIP theory, groups perform three functions: (1) production, (2) member support, and (3) group well-being. The functions are achieved by carrying out activities in one of four modes:

Mode I: Activities related to choosing goals and objectives
Mode II: Activities related to solutions of technical issues with regard to how to achieve the group's goals
Mode III: Activities related to conflict resolution
Mode IV: Activities related to execution of the requirements of the group's task

Developing relational links involves performing activities related to the member support and group well-being functions. These activities include, for example, establishing position or group status of members, defining task roles of group members, and establishing norms for group interaction. Activities that define relational development are most common after a group experiences a significant transition, such as the group's inception or a change in membership. Established groups spend less time on relational activities and more time on task-oriented activities, and should be more efficient in accomplishing tasks. Because CMCS reduce the amount and richness of the information that can be exchanged, it is more difficult for virtual teams to complete relationship-developing activities compared to face-to-face teams.

A question that has been raised by some researchers relates to whether the limitations of computer-mediated communication systems prevent groups from developing relational links as strong as face-to-face groups or whether the limitations simply increase the time it takes for these relational links to develop (Burke & Chidambaram, 1995; Chidambaram, 1996; Chidambaram & Bostrom, 1993). These researchers argued that, with time, CMCS groups would overcome the limitations of the media and achieve the same level of relational links and, therefore, the same level of performance as face-to-face groups.

Therefore, comparative research studies should allow virtual teams sufficient time to develop the same level of relational links as face-to-face groups. Further, much of the research that has investigated relational links in virtual teams has used synchronous systems such as computer conferencing and group support systems with "colocated groups" (Chidambaram, 1996). In a synchronous meeting, the effect of an inefficient communication medium would be felt to a greater extent than in an asynchronous meeting. Time pressures present in synchronous meetings are not necessarily present in asynchronous meetings. A participant in an asynchronous meeting has more time to consider his or her message, decide what to say, take the time necessary to convey his or her thoughts, and edit the message as much as necessary to achieve clarity. The receiver of the message can read it at his or her leisure and consider it carefully before responding. This allows more time to include social-emotional information in the message in addition to the information required to accomplish the task. However, due to the leanness of the medium and the limited modes of communication, it should still be more difficult to form strong relational links in groups using asynchronous CMCS than for face-to-face groups. Thus, our first hypothesis is:

H1: Face-to-face teams will exhibit stronger relational links than virtual (CMCS) teams.

Stronger relational links in groups have been associated with higher performance. The task used in this study is one that requires the groups to exchange information effectively. Previous studies have shown that both face-to-face groups and groups using synchronous CMCS exchange information poorly (Hightower &

Sayeed, 1995, 1996; Stasser & Titus, 1985, 1987). Asynchronous CMCS provide a distinct advantage for this type of task over both synchronous CMCS and face-to-face communication. Group members can take the time necessary to compose clear and complete messages. As a result, time pressures or information load should not affect the group's performance.

Information exchange is also affected strongly by the group's internal dynamics or relational links. Two factors that affect information exchange are opportunity and motivation to contribute information (Hightower & Sayeed, 1996). Opportunity is affected in part by the effects of social status; group members of lower social status often do not have the same opportunities to contribute as higher status members. Motivation is affected by the willingness of group members to contribute information that may contradict their own opinions or those of other group members. Motivation is also affected by whether the group member feels he or she has a stake in the group's outcome. Despite the advantages that asynchronous CMCS offer for exchanging information, stronger relational links will allow face-to-face groups to exchange information more effectively. Our second hypothesis is divided into two parts:

> H2a: Face-to-face teams will exhibit higher performance results, as indicated by information exchange effectiveness, than virtual (CMCS) teams.
> H2b: Information exchange effectiveness will be positively associated with relational links.

The measure of information exchange effectiveness used in this study is identical to the one used by Hightower and Sayeed (1995, 1996), described in the Instrument section below.

The Study

This research study used teams comprised of three members who completed an information-sharing task. Teams used either asynchronous CMCS or face-to-face communications. The following sections describe the task, the subjects, the CMCS itself, the research procedure, and the research instrument.

The Task

We adapted a case from one described by Pfeiffer and Jones (1977), which involves choosing the most likely suspect in a murder mystery. The subjects were supplied with the case description and information about three suspects in a murder. The subjects were told that the descriptions were the result of their initial investigation, and that they were now asked to collaborate with two other investigators who have also performed preliminary investigations in order to solve the crime. Exam-

TABLE 10.1 Information Contained in the Murder Mystery Case

Case Characteristic	Incriminating	Vindicating
Your initial investigation has revealed that the murderer entered the house through a secret passage that bypassed the security system.	Suspect was one of the contractors for the original construction.	Suspect had no apparent knowledge of the house.
The victim's allergic reaction to bee stings was not common knowledge.	Suspect was the victim's doctor.	Unknown if suspect had any knowledge of the allergy.

ples of the information contained in the case are shown in Table 10.1. This established task was selected rather than a business-oriented case because it does not require background functional knowledge such as accounting, finance, marketing, etc., and therefore isolates the communication aspects of solving the simple task. The case can be solved using common sense, and our experience has shown that this type of case engenders a high level of interest and motivation among the students used in this experiment (Hightower & Sayeed, 1995, 1996).

The case description was a half-page in length and mentioned eight attributes considered important for identifying the murderer. The suspect descriptions listed attributes about the suspects that were consistent with the suspect having committed the crime and attributes that were not consistent with the suspect having committed the crime. The exchange of unique information was a key research variable. Some of the items appeared on all three subjects' descriptions within one team (common information) while other items appeared on only one team member's description (unique information). The unique information could not be known and considered by the entire team unless the member who was privy to it chose to share it with the rest of the group. This information exchange was a key research variable.

This task was an "intellective task" according to Laughlin's (1980) typology, which is a task with a correct answer to be found by the group. Further, because the correct answer can be found using common sense, the task can be categorized as relatively low on the complexity continuum—once the team members each "lay their cards on the table," the solution is apparent. In other words, the fundamental requirement to solve the problem is effective communication.

Subjects

The subjects, who were undergraduate students at three different large universities, completed the experiment as part of a course requirement. The participating universities were Northeastern University, which is a large private university in

Boston; and Kansas State University and San Francisco State University, both of which are large state universities. The course grade the subjects received was based, in part, on their participation in the experiment, providing incentive to solve the mystery, which required collaboration among the team members. Thirty-three subjects (comprised entirely of students at Northeastern University) collaborated in face-to-face meetings two days after their clues were disclosed to them. These three-person, face-to-face team members were randomly assigned to their respective teams. Another 39 subjects (three-person virtual teams comprised of one student randomly assigned from each university) collaborated with the support of Meeting-Web™ software, described below. A total of 13 virtual teams and 11 face-to-face teams participated in the study, comprised of 72 individual team members who completed the survey instrument. Thus, the sample size was 72. These individuals and their teams were comparable in all meaningful ways, as discussed below.

Procedure and Teams

Subjects in the face-to-face groups were provided with the case description two days before their meeting time and were told to study the clues carefully. On arrival to their meeting, subjects surrendered the case description (with the suspect clues) to the experimenter. The groups were told that their goal was to discuss the case and to try to form a consensus as to the most likely suspect in the crime. They then met for approximately 25 minutes, until each team reached a consensus decision. A post-test was administered at the end of the meeting.

The virtual teams (or "CMCS groups") obviously required considerably more than 25 minutes to complete their collaboration due to the asynchronous medium, which required "turnaround time" to read and respond to messages posted to their computer conferences. The need for additional time was exacerbated by differences in time zones and class schedules, and the need to access the conference from university computer labs. The virtual teams were provided with the case descriptions and were given three weeks to complete their collaboration and solve the murder mystery. They were told that their partners may be at other universities, but no information concerning the location of their partners was provided by the researchers, the software, or by their usernames. As they collaborated, subjects were allowed to retain their case descriptions (with the suspect clues). At the completion of their three-week interval, the post-test was administered.

These 72 individuals and their 24 teams were comparable based on several factors. All 72 subjects were undergraduate business majors who were given a course grade incentive to succeed in solving the murder mystery. Beyond the individual demographic parity and motivational equality, the teams themselves were very similar except for the communication medium. All teams were comprised of three individuals with no assigned leader. All teams engaged in discussion concerning the murder and the available clues. All subjects were given sufficient time to evaluate the clues individually and to collaborate with teammates. Although the face-to-face teams were given only two days to evaluate the clues versus the three-week time allowance given the virtual teams (to compensate for the constraints imposed by time differences and technology), all participants reported that they had sufficient time to evaluate the clues and consider the mystery.

The System

The asynchronous CMCS used in this study was MeetingWeb™, a secure, moderated bulletin board system accessible from the World Wide Web. MeetingWeb™ is a custom proprietary collaboration software system residing on the Northeastern University College of Business Administration (CBA) web server and accessible to anyone with a connection to the Internet (such as an ISP), any web client (browser) software (such as Netscape), a valid username, and a valid password. It is a computer conferencing system that provides textual and graphical communication capabilities to its users.

MeetingWeb™ was designed to have a familiar look and feel to users of the World Wide Web, a new standard platform for computer communications. "The interface *is* the system for most users. However well or poorly designed, it stands as the representation of the system" (Kendall & Kendall, 1995, p. 635). The MeetingWeb™ system is easy to use; pilot tests confirmed that the participants could learn and use the system with only a brief introduction. The system permits group members to communicate by "posting" messages in a hierarchical manner. A "comment" (message) can be posted as a new "topic" (leftmost in the hierarchy), as a reply to a topic (indented under that topic), or as a reply to a reply. Usenet newsgroups term this structure a "threaded discussion." The indenting scheme appears as a familiar outline format. This intuitive structure makes the organization of the messages clear and unambiguous. Furthermore, the source of each message is clearly identified; the system provides eponymity.

Characteristics of the system other than its ability to facilitate communication among team members did not appear to be a factor in the study. Parenthetically, the system's default feature of displaying only *<new or previously unread>* comments, unless reconfigured to show *<all>* comments, may have slowed the adoption of the software by a few participants until the feature was demonstrated to them. (They thought their previously read messages were "gone"!) This unanticipated anecdotal factor, however, no longer created a distinction among groups once all participants were "retrained" to reconfigure their views.

MeetingWeb™ was developed by and licensed from CitySource Inc., and has been further customized for CBA's use with custom extensions. Figure 10.1 shows a representative screen of the MeetingWeb™ conference system. More information about MeetingWeb™ can be found at http://www.cba.neu.edu/MeetingWeb.

The near ubiquity of the World Wide Web today makes MeetingWeb™ (and other web-based CMCS) extremely accessible to a broad audience. Further, the protocol of the web (hypertext transfer protocol, or HTTP) is hardware independent, so it

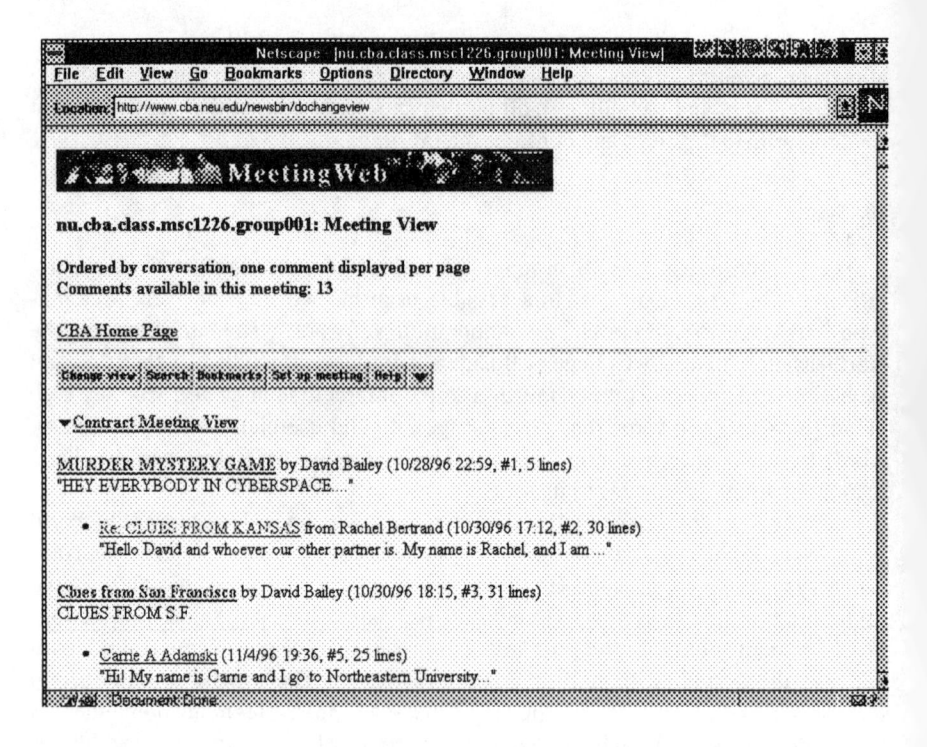

Figure 10.1. Sample Screen From MeetingWeb™

provides an essentially universal platform for communication support among virtual team members.

The Instrument

Three sets of variables were measured using the post-test instrument: Measures of Relational Links, Group Performance Measures, and User WWW Use variables. Three relational variables were measured: Group Cohesiveness, Perceptions of Group Interaction Process, and Satisfaction with Group Outcomes (see Table 10.2).

Cohesiveness is defined as the extent to which the group members are attracted to the group and each other, and has been found to be related to many desirable traits in groups (Chidambaram, 1996). Perceptions of a group's interaction process include such aspects as trust, openness, and participatory equality. Positive perceptions of the interaction process have been associated with process gains while negative perceptions are associated with process losses (Steiner, 1972). Satisfaction with outcomes is related, in part, to the attitudes of the group members toward one another (Chidambaram). As group members develop more positive attitudes toward

TABLE 10.2 Factors Influencing Relational Links Among Team Members

Relational Variable	Definition
Perceptions of group cohesiveness	The extent to which the group members are attracted to the group and to each other
Perceptions of group interaction process	Includes aspects of trust, openness, and participatory equality
Satisfaction with group outcomes	Related to positive attitudes of group members toward one another

SOURCE: Chidambarum (1996).

one another, their satisfaction with the group's work increases. Cohesiveness was measured using Seashore's (1954) Index of Group Cohesiveness, while the remaining variables were measured using an instrument developed by Chidambaram.

Two types of data were collected to measure group performance. Each of the subjects also individually indicated who he or she thought was the most likely suspect and rated the certainty of this preference on a 7-point Likert scale. First, each group's choice of the most likely suspect was indicated. Second, subjects individually wrote down everything they knew about the three suspects, including what they learned from their own material and what they learned through group discussion. A measure of information exchange effectiveness was obtained by counting the number of unique information items on each subject's post-test that they could not have known prior to discussion. This number was then divided by the total possible number of unique information items the subject could not have known before discussion, the result being the unique information-exchanged variable. The measure of information exchange effectiveness is identical to the one used by Hightower and Sayeed (1995, 1996).

Data were also collected from the CMCS group members to measure the subjects' level of experience with CMCS and the WWW. An excerpt of the instrument used for the virtual teams appears in the Appendix. The instrument used for the face-to-face teams was nearly identical.

Results

H1 proposes that face-to-face groups will have stronger relational links than CMCS groups. Data analysis supported this hypothesis. A MANOVA indicated a difference in the three relational variables between the two team categories ($F = 3.05$, $p = .0422$). Table 10.3 shows the results of ANOVA performed for each of the relational variables. Cohesion, Perceptions of Group Interaction Process, and Satisfaction with Outcomes are all significant. The means for the three relational variables are shown

TABLE 10.3 Results of ANOVA for Hypothesis 1

Variable	F (df = 1, 24)	p Value
Cohesion	7.78	.0107
Perceptions of Group Interaction Process	7.36	.0127
Satisfaction with Outcomes	11.64	.0025

TABLE 10.4 Means of Relational Variables

Dependent Variable	Remote (n = 13)	Face-to-Face (n = 11)
Cohesion (25)	16.7	19.7
Perceptions of Group Interaction Process (35)	23.8	29.0
Satisfaction with Outcomes (28)	19.8	25.2

NOTE: Values in parentheses show maximum values for each dependent variable.

in Table 10.4. Face-to-face groups reported a higher degree of cohesion, were more satisfied with the decision process followed by the groups, and were more satisfied with the team's outcome.

H2a states that face-to-face groups will exchange information more effectively than CMCS groups. Data analysis did not support this hypothesis. An ANOVA indicated no statistically significant difference in the proportion of unique information items exchanged between the two team types or categories ($F = 3.84, p = .065$). The mean of the dependent variable (the proportion of unique information items exchanged) for the face-to-face groups (.439) was higher than the mean for the virtual teams (.318). Although not statistically significant, face-to-face groups exchanged more unique information in one meeting than CMCS groups did in three weeks of online communications.

H2b proposes that information exchange will be higher for groups with stronger relational links. A stepwise regression analysis, with the unique information exchanged as the dependent variable and the four relational links as the independent variables, was conducted to test this hypothesis. The results are shown in Table 10.5. The only significant predictor to enter the model at a .05 level of significance was the Perceptions of Group Interaction Process variable ($F = 5.57, p = .021$). The coefficient indicates that groups with higher cohesion exchanged information more effectively than groups with lower cohesion. However, the resulting R^2 was only .072, indicating that a substantial proportion of the dependent variable remained unexplained by the relational links.

TABLE 10.5 Results of Regression Analysis of Relational Variables on Unique Information Exchanged Variable

Variable	Coefficient	Partial R^2	t Statistic	p Value
Perceptions of Group Interaction Process	0.01	.072	5.57	.021

Discussion and Conclusions

The findings of the present study provide several insights into the communication process of virtual groups. First, the advantages of collaboration technologies may not always outweigh their disadvantages. While collaboration technologies have the capability of creating a communication environment for virtual partners who are separated by time and/or space, they may hinder the development of a strong sense of cohesion and satisfaction with the group's interaction process. Second, the strength of relational links is positively associated with the effectiveness of information exchange.

Therefore, the loss of relationship building in virtual teams implies that the use of traditional meetings as a supplement to the use of CMCS might be useful (preferably in an early stage) for creating a sense of belonging to a group. McGrath (1990) suggested that teams spend proportionally more time on relationship development activities during periods of significant transition, such as the group's inception or a change in membership. Established groups spend more time on task-oriented activities. In the absence of the ability to have an initial face-to-face meeting, other avenues for building strong relationships are advised to ensure the cohesiveness and effectiveness of the team's interaction. Figure 10.2 shows both task-oriented communication and relational development messages for one virtual team.

The findings of this study are exploratory in nature. Using a CMCS was a unique experience for most of these participants. It is likely that people would become more effective using a CMCS with practice (Hollingshead, McGrath, & O'Connor, 1993). Frequent users of discussion forums on the Internet and online services develop ways to convey more meaning in their messages as a means of replacing paraverbal and nonverbal cues. The use of symbols called "emoticons" is one example (McGrath & Hollingshead, 1994). One only needs to spend some time reading the messages posted on some of the more controversial online forums to determine that quite detailed and emotional discussions are possible. Asynchronous media such as email, electronic bulletin boards, and the MeetingWeb™ system used in this study are more conducive to carefully constructed dialogue than synchronous conferencing systems such as GroupSystems V and videoconference systems. This is supported by the data in Table 10.6, which shows the correlations between self-reported User WWW/computer experience variables and the three relational variables. Only

254 EMERGING INFORMATION TECHNOLOGIES

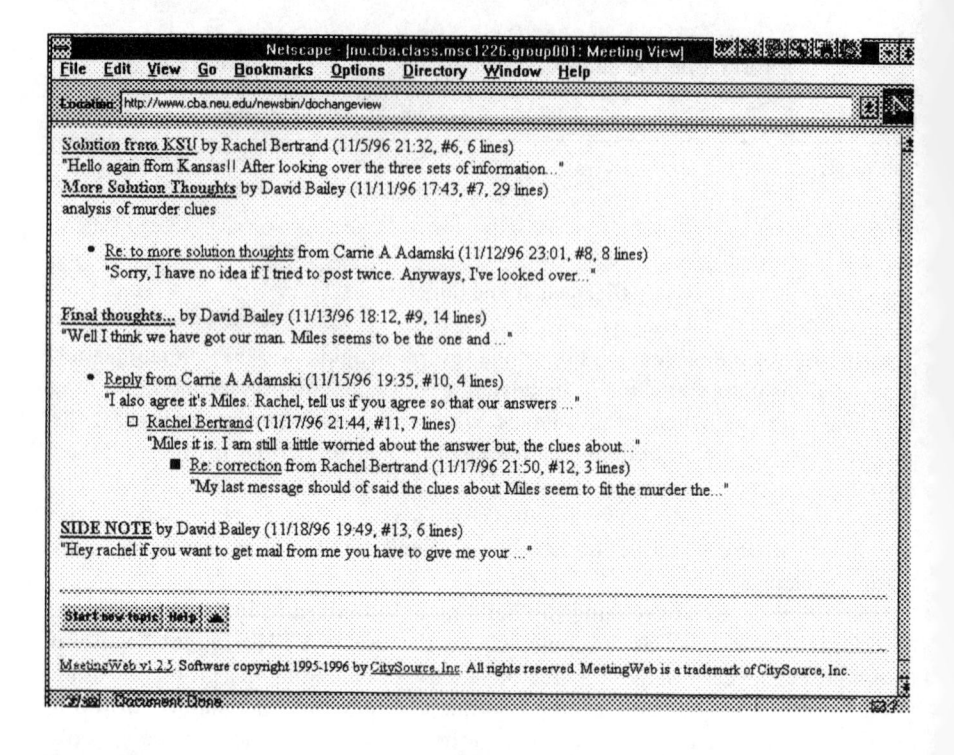

Figure 10.2. Illustrative Screen From One Virtual Team

two correlations are significant at the .05 level. WWW use was positively correlated with Perceptions of Group Interaction Process and Cohesion. This means that relational links were stronger in groups whose members reported more frequent use of the WWW than other groups. Being more familiar with the WWW may allow frequent users to concentrate on their interaction with other group members rather than on the system itself.

Creating Virtual Teams: Guidelines for Organizations on the Bleeding Edge

While face-to-face teams reported greater satisfaction with the group interaction process, the exchange of information was no more effective than that in virtual teams. In other words, there was no statistically significant difference between the effectiveness of communication (as measured by information exchange), but the traditional teams have more positive perceptions of the interactivity and the results. Therefore, since virtual teams are becoming a necessary tool, organizations must strive to bolster the satisfaction level of CMCS. If this were done, there would be

TABLE 10.6 Correlation of Relational Variables With WWW Use of Team Members

	Outcomes	Process	Cohesion
WWW use	.4587	**.5667**	**.6023**

NOTE: Bold values are significant at .05 level.

no significant drawback to the use of virtual teams, which can be made more acceptable and satisfying in several ways.

While a large amount of research about technology-supported work groups has been conducted and published, there are relatively few axioms that can be identified due to the complexity of this technological-social realm. Deep understanding of the social and psychological aspects is probably more elusive. It may also be more difficult to codify the social and psychological aspects than the technological factors employed in creating and managing CMCS. Nevertheless, an attempt to identify some of the general principles that can be used by organizations seeking to capture the advantages of these emerging technologies is warranted.

Jay (1976) suggested a set of guidelines for organizing and conducting a meeting that offers useful insights for the CMCS designer. He started by insisting on defining the objective of the meeting, and defined ways to assess each agenda item. He noted that proper preparation is required to ensure the group's success, including the identification of appropriate participants, the distribution of all appropriate documents beforehand, and establishment of the role of the leader. Among his guidelines for conducting a meeting were "draw out the silent," "protect the weak," and "encourage the clash of ideas."

The decision to implement CMCS is often based on necessity stemming from geographic separation of group members. Ideally, however, the unique characteristics of CMCS when compared to face-to-face and other communication modes should dictate when they are used. Zack (1993) showed that the highly interactive nature of face-to-face meetings makes this mode "appropriate for building a shared interpretive context among group members, while [CMCS], being less interactive, is more appropriate for communicating within an established context" (p. 207), such as ongoing discourse consisting primarily of "adjacency pairs." Ongoing groups have an established culture and set of routines, and may have a greater commitment to achieving effective communications. Further, Zack suggested that while "social presence" (a sense of belonging) is diminished in CMCS, it is the lack of interactivity that primarily constrains computer-mediated communication.

Another factor to consider when creating effective virtual teams is the psychological profile and personality characteristics of the specific team members. In order to be successful in this environment, participants must possess patience, persistence, and perseverance, along with a certain degree of tolerance, flexibility, and understanding. The traditional methods of control and influence that we are socialized to utilize as children may not be effective in computer-mediated environments. Users of CMCS must exercise leadership and influence with little means of social control, and some members may become "lost in cyberspace" and may "drop out" of virtual teams in the void of familiar communications patterns. Care must be exercised to develop and foster familiarity and proficiency with these new tools and techniques of social interaction. This represents an entirely new paradigm of communication that must be learned, much like the rules and methods of face-to-face communications that must be learned by all children.

The most important goal of CMCS is to foster interaction, inclusion, and participation (McGrath, 1991), which are all related to the feeling of "being there," or social presence. Social presence defines the extent to which a communication medium allows participants to experience each other as being psychologically close or present (Fulk & Boyd, 1991). Face-to-face communication, for example, is characterized by social cues such as nonverbal and paraverbal communications channels and continuous feedback (Rogers, 1986). The success of computer-mediated communication systems lies in part on their ability to provide the participants with socioemotional content sharing. Clearly, videoconferencing offers a greater opportunity for sharing these social cues than text-based communications modes, yet the latter do not entirely lack such cues (Rice & Love, 1987; Walther & Burgoon, 1992). Designers of CMCS should work explicitly to incorporate innovative methods and channels for sharing various cues between participants. For example, users might be trained in the use of "emoticons" (also known as "smileys") to increase the media richness of their communications. Numerous linguistic conveniences in computer messages are evident in the culture of CMCS users, such as "BTW" for "by the way" and "IMHO" for "in my humble opinion," can also create a more familiar or informal sense for the communications exchange, which can serve to increase social presence. Whereas many first-time users of CMCS such as email might write formal messages that read like a business letter, the messages of high-volume users usually evolve into a far more familiar tone with personal comments that serve to create a greater sense of actually speaking with someone.

Kraut, Fish, Root, and Chalfonte (1993) suggested that whereas formal communication is characterized by preset agendas between arranged participants scheduled in advance with "impoverished content," informal communication often occurs spontaneously with no arranged agenda between random participants with richer content. Further, they showed that informal encounters create a common context and perspective that support planning and coordination of group work. Without informal exchanges, "collaboration is less likely to start and less productive if it does occur" (Kraut et al., p. 313). Participants in purely computer-mediated systems who have never met and exchanged informal conversation have exhibited a strong desire to do so when given the opportunity. Whenever the environment affords the opportunity, it would behoove CMCS developers to facilitate informal face-to-face contact early in the project life cycle.

Managers who wish to introduce these technologies into the workplace should capitalize on the beneficial differences inherent in computer-mediated communications and mitigate the negative differences. New communication technologies such as the MeetingWeb™ allow organizations to create virtual teams as needs arise without regard for the geographical location of the team members. Many of the technologies are still evolving, and unique issues arise as new organizational structures are implemented. As a result, each scenario is likely to provide novel problems, and modern managers must be flexible to restructure their sociotechnical system as such problems are encountered. This requires that managers become familiar with the strengths and limitations of the relevant technologies. This study highlighted some of the characteristics of a Web-based conferencing system. The relevance of this type of system will grow as corporate "intranets" become a widespread platform for intraorganizational communications.

Future Research

The findings of the present study suggest several avenues for future research. First, this study might be replicated with experienced users to determine whether significantly higher levels of computer familiarity and web use might contribute to any interesting differences between face-to-face and virtual teams. Second, not all teams are strictly virtual or strictly face-to-face. Examination of various combinations of amalgamated teams (with both types of interaction for all members or with only some members using one or the other medium exclusively) might be illustrative.

Third, the group's ability to perform the three group functions described by the TIP theory can be investigated (McGrath, 1991). For example, this may involve a detailed analysis of the group interactions to track what activities are performed by the groups and how well they are accomplished. The development of relational links may be tracked over time to determine whether relationship-developing activities are as effective in CMCS groups as in face-to-face groups and whether CMCS groups can achieve the same level of relational links as face-to-face groups.

Another avenue of research is to examine which media virtual team members select for specific tasks and whether they choose appropriate media based on media richness or social presence. A related question is how a virtual group's performance is affected by the use of different combinations of communication media. Another topic of interest is the effect of cultural factors on virtual team processes and outcomes. A comprehensive contingency framework might be developed to incorporate many of these relationships between and among system and environmental factors, which could serve as a guide to CMCS researchers and practitioners alike.

Another factor that may affect how users accept CMCS is organizational subcultures. Research has suggested that membership in a particular subculture may be more useful for predicting a user's satisfaction with an information system than other variables, such as demographic measures (Kendall, Buffington, & Kendall, 1987). The implications of subcultures for the use of CMCS is unknown, although it might be reasonable to assume that, as with satisfaction with other information systems, satisfaction with CMCS may be affected by subculture membership.

However, with virtual teams, an additional factor that must be considered is that team members may not even be members of the same organization or may be members of independent divisions of the same organization. Thus, the organizational cultures of the team members may be very different. The effect this may have on a team's performance and satisfaction remains an interesting and largely unanswered question.

Appendix: Survey Instrument (for Virtual Teams)

Group Cohesiveness

1. Do you feel that you were really a part of this team?
   - ☐ Really a part of my work team
   - ☐ Included in most ways
   - ☐ Included in some ways
   - ☐ Didn't feel I really belonged too much
   - ☐ Didn't feel I belonged at all

2. If you had a chance to do the same kind of work again, how would you feel about moving to another team versus staying in the same team?
   - ☐ Would want very much to stay in the same team
   - ☐ Would rather stay in the same team than move to another team
   - ☐ Would make no difference to me
   - ☐ Would rather move to another team than stay in the same team
   - ☐ Would want very much to move to another team

How does this group compare with other teams on each of the following points?

The way people:	Very Much Better	Better Than Most	About The Same	Worse Than Most	Very Much Worse
3. got along together	☐	☐	☐	☐	☐
4. worked together	☐	☐	☐	☐	☐
5. helped each other	☐	☐	☐	☐	☐

Perceptions of process

To a very little extent				*To some extent*			*To a very great extent*
1	2	3	4	5	6	7

6. Were team members committed to the goals and objectives of the team (during this project)?
      1   2   3   4   5   6   7
7. To what extent was trust exhibited within the team (during this project)?
      1   2   3   4   5   6   7
8. Did members have a strong sense of belonging to the team (during this project)?
      1   2   3   4   5   6   7
9. Did team members recognize and respect individual differences and contributions (during this project)?
      1   2   3   4   5   6   7
10. Were team members open and frank in expressing their ideas and feelings (during this project)?
       1   2   3   4   5   6   7

Satisfaction With Outcomes

Strongly Disagree — *Undecided* — *Strongly Agree*

1 2 3 4 5 6 7

11. Overall, I was personally satisfied with the team decision process.

    1 2 3 4 5 6 7

12. This team produced effective and valuable results during this project.

    1 2 3 4 5 6 7

13. I agree with the final decision of the team.

    1 2 3 4 5 6 7

14. Overall, the quality of this meeting team's interaction was high.

    1 2 3 4 5 6 7

Yourself

15. Describe (rate) your *general* skill level with computers:

0	1	2	3	4	5
None ("illiterate")	Very Low ("newbie")	Low (novice)	Medium (intermediate)	High (advanced)	Very High (expert)

16. Describe (rate) your skill level with using the *World Wide Web*:

0	1	2	3	4	5
None ("illiterate")	Very Low ("newbie")	Low (novice)	Medium (intermediate)	High (advanced)	Very High (expert)

17. How often do you use the WWW?

0	1	2	3	4	5
Never	Rarely	Occasionally or Monthly	Regularly or Weekly	Frequently (Almost Daily)	"Constantly" or Daily

References

Alavi, M., & Keen, P. G. W. (1989). Business teams in an information age. *The Information Society,* 6(4), 179-195.

Baecker, R. M. (1993). *Readings in groupware and computer-supported cooperative work.* San Mateo, CA: Morgan Kaufmann.

Burke, K., & Chidambaram, L. (1995). Developmental differences between distributed and face-to-face groups in electronically supported meeting environments: An exploratory investigation. *Group Decision and Negotiation,* 4(3), 213-233.

Chidambaram, L. (1996). Relational development in computer-supported groups. *MIS Quarterly,* 20(2), 143-163.

Chidambaram, L., & Bostrom, R. P. (1993). Evolution of group performance over time: A repeated measures study of GDSS effects. *Journal of Organizational Computing,* 3(4), 443-470.

Culnan, M. J., & Markus, M. L. (1987). Information technologies. In F. M. Jablin, L. L. Putnam, K. H. Roberts, & L. W. Porter (Eds.), *Handbook of organizational communications: An interdisciplinary perspective* (pp. 420-443). Newbury Park, CA: Sage.

Daft, R. L., & Lengel, R. H. (1986). Organizational information requirements, media richness, and structural design. *Management Science, 32*(5), 554-571.

DeSanctis, G., & Gallupe, B. (1987). A foundation for the study of group decision support systems. *Management Science, 33*(12), 1589-1609.

Fulk, J., & Boyd, B. (1991). Emerging theories of communication in organizations. *Journal of Management, 17*(2), 407-446.

Galegher, J., & Kraut, R. (1994). Computer-mediated communication for intellectual teamwork: An experiment in group writing. *Information Systems Research, 5*(2), 110-138.

Hightower, R. T., & Hagmann, C. (1995). Social influence on remote group interactions. *Journal of International Information Management, 4*(2), 17-32.

Hightower, R. T., & Sayeed, L. (1995). The impact of computer mediated communication systems on biased group discussion. *Computers in Human Behavior, 11*(1), 33-44.

Hightower, R. T., & Sayeed, L. (1996). Effects of communication mode and prediscussion information distribution characteristics on information exchange in groups. *Information Systems Research, 7*(4), 451-465.

Hightower, R. T., Sayeed, L., Warkentin, M. E., & McHaney, R. (1997). Information exchange in virtual work groups. In M. Igbaria & M. Tan (Eds.), *The virtual workplace* (pp. 199-216). Hershey, PA: Idea Group.

Hiltz, S. R., Johnson, K., & Turoff, M. (1986). Experiments in group decision making, 1: Communications process and outcome in face-to-face vs. computerized conferences. *Human Communication Research, 13*(2), 225-252.

Hiltz, S. R., & Turoff, M. (1978). *The network nation: Human communication via computer.* Reading, MA: Addison-Wesley.

Hollingshead, A. B., McGrath, J. E., & O'Connor, K. M. (1993). Group task performance and communication technology: A longitudinal study of computer-mediated versus face-to-face work groups. *Small Group Research, 24*(3), 307-333.

Jay, A. (1976, March/April). How to run a meeting. *Harvard Business Review*, pp. 43-57.

Johansen, R. (1988). *Groupware: Computer support for business teams.* New York: Free Press.

Kendall, K. E., Buffington, J., & Kendall, J. E. (1987). The relationship of organizational subcultures to DSS user satisfaction. *Human Systems Management, 7*(1), 31-39.

Kendall, K. E., & Kendall, J. E. (1995). *Systems analysis and design* (3rd ed.). Upper Saddle River, NJ: Prentice Hall.

Kiesler, S., & Sproull, L. (1992). Group decision making and communication technology. *Organizational Behavior and Human Decision Processes, 52*(1), 96-123.

Kinney, S. T., & Panko, R. R. (1996). Project teams: Profiles and member perceptions—Implications for group support system research and products. In *Proceedings of the Twenty-Ninth Hawaii International Conference on System Sciences* (pp. 128-137). Kihei, Maui.

Kraut, R. E., Fish, R. S., Root, R. W., & Chalfonte, B. L. (1993). Information communication in organizations: Form, function, and technology. In R. M. Baecker (Ed.), *Readings in groupware and computer-supported cooperative work* (pp. 287-314). San Mateo, CA: Morgan Kaufmann.

Laughlin, P. R. (1980). Social combination processes of cooperative, problem-solving groups as verbal intellectual tasks. In M. Fishbein (Ed.), *Progress in social psychology* (Vol. 1). Hillsdale, NJ: Erlbaum.

McGrath, J. E. (1990). Time matters in groups. In J. Galegher, R. E. Kraut, & C. Egido (Eds.), *Intellectual teamwork: Social and technological foundations of cooperative work* (pp. 23-62). Hillsdale, NJ: Lawrence Erlbaum.

McGrath, J. E. (1991). Time, interaction, and performance (TIP): A theory of groups. *Small Group Research, 22*(2), 147-174.

McGrath, J. E., & Hollingshead, A. B. (1993). Putting the "group" back in group support systems: Some theoretical issues about dynamic processes in groups with technological enhancements. In L. M. Jessup & J. S. Valacich (Eds.), *Group support systems: New perspectives*. New York: Macmillan.

McGrath, J. E., & Hollingshead, A. B. (1994). *Groups interacting with technology: Ideas, evidence, issues and an agenda*. London: Sage.

Panko, R. R. (1992). Patterns of managerial communication. *Journal of Organizational Computing, 2*(1), 95-122.

Pfeiffer, J. W., & Jones, J. E. (1977). *A handbook of structured experiences for human relations training* (Vol. 4). La Jolla, CA: University Associates.

Rice, R. E., & Love, G. (1987). Electronic emotion: Socioemotional content in a computer-mediated communication network. *Communication Research, 14*(1), 85-108.

Rogers, E. M. (1986). *Communications technology: The new media in society*. New York: Free Press.

Seashore, S. E. (1954). *Group cohesiveness in the industrial work group*. Ann Arbor: University of Michigan Press.

Siegal, J., Dubrovsky, S., Kiesler, S., & McGuire, T. W. (1986). Group processes in computer-mediated communication. *Organizational Behavior and Human Decision Processes, 37*(2), 221-249.

Stasser, G., & Titus, W. (1985). Pooling of unshared information in group decision making: Biased information sampling during group discussion. *Journal of Personality and Social Psychology, 48*(6), 1467-1478.

Stasser, G., & Titus, W. (1987). Effects of information load and percentage of shared information on the dissemination of unshared information during group discussion. *Journal of Personality and Social Psychology, 53*(1), 81-93.

Steiner, I. D. (1972). *Group process and productivity*. New York: Academic Press.

Straub, D. W., & Karahanna, E. (1990). *The changing role of telecommunications technologies in the workplace: E-mail, voice-mail & fax*. Working Paper Series, MISRC-WP-90-10, Management Information Systems Research Center, University of Minnesota.

Walther, J. B., & Burgoon, J. K. (1992). Relational communication in computer-mediated interaction. *Human Communication Research, 19*(1), 50-88.

Weisband, S., Schneider, S. K., & Connolly, T. (1995). Computer-mediated communication and social information: Status salience and status differences. *Academy of Management Journal, 38*(4), 1124-1151.

Zack, M. H. (1993). Interactivity and communication mode choice in ongoing management groups. *Information Systems Research, 4*(3), 207-239.

PART THREE

INFRASTRUCTURE-ENABLING TECHNOLOGIES

CHAPTER
ELEVEN

Web Pull and Push Technologies

The Emergence and Future of Information Delivery Systems

JULIE E. KENDALL
KENNETH E. KENDALL

The Web today is often a wildly growing and chaotic jungle, where the metaphorical traveler has no guide. A user clicks on a link but has very little information about where that path will take him or her. The traveler has to struggle, seek, and find the types of landmarks (information) that will help achieve his or her objectives. As Web technologies improve, the traveler's journey is eased. The traveler will hire an experienced guide, then hire and teach a new guide to look for more specialized items, and still later will encourage the guide to develop its own new methods of discovery.

While this is occurring, parties interested in the commercial aspects of the journey (travel companies) are trying to make the experience better for the traveler. At first, information of a general nature is broadcast to all travelers. Next, select information, resulting from interviews with the traveler about his or her wants, is bundled, and the product is packaged and conveyed back to the traveler. After a while, the industry advances and now only key information, based on the past behavior of that traveler, is sent. Finally, the industry develops to such a degree that key information is selected, filtered, and processed according to the needs, rather than the wants, of the traveler.

The above metaphorical narrative briefly chronicles the development of information delivery systems (IDSs) as an emerging technology in today's world. (See Kendall & Kendall, 1993, for more about metaphors and information systems methodologies.) The first part discussed a traveler making use of pull technology, or seeking out information on the Web. The term *pull technology* can describe anything from personally surfing the Net to allowing an ever changing, independent evolutionary agent to explore the Web for you.

The second part of the narrative describes the development of push technology. Push technologies, also referred to as Webcasting, will not be limited to the desktop. True push technologies will find your pager, digital phone, or Palm Pilot and inform you about traffic congestion, a tornado warning, or possibly an art exhibit en route between your office and home. Push technologies will therefore be intelligent, know your interests and preferences, and also know, if you choose to let them, your current location. The term *push technology* can be used to describe anything from broadcasting to selective content delivery using sophisticated evolutionary filtering agents.

We use the term *information delivery system,* or IDS, to describe the advanced form of both pull and push technologies for obtaining materials over the Internet (and its successors). But perhaps we are getting ahead at this point. We will first define and examine different types of pull and push technologies. Following that, we will explore their implications for managerial decision making and society as a whole. Our goal in writing this chapter is to enhance your understanding of information delivery systems and their future.

Pull Technologies

Everyone who has attempted to find information on the Web has experienced pull technology. The word *pull* connotes grabbing and yanking something from the Internet. When people go to the library, they pull a book off the shelf; similarly, they pull a piece of information from the Web. Users summon the information they desire.

Pull technologies come in many flavors. To make them easier to discuss, we have created an original category system that classifies each of four technologies as shown in Table 11.1. Each technology builds on and refines the features of the technology in the preceding category. We name each technology, describe it, provide a predominant metaphor being used in conjunction with the technology, and then add a statement about which aspects of user wants or needs the technology addresses.

Alpha-Pull (α-Pull) Technology

We place the pull technologies into four categories, from the simplest to the most elaborate, beginning with α-pull (alpha-pull). An example of α-pull technology is the basic searching techniques of a surfer, who is navigating the Web by clicking on a hypertext link.

Software to help the surfer is somewhat limited. Some products, such as WebWacker, aid the surfer in quickly downloading entire Web sites to his or her hard drive. In this way, the surfer can browse sites off-line at his or her own pace.

Other products that aid surfers include browser accelerators. Most of these are set up as proxy servers. Three such accelerators are PeakJet, Speed Surfer, and NetAccelerator. Most of these support off-line browsing as well.

There are also bookmark managers, such as Quicklink Explorer or Linkman. Utilities, such as GoZilla, work to find the quickest site from which to download a file (Keller, Lake, & Littman, 1998). All of these utilities have one thing in common— they help users to pull material from the Web in a simple, alpha-pull manner.

TABLE 11.1 Pull Technologies: Their Descriptions, Metaphors, and Objectives

Name		Description	Metaphor for the User	Accesses What Users
α-pull	Alpha-pull	Clicking on links	Surfing the Net	Imagine they want
β-pull	Beta-pull	Using a search engine	Using a guide; asking a librarian	Strongly think they want
γ-pull	Gamma-pull	Adopting an autonomous agent	Hiring a personal spider or bot	Really want
δ-pull	Delta-pull	Creating an evolutionary agent	Creating a friendly bot that understands the user and changes over time	Really need

Alpha-pull technology (as shown in Figure 11.1) is simply going to the Web, seeking out sites of interest, and bookmarking them for future reference. This has been called "surfing the Web."

Beta-Pull (β-Pull) Technology

The second type, beta-pull technology, is more sophisticated, but somewhat limited, search engine technology. Examples of this include the early search engines of Infoseek, Excite, AltaVista, Lycos, HotBot, Yahoo!, and Northern Light. We will return to these a bit later.

When users access a search engine to find a Website, they are not, of course, searching the Web. Instead, they are searching one of the many databases consisting of Website addresses that are set up in advance and periodically updated. Each of the databases has certain peculiar characteristics. (In 1997, Alta Vista allowed users to limit languages, HotBot was particularly good in its ability to set page depth, and some are simply more flexible in Boolean searching.) In 1997, HotBot claimed to have about 50 million pages in its database (Notess, 1997) at a time when there were an estimated 250 million to 300 million Web pages in existence.

Search engines concentrate on text and, more precisely, keywords. Many people are more visual or want to find digital images and video elements on the Web. Chang, Smith, Beigi, and Benitez (1997) use an analysis of WebSEEk, an Internet-based system, to examine current and future concerns about search and retrieval of information from large, distributed, on-line visual information repositories. Additionally, they assess a prototype of an Internet metavisual information retrieval system called MetaSEEk, which they describe as analogous to text-based meta-search engines on the Web.

Search engines are impersonal and can be frustrating. An approach that evolved as a result of this dissatisfaction is the Web ring (Basch, 1998). In a Web ring, each site is linked to the one before and after it. The advantage over traditional search engines is clear. When a user follows links from the traditional search engines, there

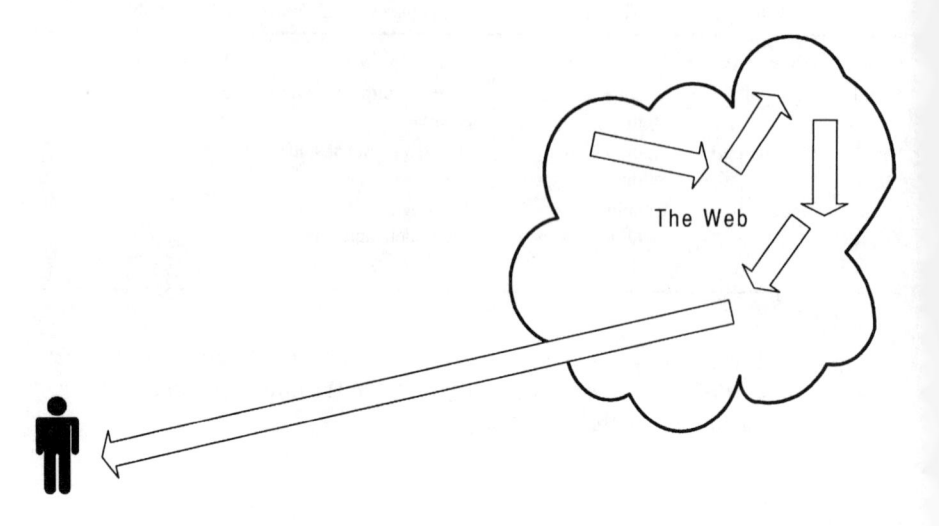

Figure 11.1. Using α-Pull Technology, the User Pulls Information by Surfing the Web

is a tendency to drift far away from the original intent of the search. When users navigate an established ring, they can always get back to their starting point.

Beta-pull technology uses general spiders or bots to gather information that may be of use to a wide audience of users, and it organizes the information so that users can refine their searches, as shown in Figure 11.2. Users depend on these rather impersonal bots to find the information for which they are looking. The impersonal beta bots are superior to the surfer, but they are still inadequate.

Gamma-Pull (γ-Pull) Technology

Gamma-pull (γ-pull) technology allows the user to control the search for Web sites directly. Originally, the agent that gathered information about Web sites was called a spider or bot (short for robot), but more generally, we refer to it as an autonomous agent.

Search engines use spiders to build their catalogs. The problem is, of course, that each of these spiders has a different set of algorithms or heuristics it uses to crawl around the Web looking for meaningful sites. Because search engine bots are meant for a mass audience, none of these spiders acts as your own personal spider, nor do they behave in a way you would necessarily approve.

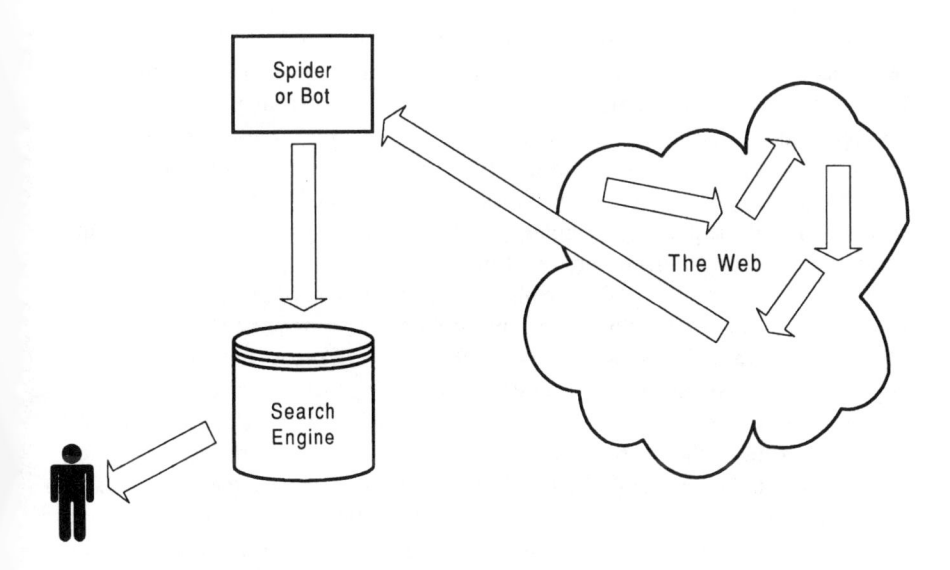

Figure 11.2. Using β-Pull Technology, the User Pulls Information From the Search Engine Database, Which Obtained the Information From the Web Using a Spider or Bot

Gamma-pull technologies make assumptions. In a recent search on Excite to locate the film and theatre director Nicolas Hytner, the search engine suggested that we add one or more of the following words: forger, breathless, fiennes, movieline, ralph, keaton, crucible, film, affection, and aniston. All of the suggestions related to films and film actors related to the director. None was helpful in locating a live production we were attending of Shakespeare's *Twelfth Night,* starring Helen Hunt. Similarly, it is difficult to search for a specific version of a piece of software. If you search for HyperCase 2.1 (Kendall & Kendall, 1999), you will get information about all versions of the simulation. Search engines still have rather impersonal bots.

New categories of off-line search programs are being called personal search engines or meta-search tools. With names like WebSleuth, Webseeker, WebCompass, and WebFerretPro, they will help you search from a dozen to more than 100 different search engines, help you weed out duplicate or dead links, and assist in assigning values to the more promising sites. Some will allow you to save the search, which will then be updated automatically.

WebSeeker refers to the technique of using quality keywords and phrases as a "results refining capability." Inforian Quest 98 not only allows the user to combine search engines, but it also allows the user to preview the site content and then sort and rank the results.

Copernic 98plus uses predefined channels to aid in searches. Sites are ranked by relevance; duplicate documents are eliminated; and statistics about a site, such as title, description, hit count, date found, and so on, are displayed. Copernic's configuration and search schemes can be customized for the user or search, and a channel development kit (for configuring channel sets) is being developed.

Other intelligent agents that take Web searching seriously are Headliner and Press Agent. All of these personal search engines take a step forward, but all still require significant user customization to be of much value.

The "Clever" project at IBM involves the development of an agent that locates a small set of the most authoritative information on a requested subject. Using algorithms developed by Kleinberg (1997) and Chakrabarti et al. (1998), the approach builds on Kleinberg's system called Hyperlink-Induced Topic Search (HITS). In this system, a standard search engine, such as AltaVista, is used to collect a root set of links, then expanded to include several thousand pages. Each page is assigned an "authority weight" and a "hub weight" according to the number of links that point to or from it within this group of links. After numerous calculations and recalculations, a high-quality list is generated. Rather than coming up with all possible sources, the list is, in effect, edited down to a concise (and, it is hoped, trustworthy) collection.

To realize fully the potential of gamma-pull technology, the independent agent needs to travel to foreign computers, visit them for a while, and return with useful information. In essence, these agents act like viruses living in another person's or company's computer. IBM has developed an agent based on Java applets and thus combined the two to form something called an "aglet" ("Applets With Attitude," 1997).

Gamma-pull technology (as shown in Figure 11.3) uses a personal agent to locate sites on the Web. At the time of this writing, independent agents were little more than meta-search agents. When these personal search engines allow users to specify more descriptive parameters and relay information about depth and fuzziness of the search, then they will earn the term personal spider, independent agent, or personal bot. The emphasis, like the other types of pull technology before this, is on the user's wants.

Delta-Pull (δ-Pull) Technology

Eventually, delta-pull will replace many of the searches by introducing an evolutionary agent—one that will observe, judge, act, and react in ways of its own to refine searches on the Web. The evolutionary agent of the future will initiate searches sans representation, that is, start without the underlying assumptions that tend to hold us back.

The evolutionary agent will observe a user's pattern of interaction with information—not just what is searched, but also what is used, saved, and transformed, as

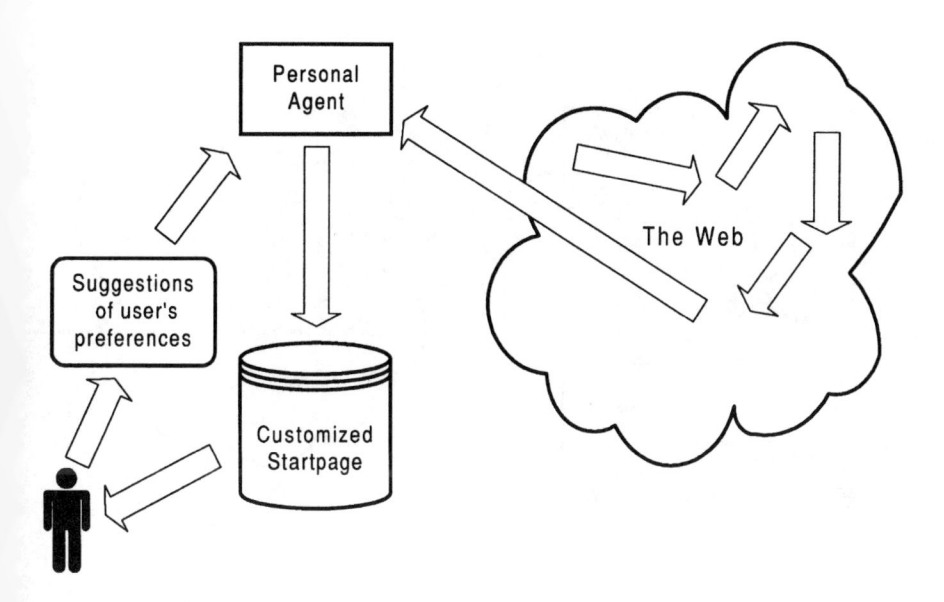

Figure 11.3. Using γ-Pull Technology, the User Sends Suggestions to a Personal Agent, Which Pulls More Specific Information From the Web and Sends It to a Customized Web

shown in Figure 11.4. In this way, the evolutionary agent minimizes the dead ends and useless information and focuses on the information needed by the decision maker.

The agent using delta-pull technology will grow and change according to the results it gets, the behavior of the decision maker, and the changing world. It will truly be, as the name implies, an evolutionary agent. A more complete discussion of the evolutionary agent appears in an earlier work on the future of artificial intelligence by Kendall (1996).

Delta-push technologies are superior to the less developed pull technologies. For example, the word *sabre* can refer to an on-line travel reservation and information system that originated with American Airlines, or it could refer to many other nonrelated items. A sabre can be the name of a freelance art studio, an automobile (either a Honda Sabre or a Buick Le Sabre), a stairlift system, a yacht company, a seminar program at the Nanyang Business School, a foundation that donates books to needy individuals in Eastern Europe, or any number of players in the Buffalo Sabres hockey franchise. Depending on the gamma-pull search engine used, you will get strikingly different results.

On the other hand, delta-pull technology is able to observe the behavior of the user and then use that information to be more selective when identifying links. If

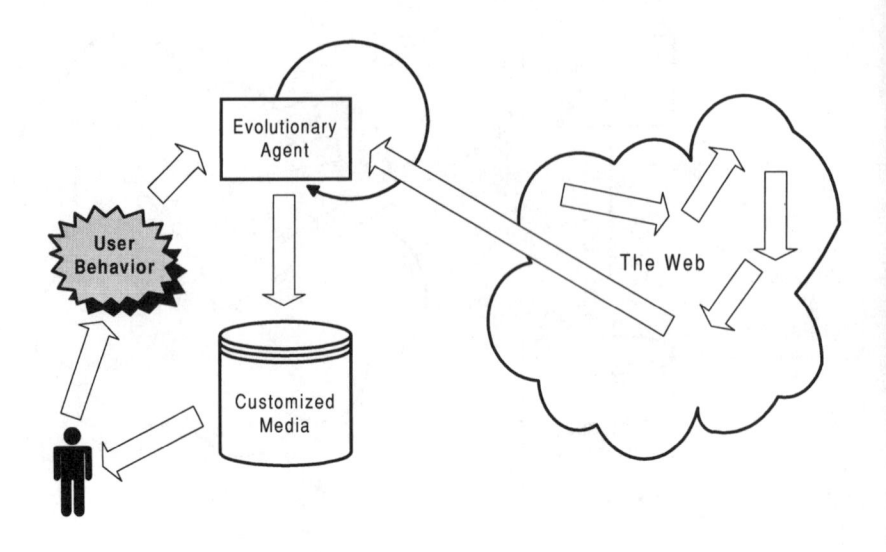

Figure 11.4. Using δ-Pull Technology, the Evolutionary Agent Captures Data on User Behavior Through an Iterative Process, Pulls the Information the User Needs From the Web, and Sends the Information to Customized Media the User Can View

the user has subscribed previously to a sports channel and indicated a preference for hockey stories, the evolutionary agent will assume an interest in hockey and consequently would list all of the Sabres hockey pages first.

There will always be a debate about whether an independent or evolutionary agent performs as well as a human on a particular task. Wegner (1997) provides a convincing argument that algorithms are inferior and that a paradigm shift will occur away from algorithms to interaction. But the lure of an automated personal assistant (evolutionary agent) that will understand your wants and needs is powerful. Users will insist on delta-push technology as soon as it is practical. It is unclear whether we will be better for it.

Furthermore, an evolutionary agent may make it more difficult to make intuitive leaps. That is, it may be much more difficult to obtain information that is outside the scope of the original search generated by the evolutionary agent. This is, in effect, getting stuck in a rut.

In the next section, we introduce four categories of push technologies that we compare and contrast with the four pull technology categories. Push technologies push a variety of contents, in some instances personalized or customized, to the user.

TABLE 11.2 Push Technologies: Their Descriptions, Metaphors, and Objectives

	Name	Description	Metaphor for the Provider	Accesses What Users
α-push	Alpha-push	Broadcasting; Webcasting	Broadcasting content much like TV	Imagine they want
β-push	Beta-push	Filtered messaging	Providing useful content though selective channel casting	Strongly think they want
γ-push	Gamma-push	Directed messaging using memes	Knowing what the user wants and pushing that content in a timely manner	Really want
δ-push	Delta-push	Evolutionary push provider	Providing for the exact needs of the user	Really need

Push Technologies

Push technologies also come in many flavors. We have created an original category system that classifies each of the four push technologies as shown in Table 11.2. Once again, we name each technology, beginning with α-push (alpha-push) technology, which describes basic Webcasting. Each of the other types (beta-, gamma-, and delta-push technology) builds on and refines the features of the technology in the preceding category. We provide a predominant metaphor being used in conjunction with the technology, and then we add a statement about which aspects of user wants or needs the technology attempts to reach.

Alpha-Push (α-Push) Technology

The most elementary form of push is broadcasting, similar to television broadcasting. This category includes everything we generally refer to as Webcasting: electronic news services, live streaming, and event reproduction. Webcasting has managed to earn a bad reputation among librarians and executives alike, not because of a dearth of content but because of a lack of *quality* content (Bing, 1997). Some even proclaim that push is dead (Pflug, 1997). Other voices call for less, more selective content proclaiming that "less is more" (Cronin, 1997). As push technologies begin to emerge, other experts assert that push is nothing new or special, consisting solely of repackaged shortcuts to Web pages (Poynder, 1997).

Early on-line news services, such as CNN Interactive, *The London Times, The New York Times,* and ABC News were simply passive Web sites and were not personalized in any way. Text and still photos, although effective, would not satisfy anyone but the least demanding Web surfer.

Animation, audio, and video clips were incorporated into news channels quickly, and plug-ins such as Shockwave (from Macromedia) set the standard for animation. RealAudio, followed by RealPlayer (from RealNetworks, Inc.) became the prominent audio and video plug-in for browsers. RealNetworks has adopted a standard called RealTime streaming protocol (RTSP), whereas Microsoft is trying to compete with NetShow, which will have intelligent streaming at different bit rates.

Streaming, a method that allows users to enjoy audio or video content while they are receiving it, has been the key to early success. Rather than downloading extremely large files to play later, streaming buffers the content, yielding only a very slight delay. But network performance can suffer, because streaming video takes place with no feedback as to the congestion it might cause (Radosevich & Fitzloff, 1998). Service providers and bandwidth management vendors are getting involved to improve streaming.

RealPlayerPlus allows users to choose headline news channels such as CNN, NPR, and ABC, as well as select among special interest channels in sports, finance, entertainment, and technology. In addition, numerous audio music and news channels are preset.

Broadcast.com (previously called AudioNet) is a Web site that serves as a home page or directory for live broadcasts on the Web. Acting as an on-line broadcasting guide, broadcast.com at the present time will simply guide you to the video or audio presentation or let you browse the schedule of upcoming events, some of which will be enhanced by other forms of communication, such as text.

Some claim that event reproduction is "better than seeing it live." It is possible to watch a video broadcast of some event and read about it at the same time using a split screen. For example, you can watch a sporting event and call up statistics on a particular player, or you can view a performance and access real-time critical reviews of the performance. In a broadcast of a shareholders' meeting, you can actually see the visual aids being presented in the room, because you can zoom in on them at will.

Internet videoconferencing comes to the desktop with software such as Microsoft NetMeeting and White Pine Software's CU-SeeMe. These packages make it possible for everyone to broadcast their own channels.

Not everyone is thrilled with the possibility of unlimited broadcasting. Webcasters download semipermanent cookies to keep track of subscriptions and demographics, as well as to store graphics on the client computer to speed up processing. Caches have to be cleared out occasionally. Finally, some feel that the advertising that goes along with push media is unsolicited garbage, or "spam."

Alpha-push technology is simple broadcasting or Webcasting, whether it is a news service, streaming video, or event reproduction. Alpha-push technology is depicted in Figure 11.5.

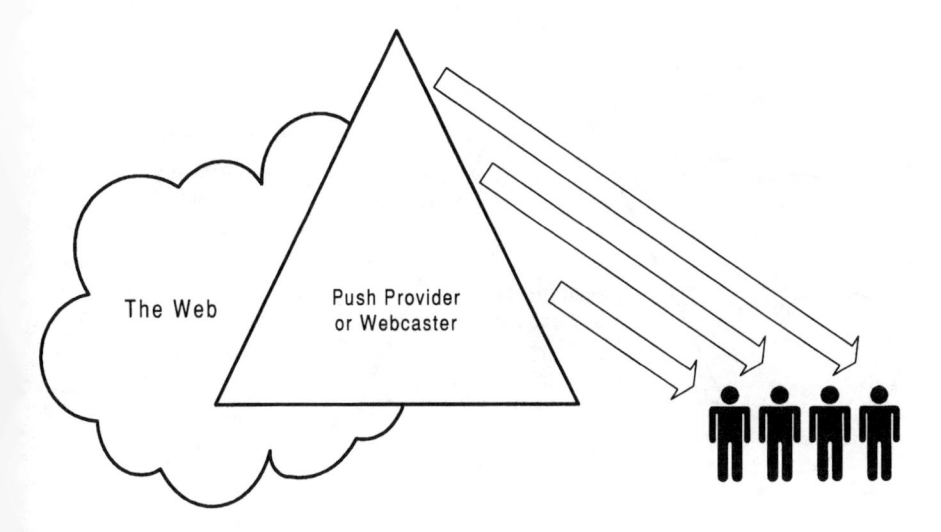

Figure 11.5. Using α-Push Technology, the Webcaster Pushes Information by Broadcasting It to a General Audience

Beta-Push (β-Push) Technology

Push technologies download information to local hard drives. Users have been known to get frustrated with long downloading times and the mindless cluttering of disk space with stories they do not care to read. Therefore push technologies such as PointCast, Marimba Castanet, Microsoft Webcaster, and Netscape's Netcaster were all developed with the idea that the user wants control over the channels received.

Selecting channels, however, isn't the same as choosing key words. So users get a mix of stories, information, and, of course, commercials having little to do with their interests. PointCast allows users to choose up to 12 channels, but many of the stories in the news services are redundant. Also a user in the United States might want to read stories about England but can select only "International" to filter the messages.

To complicate further the already chaotic clamor of criticisms regarding the content and use of push technologies, the industry has not yet agreed on a standard for push. Netscape is using an Apple format called MCF (Meta-Content format), whereas Microsoft is calling their format CDF (Channel Definition Format) (Dugan, 1998). Marimba has a partnership with Netscape, whereas PointCast and BackWeb are leaning toward Microsoft. Other Webmasters will have to choose a format. At this time, it is not clear which standard will win, but the general public will not receive push until this is resolved.

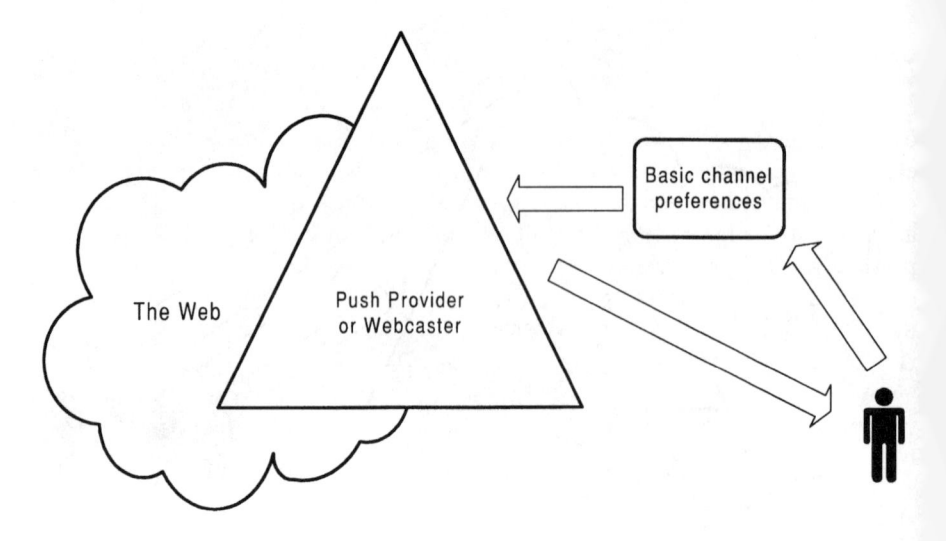

Figure 11.6. Using β-Push Technology, the Webcaster Pushes Channels of Information the User May Want Based on User Preferences

Beta-push technology is shown in Figure 11.6. Beta-push is still concerned with what push providers want to broadcast. They select the channels, then the subchannel. They choose when to subscribe and when to update. Beta-push has its limitations, but the result is obtaining more specific and more useful information than can be captured by the volumes of data coming our way through simple Webcasting.

Gamma-Push (γ-Push) Technology

The next level of push technologies involves push enterprises analyzing the user and suggesting what the user needs. The difference, therefore, is that β-push gives customers want *they* think they want and γ-push gives customers what the *push provider* thinks they want. Simple gamma-push technology is now used to push software patches (euphemistically called "upgrades") automatically if users set up their program to always check the manufacturer's Web site. An example of this is Quicken98. Products such as OilChange attempt to perform this function for all software, but they are not seamless, nor are they unobtrusive. They still need to develop further before they are truly useful. Information is stored on a user's hard drive in the form of "cookies" so that the push provider can quickly see whether an upgrade is needed.

The beginnings of this trend are evident now. Countless companies are competing to serve as a user's "personal startpage." Microsoft now has InternetStart, and Netscape has Netcenter, but they are limited compared with personal startpages such as Yahoo, Excite, Infoseek, Lycos, and Snap.

Even though each of these allows extensive customization, that customization is still very limited. For example, in Excite, you can choose the general type of entertainment (the arts) but not the specific art (opera); or, you can select the type of sport (NHL Hockey) but not the team (Buffalo Sabres). Consequently, the user ends up with an oddly fragmented collection of stories holding little or no interest.

Furthermore, these personal startpages (also known as portal sites, because they are a door to the Internet) not only allow shopping, they encourage it. On Excite's personal startpage, there appear several column inches dedicated to "My Services." (Note that these are not actually services chosen by the user; rather, they are ones that are recommended by Excite—and at the present time, the user cannot change this list.)

Innovative products such as Wayfarer and BackWeb are oriented toward the corporate world. Their approach is to develop systems that executives can use to help them make key decisions. Elements include tracking corporate resources, data warehouses, financial applications, and report generators, while monitoring both internal and external Web pages for new information. Wayfarer also provides templates for employees to send messages and reports.

The objective in gamma-push technology is not only to automate information gathering, but ultimately to steer the user in the direction it thinks the user needs to go. For example, Amazon.com, the large on-line bookseller, uses bots to track customers' preferences.

When bots are used in pull technology, they can find cheaper airfares, interesting books to purchase, parts to fix that broken phone you wanted to save, or stock tips and opportunities. When bots are used for push technologies, they can identify travelers and send email about travel packages, suggest books to read, send a telephone catalog with the latest new phones, and have stockbrokers make cold calls to potential investors. Some of these activities may be deemed desirable, whereas others may not.

Advertising and cold calls are intrusive irritations. The potential abuse of gamma-push technology does not reside in minor annoyances, but rather with the possibility of broadcasting destructive propaganda. Webcasters can broadcast memes that are potentially dangerous. We will discuss some of these concerns later.

Gamma-push technology, as depicted in Figure 11.7, tries to match up what the push provider wants to send and what it thinks users want to receive. This assumes a lot about the push technology actually *knowing* what the user wants. Powerful models, as well as insights about human behavior, are necessary to capture, analyze, and act on information collected about users.

Delta-Push (δ-Push) Technology

In the future, stories and services will be custom designed for the individual. Based on demographics and data mining, stories, services, and advertising will be targeted directly toward the user. The links featured on startpages will come from

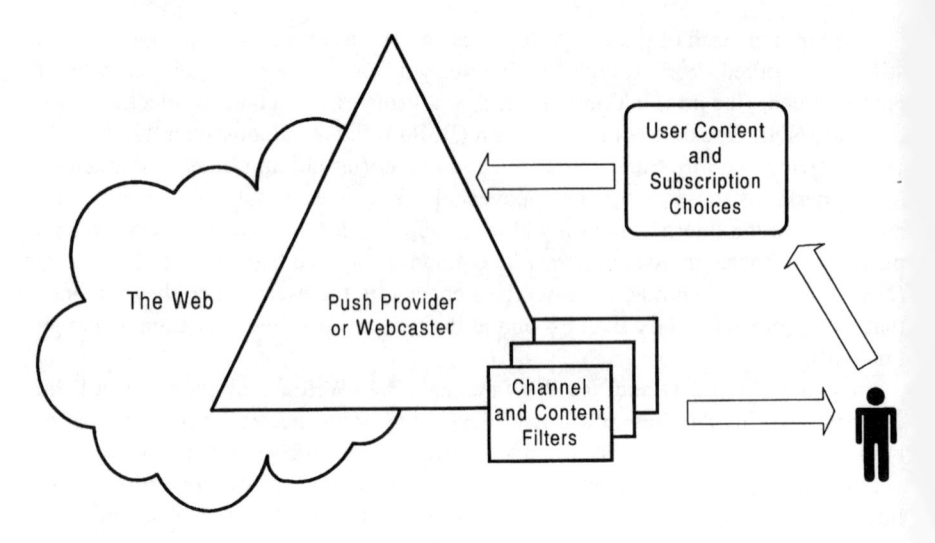

Figure 11.7. Using γ-Push Technology, the Webcaster Pushes Specific Content That the User Wants Based on Choices the User Made

an autonomous agent observing the user clicking on links and then choosing similar sites that the user might find interesting.

Alexa is the first easy-to-obtain product to attempt this. First described as a "navigation utility," this toolbar works with a browser to accomplish what the search engines do and more. Alexa gives detailed statistics about the sites (owner address, quality, and popularity) and even explanations about where the data came from. Alexa suggests where you might want to go next, and it attempts to match up related sites for you. Of course, Alexa does not actually look at or analyze individual decision-making behavior, so it cannot be called a true delta-push technology. Alexa is still in development and still a long way from achieving the potential of delta push.

Delta-push technology will involve bots, but each time a user reads a story that was downloaded from a push channel, the bots take note. Then, the bots will evolve based on those reactions and send new channels or information. Advances in genetic agents in AI are making this possible, of course. In this world, a generation occurs each time the user makes another purchase or changes a preference.

An example drawn from the realm of politics readily illustrates potential problems with delta-push. A liberal might prefer not to be bombarded with conservative viewpoints, and the opposite probably also holds true. Delta-push technology would be highly effective in screening out propaganda harboring a particular bias, and the user might be very pleased with the results. However, it might be in the better interests of the person and the society to see *both* sides of a political issue in order to make a more intelligent choice during a policy decision or when voting on a candidate.

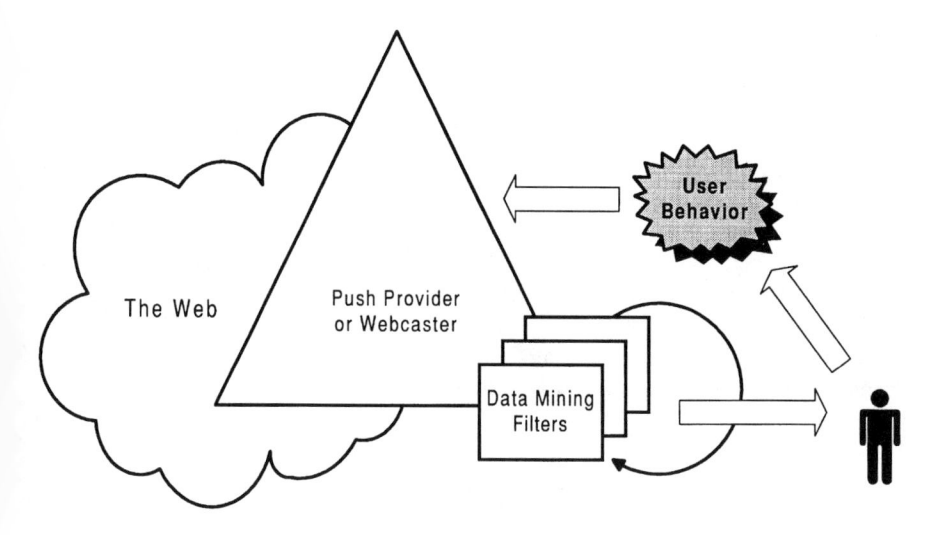

Figure 11.8. Using δ-Push Technology, the Webcaster Pushes What the User Needs After Analyzing User Behavior Through an Iterative Process

The same types of error can occur in the corporate world. If companies push the data they *think* their employees need, they may filter out useful information that would be in the best interest of the company in the long run. Therefore, we should welcome this new technology and simultaneously guard against any misuse or abuse.

It is apparent that the schemes that are part of delta-pull resemble techniques being developed in data mining. The data mining literature is addressing issues concerning obtaining and using information about people (Codd, 1995; Gray & Watson, 1998; Watson & Haley, 1997).

Delta-push technology is shown in Figure 11.8. The key here is evolution. The push provider, now properly described as an "evolutionary push agent," examines the behavior of the user—in this case, what the user reads, saves, and uses in decision making—to further fine-tune the information that is pushed to him or her.

At this stage, push providers focus on what they think users *need*. This is very different from early types of push technologies. When push providers' motives are honorable, useful information (and only useful information) is passed on to users. When push providers are less than honorable, the users can be subject to a barrage of memes or even become infected by virus memes. (See Brodie, 1996, for a further explanation of the science of memetics.)

The advantages and disadvantages of delta-push technology are still being defined, but some assessments are now possible. Currently, the advantages appear at the corporate, consumer, and commercial levels. In organizations, executives will use truly dynamic executive information systems growing from delta-push technology. In the personal realm, consumers will receive only the information they need to make their purchases. Merchants will be pleased that they can target their audience with precision and efficiency. People will be happy because evolutionary, data-mining bots will do what was once unproductive and frustrating work for them, with much greater success. Any annoyances of delta-push technology will disappear, it is claimed, because users actually will *need* the information they get.

However, assessments of delta-push technology should not be limited to overly optimistic scenarios of the future. There are clear disadvantages. Not only do we risk having destructive memes thrust upon us, but these memes can also mutate or evolve accordingly. When memes mutate and spread, they can be referred to as thought viruses, ideas we willingly pass on and even preach to others. Push technologies can push ideas too far.

Information Delivery Systems in the Corporate World

Push technology will come into its own when push is used to deliver information within the organization. As corporations recognize the value of intranets, the full potential of using push technologies on the corporate level will be discovered.

For example, National Semiconductor added its own channel to PointCast. This channel, called National Advisor, delivers three types of product-related data. The first type is the more traditional sales data and other information captured by the sales staff in the field. The second type of data is captured from the Web site. These data include the number of hits, type of product information for which a potential customer is searching, and requests for samples. The third type of data is generated from looking at email questions (Cronin, 1997).

Push systems have many advantages. They get the information to users in a timely manner. Getting information delivered by push is much faster than waiting for a weekly printout. Some people even believe that inexpensive and ubiquitous push technology spells the end of typically boring and media-free office environments ("Push!" 1997).

Push can also get the information to the person who needs it. Broadcasting information to all employees is cheaper than printing out information to a select few, and managers do not need to be concerned with whether a particular employee should get a report.

Furthermore, push technologies can be more flexible. When data are delivered over an intranet to a personal computer, the user is able to take the data and customize it in many different ways. For example, an employee may decide to look at a single product, or he or she may want to generate a graph of sales over time. This is made possible because all of the relevant data is being pushed to the right person at the best possible time.

National Semiconductor is not alone is its development of a push technology intranet. Wheat First Securities uses Wayfarer to deliver information to its brokers. MCI's network operations group uses PointCast to send information about outage alerts to its 7,000 employees who run its long-distance network. Church and Dwight, the maker of Arm and Hammer baking soda products, is developing an information delivery system using Diffusion, Inc.'s technologies (Sliwa & Stedman, 1998). Other push platforms for corporate intranets include Astound Webcast and Intermind Communicator (Strom, 1997).

Managerial Implications of IDSs

Considering the many dimensions of managerial work, managers' jobs will become easier and more interesting because of push and pull technologies. Decision making can be supported with push technologies that bring together industry data, daily user statistics from hits on a Web site, and the most recently enunciated corporate objectives for use in a forecasting model. Decision makers will be able to customize displays, seeing different data in different ways in real time, and in general "play" with data. This is a bonus for creativity and certainly frees the decision maker to think about how to achieve goals in a creative fashion, combining sources and strategies in new ways rather than solving problems with a traditional approach.

Additionally, there is great potential for sharing what one is thinking with colleagues, no matter where they happen to be at the moment. For example, corporate uses of push technology mean that rather than sending a text-only email message, you can send an entire hyperlinked multimedia message to someone via email. An example of push technology is given by Downes and Mui (1998), who write:

> Why not send everyone in the company a copy of the complete text of an interesting article, including active hyperlinks to the references, when doing so takes only a few keystrokes, no matter if the recipients are down the hall or in Sri Lanka? E-mail, as a killer app, starts by taking out the post office but may end by redefining human communications. (p. 19)

In this case, the decision maker becomes the content creator and provider by being able to create and send an entire hyperlinked multimedia message.

Lederer, Mirchandani, and Sims (1998) point to a survey they conducted that indicated that businesses adopting Web-based information systems (WISs) responded that the most important benefit of being on the Web was to "Enhance competitiveness or create strategic advantage." Not far behind in their estimation was to "Enable easier access to information," followed by to "Provide new products or services to customers." Then, they cited being able to "Improve the flexibility of information requests," and fifth on their list was to "Improve customer relations." However, managers must be empowered to comprehend that push technologies will help reap these benefits only by acting together in (as yet undiscovered) synergistic and dynamic modes that are unlike what managers or their media typically do today.

The blurring of lines between being a content creator and being merely a user is another important managerial implication of push technologies. Managers will be praised not only for their own creative approaches to problem solving but also for their ability to combine multimedia material, pushing it via intranets in a way that motivates peers and subordinates to solve problems in an innovative manner.

Organizationally, push and pull technologies can dynamically alter the structure of the enterprise so that for some projects, one manager is charge, and in a second project, he or she is not the leader but a consulting expert or even technical support for the duration of the problem (see Kendall, Kendall, Smithson, & Angell, 1992). No formal redrawing of the organizational chart is necessary, no hiring and firing of specialists du jour, because the power over the interaction is determined by the content being pushed or pulled.

Managers, as human beings, are subject to the same problems of information overload, disorientation, and frustration that any other user of push and pull technologies might experience. Already, executives (including Bill Gates) set aside days when they are purposely not reachable by electronic means (or can be reached only in an emergency), where they go to interact face-to-face with peers, sans the intrusion of technology. The wealth of ideas flowing from this type of brainstorming makes it a valuable managerial alternative to 24-hour connectivity.

However, one philosopher suggests that it is not the *length* of time we are free from our technological connections but the reflections that we have during that time (Heim, 1993) that are important. Indeed, some religious groups encourage the same kind of reflection in retreats away from television and other technologies (Yuen, 1998) in order to reconnect with spiritual values and other ways of viewing the world. The intention is that by introducing managers to alternatives unavailable via push or pull technologies, they might be less susceptible to groupthink and more likely to come up with imaginative approaches to developing their organizations, their employees, and themselves when they reconnect.

Societal Implications of IDSs

The societal implications of push and pull technologies are far reaching. Push and pull technologies are enabling a revolution. How societies, organizations, and individuals will react to, embrace, or scorn them will shape our future. The revolution is paradoxical in that it expands to vast proportions our awareness of the many worlds outside ourselves, and yet it permits what Turoff and Hiltz (1998) discuss as "superconnectivity," where one human communicates so specifically with another that their electronic interchange may be regarding matters that are of interest only to the two people involved, who may be physically far apart.

Decision makers' lives and, hence, habits are changing. Their lives are busy; their schedules are fragmented and diverse. This is a revolution in the way that we structure our discourse, in the way that we talk and think about the world. It is a change in the very way we tell stories. It is doing away with the narrative structure. To fully grasp what is happening, we must understand it as a revolution.

Postman (1984) observed that:

> Any major new medium changes the structure of discourse; it does so by encouraging certain uses of intellect, by favoring certain definitions of intelligence and wisdom, and by demanding a certain kind of content-in-a-phrase, by creating new forms of truth-telling.... We have reached ... a critical mass in that electronic media have decisively and irreversibly changed the character of our symbolic environment. We are now a culture whose information, ideas and epistemology are given form by television, but not by the printed word.... Print is now a residual epistemology, and it will remain so, aided to some extent by the computer, and newspapers and magazines made to look like television screens. (pp. 27, 28)

In the intervening years since Postman wrote this commentary, the advent of push and pull technologies is proving his words true. These technologies have taken the technological revolution to a point where television broadcasting could not go in terms of personalization of content and customization of display and timing. News media can be customized to address the different ways that people live. Rather than being tethered to something like an evening broadcast of the news, those who use the World Wide Web push technologies can have news when they like it. This trend will certainly continue. According to the Pew Research Center, in 1995, 4% of Americans used a news Web site; in 1998, 20% did ("The News Business," 1998). More and more people all over the world will avail themselves of news on the Web, many of them taking advantage of push technology to do so.

One important difference between push technologies and traditional broadcasting is that push has a much greater level of personalization. The user can configure the system to show only content in which he or she is specifically interested. The type of information that is considered to be "news" is also being shaped by the possibility to customize or personalize the content that is being pushed. With the advent of Webcasting, people need not struggle to see the relevance of the news or other content to their lives. They have chosen their display from among the pushed content available because they assume that it most assuredly will be relevant to them. What they see is of their own choosing, and in many ways, it can be said that their world is of their own making.

In addition to understanding the revolutionary aspects of push and pull technologies, we also need to educate businesspeople and organizational leaders about how push and pull technologies are changing the structure of our public debates. We can also educate decision makers and other users of pull media about the need for balance in what is subscribed to and how media are used.

Designers of information delivery systems must also study how their designs affect users' perception and understanding. Although the print culture is no longer dominant, a coherent story with a recognizable, linear narrative still may be important. Experimentation with Web development has led some researchers to assert that niceties such as standard, Windows-type interface conventions are still important to Web users (Dennis, 1998). Although push sites permit users to jump to hyperlinked topics to find out more, humans still need to be presented with *enough* information to pique their curiosity and prompt them to ask the next question or click on the next link.

The countries of the world will face some very real problems pertaining to information overload and diversity of perspectives because of push and pull technologies. How much information should be filtered by governments, businesses, religious groups, schools, or families? This raises questions about censorship, as well as questions concerning the legitimacy of commercial versus individual information, and whether push and pull technologies ultimately demand that only free societies will evolve.

We do not know how much information people can handle, nor do we know what the effects are of continuous connection, instant access, or even bombardment with information. We know that information *does* affect human beings, and that those with addictions to surfing the Web are following patterns similar to other addicts, where normal endeavors and lifestyles are displaced by Web-based activities, leading in turn to loss of jobs, break up of homes, and so on. Crabb (see Kelley, 1998) notes that without private times and spaces, human beings in any culture become stressed and sick. Other researchers, such as Friedman (see Kelley, 1998), worry that connection to the Web does not automatically translate into higher productivity or a better quality of life overall.

The kaleidoscope of relationships between push and pull technologies, selectivity and quality of information versus overload, and commercial versus individual and public uses should be debated openly throughout society for many years to come. Awareness, understanding, and education can help us recognize that many of these issues require joint decision making with users and providers who have come to realize that the impact of their choices can be tremendous.

Conclusion and Future Implications for IDSs

We have created the term *information delivery systems,* or IDSs, to denote emerging information technologies that include push and pull technologies and whose providers are intent on enabling users to handle Web information in useful ways. Using IDS, organizations, managers, and other users find out what content is available on the Web, and then they locate it, analyze it, and make it meaningful in a way that will help ensure competitive advantage. Because of the type of push and pull technologies that are emerging, users will also be able to substantiate and enrich the immediacy, reliability, completeness, and accuracy of information used to make strategic decisions.

We have identified and classified eight types of information delivery systems that we refer to as alpha-, beta-, gamma-, and delta-pull technologies, as well as alpha-, beta-, gamma-, and delta-push technologies. It is clear from our analysis here that

IDSs are emerging and will continue to gain acceptance as organizations put them to new uses. Particularly striking will be the use of push technologies on corporate intranets that will enable managers to push a variety of visual displays and other data together in new and stimulating ways. Pull technologies will also grow in use and acceptance as evolutionary agents are refined and searches become more easily personalized with better, more accurate results.

We believe that the future of pull technologies will include an evolutionary agent, one that will observe a user's pattern of interaction with information—including what is searched, what is used, what is saved, and how it is transformed into information used in decision making. The term *evolutionary* implies that the agent will change according to what it observes, and, it is hoped, improve as time goes on. This agent, which we refer to as delta-pull technology, will seek out the information the user needs.

When delta-pull technology is fully engaged, the evolutionary agent will relieve some of the burden of searching because it will observe and understand a user's behavior and seek out the information the user wants. Additionally, searches on the Web will be more efficient. It follows that more satisfying results from initial searches also mean that the searches will be more effective.

On the push side, we refer to delta technology, which is an advanced form of push that uses concepts from data mining and the evolutionary agent to observe users' behavior and then deliver (or Webcast) only what they need. This includes delivering information, software upgrades, corporate data, and, of course, advertising. Just as in delta-pull, the process will be evolutionary, so delivery will change according to what is observed about the user's decision-making behavior.

The advent and use of the evolutionary push agent will make it possible for Webcasters (including corporations) to deliver what the users need at the time that they want it. Additionally, push providers will be able to influence users in many more significant ways. Steering a user toward a particular product is one application, but a more powerful use may be corporations influencing decision makers to focus on key issues simply by filtering data and messages to them. Furthermore, delta-push technologies will make it possible to reduce the amount of useless information now being received by users who simply do not want it, so most users will be satisfied with the quantity of information received, which is a key attribute of decision data.

Societies and corporations alike face many issues regarding the adoption and use of information delivery systems. Reactions are spanning a wide range of behaviors. For example, some companies are beginning to experiment with push technology, whereas other enterprises are skeptical of it, viewing it merely as a toy or game of which employees will gradually, but inevitably, tire. To them, it is a benign technology, but ultimately boring.

We believe that information delivery systems will continue to evolve. IDSs are an emerging technology. There will be barriers to overcome, but both pull and push technologies will advance—but not necessarily in the ways we currently anticipate. We will explore a couple of the more imaginative possibilities here. The first deals with IDSs through delivery to devices more personal than cathode ray tubes, and the second explores IDSs that use new technology that has the look and feel of paper.

One way in which an IDS can gain acceptance is by delivering personal information more personally. What if all of your small, portable personal devices (mobile phones, palmtops, pagers, watches) could communicate together with computers in an ad hoc fashion? No more productivity curtailed because of travel, no more cumbersome cables, and any emails written on a plane could be automatically sent (without you having to boot your laptop or connect it) as soon as you landed. Bluetooth (named for Harald Bluetooth, a 10th-century Viking king) is the code name for a new international consortium composed of telecommunications and computing companies, including Ericsson, IBM, Intel, Nokia, and Toshiba. They are developing a new technology consisting of a low-cost, low-power, radio-based cable replacement, or wireless link, and along with this, they hope to specify a global specification for wireless connectivity (Kelly, 1998; see also www.bluetooth.com/news/text.Techback.htm). If only one of the devices has ISP dial-up capability, then all of them can be connected to the Internet. This technology encourages the use of IDSs by delivering the information to more personal destinations—your mobile phone or palm computer, for example. Users will prefer to use pull technology and receive push technology at the point where the situation calls for it.

After we have spent considerable time dwelling on what is displayed to users on their computer screens, we must caution that the latest push technology does not necessarily have to come to a conventional computer screen near you. It may come to users on what some have dubbed "the last book," which is an electronic information display medium "comprised of hundreds of electronically addressable display pages printed on real paper substrates. Such pages may be typeset *in situ*, thus giving such a book the capability to be any book" (Jacobson, Comiskey, Turner, Albert, & Tsao, 1997, p. 457). When a user has finished with the content, the medium can electronically change the charges displayed, and all new content will appear. Even though the medium can be recycled electronically, it will have the look and feel of traditional paper. There are ongoing efforts at MIT, in conjunction with a company called E Ink Corp. (early investors are Motorola and the Hearst Corp.) to develop this type of flexible, lightweight, and rechargeable medium (Peterson, 1998).

Information delivery systems (IDSs) are an emerging technology. Many users are frustrated with today's pull technology, and some critics claim that push is dead. They fail to see the entire picture. As new technologies make it possible to obtain the information we need, when and where we need it, the IDS will come into its own. IDSs are coming, but perhaps not in the way we currently envision them.

References

Applets with attitude. (1997, May 17). *The Economist*, p. 89.
Basch, R. (1998). Web rings offer a new way to sift through loads of information. *Computerlife, 5*(1), 62-64.

Bing, M. (1997). Implementing Webcasting as a communication tool. *Database, 20*(6), 42-44.
Brodie, R. (1996). *Virus of the mind.* Seattle, WA: Integral Press.
Chakrabarti, S., Dom, B., Gibson, D., Kleinberg, J., Raghavan, P., & Rajagopalan, S. (1998). Automatic resource compilation by analyzing hyperlink structure and associated text. In *Proceedings of the 7th World-Wide Web conference.* Amsterdam: Elsevier Sciences. Available: http://decweb.ethz.ch/WWW7/1898/com1898.htm.
Chang, S., Smith, J. R., Beigi, M., & Benitez, A. (1997). Visual information retrieval from large distributed on-line repositories. *Communications of the ACM, 40*(12), 112-113.
Codd, E. F. (1995, April 13). Twelve rules for on-line analytic processing. *Computerworld,* pp. 84-87.
Cronin, M. (1997, September 29). Using the Web to push key data to decision makers *Fortune,* p. 254.
Dennis, A. (1998). Lessons from three years of Web development. *Communications of the ACM, 41*(7), 112-113.
Downes, L., & Mui, C. (1998). *Unleashing the killer app: Digital strategies for market dominance.* Boston: Harvard Business School Press.
Dugan, D. (1998, January 26). Who will win the push war? *Infoworld, 20*(4), 81.
Gray, P., & Watson, H. J. (1998). *Decision support in the data warehouse.* Upper Saddle River, NJ: Prentice Hall.
Heim, M. (1993). *The metaphysics of virtual reality.* New York: Oxford University Press.
Jacobson, J., Comiskey, B., Turner, C., Albert, J., & Tsao, P. (1997). The last book. *IBM Systems Journal, 36*(3), 457.
Keller, A., Lake, M., & Littman, D. (1998, July). Pump up your browser. *PC World,* pp. 171-174, 178, 180.
Kelley, T. (1998, June 28). Only disconnect (for a while, anyway): A few of the well-connected who take time off from e-mail, and survive. *The New York Times,* pp. G1, G8.
Kelly, S. (1998). Viking radio. *Equip, 3*(1), 128.
Kendall, J. E., & Kendall, K. E. (1993). Metaphors and methodologies: Living beyond the systems machine. *MIS Quarterly, 17*(2), 149-171.
Kendall, J. E., Kendall, K. E., Smithson, S., & Angell, I. O. (1992). SEER: A divergent methodology applied to forecasting the future roles of the systems analyst. *Human Systems Management, 11*(3), 123-135.
Kendall, K. E. (1996). Artificial intelligence and Götterdämerung: The evolutionary paradigm of the future. *The DATA BASE for Advances in Information Systems, 27*(4), 99-115.
Kendall, K. E., & Kendall, J. E. (1999). *Systems analysis and design* (4th ed.). Upper Saddle River, NJ: Prentice Hall.
Kleinberg, J. (1997). Authoritative sources in a hyperlinked environment. In *Proceedings of the 9th ACM-SIAM Symposium on Discrete Algorithms.* Available: http://www.cs.cornell.edu/home/kleinber/auth.ps.
Lederer, A. L., Mirchandandi, D. A., & Sims, K. (1998), Using WISs to enhance competitiveness. *Communications of the ACM, 41*(7), 94-95.
The news business. (1998, July 4). *The Economist,* pp. 17-19.
Notess, G. R. (1997). Refining the Internet in '97. *Database, 20*(6), 62.
Peterson, I. (1998). Rethinking ink: Printing the pages of an electronic book. *Science News OnLine* at www.sciencenews.org/sn_arc98/6_20_98/bob2.htm.
Pflug, O. (1997, January 27). Push technology: Dead on arrival. *Computerworld,* p. 37.
Postman, N. (1984). *Amusing ourselves to death: Public discourse in the age of show business.* New York: Penguin.
Poynder, R. (1997). It's "Push," Jim, but not as we know it. *Information Today, 14*(11), 18, 20.
Push! Kiss your browser goodbye: The radical future of media beyond the Web. (1997, March). *Wired,* cover, pp. 12-23.
Radosevich, L., & Fitzloff, E. (1998, March 2). Damming the stream. *Infoworld,* pp. 1, 18.
Sliwa, C., & Stedman, C. (1998, March 23). "Push" gets pulled onto intranets. *Computerworld,* p. 6.
Strom, D. (1997). Tune in to the company channel. *Windows Sources, 5*(9), 149-150, 154, 156, 158.

Turoff, M., & Hiltz, S. R. (1998). Superconnectivity. *Communications of the ACM, 41*(7), 116.
Watson, H. J., & Haley, B. (1997). A framework for data warehousing. *Data Warehousing Journal, 2*(1), 10-17.
Wegner, P. (1997). Why interaction is more powerful than algorithms. *Communications of the ACM, 40*(5), 81-91.
Yuen, E. (1998, July 12). An ideal Buddhist vacation: Travel combined with mindfulness meditation. *Philadelphia Inquirer,* p. H7.

CHAPTER
TWELVE

Structure and Macro-Level Impacts of Electronic Commerce

From Technological Infrastructure to Electronic Marketplaces

VLADIMIR ZWASS

Introduction: From Traditional to Internet-Driven Electronic Commerce

As electronic commerce is being redefined by the dynamics of the Internet, we wish to analyze the present structure of the enterprise defined by this term and look forward to future developments. We shall thus present a hierarchical framework for electronic commerce, within which we shall analytically survey the mutually reinforcing changes in the business practices and in the underlying information technologies.

Electronic commerce (E-commerce) is sharing business information, maintaining business relationships, and conducting business transactions by means of telecommunications networks. In today's business environment, where the operational boundaries between firms have become fluid, it is often both pragmatically and analytically unfruitful to separate the interorganizational business processes from the intraorganizational ones. Therefore, in our understanding, E-commerce includes the relationships and transactions between companies, as well as the corporate processes that support the commerce within individual firms.

Electronic commerce is a new and certainly trendy name, but the practice to which it refers originated a half-century ago in the Berlin airlift (Seideman, 1996). This practice became electronic data interchange (EDI), the computer-to-computer exchange of standardized electronic transaction documents. Although what can now be called traditional E-commerce has not been limited to EDI and has included business practices built around computer-to-computer transmissions of a variety of message forms, bar codes, and files, the use of EDI has arguably led to the most significant organizational transformations and market initiatives (e.g., see Jelassi & Figon, 1994). Some of the well-known cases in point are Wal-Mart, Levi Strauss,

General Motors, and other companies that have built new kinds of relationships with their suppliers and customers through bilateral electronic linkages. Electronic integration, supported by EDI and other information technologies, drastically reduces time and space buffers that shelter a firm but that also limit the firm's competitive opportunities.

Electronic integration has led to dramatic shifts in the definition of a firm with the emergence of virtual companies, whose capabilities of delivering their products to the market are defined largely by their ability to organize and maintain a network of business relationships rather than by their ability to manufacture a product or deliver a service. Extensive business networks have been formed by relying on this form of integration; the local and global business communities using TradeNet in Singapore can serve as an example (and have done so—to the authorities of the Port of Rotterdam in The Netherlands, for instance). Entire industries are being radically changed; for instance, U.S. grocery retailing is being reshaped by the EDI-based Efficient Consumer Response initiative, which is expected to save tens of billions of dollars in the distribution channel ("H.E. Butt," 1994). To understand and rationalize the operations of an individual firm, it is now necessary to study the business networks in which the firm is embedded.

It is the arrival of the commercial use of the Internet, driven by its World Wide Web subset, that has been defining new E-commerce since 1993.[1] E-commerce now emerges from the convergence of several major information technologies and business practices. Among the principal technologies directly enabling modern E-commerce are computer networking and telecommunications; client/server computing; multimedia, and hypermedia in particular; information retrieval systems; EDI; message handling and workflow management systems; groupware and electronic meeting systems; and public key cryptography. In a broader sense, all of the major computer and telecommunications technologies, and database management in particular, undergird E-commerce. The set of technologies driving E-commerce is embodied (for want of a better word) today in the Internet. This conglomerate is a transformational technology (in the sense of Fedorowicz & Konsynski, 1992) that has challenged old assumptions and helps shape new workplaces, organizations, and markets. The Internet offers an open platform for new E-commerce, removing the long lead times, asset specificity, and bilaterality of E-commerce based on the traditional proprietary EDI.

It would be entirely wrong to interpret E-commerce as a largely technological development. This way of doing business can be understood as the deployment of information technologies together with the organizational and management advances that pull the technology and are pushed by it in turn. Team-centered work organization, with international teams working around the clock if desired; telework; moving products and operations to virtual value chains; demassing the firm by building it around core competencies; and transnational organizations are some of these advances. In the process of creative destruction described by Schumpeter (1950/1975), the use of transformational technologies challenges the preexisting ways of doing business, collaborating, and competing. In a wider realm, the underlying technology of global, accessible, and nonproprietary connectivity changes many aspects of our lives in the public and private domains.

The chapter first presents a systematic view of the complex enterprise of E-commerce within a hierarchical framework, extending from the networking infrastructure to global marketplaces. It then analyzes some of the nodal impacts of E-commerce, relating them to this framework. A number of open questions emerge from this analysis.

The Framework of Electronic Commerce

The Hierarchical Framework of E-Commerce and Its Metalevels

The established way to both analyze and develop very complex systems, such as that of E-commerce, is to structure them as a hierarchy of several levels, with each of the lower ones delivering a well-defined functional support to the higher ones. Such a hierarchical framework of E-commerce is shown in Table 12.1, updated from Zwass (1996). The framework will help us in the sensemaking and in our subsequent analysis of the impacts of E-commerce.

The framework recognizes that E-commerce consists of three metalevels:

I. *Infrastructure*—the hardware, software, databases, and telecommunications that are deployed to deliver such functionality as the World Wide Web over the Internet, or to support EDI and other forms of messaging over the Internet or over value-added networks

II. *Services*—messaging and a variety of services enabling the finding and delivery (on business terms, if desired) of information, including a search for potential business partners, as well as the negotiation and settlement of a business transaction

III. *Products and Structures*—direct provision of commercial information-based goods and services to consumers and business partners; intra- and interorganizational information sharing and collaboration; and organization of electronic marketplaces and supply chains

We shall now discuss the individual levels that constitute these three metalevels, and we will examine the impacts engendered by their functions later in the chapter.

Technological Infrastructure

The first three levels of the hierarchical framework are the technological infrastructure of E-commerce. The foundation is the intermeshed network of wide area telecommunications networks, extended by the metropolitan and local area nets. Deploying both guided (such as the fiber optic and coaxial cable) and wireless transmission media (such as the satellite microwave and the radio) under computerized control, these networks span the globe. Thus, E-commerce is inherently

TABLE 12.1 The Hierarchical Framework of E-Commerce

Metalevel	Level	Function	Examples
Products and structures	7	Electronic marketplaces and electronic hierarchies	Electronic auctions, brokerages, dealerships, and direct search markets Interorganizational supply-chain management
	6	Products and systems	Remote consumer services (retailing, banking, stock brokerage) Infotainment-on-demand (fee-based content sites, educational offerings) Supplier-customer linkages On-line marketing Electronic benefit systems Intranet- and extranet-based collaboration
Services	5	Enabling services	Electronic catalogs/directories, smart agents E-money, smart-card systems Digital authentication services Digital libraries, copyright protection services Traffic auditing
	4	Secure messaging	EDI, e-mail, EFT
Infrastructure	3	Hypermedia/multimedia object management	World Wide Web with Java
	2	Public and private communication utilities	Internet and value-added networks (VANs)
	1	Wide area telecommunications infrastructure	Guided- and wireless-media networks

global. Yet there are, and will persist, major differences in national and regional development of the infrastructure, as well as in the national governance of telecommunications, with government monopolies in a number of countries limiting the development and imposing high telecommunications costs. In Europe and, to a degree, in Latin America, a movement toward privatization has produced, or is expected to produce, beneficial effects on prices and services. In salutary cases of government intervention, such as in Singapore, national development programs support the development of E-commerce. The inadequacies of the telecommunications infrastructure in many developing countries make it impossible for them to partake of the benefits of E-commerce and perpetuate their underdevelopment (Dutta, 1997).

The telecommunications capabilities are delivered for business use through two essential means. The older order is proprietary value-added networks (VANs), established by vendors to deliver services over and above those of common carriers that are licensed by governments to provide communications services to the public. The new order is the Internet, which has become the principal vehicle of E-commerce. The history of the almost organic emergence of today's Internet from its

U.S. Department of Defense-sponsored origins as a network for research support is well known. The salient features, conditioned by the development trajectory of this de facto global information infrastructure, are its easy and relatively inexpensive public access in the more developed countries of the world; absence of centralized control and the consequent organic growth, combined with the limited security, reliability, and bandwidth; reliance on an open and simple packet-switching protocol suite (TCP/IP), and thus the ease of linking in additional networks with routers, with the standardization managed by the Internet Society and its subsidiary bodies, such as the Internet Architecture Board.

The Internet has become the driver for E-commerce thanks to the invention of the World Wide Web as a principal means of sharing information, and of the browser as the universal front end. The Web has turned the Internet into a global, distributed, and hyperlinked multimedia database. By relying on the client/server architecture, the Web further builds on the decentralized model of the Internet. It is easy to join, and it is easy to organize an information space for a small or a very large group. Internet communities can carve out and shape the space that suits their purposes (Armstrong & Hagel, 1996). The Web can serve as a medium for presentation, distribution, and use-based sale of passive or active (in the sense of software) information objects. Specialized platform-independent programming languages, such as Java, facilitate making the electronic pages of the Web into a source of active software objects. It needs to be seen clearly that as a separate and software-based layer, the Web can and may be replaced in the future by an information management mechanism that would better meet the demands of very large-scale use of the global network of networks.

Services: Enablers of Business Communication and Commerce

The metalevel of services consists of provision of secure messaging and enabling services for E-commerce. Taken together, these services provide the *business* infrastructure for E-commerce.

As opposed to the traditional, EDI-based E-commerce relying on secured private VANs, the public communication utility of new E-commerce is based on the TCP/IP protocol suite that was developed to share information freely rather than to underlie a marketplace. The fundamental security flaws in the Internet infrastructure include the ability of any computer that lies on the path of a communication between two parties to eavesdrop (and potentially be a tool in stealing information, such as a credit card number); the absence of authentication of the communicating parties (making impersonation at either end possible); and no precautions against altering the contents of a message's packets (Bhimani, 1996).

Secure messaging for business transaction processing has to feature the following attributes: confidentiality (generally accomplished through encryption, but secure key logistics remains a problem even in the public key systems); message integrity (achieved with hash totals or similar tokens accompanying the message); authentication of both parties (generally via a digital signature and possession of a private key); and nonrepudiation by either party (achieved through a combination of the means mentioned previously). Some transactions require additional attributes; thus, generation of electronic cash requires anonymity of the receiving party (accomplished with a blinding factor during the encryption).

Considering the limitations of the Internet's protocol suite, the attributes of secure messaging have to be provided by other means, and the organization's own information systems are generally separated from the public Internet by a firewall system that screens out unauthorized traffic. A number of secure protocols are being considered actively for various levels of communication, from the network to applications. A notable example is the Secure Electronic Transaction (SET) protocol layer, developed by the Visa and MasterCard organizations to secure credit card transactions over the Internet, which relies on digital certificates to be issued to cardholders and presented by them when making a purchase. At this time, a uniform secure environment has not been created, and the perceived lack of security remains a fundamental obstacle to E-commerce. In particular, by often making it necessary to separate the settlement from the informational and contracting steps in an acquisition, the security concern is a serious obstacle to consumer-oriented E-commerce.

The principal messaging services include EDI, electronic funds transfer (EFT), and e-mail; voice messaging and telefacsimile are also available and have high potential as business initiatives when placed on the Internet. The basic motivation for implementing EDI is economy. Thus, corporations spend an average of $150 to process a paper order but only about $25 to process an electronic order (Verity, 1996). Beyond economy, companies seek strategic benefits, such as a compressed business cycle and intensified relationships with business partners. Time-based competitive moves of quick-response retailing by "pulling in" demanded products from the supply chain, and just-in-time manufacturing with close-to-zero inventories, are enabled by EDI.

Traditional EDI relies largely on the hub-and-spoke model, with a dominant business partner (the hub) gradually surrounding itself with the spokes of its supplier, customer, and collaborator firms. This form of EDI is still largely VAN based, with proprietary standards and relatively high costs of bundled-in services. Although industry standards have emerged in such segments as grocery or railroads, the international EDIFACT standard has found only a limited measure of adoption. At this time, many leading companies are moving their EDI communications to the Internet, seeking the benefits of lower costs and seamless global connectivity. This move will have important consequences for industries and entire economies, even more so when combined with a semantically enriched open-EDI. Such open-EDI will offer public, international standards for common business scenarios. The objective is to interact spontaneously with a new trading partner and without a prior agreement on a common protocol of interaction. Multilateral interactions may be facilitated as well. Global business-to-business E-commerce is expected to benefit hugely by moving forward from the simple transaction sets of the traditional EDI, which are basically electronic equivalents of paper forms, to far more elaborate, validated, and customizable business scenarios of open-EDI (Bons, Lee, & Wagenaar, in press; "The Open-edi," 1996).

A form of messaging is also a special type of secure EDI used in electronic funds transfer systems (EFTS), which enable interbank transfers of funds in the form of information. Electronic mail (e-mail) has become a ubiquitous means of communication and organizational integration, often with profound organizational effects.[2] E-mail remains the most popular use of the Internet. It may be expected to remain such, incorporating the transmission of multimedia documents and combined with such enabling services as negotiation tools and smart software agents.

The most turbulent technological and entrepreneurial activity is taking place at the level of enabling services. These services facilitate searches for business information as well as for business partners, negotiation and maintaining a business relationship, and consummation of business transactions by financial settlements and other information-equivalent transfers. This E-commerce level includes (or will include) digital libraries (Fox, Akscyn, Furuta, & Leggett, 1995); electronic catalogs and directories; smart agents helping to seek out a desired good or service; electronic authentication services helping to establish the bona fides of a partner; copyright protection services (perhaps relying on digital watermarks); traffic auditing to establish the worth of an electronic site for advertising purposes (the dominant revenue source for many Web sites that do have significant revenue); smart-card systems that enable financial and information transfers of various kinds; and a variety of other services that are being invented and introduced (Kalakota & Whinston, 1996).

In particular, the development of electronic money (E-money) is the subject of much work and popular excitement. Called reengineering of money by some (Clemons, Croson, & Weber, 1996-1997), it may be expected to further limit the role of cash in the economy. In its various forms, E-money is expected to become a substitute for credit (e.g., credit cards) and debit instruments (e.g., checks or debit cards), or for bank notes and coins that offer anonymity to the owner (within certain legal limits in the United States) at the considerable expense of handling to commercial organizations. At present, the money supply of the United States surpasses $4 trillion, but only one tenth of that, $400 billion, exists in physical form of bills and coins. Moreover, two thirds of even that amount has been taken out of circulation, largely in the form of $100 bills, by various agents (many of them abroad) uninterested in banking (Gleick, 1996). Thus, most of the currency extant today in the United States and other developed countries already exists only as magnetized domains in the secondary storage of a computer system. Many actors other than buyers and sellers have a vested interest in the course that the development of E-money will take; these include the vendors of the new instruments, but also the banks of issue, regulators, and the agencies entrusted with national security and law enforcement.

Products and Structures of Electronic Commerce

Products and structures of E-commerce cover its three categories: consumer-oriented commerce, business-to-business commerce, and intraorganizational business. All three are experiencing vigorous developments, albeit with differing economic outcomes at this time.

The most highly touted applications of E-commerce are consumer oriented. They include remote (or home) shopping, banking, and stock brokerage, accompanied by (and in some cases so far, paid by) on-line advertising. The intended audience for this market has not reached a critical mass, although the immense potential of this segment is driving much of the interest in E-commerce, as expressed, for example, by the stock market capitalization of a number of companies that address it. The fact that the relatively successful vendors are so well known is a testimony to their dearth. These vendors include Amazon.com, a bookseller with huge, since virtual, inventory of 2.5 million titles; an impressive market capitalization, and a large following that has grown just in the third quarter of 1997 by 54% (Carvajal, 1998). CDnow and N2K are reportedly profitable sellers of recorded music and are already public companies with very high valuations relative to their sales. Virtual Vineyards, a virtual storefront selling wine and gourmet foods, and SportSite.com, which sells sports equipment and apparel, are other well-known (yet limited-size) examples. A large number of traditional vendors derive incremental revenues from E-commerce. In many cases, purchase over the Internet is a substitute for a purchase in a physical outlet. This cannibalization belies its name by its desirability. Thus, Dell Computers, for example, realizes very significant savings by selling to consumers over the Web $3 million worth per day of personal computing hardware and software.[3] A number of firms provide remote financial services. Security First National Bank has successfully introduced branchless banking over the Internet (Clark & Lee, 1998) and has been acquired by the Royal Bank of Canada at a valuation significantly exceeding that suggested by the $54.7 million in deposits accumulated by Security First. Lombard Brokerage (now Discover Brokerage Direct) was the most notable pioneer of offering securities on the Web, along with a variety of free information services. For a chance of success in the consumer marketplace, the firm must identify an actual customer need, and the firm's relationship with the customer must build on the key feature of the medium, namely, interactivity (Hoffman, Novak, & Chatterjee, 1996).

The other principal consumer-oriented segment is infotainment-on-demand. The segment builds on the Web as a new communication medium whose nature is still being explored. Infotainment ranges from education, through the delivery of specialized information, on to entertainment. Many educational offerings can respond to just-in-time, specialized requirements. Some of the educational programs and courses may be expected to bear appropriate accreditation and degrees; virtual universities are being formed, and some see the traditional university model threatened. The segment also includes such content sites as webzines (such as *HotWired* and Microsoft's *Slate,* both not viable commercially at this time); electronic newspapers and books; and access to analytical reports, expert opinions, and the experts themselves. Legitimation of expertise, packaging of knowledge and information from several sources, preservation of intellectual property, and use-based payments (including micropayments for the chunks of information bundled together) are issues to be resolved through further research, development, and experimentation in the marketplace. The entertainment side, overlapping with the informational one, includes several categories of webzines and electronic books, as well as video-on-demand, virtual reality experiences on demand, and games that can provide an engrossing and continuing experience to multiple players. The sector known as adult entertainment is reputed to be the most profitable aspect of infotainment (Weber, 1997).

The consumer-oriented category is expected to expand in many ways, only some of which can be foreseen. For example, electronic benefit systems can be used to distribute government transfers over the Internet, which can then be employed for direct payments; the multimedia capability can redefine the notion of a magazine by including, for example, film clips; and a variety of electronic interactions with "live" creators of infotainment may be expected to complement their creations.

The business-to-business, supplier-customer linkages maintained with EDI are the best-established category of E-commerce application. This category will be vastly expanded by the growth of new E-commerce, leading in many cases to interorganizational supply chain management, which we shall discuss later. The business-to-business commerce is facilitated by consortia, such as CommerceNet, and by firms that organize industrial marketplaces on the Web, such as Industry.Net. Total business-to-business purchases made on the Web in the United States in 1997 are estimated at $10 billion by the International Data Corporation ("Commerce by Numbers," 1998).

The fastest growing area on this level of E-commerce is the intranet- and extranet-based information sharing and collaboration. Intranets support the opening of organizational databases and data warehouses within the firm and the dissemination of information on Web pages, as well as geography-independent, team-oriented collaboration within the corporate firewalls. A typical intranet, employed by Morgan Stanley, displays on the globally accessible Web site automatically generated, up-to-the-minute data summarizing the company's investment positions. More active uses of intranets are being developed and include on-line collaboration on common projects by working on electronic documents and communicating via videoconferencing. Thus, Ford Motor Company has linked with an intranet its design centers in the United States, Asia, and Europe, enabling the engineers to develop on-line electronic prototypes of automobiles and their components. The intranet-based use of the Internet facilities may lead to spectacular returns on investment ("The Chief Executive," 1998). An extranet accessible to Harley-Davidson's dealers enables them to file warranty claims, check recall status, and submit financial statements to the motorcycle manufacturer, with the capability to order parts and accessories being implemented. It has become an inexpensive means of converting paperwork to electronic communications (Kalin, 1998).

At the apex of the E-commerce framework are the electronic marketplaces and electronic hierarchies that facilitate business relationships and transactions between firms. Electronic marketplaces are created to facilitate transactions over telecommunications networks between multiple buyers and multiple suppliers. Electronic hierarchies are long-lasting supplier-customer relationships between firms that are maintained with telecommunications networks and coordinated largely by management, rather than by the market forces.

Market-based coordination can be classified into four categories (Garbade, 1982): direct-search markets (where the future partners seek out one another), brokered markets (with the brokers assuming the search function), dealer markets (with the dealers holding inventories against which they buy and sell), and auction markets. Industry.Net is an example of an established direct-search market for industrial products; OnSale provides an electronic auction market. Lee and Clark (1996) offer further analysis of several electronic marketplaces.

The formation of interorganizational electronic hierarchies is being supported by the fashioning of integrated supply chains that promote just-in-time manufacturing pulled by the actual customer orders. The partners' value chains are integrated to a significant extent with the use of information systems and telecommunications networks. The visibility of stocking levels throughout the supply chain helps to minimize inventories and reduce working capital. This mode of operation imposes tight constraints on intra- and interorganizational coordination, in which intranets, extranets, and the Internet in general may be expected to play a significant role. Indeed, the reliance by all three on the same fundamental technology package is vital for the integration. By securely linking its subnetworks with those of business partners in an extranet that relies on the Internet connectivity and software, the enterprise and the involved partners can coordinate product development, production, and delivery. Heineken U.S.A., for example, uses its HOPS extranet to collaborate with the distributors and suppliers on scheduling, forecasting, and just-in-time replenishment of supplies, consistently moving toward an electronically integrated supply chain. New intra- and interorganizational structures are necessary to take advantage of the Internet technologies in supply chain management.

The hierarchies of individual firms and the open marketplaces may be considered the two ends of the continuum of business governance, with electronic hierarchies situated in the middle. As the next section elaborates, the spreading of new E-commerce will alter the comparative advantage between the hierarchy-based and market-based coordination, and among the various ways of structuring the market. Many and serious questions about the effects of E-commerce on business governance remain open.

The Impacts and Issues of Electronic Commerce

The business, societal, and research problematic of E-commerce spans an immense range that reflects the depth of change being caused by this rapidly expanding mode of doing business (any business, including that of governing and educating). It is, of course, possible here to point only to some nodal impacts and issues within the hierarchical framework we have discussed. In keeping with the nature of our framework, we are discussing the problematic at the macro level.

In discussing the issues of E-commerce, we shall move up the hierarchy of Table 12.1, from the infrastructure to the business governance. The following aspects of E-commerce will be discussed: the limitations and asymmetries of the technological infrastructure of the Internet, the integration of the transaction process in consumer-oriented E-commerce by incorporating the payment stage into it, the building of the consumer marketplace, moving products and stages of supply chains into marketspace, changes in business governance, and the new intermediation in the electronic marketplaces.

Limitations and Asymmetries of Infrastructure

Although we should be wary of a technology-centered, "field-of-dreams" view of success factors, an appropriate technological infrastructure is necessary for the development of E-commerce. The infrastructure of the Internet, which acts as the current global information infrastructure, has acknowledged problems. The issues turn on the provision of sufficient bandwidth for the surging use that is also moving to multimedia transmissions, and on the problems fostered by the decentralized nature of the Internet.

The bandwidth of the telecommunication infrastructure is considered a serious limitation by many analysts. The current Internet 2.0 backbone operates at 45 to 155 megabits per second, which enables the World Wide Web (Bell & Gemmell, 1996) but is not sufficient for the massive use of video-on-demand, for example. However, the poor performance experienced by users often stems from the limitations of the equipment and of the connectivity of their access providers, rather than from the limited backbone bandwidth. Significant asymmetries exist between the bandwidth actually available to larger organizations and that available to small businesses and homes (where the consumers, telecommuters, and increasing numbers of very small businesses are). Solving the latter problem, known as the "last mile problem" or "fiber to the home," outside urban areas by rewiring is prohibitively expensive. The mitigating factor is the increasing use of high-bandwidth T-1 lines, and of the newer and cheaper Digital Subscriber Line (DSL) technology. The issues pale in comparison with limitations of the infrastructure in a number of (slowly) developing countries. Fifty countries, some of them admittedly small island nations, that bring up the rear of the host survey by Market Wizards as of January 1998 currently run nine host machines out of the total of about 30 million Internet hosts ("Distribution," 1998).

Market-oriented solutions, in some cases stimulated by a government intervention, are in view in the developed and rapidly developing countries. A number of U.S. corporations are acquiring the requisite bandwidth on parallel for-profit networks with premium high-bandwidth links, using the services of companies that offer connections via direct leased circuits (such as Digital Island in Oahu, Hawaii), and they are accessing commercial duplicate Web sites. The trend to the provision of premium, high-bandwidth services with multitier pricing may be expected to expand greatly. This will split the issue of public access from that of open systems. As the provision of premium infrastructural services accelerates, and as the data traffic begins to dominate the voice, pressures will develop on the providers of local telecommunications services, generally sheltered from competition until now. New and powerful entrants appear in the marketplace to compete for the provision of the "Web tone"—instant and wide-bandwidth connection to the Internet (Woolley, 1998).

The future development of the multimedia Internet 3.0 backbone that would be able to carry simultaneously data, video, and voice communications is a widely open issue. Aside from the financial risk and technological problems, public policy questions of access will arise. Regulatory changes may be expected to attempt to facilitate funding.

As the use of its facilities expands exponentially, Internet protocols require updating as well. In a longer view, the shortage of Internet addresses in the current IPv4 protocol that relies on a 32-bit address system is considered a serious limitation as we are moving into the era of Internet-connected appliances, from personal digital assistants to cars. The proposed IPv6 protocol, with its 128-bit addressing, has not yet been adopted by the makers of the Internet equipment, such as routers.

A number of limitations are apparent on the Web level of the infrastructure, and they do translate into business problems. Many of the integration solutions are provided by middleware, or systems placed between the client and the server software. Because of the sessionless nature of the hypertext transfer protocol (HTTP), you would need to identify yourself to every electronic page of a site during a single session in order to do business. There is no built-in way to maintain the continuity of a connection—and perhaps make another offer the next time the caller dials in. This clearly highlights the business effects of technological limitations—and their unintended consequences, which, in this case, is the attack on privacy. "Dropping a cookie" into a caller's system is a way around this limitation, but it is invasive of the user's privacy. Stored as a text file by the accessed Web server in the user's computer system, a cookie identifies the user, along with the user's preferences and past purchases, to the server during future accesses.

Major infrastructural questions remain, such as the following: Assuming that the Internet will further evolve as the global information infrastructure, will it remain fundamentally decentralized? How do we create a protected, secure, and reliable business environment in a decentralized infrastructure? Has the time come for a more transparent organizational structure in Internet management? Is the limited bandwidth a real barrier for the consumer, or are there other, more lasting forces at work? What infrastructure can be provided to enhance the ability of vendors to differentiate their offerings and the ability of customers to compare them? (Baty & Lee, 1995, present one such attempt.)

Integrating Electronic Payment Into the Buying Process

Consumer-oriented E-commerce is significantly lagging behind its business-to-business segment, and current estimates place it at less than 10% of the total volume. The settlement phase of transacting on the Web is often pointed to as one of the limiting factors. The consumer should be able to pay for a purchase on the Web easily and with a perception of security. Although the overall shopping experience, product perceptions, and customer service on the Web today lead to a dissatisfaction of potential customers (Jarvenpaa & Todd, 1996-1997) and require attention of marketers and researchers, the problem of settlement is the one capable of a systemic solution. As stated earlier in the chapter, electronic equivalents of all of the payment instruments in use today are appearing on the Web ("Electronic Money," 1997).

The most excitement is occasioned by the development of electronic cash, the informational equivalent of physical banknotes and coins. Electronic cash can offer such benefits as the anonymity of the buyer, global acceptance, and divisibility that can cost-effectively go beyond that of real cash in the case of so-called micropayments (such as paying $0.10 for the one-time use of a software object or $0.19 for reading a literary essay on the *http://www.bylines.org* content site that plans to switch to electronic cash). Widespread use of electronic cash would have serious implications for the national banking systems and for the banks of issue, which would partly lose their seignorage profits and control of the quantity of money in circulation.

At this time, an electronic cash system called ecash has been implemented by Digicash (of Amsterdam) together with the Mark Twain Bank of Missouri (http://www.digicash.com), and it is now offered by such major banks as Deutsche Bank and Bank Austria. The major U.S. banks have adopted a posture of watchful waiting, accompanied by internal research on the potential impacts of electronic cash. Mondex (http://www.mondex.com), a cashlike system relying on a smart card, has been tested locally in several countries with very limited acceptance results (Clemons et al., 1996-1997; Westland, Kwok, Shu, Kwok, & Ho, 1998). Mondex International Limited, a joint venture of a number of banking institutions, licenses the rights to the Mondex technology. The NetCheque system, developed at the Information Sciences Institute of the University of Southern California, allows its registered users to "write" electronic checks (http://gost.isi.edu/info/netcheque). On the other side of the payment issue are the financial intermediaries, such as First Virtual Holdings, which facilitate settlements for E-commerce transactions by external means without the financial tokens (such as the credit card numbers or bank account information) ever appearing on the Internet (http://www.fv.com). The proponents of this mode of operation consider the Internet to be fundamentally insecure for financial transactions (Borenstein et al., 1996). At this time, the apparently prevalent informed opinion is that the financial transactions on the Internet are no less secure from the consumer's point of view than today's physical-world transactions, with the admixture of a fear that "a big hit from cyberspace" is possible because of the complexity and globally distributed nature of the system.

The multifaceted impacts of electronic banking call for much research on the acceptability of various solutions to consumers, the apportioning of the risk, the institutional framework, the effects of the electronic cash on the economy, and, certainly not least, making secure the electronic settlement of transactions.

Building the Electronic Consumer Marketplace

Some would argue that the main question of E-commerce today is how to convert Web surfers from browsers to consumers by creating an encompassing marketspace for information, services, and goods. The statistics of the phenomenal growth of Internet use—with 29.2 million Web users in the United States as of the end of 1997 ("Commerce by Numbers," 1998), and with 27.8 million unique visitors during January 1998 to the top-ranked site, Yahoo! ("Top 20 Sites," 1998), all of which was accomplished within some 4 years—have to be counterbalanced by the modest statistics of the actual consumer buying. Yet rapid growth is apparent in this sector as well. The approximately $132 million spent by the consumers in 1995 (according to Martin, 1996) has reportedly grown into $1 billion spent during just the fourth quarter of 1997 (according to Forrester Research; Guglielmo, 1998), a figure that appears too high when placed in the context of other estimates. A large number of widely diverging yet generally highly optimistic forecasts of future growth exist (Foley & Sutton, 1998). The statistics, and especially the projections, are debatable, yet the growth trend is not.

The consumer marketplace encompasses auction sites, reverse markets, and digital retail outlets. As we have said before, the auction approach is a successful means to capitalize on the ubiquitous accessibility of the Internet medium. Along with other roles, an auction intermediary facilitates price discovery. Such sites as OnSale, which auctions computer and electronics equipment, and eBay, which auctions collectibles, are relatively limited-size, U.S.-based, virtual auction houses. The two sites are built on two different business models. OnSale, a public company by now, is a dealership type of marketplace that takes an active role in the ownership and delivery of goods, as well as in customer service. This is reflected in the much higher net revenue as a percentage of sales than that of eBay, which simply provides the sites as a form of digital agora, accessible to sellers and buyers, and realizes a commission of 1.5% to 5% of an item's price. The success of both sites points up the variety of approaches that can be taken in the Web-based consumer market. Auction houses have the potential to coalesce into large and multifaceted marketplaces that take on additional intermediary responsibilities in lowering the risk of the transacting parties by certifying the quality of goods and facilitating logistics.

Reverse markets are also based on the inexpensive ubiquity of the Internet medium and place the consumer in the driver's seat. By broadcasting the need over the Internet, the prospective buyer of a product or service (or a job, though ceasing to be a consumer in this relationship) is able to increase the consumer's surplus by extracting more favorable offers than those available publicly. A number of facilitators of reverse markets provide "wanted" sites.

Several approaches have been identified within the general business model of Web-based digital retailing at fixed prices (as opposed to creating marketplaces that include price discovery). These on-line retailing outlets have been classified by Hoffman et al. (1996) into (a) on-line storefronts or catalogs actually selling products or just establishing awareness of them; (b) content sites providing information and support; and (c) Web traffic control sites, such as malls and search engines. Westland and Au (1997-1998) classify the digital retailing approaches into catalog sites, bundling outlets, and virtual reality storefronts. The bundling and virtual reality approaches may be considered of particular promise in experimenting with Web retailing. Theoretical work indicates that the bundling of goods is attractive for the goods of low marginal cost, with uncorrelated demand, and of approximately equal consumer valuation, with information goods (such as software) being a prime example (Bakos & Brynjolfsson, 1997). Bundling is also seen as promising for such goods as flower arrangements and gifts, where the consumer can conveniently limit the extent of necessary decision making and the vendor can substitute products at will. In a kiosk-based experiment, Westland and Au (1997-1998) find that the additional time necessary to interact with a virtual reality storefront does not result in a greater consumer spending.

Spiller and Lohse (1997-1998) further classify empirically the catalog-type on-line sites actually available on the Web into five categories, summarized in Table 12.2. Note that several categories of digital retailers include on their sites what we call bonding features, which are expected to motivate repeated visits. Such features include product-related webzines, lotteries, and tips. These researchers find that digital retailing outlets offer limited product selection, few service features, and poor interfaces. As a confirmation of these perceptions, consumers find offering lists to be shallow and are also concerned about the performance and personal risks, such as payment-related security and privacy (Jarvenpaa & Todd, 1996-1997).

Digital retailing has low entry thresholds at its lower end. Claims are made that multinational corporations may find themselves challenged on the Web by small upstarts, and it is suggested that they need to review their business models (Ghosh, 1998; Quelch & Klein, 1996). However, the cost to build an "aggressive" Web site, that is, a site that is interactive, transactional, and dynamic, is estimated at more than $1 million ("Commerce by Numbers," 1998). It is to be expected that the usual advantages of scale, scope, and existing brand will translate into Web retailing advantages when consumer-oriented E-commerce matures.

In the case of digital products, such as software, music, or multimedia, the Internet plays the role of distribution medium. For example, a number of firms, including Cybermedia, TestDrive, and Tuneup.com, market software over the Internet. Worth watching is the future of renamed Egghead.com, which, under competitive pressures, moved its software retailing business from the brick-and-mortar outlets of limited size to the Internet in September 1997, with encouraging initial results. The range of digital products will vastly expand with the growth of E-commerce,

TABLE 12.2 Empirical Classification of Catalog-Type Digital Retailing Strategies

Strategy	Main Features	Examples
Superstore	Large catalog size Navigation tools Bonding features Extensive information and hand-holding	L.L. Bean Online Sports
Promotional store	Limited product range Extensive company information Bonding features Community-oriented information	AWEAR Cheyenne Outfitters
Plain sales catalog	Medium-size or large catalog Large images and thumbnails	Milano First Lady
One-page catalog	Limited catalog size Product-browse function	Alaska Mountaineering Close To You
Product listing	Medium-size catalog Small product images Few hierarchical levels	Rocky Mountain Outfitters Dance Supplies

NOTE: Modified from Spiller and Lohse (1997-1998).

with many new products emerging as, for example, symbolic tokens replacing hard goods (Choi, Stahl, & Whinston, 1997). Later, we shall discuss further the virtualization of products.

An emblematic trajectory taken by a small merchant on the Web is that of GolfWeb, which had painstakingly built up a following—a golf-centered community—on its electronic site before turning it into a retail outlet. By providing extensive golf-related features and information, GolfWeb had been able to attract some 500,000 hits a day to its 25,000 pages and had relied on advertisers for any revenue before starting its virtual pro shop to produce sales. The firm does treat the Web as a new medium by providing such interactive features as virtual equipment fitting for customers. Yet questions remain: Will many smaller firms, encountering a relatively low entry threshold ($1.7 million of venture capital in the case of GolfWeb), make money on the Web? Will the business model, such as that of GolfWeb, ultimately lead to profits? What are the successful consumer-oriented business models for the Internet? And how do we measure what is actually happening on the Internet?

The potential in the expansion of the Internet-based consumer marketplace can be seen in experimentation going beyond the facilitation of consumer search and order taking. Building demand for the products, customizing products to the individual requirements, and developing lasting relationships between the vendor and the customer are the long-term objectives of Web sites. Specifically, stimulating sites can build demand for products regardless of the ultimate manner of purchase.

The interactivity of the medium gives a vast opportunity to customize, and thus engage in, one-to-one marketing at relatively low incremental costs. If it appears unlikely that one would purchase a pair of shoes over the Internet, it is far more likely that one would if offered a customized product, based on the measurements transmitted over the network, such as the services currently available in some brick-and-mortar outlets.

The sites can be used to build lasting relationships with individuals, and thus develop brands. Of particular importance at this stage of the development of consumer-oriented E-commerce are community-building features of Web sites. These features attract an individual to a community of "birds of a feather," along demographic, interest, or even affliction (that may be alleviated) lines. Community sites attract voluminous traffic by committed members and serve for them as the portal to the Web, making such sites highly attractive to advertisers. Sensitivity to the needs of the particular community is crucial to success. The sale of Tripod, a 2-year-old company that runs a site with 2.7 million unique visitors a month, for $58 million to Lycos in 1998 places a financial estimate on the value of such communities. GeoCities is another community-oriented firm that has attracted significant investment. Technology can be used creatively to reinforce the sense of community while pursuing marketing objectives (doing well and good at the same time). Firefly technology (http://www.firefly.com), for example, is notable for inferring the purchasing needs of an individual from those of the community members with similar profiles, and offering products accordingly. The company's sensitive privacy policy made it an attractive acquisition target for Microsoft.

Selling on the Web can provide on-line demonstration, consultation, and assistance to these virtual communities. Clearly, the nature of many existing electronic communities is antithetical to commerce, and a pull-model of doing business has to be built for them. Will the community-oriented model of digital retailing prove to be only a stage in acculturating consumers to the new buying venue? Will the purely transactional approach take over for the appropriate products as Internet selling matures? The digital retailing practice has to embrace the broad approach to the opportunities offered by an interactive medium that attracts many millions of potential buyers. The future research on building consumer marketplaces would do well by adopting this broader approach to Web sites as well, which would, of course, require a longer experience and longitudinal studies.

Moving Supply Chains and Products Into Marketspace

It is recognized that the networked infrastructure offers new opportunities for adding value by moving the stages of corporate value chains into the realm of information processing, saving money and time in the process (Rayport & Sviokla, 1994). We are witnessing the virtualization of value-chain segments and, in the future, perhaps also of an increasing number of products. Business processes can be moved into the virtual, informational value chains, be they paperless transaction processing or electronic prototyping. The development of the Boeing 777 airplane based on virtual prototyping is probably the best known example. Rapid prototyping and rapid manufacturing technologies move the electronic model of a product directly from the computer-aided design (CAD) file into the machine that builds up a final, physical prototype—or the final product—layer by layer or powdered particle by powdered particle (Bylinsky, 1998). A virtual reality-based system for developing customized clothes, called Virtuosi, affords three-dimensional viewing and manipulation of fashion designs over the Web; voice-controlled mannequins demonstrate the clothes on the virtual runway in this experimental system (Gray, 1998). Indeed, a computer hardware design can be sent over the Web when field-programmable gate arrays are used (Mangione-Smith et al., 1997).

This virtualization of products and processes is only at its origins, and we may expect very significant development and efficiencies to derive from it. As they move from purely informational to collaborative use, corporate intranets can serve as vehicles for these virtual elements of value chains. Corporate extranets, open to business partners, suppliers, and customers, can become secured extensions of the Internet in the interorganizational marketspace networks.

Which goods and services can be converted to information that can be moved around and traded over the electronic marketplace? Rayport and Sviokla (1995) offer an example of the answering machine. Cash is another example of a good that can be virtualized (a special kind of good that it is), videocassettes are another such good, retail services are already delivered over the Web instead of in physical stores, and many personal computers may be converted to appropriate over-the-network services. After all, a network computer is just such an attempt. Many questions regarding the relative economic efficiency of physical-versus-virtual organization of work and product delivery need to be formulated and researched.

Changes in Business Governance

Our understanding of a firm as a monolith has been problematized by Coase's (1937) milestone paper. Transaction cost economics that arose from this work help us see the boundary of the firm as defined by the equilibrium between the advantages of the lower transaction costs of internal production, on one hand, and the lower agency costs (such as the costs of management) and economies of scale and scope of outside procurement on the other (Williamson, 1975). In other words, the costs of conducting marketplace transactions (i.e., information seeking, negotiating the terms, and settlement) define to a large extent what a firm will buy, instead of making it. Because these coordination costs are lowered in E-commerce, a general agreement exists (following the analysis by Malone, Benjamin, & Yates, 1987) that more outsourcing—buying rather than making in-house—will take place. There is considerable evidence that the use of information technologies is indeed associated with the emergence of small firms as the result of outsourcing of noncore activities (Brynjolfsson, Malone, Gurbaxani, & Kambil, 1994). Will the Internet reaffirm and amplify this trend? Will the maturing Internet enhance the opportunities for smaller firms, and, if so, to what extent?

Going beyond the boundaries-of-the-firm analysis, the electronic market hypothesis offered by Malone et al. (1987) suggests that the development of interorganizational systems based on telecommunications networks will move the governance toward the market end of the spectrum, with increased transaction-oriented buying from multiple suppliers. Yet the move-to-the-middle hypothesis by Clemons, Reddi, and Row (1993) postulates that the outsourcing will go only as far as long-term collaboration with a limited number of suppliers. Likewise, Bakos and Brynjolfsson (1993) argue that the consideration of coordination costs needs to be combined with the incentives for noncontractable investments that suppliers need to make to maintain a relationship with a buyer. These relationship-specific investments have to be made to ensure, for example, the appropriate quality control, the implementation of information-sharing systems, and the modification of business processes. This consideration leads the authors to postulate the move to the middle as well.

The evidence available at this time tends to support the second hypothesis. For example, a study of computerized loan-origination systems found no move to the market (Hess & Kemerer, 1994). A study of the effects of the French Teletel system, whose Minitel terminals are a part of the landscape in that country (40% of non-retired population has access), found stable customer-supplier relationships as a result (Streeter, Kraut, Lucas, & Caby, 1996). However, new E-commerce relies on tools that are radically different from, for example, the French Teletel (whose technology is outdated), and the developments surrounding the Internet (e.g., open-EDI that would foster a transactional approach to the marketplace) are certain to lead to further analyses of the issue.

Within the market governance, profound changes can be expected. For example, the global reach and the low access cost of the Internet can be expected to promote the growth of auction markets.[4] Electronic auction companies that are able to tap into an enthusiastic user community are almost instantaneously successful. Reverse markets, where willing buyers seek out sellers, are expanding as well. This naturally leads to the next question: Will there be a role for business intermediaries in a business world where the ultimate agents—the buyer and the seller—can seek out one another, negotiate the terms, and settle the trade over the Internet or a similar global open network?

New Intermediation and Impacts on the Distribution Channel

An argument is being commonly advanced that the greater reliance on the open telecommunications networks for doing business will lead to disintermediation: the disappearing role of an intermediary, such as a dealer or a broker. Indeed, a perceptible pressure can be felt on the role of car dealers (Armstrong, 1998). Electronic commodity and stock exchanges are being created that will squeeze out some intermediaries to the trade, as it has happened at the London Stock Exchange or at the Swiss Electronic Exchange. Removing intermediaries from a supply chain can result in significant economies, with much of the savings competed away and returned as a part of consumer surplus (Benjamin & Wigand, 1995).

Powerful social and organizational barriers counteract many of these developments (Lee & Clark, 1996). Beyond that, intermediaries do play an important economic role in business exchanges by limiting the risk of the trading parties, creating economies of scale and scope, and facilitating transactions. The latter role includes the assistance in the search for a trading partner, in negotiation (or price discovery in auction markets), and in settlement. It may even be argued that the role of intermediaries will be reinforced in E-commerce (Sarkar, Butler, & Steinfield, 1996).

New types of electronic intermediaries (so-called cybermediaries) can become valuable. They can facilitate product search, evaluation, and distribution in the form of virtual malls or on-line auctioneers. Buyer search costs are an important factor in the market behavior and in the efficiency of allocation (Bakos, 1991) and intermediation may be necessary for products of more complex description. New E-commerce has given rise to a new category of Web-based niche intermediaries that are able to create a business model by reducing search costs in industry-specific marketplaces. Realbid has created a site (http://www.realbid.com) that brings together the buyers and sellers of commercial real estate (Jones, 1998). The firm attracts to the site with e-mail notices the potential buyers identified with its growing database. The firm's offering consists in removing the need for the buyer to study multiple, several-hundred-page-long proposals to find likely purchase candidates. In another industry, Cattle Offerings Worldwide posts on its site the pedigree and genetic traits of cattle embryos and lets cattle buyers bid on them. Industry segments with widely dispersed sellers and buyers, and complex offerings that lend themselves to simplification with a searchable database, are promising targets for this intermediation.

Quality certification plays a crucial role in the success of the AUCNET, the electronic auction house for used cars in Japan (Lee, 1998). AUCNET is able to extract, on the average, higher prices in its electronic auctions than the traditional auction houses in that country are able to do. This can be accounted for by the avoidance of the need to transport the car to an auction, with the lower transaction costs and wider reach thus attracting better cars on the seller side, and the local availability of cars producing savings for buyers. The virtuous spiral attracts higher-quality cars, naturally commanding higher prices.

New intermediaries can provide packaging and enhancement of information-based goods, for example, by delivering customized targeted multimedia information packages, with use-based payments to the holders of intellectual property rights and with access to the authors as a premium service. Suppliers receive the efficiency of a single payment; customers save on search costs and get a more focused and comprehensive product. Intermediaries can track the copyrights and licensing payments and enforce site-license agreements. In the future, if persistent software opies will not need to be made for many products, but simply downloaded for each use, appropriate billing can be provided by an intermediary. Intermediaries can also handle support services and updating of information-based products. At the same time, those traditional publishers and resellers of information-based products that cease to provide value in the new constellation may indeed be disintermediated.

An excellent example of a territory being carved out by a new intermediary is Healtheon, a company formed by Jim Clark, the founder of Silicon Graphics and Netscape Communications. Healtheon expects to sell its services to insurers and health maintenance organizations, which will use the firm's software to present their own services to employers and to register their employees. The firm will also provide health plan management for these employers. It will use the Web as its operations platform and has prospects to expand into a ubiquitous electronic network for health care.

Traditional intermediaries can adapt to deliver enhanced value. Marshall Industries, a distributor of electronic products, has exploited the capabilities of the Web by establishing a site (http://www.marshall.com) that is frequented by millions of engineers from around the globe. The site offers up-to-date data sheets, prices, and inventory information on the products of 150 major suppliers in a format that can be customized on demand. In addition, the site makes available software that can be downloaded to the customer's site in order to design virtual chips that will work with the chips distributed by Marshall Industries. The software code describing the newly designed chips then can be uploaded to the distributor via the site. The distributor immediately burns the designs into prototype chips that are mailed to the customer. By inserting itself into the virtual value chain of the ultimate customer, the intermediary makes itself indispensable to both its suppliers and its customers (Hartman, 1997).

The principal expected impacts of E-commerce on distribution channels have been summarized in Table 12.3. The table allocates the factor to the channel's actor where the impact is expected to be felt most. For example, although the size of both the seller and the buyer is not directly transparent on the Internet, it is the partly opaque size of the seller that has the greatest effect on the course of a transaction. Notable is the price pressure on the sellers, which emerges from the reduced buyer search costs (Bakos, 1991, 1997). All of the channel impacts listed in the table require further study.

The revenue stream extracted by the new intermediary will depend on the value added by its activities; this value added then may be hypothesized to correlate with the level in the framework of Table 12.1 that the intermediary operates on, with higher-level products and services yielding higher margins.[5] Multiple questions present themselves: Which intermediaries are doomed? How can intermediaries add value in E-commerce? What are the successful new business models for intermediaries? How can traditional intermediaries become new intermediaries? What will be the categories and the role of the new intermediaries? How will the profits and welfare be redistributed among the parties in the business transactions?

TABLE 12.3 Principal Channel Impacts of E-Commerce

Sellers	Intermediaries	Buyer
Partly opaque firm size	Bypass possibility	Possibility of enacting reverse markers
Increased price competition	Traditional ones may be replaces by cybermediaries	Reduced search costs
Price discrimination possible	Increased role in price discovery possible	Increased risks
Rich product description may be needed	May be material as third-party guarantors	Network effect (increased benefit with increased number of sellers)
Reduced search costs in finding buyers		
Observable and measurable buyer behavior		
Product quality and settlement terms may have to be independently certified		
Goods movement and storage costs may be reduced		
Network effect (increased benefit with increased number of buyers)		

Conclusions

New E-commerce is still in its formative stage. E-commerce is currently dominated by the business-to-business and intraorganizational segments. Many major digital retailers are still in the investment and brand-building mode and show no profits; yet many established retailers realize profits from the new selling channel. Buoyant growth is apparent throughout.

The hierarchical framework presented above offers an opportunity to separate concerns and analyze the specific aspects of this enterprise. The technological infrastructure currently imposes several limitations on the development of a global marketspace and on the personal convenience of the participants. An integrated, consumer-oriented transaction space is yet to emerge. The consumer marketplace is being developed by a large number of entrepreneurial initiatives, many of them experimenting on the frontiers. Moving the links of supply chains and products into marketspace offers a major promise in raising economic efficiency of both manufacturing and service industries. As these moves take place, and as the supply chains are reconfigured, many new firms may be expected to emerge and specialize around newly redefined core capabilities. The business models of many existing firms will be threatened. Although several intermediary roles are threatened by E-commerce, others are not, and new intermediary opportunities emerge.

The capabilities of the new marketplace that combines the properties of a medium with that of a global (virtual) location will be exploited to redefine many products and marketplaces. Notable are the possibilities to provide customized products, in the process moving ever larger segments of the supply chains to the Internet; branding through bonding to a Web site and thus to its sponsor; the advantages of virtual auctions; and the possibility to create large reverse markets.

New E-commerce will present over time countless opportunities and challenges to our economies and societies. Expansion of commerce and technological innovations are two of the levers of economic growth (Mokyr, 1990). These forces are combined in the progress of E-commerce. The macroeconomic effects of E-commerce on the national and regional economies, and on the international trade and its terms, will need to be assessed and analyzed. The prevailing judgment at this stage of E-commerce development is to allow free-market forces to assert themselves unhampered by excessive government regulation ("A Framework," 1997). The traditional institutions, such as banks of issue, commercial banks, universities, established business intermediaries, and media and publishing companies, will find a need to redefine their roles in the new environment. The taxability of products traded globally over the Internet is still an open issue. Intellectual property that can be converted to on-line content may find itself revalued in the global marketplace.

The tension between the transactional efficiency of spot purchasing facilitated by electronic markets and the need for long-term relationships of trust and forbearance, enabled by electronic hierarchies, will persist and call for much study. The geographical limitations that have bound the place of residence to the place of work, and that have already been eroded by the growth of telework, may be expected to be even less binding. Indeed, the possibilities of the loss of rural space to the new ex-urbanites are already causing environmental alarms (Snider & Moody, 1995). A number of countries that had been marginalized by their geographical position take an extremely active interest in E-commerce as the means to move to the center of the virtual geography. The redistribution of work has to be studied from multiple perspectives.

E-commerce has entered a stage of rapid and sustained development, and a large number of business models have been enabled by it. A number of questions have been posed here. All of these and many others will require further experimentation, experience, observation, analysis, and research.

Notes

1. The World Wide Web, which has brought people to the Internet, was devised by Tim Berners-Lee in 1989 as a means of collaboration for the physicists working on the projects of the international research center CERN. However, it is actually the first popular Web browser, NCSA Mosaic (designed by Marc Andreessen, not much later a founder of Netscape), that began to bring people and businesses to the Web in the spring of 1993. That year may be considered the beginning point of new E-commerce.

2. According to John Gage, the director of the science office of Sun Microsystems:

Your E-mail flow determines whether you're really part of the organization; the mailing lists you're on say a lot about the power you have. I've been part of the Java group at Sun for four or five years. Recently, by mistake, someone removed my name from the Java E-mail list. My flow of information just stopped—and I stopped being part of the organization, no matter what the org chart said. . . . The best way to understand what's happening in a company is to get its alias file—the master list of all its E-mail lists. (Rapaport, 1996, p. 118)

3. "The Internet for us is like a wonderful dream come true. It's like zero variable cost transactions. The only better thing would be mental telepathy," said Dell Computer CEO Michael Dell ("The Chief Executive," 1998, p. 22).

4. An interesting system that shows the potential of almost frictionless auction markets has been developed at Xerox Corporation. The system auctions off cool or hot air in a building to the individual rooms. Software agents track the temperature in the rooms and bid accordingly for heating or cooling. The system holds about 1,500 auctions a day, more than one a minute. The "market-based" system was found to distribute warm and cool air throughout the building better than the traditional, "hierarchical" systems (Markoff, 1996).

5. Here is an example of a trajectory to the new intermediation. Andrew Klein, founder and president of Spring Street Brewing Company, was the first to complete the initial public offering (IPO) of his company's stock on the Internet—disintermediating the investment bankers. He has since launched Wit Capital Corporation, an investment bank that will specialize in Internet IPOs. The firm is currently taking orders for its solely managed over-the-Net offering—appropriately, of the shares of an Internet game developer called Sandbox Entertainment (Schifrin, 1998). One can speculate that by moving the function of IPO from the top level in Table 12.1 to Level 5, the entrepreneur will be able to extract a smaller surplus than the traditional intermediaries.

References

A Framework for Global Electronic Commerce. (1997). The White House. http://www.ecommerce.gov/framewrk.htm.
Armstrong, A., & Hagel, J., III. (1996, May-June). The real value of on-line communities. *Harvard Business Review*, pp. 134-141.
Armstrong, L. (1998, March 9). Downloading their dream cars. *Business Week*, pp. 93-94.
Bakos, J. Y. (1991). A strategic analysis of electronic marketplaces. *MIS Quarterly, 15*, 295-310.
Bakos, J. Y. (1997). Reducing buyer search costs: Implications for electronic marketplaces. *Management Science, 43*, 1676-1692.
Bakos, J. Y., & Brynjolfsson, E. (1993). Information technology, incentives, and the optimal number of suppliers. *Journal of Management Information Systems, 10*(2), 37-54.
Bakos, J. Y., & Brynjolfsson, E. (1997). *Bundling information goods: Pricing, profits and efficiency.* Working paper, Sloan School of Management, MIT, http://www.gsm.uci.edu/bakos/big/big.html.
Baty, J. B., II, & Lee, R. (1995). InterShop: Enhancing the vendor/customer dialectic in electronic shopping. *Journal of Management Information Systems, 11*(4), 9-32.
Bell, G., & Gemmell, J. (1996). On-ramp prospects for the information superhighway dream. *Communications of the ACM, 39*(7), 55-61.
Benjamin, R., & Wigand, R. (1995). Electronic markets and virtual value chains on the information superhighway. *Sloan Management Review, 37,* 62-72.
Bhimani, A. (1996). Securing the commercial Internet. *Communications of the ACM, 39*(6), 29-35.
Bons, R. W. H., Lee, R. M., & Wagenaar, R. W. (in press). Designing trustworthy interorganizational trade procedures for open electronic commerce. *International Journal of Electronic Commerce.*
Borenstein, N. et al. (1996). Perils and pitfalls of practical cyber-commerce. *Communications of the ACM, 39*(6), 36-45.

Brynjolfsson, E., Malone, T. W., Gurbaxani, V., & Kambil, A. (1994). Does information technology lead to smaller firms? *Management Science, 40,* 1628-1644.
Bylinsky, G. (1998, January 12). Industry's amazing instant prototypes. *Fortune,* pp. 120b-120c.
Carvajal, D. (1998, January 5). In the publishing industry, the high-technology plot thickens. *The New York Times,* p. D18.
The Chief Executive's Guide to the Internet. (1998, January). *Supplement to CIO.*
Choi, S.-Y., Stahl, D. O., & Whinston, A. B. (1997). *The economics of electronic commerce.* Indianapolis, IN: Macmillan Technical.
Clark, T. H., & Lee, H. G. (1998). Security First National Bank: A case study of an Internet pioneer. In R. W. Blanning & D. R. King (Eds.), *Proceedings of the 31st Annual Hawaii International Conference on System Sciences* (Vol. 4, pp. 73-82). Los Alamitos, CA: IEEE Computer Society Press.
Clemons, E. K., Croson, D. C., & Weber, B. W. (1996-97). Reengineering money: The Mondex stored value card and beyond. *International Journal of Electronic Commerce, 1*(2), 5-31.
Clemons, E. K., Reddi, S. P., & Row, M. C. (1993). The impact of information technology on the organization of economic activity: The "move to the middle" hypothesis. *Journal of Management Information Systems, 10*(2), 9-36.
Coase, R. H. (1937). The nature of the firm. *Economica, 4,* 386-405.
Commerce by Numbers. (1998, January 26). *Computerworld Emmerce,* http://www2.computerworld.com/home/emmerce.nsf.
Distribution by Top-Level Domain Name by Host Count. (1998). *Internet domain survey of January 1998.* http://www.nw.com/zone/WWW/dist-bynum.html.
Dutta, A. (1997). The physical infrastructure for electronic commerce in developing nations: Historical trends and the impact of privatization. *International Journal of Electronic Commerce, 2*(1), 61-83.
Electronic Money: Toward a Virtual Wallet. (1997). *IEEE Spectrum, 34*(2), 18-80.
Fedorowicz, J., & Konsynski, B. (1992). Organizational support systems: Bridging business and decision processes. *Journal of Management Information Systems, 8*(4), 5-25.
Foley, P., & Sutton, D. (1998). The potential for trade facilitated by the Internet 1996-2000: A review of demand, supply and Internet trade models. In R. W. Blanning & D. R. King (Eds.), *Proceedings of the 31st Annual Hawaii International Conference on System Sciences* (Vol. 4, pp. 210-221). Los Alamitos, CA: IEEE Computer Society Press.
Fox, E., Akscyn, R. M., Furuta, R. K., & Leggett, J. J. (Eds.). (1995). Digital libraries [Special section]. *Communications of the ACM, 38*(4), 23-96.
Garbade, K. (1982). *Securities markets.* New York: McGraw-Hill.
Ghosh, S. (1998, March-April). Making business sense of the Internet. *Harvard Business Review,* pp. 127-135.
Gleick, J. (1996, June 16). Dead as a dollar. *The New York Times Magazine,* pp. 26-30+.
Gray, S. (1998). In virtual fashion. *IEEE Spectrum, 35*(2), 19-25.
Guglielmo, C. (1998, February 9) The mezzanine may be closed for merchants. *Inter@active Week,* p. 44.
Hartman, C. (1997, June-July). Sales force. *Fast Company,* pp. 134-146.
H.E. Butt Grocery Company: A Leader in ECR Implementation. (1994). Harvard Business School Case #196-061.
Hess, C. M., & Kemerer, C. F. (1994). Computerized loan origination systems: An industry case study of the electronic markets. *MIS Quarterly, 18,* 251-275.
Hoffman, D. L., Novak, T. P., & Chatterjee, P. (1996). Commercial scenarios for the Web: Opportunities and challenges. *Journal of Computer-Mediated Communication, 1*(3), http://www.usc.edu/dept/annenberg/journal.html.
Jarvenpaa, S. L., & Todd, P. T. (1996-97). Consumer reactions to electronic shopping on the World Wide Web. *International Journal of Electronic Commerce, 2*(1), 59-88.

Jelassi, T., & Figon, O. (1994). Competing through EDI at Brun Passot: Achievements in France and ambitions for the single European market. *MIS Quarterly, 18,* 337-352.
Jones, K. (1998, March 23). Vortex businesses find vitality on the net. *Inter@active Week,* pp. 60-61.
Kalakota, R., & Whinston, A. B. (1996). *Frontiers of electronic commerce.* Reading, MA: Addison-Wesley.
Kalin, S. (1998, April 1). The fast lane. *CIO Web Business,* pp. 28-35.
Lee, H. G. (1998). Do electronic marketplaces lower the price of goods? *Communications of the ACM, 41*(1), 73-80.
Lee, H. G., & Clark, T. (1996). Impacts of electronic marketplace on transaction cost and market structure. *International Journal of Electronic Commerce, 1*(1), 127-149.
Malone, T. W., Benjamin, R. I., & Yates, J. (1987). Electronic markets and electronic hierarchies: Effects of information technology on market structure and corporate strategies. *Communications of the ACM, 30*(6), 484-497.
Mangione-Smith, W. H., Hutchings, B., Andrews, D., DeHon, A., Ebeling, C., Hartenstein, R., Mencer, O., Morris, J., Palem, K., Prasanna, V., & Spaanenburg, H. A. E. (1997). Seeking solutions in configurable computing. *Computer, 30*(12), 38-43.
Markoff, J. (1996, June 24). Can Xerox auction off hot air? *The New York Times,* p. D5.
Martin, M. H. (1996, February 5). Why the Web is still a no shop zone. *Fortune,* pp. 127-128.
Mokyr, J. (1990). *The lever of riches: Technological creativity and economic progress.* New York: Oxford University Press.
The Open-EDI Reference Model. (1996). IS 14662, ISO/IEC JTC1/SC30, International Standards Organization.
Quelch, J. A., & Klein, L. R. (1996). The Internet and international marketing. *Sloan Management Review, 37,* 60-75.
Rapaport, R. (1996, April-May). Interview with John Gage. *Fast Company,* pp. 116-121.
Rayport, J. F., & Sviokla, J. J. (1994, November-December). Managing in the marketspace. *Harvard Business Review,* pp. 141-150.
Rayport, J. F., & Sviokla, J. J. (1995, November-December). Exploiting the virtual value chain. *Harvard Business Review,* pp. 75-85.
Sarkar, M. B., Butler, B., & Steinfield, C. (1996). Intermediaries and cybermediaries: A continuing role for mediating players in the electronic marketplace. *Journal of Computer-Mediated Communication, 1*(3), http://www.usc.edu/dept/annenberg/journal.html.
Schifrin, M. (1998, January 12). E-threat. *Forbes,* pp. 152-153.
Schumpeter, J. A. (1975). *Capitalism, socialism and democracy* (3rd ed.). New York: Harper & Row. (Original work published in 1950)
Seideman, T. (1996, Spring). What Sam Walton learned from the Berlin airlift. *Audacity: The Magazine of Business Experience,* pp. 52-61.
Snider, J. H., & Moody, A. (1995, March-April). The information superhighway as environmental menace. *Futurist,* pp. 16-21.
Spiller, P., & Lohse, G. L. (1997-98). A classification of Internet retail stores. *International Journal of Electronic Commerce, 2*(2), 29-56.
Streeter, L. A., Kraut, R. E., Lucas, H. C., Jr., & Caby, L. (1996). How open data networks influence business performance and market structure. *Communications of the ACM, 39*(7), 62-73.
Top 20 Sites. (1998, February 9). *Inter@active Week,* p. 16.
Verity, J. W. (1996, June 10). Invoice? What's an invoice? *Business Week,* pp. 110-112.
Weber, T. E. (1997, May 20). For those who scoff at Internet commerce, here's a hot market. *The Wall Street Journal,* pp. A1, A8.
Westland, J. C., & Au, G. (1997-98). A comparison of shopping experiences across three competing digital retailing interfaces. *International Journal of Electronic Commerce, 2*(2), 57-69.
Westland, J. C., Kwok, M., Shu, J., Kwok, T., & Ho, H. (1998). Customer and merchant acceptance of electronic cash: Evidence from Mondex in Hong Kong. *International Journal of Electronic Commerce, 2*(4), 5-26.

Williamson, O. E. (1975). *Markets and hierarchies: Analysis and anti-trust implications.* New York: Free Press.
Woolley, S. (1998, January 26). Dial tones? No, Web tones. *Forbes,* pp. 84-85.
Zwass, V. (1996). Electronic commerce: Structures and issues. *International Journal of Electronic Commerce, 1*(1), 3-23.

CHAPTER
THIRTEEN

Client/Server System Success

Exploring the Human Side

TOR GUIMARAES
MAGID IGBARIA

As an emerging technology, the results from client/server systems (CSS) implementation look quite mixed. On one hand, an increasing number of companies are making substantial investments in the technology, and some organizations are claiming good results. About 90% of the CIOs in one survey said that expenditures on client/server projects would increase "significantly" or "somewhat." Even companies with revenues of less than $100 million foresaw sizable increases in expenditures. The survey revealed that client/server architectures had risen from 27% of all newly developed applications in 1993 to 43% in 1994 (Plewa & Pliskin, 1995). However, the extent to which specific organizations have converted legacy systems to CSS or developed new systems using a client/server architecture varies dramatically from company to company. Some organizations have made significant progress in converting their application portfolio; for example, Textron managers put its application portfolio at 60% mainframe based and 40% client/server based (Bucken, 1996). Some of these organizations claim substantial benefits from CSS applications. According to a 1995 Sentry Market Research study (SMR, 1995), of the sites surveyed, 25% had deployed client/server applications. Another 18% were in the pilot or test stages, 32% had applications in development, and 15% were at the design stage. Only 10% of the sites were completely uncommitted to CSS applications. Of a total of 711 IS managers participating in an InfoWorld survey (Willett, 1994), 70% were using CSS at the time, or were planning to do so in the next 18 months. Far from being minor experiments, many of the applications supported by CSS are quite important to the organization. Approximately 25% of the respondents said they are moving "mission-critical" applications to CSS platforms. Also, another survey indicated that major business process reengineering had been conducted in 78% of the sites moving mission-critical applications to a client/server environment

---

Reprinted by permission from *Decision Sciences,* Volume 28, Number 4, Fall 1997.

(Cox, 1995). Thus, CSS are being used to support "dramatic changes" in business processes, not just to automate existing ones.

On the other hand, despite the serious organizational commitments to CSS, implementation success is far from assured, and there remain many problems (Hufnagel, 1994). In many companies, only 9% of CSS development projects come in on time and on budget, and the average time overrun is 230% of the original estimate. Late delivery has become a serious problem and a key factor behind high CIO turnover (Radosevich, 1995). A Gartner Group study of 117 CSS projects worldwide found that 55% of the participants reported that projects took longer then expected. Half of the respondents said projects cost more, and 59% said projects were more complicated than expected. Despite these disappointments, only 4% of respondents felt their projects were unsuccessful, and 27% said it was too soon to tell (Glaser, 1996). Apparently, managers are willing to slowly climb the CSS learning curve.

Thus, in summary, despite the many potential implementation problems, significant rewards can be derived from CSS implementation. As put by an IS director summarizing CSS benefits, problems, and success factors from an informal CSS user group meeting attended by one of the authors:

> Seems as if there is a lot of hype, but for good reasons. End users are happy with the new system interfaces. The development tools are state-of-the-art so developers' interest is high. The only question is whether or not the companies have the resources and time to do it efficiently. Clearly, there is need for a better understanding of the important factors in CSS implementation.

The CSS Difference and Study Motivation

As defined by Sinha (1992, p. 79), "In the Client-Server computing paradigm, one or more Clients and one or more Servers, along with the underlying operating system and interprocess communication systems, form a composite system allowing distributed computation, analysis, and presentation." A client provides an end-user/system interface and the means of data retrieval and analysis, and of presenting the results. A server provides a service to one or more clients. It responds to the queries or commands from the clients. In a multiserver environment, the servers may communicate with one another to provide service to the client. As much as possible, it is desirable that the work necessary to provide the service be transparent to the end user interacting with the client. From an IS management perspective, CSS represent a marriage between end-user computing operations and more traditional IS development approaches. The client embodies the end-user friendliness of microcomputer tools, while the server side calls for more methodical systems development. For most projects, the development process is just too large and complex for end users to undertake on their own, requiring IS department participation and leadership.

Without any doubt, by designing applications separated into their client and server components, and concurrently using an object-oriented approach to systems development, CSS development represents a considerably different approach to systems development. The costs and time utilization are high, and the implementation difficulties are many, as discussed above. Why then would business managers take the plunge into this risky undertaking? To the end user, the benefit from CSS is the ability to get the required information through a significantly more user-friendly machine interface. As put by Atre (1994), a primary objective of CSS is "to give end-users the ability to point and click to retrieve data from any source" (p. 72). Ease of use and access to information are the value to "business unit managers who are providing the emotional impetus" for CSS (Brousell, 1995, p. 6). Similarly, Baum and Teach (1996) saw the primary benefit of CSS as "pushing decision making and computing power to end-users" (p. 53). The emphasis is definitely on user satisfaction with the system. As declared by Seymour (1994, p. 55), "Everyone feels such a sense of satisfaction" with CSS. In some cases, the satisfaction extends beyond company boundaries, where costs of CSS development and conversion from legacy systems were considerably less than the gains related to better customer service and greater customer satisfaction (Nielsen, 1994).

As discussed above, the motivating force for CSS lies in further improving the human aspects of computer utilization: ease of learning, ease of use, user satisfaction with the system, and the impact of the system on quality of life and jobs. This CSS emphasis on human aspects of computing, and the extent to which dramatically different systems development approaches have been employed at considerable costs to the host organizations, represent a new research opportunity. The CSS human focus is even more striking in light of continuing trends in the application of other emerging technologies. With most projects dealing with other emerging technologies, the people-related factors tend to take a back seat. For example, some studies have indicated that U.S. manufacturing companies have experienced somewhere between 50% and 75% failure rates while trying to implement advanced technologies, mostly due to neglect of human factors (Saraph & Sebastian, 1992). For these reasons, this study is focused on the people-related factors of CSS. Its main purpose is to test a theoretically well-grounded model dealing with three human elements of CSS implementation: end users, developers, and the organization. Specifically, four major factors important to the success of this emerging technology are studied: the degree of end-user involvement in the CSS development process, end-user characteristics, developer skills, and management support for the CSS project. The measures of CSS success studied here are end-user satisfaction, system usage, and its impact on end-users' jobs. Because the primary motivation for the trend toward CSS is their friendliness and appeal to the end users, we expect that these independent variables will have a relatively strong effect on the success measures.

There are three major reasons why undertaking this study is important: (1) The theoretical basis for this work is relatively strong; consequently, the constructs and the proposed relationships are widely known. Thus, one may ask, why test them again in the context of CSS? The independent variables have been found to be determinants of non-CSS implementation success. They are hypothesized also to be relevant in the case of CSS. However, given the fact that CSS represent a dramatically different approach to systems development, one should not make such assumptions without at least some empirical testing. No test has been found in the existing literature. (2) Testing this model in the CSS context is particularly relevant since, as discussed earlier, the strong emergence of CSS is primarily motivated by improved system friendliness toward the user community, thus implicitly promising substantial differences from more traditional IS along the main constructs studied here. (3) The measure used for one of the dependent variables (system impact on end-users' jobs) is a major improvement on previous measures. However, its reliability is much less established than for the other two dependent variables (system usage and user satisfaction with the system). This study is one of the few in which such a measure is evaluated, thus providing valuable information for future research on an exceedingly important construct. Further, given that end users provide the impetus for CSS emergence, CSS impact on their jobs represents a special phenomenon. It complements the work done by Yoon and Guimaraes (1995) on expert systems' job impact in that expert systems are generally more threatening to the user community, thus placing them opposite to CSS, which are primarily motivated by their attractiveness to the user community.

The Theoretical Model: The Human Side of CSS

The theoretical foundation for this study is relatively well established. Two models have been used by MIS researchers as a theoretical foundation for research on the factors affecting the user acceptance of computer technology: Fishbein and Ajzen's (1975) theory of reasoned action (TRA) and the technology acceptance model (TAM) by Davis, Bargozzi, and Warshaw (1989). Hubona and Cheney (1986) discussed both models, their relationship, and implications in more detail. The TAM adapted the generic TRA model to the particular domain of user acceptance of computer technology, replacing the TRA's attitudinal determinants, derived separately for each behavior, with a set of two variables (perceived ease of use and perceived usefulness). Both models were found to predict user intentions and usage satisfactorily; the TAM, however, was found to be a much simpler, easier to use, and more powerful model of the determinants of user acceptance of computer technology. In addition, the TAM attitudinal determinants outperformed the TRA's much larger set of measures. Adams, Nelson, and Todd (1992), Davis et al. (1989), and Mathieson (1991) provided insights into the acceptance of computer technology using the TAM.

In more general terms, much of the research on computer systems implementation has been focused on identifying the factors that appear to be conducive to either success or failure of computer-based information systems (Cheney, Mann, & Amoroso, 1986; Guimaraes, Igbaria, & Lu, 1992; Liang, 1986; Rivard & Huff, 1988; Swanson, 1988). Prior research has employed various measures of system success (DeLone & McLean, 1992), including the ones in the model proposed here: end-user satisfaction (Galletta & Lederer, 1989; Kendall, Buffington, & Kendall, 1987; Mahmood & Sniezek, 1989; Yoon, Guimaraes, & O'Neal, 1995), impact on end-users' jobs (Byrd, 1992; Sviokla, 1990; Yoon & Guimaraes, 1995; Yoon, Guimaraes, & Clevenson, 1996), and level of system usage (Fuerst & Cheney, 1982; Igbaria, Guimaraes, & Davis, 1995; Mykytyn, 1988). As mentioned by DeLone and McLean (1992), the choice of the "best" measure for system success depends on the study objectives. A variety of factors affecting information system success have also been studied previously, including end-user involvement (Barki & Hartwick, 1989; Baronas & Louis, 1988; Yoon et al., 1995), management support (Lee, 1986; Leitheiser & Wetherbe, 1986; Yoon et al., 1995), end-users' expectation and attitude (Ginzberg, 1981; Maish, 1979; Robey, 1979), politics (Markus, 1983), communications between developers and end users (Igbaria et al., 1995), task structure (Guimaraes et al., 1992; Sanders & Courtney, 1985), and end-users' training and experience (Fuerst & Cheney, 1982; Nelson & Cheney, 1987).

Targeting an emerging technology that emphasizes the human side of computing, the main premise in this study is that CSS implementation success, defined alternatively by three widely accepted people-related constructs, is dependent on a small set of widely accepted people-related factors. The parsimonious model in this case specifically tests the relationship among management support, end-user characteristics, developer skills, and end-user involvement in the CSS development process with these "system success" measures: end-user satisfaction, usage, and impact on end-users' jobs. Figure 13.1 graphically presents the model of CSS success examined in this study. In the next section, the CSS success variables are addressed in more detail, followed by a discussion of the major independent variables and the proposed relationships.

CSS Impact on End-User Jobs

In the study of IS impact on end-user jobs, DeLone and McLean (1992) presented two factors affecting the IS impact on individual jobs: end-user satisfaction and usage. Several different measures for the impact of computer-based systems on end-user jobs have been previously reported. Benbasat and Dexter (1982) used the average time to make a decision as a measure. Chervany and Dickson (1974) measured confidence in the decision made. Byrd (1992) assessed impact based on fear of loss of control and fear of loss of jobs. Sviokla (1990) measured the impact of XCON on end-user jobs by examining the changes on input and output, the increase in task accuracy and amount of work completed, the shifts in end-user roles and responsibilities, and job satisfaction. Most prior studies have used one or two items to measure system impact on end-user jobs. Similar to previous studies (Yoon & Guimaraes, 1995; Yoon et al., 1996), we employed 11 variables to measure the impact of a CSS on end-user jobs. These include the change in the importance of the end-user's job, amount of work required on the job, accuracy demanded on the job, skills needed to do the job, job appeal, feedback on job performance, freedom

```
┌──────────────┐
│  Management  │─────────────────┐
│   Support    │                 │
└──────────────┘                 │
┌──────────────┐    ┌──────────────┐   ┌──────────┐   ┌──────────┐
│   End-User   │───▶│   End-User   │   │  System  │   │   C/S    │
│  Involvement │    │ Satisfaction │   │   Usage  │   │  Impact  │
└──────────────┘    └──────────────┘   └──────────┘   └──────────┘
┌──────────────┐           │                              ▲
│  Developers' │           └──────────────────────────────┘
│    Skills    │
└──────────────┘
┌──────────────┐
│   End-User   │
│Characteristics│
└──────────────┘
```

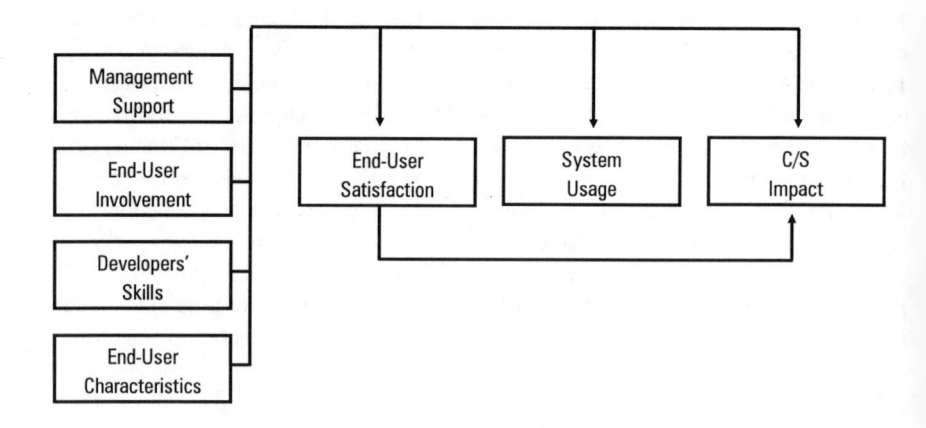

Figure 13.1. CSS Success Indicators and Determinants

in how to do the job, opportunity for advancement, job security, relationship with fellow employees, and job satisfaction.

End-User Satisfaction

End-user satisfaction with the system has been considered to be the most useful assessment of system effectiveness by Hamilton and Chervany (1981), and to be a useful substitute for objective determinants of information system effectiveness (Ives, Olson, & Baroudi, 1983). A comprehensive discussion of system success by DeLone and McLean (1992) indicated that compared to other factors, end-user satisfaction has been widely used as a surrogate measure of system success (Galletta & Lederer, 1989; Guimaraes et al., 1992; Kendall et al., 1987; Mahmood & Sniezek, 1989; McKeen, Guimaraes, & Wetherbe, 1994; Yoon et al., 1995), thus allowing interstudy comparisons.

Starting with the end-user satisfaction measure originally developed by Bailey and Pearson (1983), Ives et al. (1983) produced a shorter form by excluding 26 items from the original 39-item instrument. Raymond (1985) also adapted the instrument and developed a 20-item scale, which, by factor analysis, has been grouped into four factors: output quality, end-user-system relationship, support, and end-user relationship with EDP staff. Instead of measuring end-user satisfaction in all four areas, this study uses the 10 items assessing end-user satisfaction with the quality of the CSS output. This approach is deemed more appropriate in the case of CSS and is similar to the one used to measure the quality of a model in terms of its output, problem solution, and system interfaces with the end users (Lucas, 1978; Yoon et al., 1995, 1996). This scale excluded items not applicable to measure end-user satisfaction with CSS output quality, that is, management support, end-user relationship with

EDP staff, and vendor support. The 10 items retained are output value, usage frequency, timeliness, reliability, response/turnaround time, accuracy, completeness, easy to use, easy to learn, and the usefulness of the available documentation. As mentioned earlier, user satisfaction has been proposed by DeLone and McLean (1992) as a determinant of IS impact on user jobs. It is used as such here in the context of CSS.

System Usage

Thompson, Higgins, and Howell (1991) proposed the need for greater attention to the usage of any emerging technology, particularly the factors that cause individual resistance to computer usage. While system usage may not ensure improved end-user task performance or return on investment, it remains a critical variable for organizations to derive benefit from any emerging technology. Indeed, as mentioned earlier, a central focus of IS implementation research has been to examine the factors affecting end-user acceptance of computer technology, particularly emerging major variations such as CSS. Several models have been developed to investigate the impact of these factors on the acceptance of computer technology. Among these factors are individual, organizational, and system characteristics (Davis et al., 1989; Franz & Robey, 1986; Fuerst & Cheney, 1982; Igbaria, 1990; Igbaria et al., 1995; Lucas, 1978; Swanson, 1988; Zmud, 1979). Given its importance, CSS usage was included in this study.

The Independent Variables

As discussed earlier, DeLone and McLean (1994) have proposed user satisfaction and system usage as factors affecting system impact on end-users' jobs. Similarly, as discussed before, other authors have proposed many factors affecting user satisfaction and system usage (Benbasat & Dexter, 1979; Byrd, 1992; Sviokla, 1990). Within the human-related framework chosen for this CSS study, four widely accepted independent variables were chosen as particularly relevant to understanding the CSS phenomenon: end-user characteristics, end-user involvement in CSS development, developer skills, and management support.

End-User Characteristics

Based on the theoretical model of Zmud (1979), individual characteristics have been reported to play an important role in the eventual success of IS. The acceptance of computer technology depends on the technology itself and the level of skill or expertise of the individual using the technology (Nelson, 1990). End-user training and experience, representing individual skills and expertise, were found to be related to end-user beliefs and usage. The impact of beliefs and usage has been well documented (Igbaria, 1990; Schewe, 1976; Zmud). These studies and others suggest that end-user training plays a very important role in influencing end-user beliefs toward the system, and that training programs are likely to increase end-user confidence in their ability to master and use computers in their work (Gist, 1987). Recent research (Davis & Bostrom, 1993; Igbaria & Chakrabarti, 1990; Nelson & Cheney, 1987) provided evidence that the type of training the users receive will influence subsequent task performance and end-users' belief that they can develop skills necessary to use computers. Additionally, opportunities to gain experience using computers and information systems are thought to improve end-users' beliefs about the system (Igbaria; Rivard & Huff, 1988). End-user training and computer experience were also found to be positively related to system usage (DeLone, 1988; Fuerst & Cheney, 1982; Igbaria, Pavri, & Huff, 1989; Kraemer, Danziger, Dunkle, & King, 1993; Lee, 1986; Schewe). It was found that lack of training is a major reason for the lack of IS success. In addition, prior computer experience promoted increased computer usage. The dominant end-user characteristics affecting success include end-user attitude, end-user expectation, and end-user knowledge of CSS technology (Smith, 1988). End-user attitude has been viewed as an important factor to success since end users with a negative attitude will tend to be unhappy with the system and not use it, completely wasting development costs. Further, poor user attitude is likely to lead to lower satisfaction with the system. Based on the above discussion, it is proposed that individual characteristics will directly affect user satisfaction with the CSS, CSS usage, and its impact on end-users' jobs.

End-User Involvement

CSS are expected to be similar to most decision support systems whose development is heavily dependent on end-user involvement (Guimaraes et al., 1992; Igbaria & Guimaraes, 1994; McKeen et al., 1994) for information requirements definition. To increase end-user satisfaction and CSS usage, heavy end-user involvement is recommended to design the end-user interface and to determine the system availability and access according to their needs. Similar to the model used by Yoon et al. (1995), involvement in nine different activities was studied: initiating the project, establishing the objective of the project, determining end-user requirements, accessing ways to meet end-user requirements, identifying the sources of data/information, outlining the information flow, developing the input forms/screens, developing the output forms/screens, and determining the system availability/access. Based on the above discussion, it is proposed that user involvement will directly affect user satisfaction with the CSS, CSS usage, and its impact on end-users' jobs.

Developer Skills

A number of developer characteristics were found to affect system implementation success, that is, developers' abilities to minimize conflicts with end users (Green, 1989; Kaiser & Bostrom, 1982; Lucas, 1978; Yoon et al., 1995). White and Leifer (1986) explored the impact of developer(s) skills on IS success and reported that a range of skills, including both technical and process skills, is important for system success. Although the range of developers' skills and abilities varies slightly between studies, Nunamaker, Couger, and Davis (1982) classified skills into six general categories: people, model, system, computer, organizational, and societal. People skills refer to communication and interpersonal skills. Model skills are defined as the ability to formulate and solve models of the operation research type. System skills refers to the ability to view and define a situation as a system—specifying components, scopes, and functions. Computer skills refer to knowledge of hardware/software, programming languages, and CSS techniques. Organizational skills are defined as knowledge of the functional areas of an organization and organizational conditions. Strong knowledge of various functional areas in an organization improves developers' communication with end users and helps save everyone's time and effort. Last, societal skills generally refer to the ability to articulate and defend a personal position on important issues about information technology's impact on society. More specifically, it refers to the ability to perceive and describe the impact of a CSS on a particular part of society. Due to the special nature of CSS emphasis on system friendliness to end users and its development process (i.e., complex system design, new development methods and tools), the importance of skillful CSS developers is expected to be relatively greater than for non-CSS success. Based on the above discussion, it is proposed that developers' skills will directly affect user satisfaction with the CSS, CSS usage, and its impact on end-users' jobs.

Management Support

The importance of management support for system success has been emphasized by several authors (DePree, 1988; Keyes, 1989; Smith, 1988). Igbaria (1990) and Igbaria and Chakrabarti (1990) successfully used a measure of management support encompassing two broad categories of support: (1) end-user support, which includes the availability of system development assistance, specialized instruction, and guidance in using microcomputer applications; and (2) management support, which includes top management encouragement and allocation of resources. High levels of management support are thought to promote more favorable beliefs about the system among end users as well as IS staff (Igbaria & Chakrabarti; Lucas, 1978). Management support was found to be associated with favorable user attitude toward the system and with greater system usage. Furthermore, lack of management support is considered a critical barrier to the effective utilization of computers (Fuerst & Cheney, 1982; Igbaria; Lucas). A model proposed by Triandis (1980) and tested by Thompson et al. (1991) found that support for end users also influences system utilization. Igbaria et al. (1995) found management support directly related to system usage. Keyes reported that lack of management support was a critical barrier to system success, and Barsanti (1990) said that a key predictor to success in an organization is the existence of top-down corporate support.

Several reasons for the importance of management support can be described. First, management support is essential to receive personnel and monetary resources necessary to the system development. Without management's support, a system's development cost will not be funded, resulting in a system failure. Second, the adoption of a new technology by an organization always results in some change in the manner in which decisions are made, business tasks are performed, and power is allocated. Changes in a work environment frequently increase end-user fears about their jobs and, in turn, may generate resistance against a new system (Sloane, 1991). Since many CSS development costs seem quite expensive, and many are being used for business process reengineering, these factors may be relatively more important for CSS implementation. Based on the above discussion, it is proposed that management support will directly affect user satisfaction with the CSS, system usage, and its impact on end-user jobs.

Methodology

Sampling Procedure

A questionnaire containing the variables and their measurement scales as discussed below was developed and pilot tested for content and readability by nine CSS development managers from six different companies. Based on the managers' suggestions, some of the questions were reworded to make them easier to understand. Five hundred questionnaires were mailed out to attendees of a series of seminars for IS managers organized by vendors of CSS equipment and development services. Each questionnaire had a cover letter from the researchers explaining the purpose of the study, promising anonymity and a copy of the results upon request. The questionnaire was addressed to the IS manager, but it contained two detachable parts: one with questions for the IS managers, the second with questions for the end-user department manager most directly related to the specific CSS project being reported on. Each of the two separate parts was foldable and prestamped for mailing directly to the researchers. Multiple respondents were used to increase data validity and reduce the possibility of common method variance.

The IS managers were instructed to select the most recently implemented CSS that had been fully operational for at least one year. This directive was issued to reduce the chance that IS managers would select their "favorite" end users. The inclusion of only those CSS operational for at least one year was necessary to detect any permanent changes managers may have caused to end-user jobs, and to ensure that system usage and end-user satisfaction were not temporary. Last, the end-user department managers were instructed to answer their questions based on "this specific" system. From the 500 questionnaires mailed out, 148 matched and usable responses were obtained, along with 16 unmatched responses (9 from IS managers and 7 from end-user managers) and 5 discarded responses due to invalid data or too much missing information. The response rate of approximately 29% is considered good for surveys of this type.

Sample Demographics

Tables 13.1 and 13.2 present selected information about respondents and their organizations. Table 13.1 shows that the sample contains a broad selection of industrial sectors, with close to half of the companies from the manufacturing sector and over 13% from financial services. The sample also shows broad participation based on company gross revenues. Table 13.2 shows selected characteristics of the client/server environment, such as experience with CSS, the primary business area supported, the system's primary purpose, number of existing CSS configurations (two or three tier), and the number of database servers in the CSS configuration. The mainframe-based systems are CSS using mainframe servers necessary for large corporate databases.

Variable Measurement

Most of the measures used in this study were previously tested and published elsewhere. Most are based on the Likert and semantic differential scales, and comprise several items.

The Impact of the CSS on End-User Jobs

CSS impact was measured by perceived performance since objective measures of performance were unavailable in this field context and, at any rate, would not have been compatible across individuals with different task portfolios. Eleven questions (adapted from Millman & Hartwick, 1987) were used, which asked individuals to self-report on the perceived impact of client/server on their performance, productivity, and effectiveness in their job. Seven of these items were taken from Hackman and Oldham's (1980) research and dealt with various aspects of an individual's work (importance of the job, amount of work required on the job, accuracy demanded by the job, skills needed to do the job, amount of freedom in how to do the job, job appeal, and feedback on job performance). Four additional items dealt with other job concerns detailed within their job satisfaction literature (Bikson, Stasz, & Mankin, 1985; Kraut, Dumais, & Kock, 1989). The department managers were asked about their employees' relationship with fellow employees, job security, opportunity for advancement, and job satisfaction. Each item was measured on a 7-point Likert scale ranging from "1" (*strongly disagree*) to "7" (*strongly agree*). These questions were answered by end users.

TABLE 13.1 Company Demographics

	Frequency	Percentage
a. The primary organization's business		
Manufacturing	67	45.3
Retailer	9	6.1
Financial services	20	13.5
Insurance	9	6.1
Health care	2	1.4
Utility (electric, gas, etc.)	9	6.1
Transportation	10	6.8
Extraction of natural resources	8	5.4
Wholesaler	6	4.1
Other	8	5.4
	148	100.0
b. Organizations' gross revenues		
Less than $50 million	9	6.1
$50-$100 million	14	9.5
$101-$300 million	23	15.5
$301-$600 million	36	24.3
$601M-$1 billion	25	16.9
$1B-$10 billion	17	11.5
Over $10 billion	24	16.2
	148	100.0

System Usage

Based on several studies (Igbaria et al., 1989; Srinivasan, 1985; Thompson et al., 1991), two indicators of computer usage were included in this study: (1) the actual amount of time spent on the microcomputer system per day (based on Lee's 1986 study, individuals were asked to indicate how many hours the manager used the client/server system per day); and (2) frequency of use of client/server system. Frequency of use has been proposed by Raymond (1985) for providing a perspective on use slightly different from actual time spent. Frequency of use was measured on a 6-point scale ranging from "1" (*less than once a month*) to "6" (*several times a day*). These indicators are typical of the kinds of self-reported measures often used to operationalize system use and acceptance, particularly in cases in which objective use and acceptance metrics are not available. Self-reported utilization should not be regarded as a precise measure of actual utilization, although previous research suggests it is appropriate as a relative measure. These questions were answered by end users.

TABLE 13.2 Characteristics of the Client/Server Environment and the CSS

	Frequency	Percentage
a. Primary business area supported by its CSS		
1. Accounting	29	19.6
2. Finance	15	10.1
3. Customer service	14	9.5
4. Engineering	8	5.4
5. General management	7	4.7
6. R&D	4	2.7
7. Manufacturing	33	22.3
8. Marketing	16	10.8
9. Personnel	8	5.4
10. Logistics	8	5.4
11. Purchasing	5	4.1
b. System primary nature or purpose		
1. Transaction processing	15	10.1
2. Decision support	37	25.0
3. Both 1 and 2	96	64.9
4. Mission critical	34	23.0
5. Online	63	42.6
c. CSS configurations		
1. Two tier (clients and server only)	113	76.4
2. Three tier (clients, servers, and middleware)	35	23.6
d. Database server(s) in the CSS		
1. LAN-based (databases on one or more servers)	96	64.9
2. Middleware-based (data warehouse servers between clients and other servers)	39	26.4
3. Mainframe-based (large database on mainframe servers)	3	8.8

NOTE: Number of months the organization used CSS technology: Mean: 44.4, Standard Deviation: 13.4

End-User Satisfaction

Satisfaction was measured by a 10-item scale adapted from Yoon et al. (1995). The scale is a measure of end-user satisfaction with the CSS system. It includes items on which the CSS meet the end-user's needs regarding information content, accuracy, and timeliness; along with CSS response/turnaround time, end-user friendliness (ease of learning and ease of use), documentation, and functionality.

Each item was measured on a 7-point Likert scale ranging from "1" (*strongly disagree*) to "7" (*strongly agree*). These questions were answered by end users.

Management Support

This measure was developed by Igbaria (1990), assessing management support in terms of encouraging the use of the technology as well as providing necessary resources. It was measured by six items: management's understanding of the CSS potential benefits; encouragement by managers for the use of CSS in the employee's job; providing the necessary training, assistance, and resources needed for effective use of the CSS; and management's interest in having employees satisfied with CSS technology. The managers were asked to indicate the extent of their agreement or disagreement with six statements concerning management support on a 7-point Likert-type scale ranging from "1" (*strongly disagree*) to "7" (*strongly agree*). These questions were answered by either the IS director, the project manager, or both.

End-User Involvement

End-user involvement in the client/server system development process, adapted from Doll and Torkzadeh (1989), was measured by asking the managers how much they were actually involved in each of the nine specific client/server activities, such as initiating the project, establishing the objective of the project, determining the system availability/access, and outlining information flows. The response options, anchored on a 7-point Likert-type scale, ranged from "1" (*strongly disagree*) to "7" (*strongly agree*). These questions were answered by either the IS director, the project manager, or both.

Developers' Skills

This was assessed by a five-item scale previously developed and used by Yoon et al. (1995). It incorporates people skills, modeling skills, systems skills, computer skills, and organizational skills. The response options, anchored on a 7-point Likert-type scale, ranged from "1" (*strongly disagree*) to "7" (*strongly agree*). These questions were answered by either the IS director, the project manager, or both.

End-User Characteristics

End-user characteristics were measured by a four-item scale previously developed and used by Yoon et al. (1995). The managers were asked to indicate the extent of their agreement or disagreement with three statements concerning end-user attitudes, expectations, resistance, and computer background on a 7-point Likert-type scale ranging from "1" (*strongly disagree*) to "7" (*strongly agree*). These questions were answered by either the IS director, the project manager, or both.

Data Analysis

Partial least squares (PLS) was used to test the hypothesized relationships among the study variables. PLS is a second-generation multivariate technique that facilitates testing of the psychometric properties of the scales used to measure a variable, as well as estimation of the parameters of a structural model, that is, the strength and direction of the relationships among the model variables (Fornell, 1982; Lohmoller, 1989; Wold, 1982).

PLS embraces abstract and empirical variables simultaneously and recognizes the interplay of these two dimensions of theory development. The causal modeling technique, often termed structural equation modeling, accommodates a priori knowledge derived from theory and/or previous empirical findings. According to Fornell (1982), these methods can combine and confront theory with empirical data, offering the potential for scientific explanation that goes far beyond description and empirical association. PLS is a multivariate technique that facilitates testing of the psychometric properties of the scales used to measure a variable, as well as estimating the parameters of a structural model, that is, the magnitude and direction of the relationships among the model variables (Fornell; Lohmoller, 1989; Wold, 1982). The technique is particularly applicable in research areas in which theory is not as well developed as that demanded by LISREL (Fornell & Bookstein, 1982; Igbaria, 1990). As suggested by Lohmoller (1981, p. 7), "PLS methods are more close to the data, more explorative, more data analytic." Of particular relevance to this study is the fact that PLS does not depend on having multivariate normally distributed data (distribution free). Finally, PLS can be used with noninterval-scaled data, and importantly, with small samples.

PLS recognizes two components of a causal model: the measurement model and the structural model. Figure 13.1 represents the structural model being examined. The model describes the relationships or paths among theoretical constructs. Furthermore, for each construct in Figure 13.1, there is a related measurement model, which links the construct in the diagram with a set of items. For example, perceived usefulness is a composite of four related items. The measurement model consists of the relationships between the observed variables (items) and the constructs that they measure. The characteristics of this model demonstrate the construct validity of the research instruments, that is, the extent to which the operationalization of a construct actually measures what it purports to measure. Two important dimensions of construct validity are (1) convergent validity, including reliability, and (2) discriminant validity.

PLS is also used to test the structural model. A structural model is a regression-based technique with its roots in path analysis, is often loosely termed a causal modeling technique, and is a relatively new approach to testing multivariate models with empirical data (Wold, 1982). The structural model consists of the unobservable constructs and the theoretical relationships among them (the paths). It evaluates the explanatory power of the model, and the significance of paths in the structural model which represent hypotheses to be tested. Together, the structural and measurement models form a network of constructs and measures. The item weights and loadings indicate the strength of measures, while the estimated path coefficients indicate the strength and the sign of the theoretical relationships. The evaluation of the structural model was conducted with the total sample. The computer program used for this analysis was LVPLS 1.6 (Latent Variables Path Analysis using Partial Least Squares), developed by Lohmoller (1981, 1989). To test the estimated path coefficients, *t*-statistics were calculated using a nonparametric test of significance known as jackknifing (Tukey, 1958; Wildt, Lambert, & Durand, 1982).

The path coefficient of an exogenous variable represents the direct effect of that variable on the endogenous variable. An indirect effect represents the effect of a particular variable on the second variable through its effects on a third mediating variable. It is the product of the path coefficients along an indirect route from cause to effect via tracing arrows in the headed direction only. When more than one indirect path exists, the total indirect effect is their sum. The sum of the direct and indirect effect reflects the total effect of the variable on the endogenous variable (Alwin & Hauser, 1975; Ross, 1975).

Results

The Measurement Model

Table 13.3 presents the results of the test of the measurement model. The data show that the measures of the constructs examined in this study are robust in terms of their internal consistency reliability as indexed by coefficient alpha. The composite reliabilities of the different constructs included in the model range from .82 to .96, which exceed the recommended values in Nunnally's (1978) guidelines. The results also demonstrate satisfactory convergent and discriminant validity of the measures. Consistent with the recommendations of Fornell and Larcker (1981), average variance extracted for all constructs exceeded .50. The intercorrelations among the items measuring each construct are stronger than their correlations with items representing other constructs.

Tests of the Structural Model

The results of the multivariate test of the structural model are presented in Tables 13.3 and 13.4. Table 13.4 shows that the structural model as a whole explains 32% and 67% of the variance ($p < .001$) in end-user satisfaction and system usage, respectively. Table 13.3 shows that all the antecedent variables explained 67% of the variance in the impact on end-user jobs. Overall, this relatively parsimonious model explains a relatively high percentage of the variance in system impact on end-user jobs (total $R^2 = .67$). This fulfills the basic premise motivating this study

TABLE 13.3 Assessment of the Measurement Model

Variables	The Composite Reliability (Alpha Coefficients)	Average Variance Extracted/Explained
Independent variables		
End-user involvement	.95	.69
Management support	.86	.52
Developers' skills	.84	.51
End-user characteristics	.91	.71
Dependent variables		
End-user satisfaction	.96	.69
System usage	.82	.69
The impact on end-user jobs	.95	.62

that human factors are relatively more important than technological factors in the case of CSS, compared to more traditional systems.

Consistent with our expectations, developers' skills, end-user involvement, and end-user characteristics are positively related to end-user satisfaction ($g = .45, .19$, and $.11, p < .05$, respectively). Inconsistent with our expectations, management support had no significant effect on end-user satisfaction. It should be noted that management support is significantly correlated with end-user satisfaction ($r = .33$, $p < .05$). The insignificant effect may be due to the correlation among the independent variables.

Table 13.4 also shows that end-user characteristics had the strongest direct effects on system usage, followed by management support, developers' skills ($g = .50, .26$, and $.11, p < .05$, respectively), and end-user satisfaction ($\beta = .09, p < .05$). It should also be noted that developers' skills had an indirect effect on usage through end-user satisfaction.

The contribution of the independent variables on the impact of CSS on end-user jobs are statistically significant. Table 13.5 shows that management support had the strongest effect ($g = .43, p < .01$), followed by developers' skills ($g = .31, p < .05$), end-user involvement and end-user characteristics ($g = .08$ and $.08, p < .05$, respectively). Table 13.5 also shows that end-user satisfaction and system usage also had positive effects on CSS impact ($\beta = .09$ and $.15, p < .05$, respectively). It should be noted that end-user characteristics, developers' skills, and management support also had indirect effects on impact through satisfaction and usage.

To sum up, the tests of the structural model show that developers' skills and organizational support are the dominant factors affecting the impact of client/server systems. Developers' skills had the strongest effect on end-user satisfaction. The data also show that end-user characteristics had the strongest effect on usage.

TABLE 13.4 Prediction of End-User Satisfaction and System Usage

		System Usage		
Variables	End-User Satisfaction	Direct	Indirect	Total
End-user involvement	.19*	.02	.02	.04
Management support	.02	.26*	.00	.26*
Developers' skills	.45*	.11*	.04	.15*
End-user characteristics	.11*	.50*	.01	.51*
End-user satisfaction		.09*	.00	.09*
R^2	.32*	.67*		

*$p < .01$.

Discussion and Conclusions

The results from this study indicate that the human-related aspects of CSS implementation (i.e., end-user involvement in system development, end-user characteristics, developer skills, and management support) are very important and can explain significant portions of the variances in the widely used measures for system success studied here: end-user satisfaction, system usage, and system impact on the end-users' jobs. The results indicate that while CSS development methods and tools are also important and deserve attention from project managers (particularly in today's early stages of CSS technology evolution), CSS project managers need to pay a great deal of attention to the human aspects of CSS development and implementation. Further, as the development tools and methodologies mature and become more established and better known to developers, the relative importance of the human factors is likely to grow.

CSS technology is promoted by vendors as a particularly easy to learn and easy to use technology for end users, once the system is operational. Nevertheless, the quality of the CSS end-user interfaces will be heavily dependent on the proper definition of end-user requirements. Thus, end-users' involvement in the definition of system requirements is critically important. End-user involvement in the other stages of the development life cycle is also likely to be important to varying degrees for different types of applications. For example, for mission-critical applications in which prototyping time frames are likely to be relatively short, close end-user cooperation in all phases of the development effort is necessary. On the other hand, for CSS processing high transaction volume, detailed systems design considerations are best left to IS specialists, with the end users participating in the evaluation of the design decisions at the CSS operational testing stage. Regardless of these tactical considerations, it behooves CSS project managers to cultivate end-user participation by educating the end-user community as to the potential benefits of client/server technology in general, as well as the benefits of the particular system being

TABLE 13.5 Prediction of the Impact of Client/Server System on End-User Jobs

Variables	Direct	Indirect	Total
End-user involvement	.08*	.02	.10*
Management support	.43*	.04	.47*
Developers' skills	.31*	.06*	.37*
End-user characteristics	.08*	.09	.17*
End-user satisfaction	.09*	.01	.10*
System usage	.15*	.15*	.30*
R^2	.67*		

*$p < .01$.

developed. Good working relations with end-user department managers and a good understanding of end-user department political structures and individual end-user competencies is likely to be helpful in securing the participation of specific end users deemed most helpful to the developers of a particular CSS.

Because CSS technology is relatively young, the collection of tools and methodologies for systems development continues to proliferate at a fast pace. Previous industry experience has clearly indicated the importance of training and developer skills for systems development productivity while using new tools. Therefore, managers should either ensure an appropriate project time frame and budget (including an appropriate training budget), or outsource CSS development to more qualified developers.

It is also important that before embarking on major CSS development projects, particularly those involving highly visible business process reengineering and/or mission-critical applications, project managers understand the characteristics of the end users involved: their attitude toward the new system, any reasons why they might resist the system implementation, their prior experience with computer technology, and their expectations from the system being developed. End-user education and other activities with the specific objectives of improving end-user attitudes and keeping the level of end-user expectations within reasonable limits should be considered on a project-by-project basis. Development of a more cooperative relationship and the nurturing of a more computer-smart end-user community should be a more continuous objective to be accomplished over time. To minimize long-lasting political problems, the management of end-user resistance to a particular CSS must be addressed in cooperation with business managers responsible for the application area, under the arbitration of top management if necessary.

Last, management support is found to be an important factor for CSS to have a positive impact on end-users' jobs. The willingness of managers to encourage the CSS use, to have an interest in having employees satisfied with CSS technology, and to provide the necessary help and resources for effective CSS use are important factors for a positive system impact on end-users' jobs. For applications that need to integrate different legacy applications with distributed databases in an end-user transparent fashion, and/or applications that require relatively more friendly user interfaces, CSS configurations should be seriously considered. For those applications, particularly when end users' CSS expectations are relatively high, IS managers must lobby corporate managers for the necessary resources and develop positive management attitudes toward the application of this promising but relatively new technology.

Study Limitations and Directions for Future Research

While the present study has provided both strong support for the human-related model of CSS success and insights that in the CSS context, managers must concentrate attention on the independent variables studied here, it also raises several issues that represent substantial opportunities for future research.

1. As one of the first relatively rigorous studies on the application of CSS technology, it deliberately excluded some important factors from the research model. While the focus on the human aspects of CSS gave more depth to the study, it also sacrificed the comprehensiveness of the research model. Future studies are necessary to either expand the research model, focus on other likely determinants of CSS implementation success, or both. Specifically, there is presently a dire need for a better understanding of the impact of development tool characteristics on success, given the wild proliferation of development tools and methodologies. Important factors to be considered are the quality of the CSS development tools used and their compatibility with the existing applications and IS infrastructure. Also, as organizations attempt to apply the technology to an increasingly broader variety of business processes, it is important to have a better understanding of the application characteristics lending themselves to this fast emerging technology. Applications in which developers need to integrate different databases and systems behind relatively friendly user interfaces are likely to benefit from CSS configurations.

2. The implementation of intranet concepts such as home pages and Internet compatible protocols is likely to have a profound impact on the motivation and operational aspects of the CSS approach. The more smooth connection to the Internet is likely to speed up the conversion process from legacy applications to the object-oriented CSS paradigm for systems development. As more organizations step up Internet use to support interorganizational systems and provide information-pull applications (web pages) to internal and external end users alike, the importance of server-based software and data access/integrity control mechanisms will grow in importance. There is need for information on the advantages and disadvantages of the various combinations of these emerging technologies, and the type of applications most suited to each. Further, the success factor priorities are likely to change, new factors may become important and old ones may become

more or less important, creating the need for retesting existing predictive models for system success.

3. The ultimate test for any model is its ability to produce desired changes in an applied setting. Therefore, future research should examine whether the specific managerial actions recommended here indeed produce the expected effects. Research programs that combine theoretically oriented studies on the turnover process, using second generational multivariate analysis with field-based, quasi-experimental interventions, should provide major insights of both a theoretical and practical nature.

4. Although common method variance due to self-reporting bias is not found to be a problem in this study, researchers must strive to develop more direct and objective measures for the variables being studied, thereby reducing the likelihood of obtaining spurious results in the future. The following evidence suggests that research results are relatively bias free: (1) the data show no tendency for respondents to agree/disagree with items, regardless of content; (2) the risk of common method variance is much greater for single-item measures or poorly designed scales (Spector, 1987); and (3) correlations between objective measures (i.e., demographic variables) and suspect variables are consistent with expectations based on previous studies and experience. This study has passed the first and second tests satisfactorily. The third test is not formally possible due to the absence of other published empirical evidence regarding CSS; however, no bias is apparent to the authors and to several reviewers of this report.

References

Adams, D. A., Nelson, R. R., & Todd, P. A. (1992). Perceived usefulness, ease of use, and usage of information technology: A replication. *MIS Quarterly, 16*(2), 227-247.
Alwin, D. E., & Hauser, R. M. (1975). Decomposition of effects in path analysis. *American Sociological Review, 40*(2), 37-47.
Atre, S. (1994). Twelve steps to successful client/server. *DBMS, 7*(5), 70-76.
Bailey, J. E., & Pearson, S. W. (1983). Development of a tool for measuring and analyzing computer user satisfaction. *Management Science, 29*(5), 530-545.
Barki, H., & Hartwick, J. (1989). Rethinking the concept of user involvement. *MIS Quarterly, 13*(1), 53-63.
Baronas, A. M. K., & Louis, M. R. (1988). Restoring a sense of control during implementation: How user involvement leads to system acceptance. *MIS Quarterly, 12*(1), 111-124.
Barsanti, J. B. (1990). Expert systems: Critical success factors for their implementation. *Information Executive, 3*(1), 30-34.
Baum, D., & Teach, E. (1996). Putting client/server in charge. *CFO, 12*(1), 45-53.
Benbasat, I., & Dexter, A. S. (1982). Individual differences in the use of decision support aids. *Journal of Accounting Research, 20*, 1-11.
Bikson, T. K., Stasz, C., & Mankin, D. A. (1985). *Computer-mediated work: Individual and organizational impact in one corporate headquarters.* Santa Monica, CA: RAND.
Brousell, D. R. (1995). Can we justify client/server? *Software Magazine, 15*(9), S3-S24.

Bucken, M. (1996). Textron stays on client/server course, as legacy application migration nears completion, IS officials reflect on the journey. *Software Magazine, 16*(3), 42-43.

Byrd, T. A. (1992). Implementation and use of expert systems in organizations: Perceptions of knowledge engineers. *Journal of Management Information Systems, 8*(4), 97-116.

Cheney, P. H., Mann, R. I., & Amoroso, D. L. (1986). Organizational factors affecting the success of end-user computing. *Journal of Management Information Systems, 3*(1), 68-80.

Chervany, N. L., & Dickson, G. W. (1974). An experimental evaluation of information overload in a production environment. *Management Science, 20*(10), 1335-1349.

Cox, J. (1995). Client/server is pricey but effective. *Network World, 12*(49), 29-32.

Davis, F. D., Bargozzi, R. P., & Warshaw, P. R. (1989). User acceptance of computer technology: A comparison of two theoretical models. *Management Science, 35*(8), 982-1003.

Davis, S. A., & Bostrom, R. P. (1993). Training end users: An experimental investigation of the roles of computer interface and training methods. *MIS Quarterly, 17*(1), 61-85.

DeLone, W. H. (1988). Determinants of success for computer usage in small business. *MIS Quarterly, 12*(1), 51-61.

DeLone, W., & McLean, E. (1992). Information systems success: The quest for the dependent variable. *Information Systems Research, 3*(1), 60-95.

DePree, R. (1988). Implementing expert systems. *Micro User's Guide,* Summer Edition.

Doll, W. J., & Torkzadeh, G. (1989). Discrepancy model of end-user computing involvement. *Management Science, 35*(10), 1151-1171.

Fishbein, M., & Ajzen, I. (1975). *Belief, attitude, intentions and behavior: An introduction to theory and research.* Boston: Addison-Wesley.

Fornell, C. R. (Ed.). (1982). *A second generation of multivariate analysis, Volume I and II: Methods.* New York: Praeger Special Studies.

Fornell, C. R., & Bookstein, F. L. (1982). Two structural equation models: LISREL and PLS applied to consumer exit-voice theory. *Journal of Marketing Research, 19*(4), 440-452.

Fornell, C. R., & Larcker, D. F. (1981). Structural equation models with unobservable variables and measurement error. *Journal of Marketing Research, 18*(1), 39-50.

Franz, C. R., & Robey, D. (1986). Organizational context, user involvement, and the usefulness of information systems. *Decision Sciences, 17*(4), 329-356.

Fuerst, W., & Cheney, P. (1982). Factors affecting the perceived utilization of computer-based decision support systems in the oil industry. *Decision Sciences, 13*(4), 554-569.

Galletta, D. F., & Lederer, A. L. (1989). Some cautions on the measurement of user information satisfaction. *Decision Sciences, 20*(3), 419-438.

Ginzberg, M. J. (1981). Early diagnosis of MIS implementation failure: Promising results and unanswered questions. *Management Science, 27,* 459-478.

Gist, M. E. (1987). Self-efficacy: Implications for organizational behavioral and human resource management. *Academy of Management Review, 12*(4), 472-485.

Glaser, M. (1996). Client/server hits growing pains. *InfoWorld, 17/18*(52/1), 48.

Green, G. I. (1989). Perceived importance of system analysts' job skills, roles and non-salary incentives. *MIS Quarterly, 13*(2), 115-133.

Guimaraes, T., Igbaria, M., & Lu, M. (1992). Determinants of DSS success: An integrated model. *Decision Sciences, 23*(2), 409-430.

Hackman, J. R., & Oldham, G. R. (1980). *Work redesign.* Reading, MA: Addison-Wesley.

Hamilton, S., & Chervany, N. L. (1981). Evaluating information system effectiveness: Comparing evaluation approaches. *MIS Quarterly, 5*(1), 55-69.

Hubona, G. S., & Cheney, P. H. (1994). System effectiveness of knowledge-based technology: The relationship of user performance and attitudinal measures. In *Proceedings of the 27th Annual International Conference on Systems Sciences* (Vol. 3, pp. 532-541). Honolulu, HI.

Hufnagel, E. (1994). The hidden costs of client/server. *Network Computing Client Server,* (Suppl.), 22-27.

Igbaria, M. (1990). End-user computing effectiveness: A structural equation model. *OMEGA, 18*(6), 637-652.

Igbaria, M., & Chakrabarti, A. (1990). Computer anxiety and attitudes towards microcomputer use. *Behavior and Information Technology, 9*(3), 229-241.

Igbaria, M., & Guimaraes, T. (1994). Empirically testing the impact of user involvement on DSS success. *OMEGA, 22*(2), 157-172.

Igbaria, M., Guimaraes, T., & Davis, G. (1995). Testing the determinants of microcomputer usage via a structural equation model. *Journal of Management Information Systems, 11*(4), 87-114.

Igbaria, M., Pavri, F., & Huff, S. (1989). Microcomputer application: An empirical look at usage. *Information & Management, 16*(4), 187-196.

Ives, B., Olson, M. H., & Baroudi, J. J. (1983). The measurement of user information satisfaction. *Communications of the ACM, 26*(10), 785-793.

Kaiser, K. M., & Bostrom, R. P. (1982). Personality characteristics of MIS project teams: An empirical study and action-research design. *MIS Quarterly, 6*(4), 43-60.

Kendall, K. E., Buffington, J. R., & Kendall, J. E. (1987). The relationship of organizational subcultures to DSS user satisfaction. *Human Systems Management, 7,* 31-39.

Keyes, J. (1989). Why expert systems fail. *AI Expert, 4*(11), 50-53.

Kraemer, L., Danziger, J. N., Dunkle, D. E., & King, J. L. (1993). The usefulness of computer-based information to public managers. *MIS Quarterly, 17*(2), 129-148.

Kraut, R., Dumais, S., & Kock, S. (1989). Computerization, productivity, and quality of worklife. *Communications of the ACM, 32*(2), 220-238.

Lee, D. S. (1986). Usage patterns and sources of assistance to personal computer users. *MIS Quarterly, 10*(4), 313-325.

Leitheiser, R. L., & Wetherbe, J. C. (1986). Service support levels: An organized approach to end-user computing. *MIS Quarterly, 10*(4), 337-349.

Liang, P. L. (1986). Critical success factors of decision support systems: An experimental study. *Data Base, 17*(2), 3-16.

Lohmoller, J. B. (1981). *LVPLS 1.6: Latent variables path analysis with partial least squares estimation.* Munich: University of Federal Armed Forces.

Lohmoller, J. B. (1989). *Latent variable path modeling with partial least squares.* Heidelberg, Germany: Physica-Verlag.

Lucas, H. C. (1978). Empirical evidence for a descriptive model of implementation. *MIS Quarterly, 2*(2), 27-41.

Mahmood, M. A., & Sniezek, J. A. (1989). Defining decision support systems: An empirical assessment of end-user satisfaction. *Information Systems & Operational Research (INFOR), 27*(3), 253-271.

Maish, A. M. (1979). A user's behavior toward his MIS. *MIS Quarterly, 3*(1), 39-52.

Markus, M. L. (1983). Power, politics, and MIS implementation. *Communications of the ACM, 26*(6), 430-444.

Mathieson, K. (1991). Predicting user intentions: Comparing the technology acceptance model with the theory of planned behavior. *Information Systems Research, 2*(3), 173-191.

McKeen, J. D., Guimaraes, T., & Wetherbe, J. C. (1994). The relationship between user participation and user satisfaction: An investigation of four contingency factors. *MIS Quarterly, 18*(4), 427-451.

Millman, Z., & Hartwick, J. (1987). The impact of automated office systems on middle managers and their work. *MIS Quarterly, 11*(4), 479-491.

Mykytyn, P. P. (1988). End-user perceptions of DSS training and DSS usage. *Journal of System Management, 39*(6), 32-35.

Nelson, R. R. (1990). Individual adjustment to information-driven technologies: A critical review. *MIS Quarterly, 14*(1), 87-98.

Nelson, R., & Cheney, P. (1987). Training end users: An exploratory study. *MIS Quarterly, 11*(4), 547-559.

Nielsen, C. (1994). Improved service pays for C/S migration. *Application Development Trends, 1*(7), 32-33.
Nunamaker, J., Couger, J. D., & Davis, G. B. (1982). Information systems curriculum recommendations for the 80s: Undergraduate and graduate programs. *Communications of the ACM, 25*(11), 781-794.
Nunnally, J. C. (1978). *Psychometric theory.* New York: McGraw-Hill.
Plewa, J., & Pliskin, S. (1995). Client/server everything. *CIO, 8*(18), 30-34.
Radosevich, L. (1995). Beat the clock. *CIO, 9*(4), 64-70.
Raymond, L. (1985). Organizational characteristics and MIS success in the context of small business. *MIS Quarterly, 9*(1), 37-52.
Rivard, S., & Huff, S. (1988). Factors of success for end-user computing. *Communications of the ACM, 31*(5), 552-561.
Robey, D. (1979). User attitudes and MIS use. *Academy of Management Journal, 22*(3), 527-538.
Ross, D. R. (1975). Direct, indirect, and spurious effects: Comments on causal analysis of interorganizational relations. *Administrative Science Quarterly, 20,* 295-297.
Sanders, G. I., & Courtney, J. F. (1985). A field study of organizational factors influencing DSS success. *MIS Quarterly, 9*(1), 77-93.
Saraph, J. V., & Sebastian, R. J. (1992). Human resource strategies for effective introduction of advanced manufacturing technologies (AMT). *Production and Inventory Management Journal, 12*(1), 64-70.
Schewe, C. D. (1976). The MIS user: An exploratory behavioral analysis. *Academy of Management Journal, 19*(4), 577-590.
Seymour, P. (1994). Redeveloping legacy systems to client/server. *Application Development Trends, 1*(6), 54-59.
Sinha, A. (1992). Client/server computing. *Communications of the ACM, 35*(7), 77-79.
Sloane, S. B. (1991). The use of artificial intelligence by the United States Navy: Case study of a failure. *AI Magazine, 12*(1), 80-92.
Smith, D. L. (1988). Implementing real-world expert systems. *AI Expert, 3*(2), 51-57.
SMR. (1995). Report by Sentry Market Research.
Spector, P. (1987). Method variance as an artifact in self-reported affect and perceptions at work: Myth or significant problem. *Journal of Applied Psychology, 72*(5), 438-443.
Srinivasan, A. (1985). Alternative measures of system effectiveness: Associations and implications. *MIS Quarterly, 9*(3), 243-253.
Sviokla, J. (1990). The examination of the impact of expert systems on the firm: The case of XCON. *MIS Quarterly, 14*(2), 126-140.
Swanson, E. B. (1988). *Information system implementation: Bridging the gap between design and utilization.* Homewood, IL: Irwin.
Thompson, R. L., Higgins, C. A., & Howell, J. M. (1991). Personal computing: Toward a conceptual model of utilization. *MIS Quarterly, 15*(1), 125-143.
Triandis, H. C. (1980). Values, attitudes, and interpersonal behavior. In *Nebraska Symposium on Motivation, Beliefs, Attitudes, and Values* (pp. 195-259). Lincoln: University of Nebraska Press.
Tukey, J. W. (1958). Bias and confidence in not-quite large samples. *Annals of Mathematical Statistics, 29*(2), 614.
White, K. B., & Leifer, R. (1986). Information systems development success: Perspectives from project team participants. *MIS Quarterly, 10*(3), 215-223.
Wildt, A. R., Lambert, Z. V., & Durand, R. M. (1982). Applying the jackknife statistics in testing and interpreting canonical weights, loadings and cross-loadings. *Journal of Marketing Research, 19*(3), 99-107.
Willet, S. (1994). Strong IS support found for move to client/server platform. *InfoWorld, 16*(31), 53.
Wold, H. (1982). Soft modeling-The basic design and some extensions. In K. G. Jöreskog & H. Wold (Eds.), *Systems under indirect observation-II* (pp. 1-54). Amsterdam: North-Holland.

oon, Y., & Guimaraes, T. (1995). Assessing expert systems impact on users' jobs. *Journal of Management Information Systems, 12*(1), 225-249.

oon, Y., Guimaraes, T., & Clevenson, A. (1996). Assessing determinants of desirable ES impact on end-users' jobs (Dupont). *European Journal of Information Systems, 5,* 273-285.

oon, Y., Guimaraes, T., & O'Neal, Q. (1995). Exploring the factors associated with expert systems success. *MIS Quarterly, 19*(1), 83-106.

mud, R. W. (1979). Individual differences and MIS success: A review of the empirical literature. *Management Sciences, 25*(10), 966-979.

CHAPTER
FOURTEEN

Knowledge Work Productivity

Features and Functions of Information Technologies

GORDON B. DAVIS
J. DAVID NAUMANN

Some information technologies are a response to existing or emerging needs of individuals, groups, and organizations. Other technologies are created with the expectation that uses will emerge. An example of the first is the emergence of a set of information technology software with features and functions for productivity in knowledge work. Information technologies for knowledge work have been developed because knowledge work has become more important, and the productivity issues have become clear. The creation of technology for the organization activities of knowledge work is understood, but the mapping of technology to the detailed needs is not well defined. This chapter addresses the mapping by explaining the nature of the needs in knowledge work productivity and how these needs are met by specific features and functions of information technology.

The chapter has six sections and a summary. The first section defines knowledge work and knowledge workers, the second summarizes the knowledge work productivity problem, and the third identifies strategies for improving effectiveness and efficiency in knowledge work. The fourth section surveys information technologies and software products that support knowledge work activities. The fifth and sixth sections describe the features and functions of these technologies, mapping them to the strategies for improving knowledge work effectiveness and efficiency. The first three sections provide the context for understanding the importance and value of the information technology functions and features described in the remainder of the chapter. As a group, these functions and features represent new opportunities for improving the productivity of knowledge workers.

The Definition of Knowledge Work and Knowledge Worker[1]

Knowledge work is human mental work performed to generate useful information. In performing this type of work, knowledge workers access data, use knowledge, employ mental models, and apply significant concentration and attention.

Knowledge work results in useful information. It involves sets of activities for acquiring knowledge, designing analyses and solutions, making decisions, and communications. Examples of individual activities are scanning and monitoring information sources, searching for information, modeling problems and processes, planning, organizing, scheduling, authoring outputs, formulating problem definitions, performing analyses, selecting among alternatives, formulating action plans, presenting results of analysis, and persuading and motivating others to accept analyses and plans. Examples of knowledge workers are managers, analysts, authors, developers, planners, and so forth. In this chapter, knowledge work tasks consist of a desired output and a set of activities to achieve the results. Activities such as information search, analysis, authoring, and presentation are performed in order to complete a task.

No person does only knowledge work. Clerical work must be performed in order to accomplish knowledge work. Therefore, even when a knowledge worker is supported by clerical staff, there is personal clerical work involved such as keyboarding, formatting documents and outputs, entering queries, and so on. Almost all workers do some knowledge work, but the work of those classified as knowledge workers is dominated by knowledge work activities. Within those classified as knowledge workers, there are differences in the amount of clerical work. Some knowledge workers have little clerical work; others have more. Information technology aids productivity in both components.

The Knowledge Work Productivity Problem

The issue of productivity of knowledge workers has always existed; it has become more important because an increasing proportion of workers are knowledge workers. If only 5% of work is done by knowledge workers and 95% by manual workers, production workers, clerical workers, and other nonknowledge workers, then the productivity of knowledge workers is not as significant as the productivity of the other groups. However, when 30% to 50% of workers can be classified as knowledge workers (or mainly so), the issue is very important.

Although it is difficult to measure productivity in knowledge work, there is widespread recognition that productivity differs significantly not only among individuals doing similar tasks but also for the same individual in different time periods. Furthermore, the range of acceptable productivity for knowledge workers is much greater than for workers who perform physical or clerical tasks. For example, in a large group of computer programmers, the productivity of the best performers (using a variety of measures such as lines of correct code, function points, and so on) will be five or more times greater than the worst but acceptable programmers. This ratio of best to worst performance is much higher than productivity differences of less than two to one for workers performing physical or clerical tasks. The productivity differences among knowledge workers may be due in part to individual abilities and skills, but much of the difference may be due to individual investment in knowledge work skills, application of knowledge work management principles, and appropriate use of knowledge work information and communication technology.

A characteristic of knowledge work is significant reliance on individual structuring and management of work. A knowledge worker has responsibility for both expanding and conserving knowledge work resources. For example, high motivation to perform knowledge work expands the mental energy that may be applied to work. An example of how knowledge work resources can be conserved is by effective communication. Making operations as automatic as possible also conserves scarce mental resources. These knowledge work management responsibilities of expanding and conserving resources can benefit from task design, organization, scheduling, and use of information and communication technologies.

The solution to the productivity differences is partly an individual issue and partly an organizational and management issue (Drucker, Dyson, Handy, Saffo, & Senge, 1997). At the individual level, knowledge workers have significant individual responsibility for being productive by applying productivity principles and investing to develop appropriate skills in using the knowledge work functions and features of information and communication technologies. At the organizational level, management has responsibility for providing appropriate technology infrastructure with knowledge work functions and features, establishing organization forms and training opportunities that encourage productivity, and applying measurement methods and incentives that reward productivity. This task has been noted by Drucker (1978) as one of the most important ones for management: "To make knowledge work more productive will be the great management task of this century, just as to make manual work productive was the great management task of the last century" (p. 290).

Strategies for Improved Productivity in Knowledge Work

It is useful to classify productivity improvements for knowledge work in terms of effectiveness and efficiency (Figure 14.1). Effectiveness relates to the quality and usefulness of knowledge work outputs. Efficiency is how well knowledge work resources are managed and used. The next section identifies two approaches for improving effectiveness. The section following identifies seven strategies for improving efficiency. The remainder of the chapter presents an overview of knowledge work software and describes how these information technologies can be applied to achieve improvements in knowledge work productivity.

```
                Quality and
                Usefulness    ──▶  Effectiveness
                of Results         Strategies
                                                  ──▶ Improved
                                                  ──▶ Productivity
                Management
                and Use of    ──▶  Efficiency
                Resources          Strategies
```

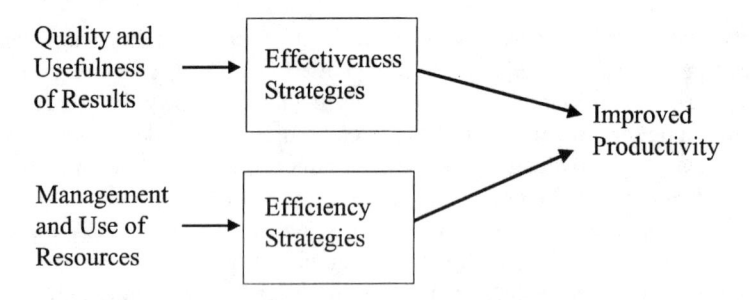

Figure 14.1. Relationship of Effectiveness and Efficiency Strategies

Strategies for Improving Effectiveness in Knowledge Work

Effectiveness in knowledge work enhances the value of the work results. Effectiveness can be improved by performing knowledge work with more expertise and creativity as well as by achieving more complete and timely results. These improvements are manifest in information technologies that either (a) expand the scope, depth, and completeness of activities or (b) provide for the application of new methods that were previously not feasible.

Effectiveness Strategy 1: Extending scope, depth, and completeness of traditional knowledge work activities. Knowledge work has several limits: time available, constraints on human cognition and effort, difficulty of communication among participants in a project, and availability of information relevant to the work and knowledge gained in similar efforts. These constraints interact to limit the scope, depth, and completeness of knowledge work activities. These constraints can be addressed by changes in organization and group structures, changes in the structure of the work, and technology (Avison, Kendall, & DeGross, 1993; Orlikowski, Walsham, Jones, & DeGross, 1996). This chapter will focus only on the use of technology to offset the limits of human cognition and effort, human communication, and information availability.

Effectiveness Strategy 2: Application of new methods not feasible without information technology. The quest for more effective knowledge work should not be constrained to extending existing methods and technologies. New methods and emerging technologies may change the underlying nature of the work. There are many analogies. An airplane is not just a flying cart; it changes the nature of transportation. It introduces new capabilities and new concepts.

In this chapter, the application of new methods focuses on new technologies. In some cases, the technologies make such large changes that the nature of the task changes. For example, a traditional method of applying past experience and expertise to forecasting problems is to establish standard operating procedures. The use of computers makes it possible to change the task of forecasting to one of dynamic data analysis using expert systems or neural nets.

Seven Strategies for Improving Efficiency in Knowledge Work

Improved efficiency in knowledge work may be achieved by a combination of improved processes, improved procedures, and more productive use of information technology. Efficiency improvements can be achieved through the application of seven strategies. These provide a framework for a discussion of the role of information technology in efficiency-based productivity improvement. The seven strategies are the following:

1. Reduce interface time and errors
2. Reduce process learning time and dual processing losses
3. Reduce time and effort to structure tasks and format outputs
4. Reduce nonproductive expansion of work
5. Reduce data and knowledge search and storage time and costs
6. Reduce communication and coordination time and costs
7. Reduce losses from human information overload

Although it is possible that each of these strategies may be implemented through process or procedural changes (at either the organizational or task structure level), the remainder of this chapter focuses on the implementation of these strategies through the use of information technologies (Figure 14.2).

Efficiency Strategy 1: Reduce interface time and errors. Many activities involve an interface with manual systems and information technology systems. When a task is begun, there is a significant time for locating materials, pulling together source documents, locating instructions, and so on. Instructions and formats for entering and retrieving data must be reviewed and understood. There are opportunities for significant errors in entering or retrieving data. Interface costs and errors can be reduced by organization standards that are consistent across applications and by tailoring interfaces (within the context of organization standards) to suit individual users. Errors in using interfaces for storing and retrieving data can be reduced by forms and by standards for naming, storing, and finding data.

Efficiency Strategy 2: Reduce process learning time and dual processing losses. Every change, such as a new process or new software package, has an associated learning time. When a knowledge worker must devote significant attention to learning a new process or the operation of the software and, at the same time, attend to the task to be achieved, the worker has two simultaneous tasks: learning the new process or software and completing the task. Two simultaneous tasks reduce productivity. Once the process or software is learned, the use of its most common

348 EMERGING INFORMATION TECHNOLOGIES

```
┌─────────────────────────┐
│ Organizational Design and│
│ Structure Strategies    │─────┐
└─────────────────────────┘     │      ┌──────────────┐
                                │      │   Changes    │
┌─────────────────────────┐     │      │      in      │
│ Task Design Changes     │─────┼─────▶│ Productivity │
└─────────────────────────┘     │      │  Efficiency  │
                                │      └──────────────┘
┌─────────────────────────┐     │
│ Use of Information      │─────┘
│ Technology              │
└─────────────────────────┘
```

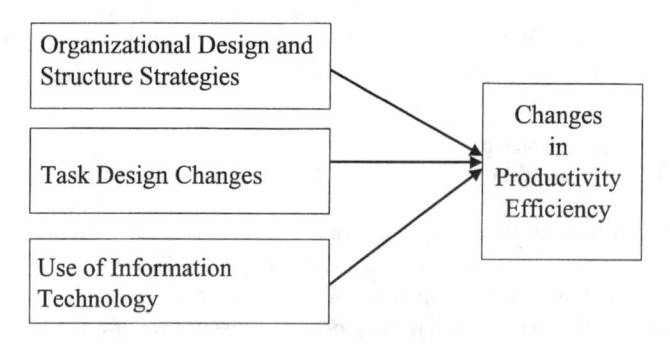

Figure 14.2. Three Ways to Implement Efficiency Strategies

features may be almost automatic, resulting in a net productivity gain. The general strategy, therefore, is to reduce dual processing losses and the amount of learning effort required by managing the frequency of process and technology changes.

Efficiency Strategy 3: Reduce time and effort to structure tasks and format outputs. A knowledge work task consists of structuring task activities, designing a format for analysis, and designing outputs. Task structuring can take a significant proportion of the total task time. Time and effort to structure tasks and format outputs can be reduced by reuse of forms, formats, and processes. Reuse can be provided by organization standards or by individual forms and templates. Reuse can also be achieved by employing the forms and processes developed by someone else in the organization who performs or has performed a similar task.

Efficiency Strategy 4: Reduce nonproductive expansion of work. One of the characteristics of knowledge work is the absence of explicit stopping rules for effort other than deadlines. In the absence of a deadline, knowledge work can expand without limit. Most manual work has a naturally observable completion point. For example, the task of entering invoices into an accounting system is completed when all invoices have been entered; a ditch-digging project is completed when the dirt has been removed. However, an information search can be expanded, analyses can be repeated with an unlimited number of assumptions, and outputs can be formatted and edited with no limit. When no deadline is specified, knowledge workers may apply implicit rules for stopping activities. Given the tendency to expand knowledge work, efficiency can be improved by incorporating explicit stopping rules in knowledge work activities and tasks.

Efficiency Strategy 5: Reduce data and knowledge search and storage time and costs. The search for data and the storage of data are part of most knowledge work tasks. The search and storage activities include both computer-based and paper files.

Because the amount of data that can be searched is usually large in comparison to the amount of data needed in a typical project, an efficient search process is important. Similarly, as work is completed, data that have been acquired, report drafts, email messages, and so forth are stored. Storing time can be minimized by efficient storage organization and naming procedures. Efficient storage supports more efficient retrieval. Efficient storage may affect the current task; it is also an investment affecting future retrieval efficiency.

In addition to traditional data storage, efficiency can be improved by storage and retrieval of organization knowledge. This knowledge consists of information about skills and experiences of other knowledge workers, experiences (including processes and formats) from similar tasks, and ideas and lessons learned by members of the organization. An efficient knowledge worker will develop a network of contacts that provide some of this knowledge; an organization may provide a system (an example is Lotus Notes) offering more complete organization knowledge for any knowledge worker who is willing to invest in learning the system.

Efficiency Strategy 6: Reduce communication and coordination time and costs. Communication and coordination take time to perform. There are delays inherent in sending and receiving communications and in coordinating with others involved in part or all of the task. Communication and coordination effort and time increase with the number of individuals involved. When staff members are added to a project, communication and coordination increase to consume a greater proportion of available time unless methods are applied to control the growth. These methods include organization mechanisms such as separation of responsibilities into smaller tasks and task groups, use of specifications and standards to reduce communication needs, and use of organization technologies for communication and coordination.

Efficiency Strategy 7: Reduce losses from human information overload. Given the amount of data that can be obtained and the proliferation of information from communication with others involved in a project, knowledge workers can be overloaded with information and communications. There are various mechanisms for dealing with overload. Some of them are organizational; others employ information technologies. The objective in both types of mechanisms is to reduce losses from human information overload by applying filtering and compression techniques to reduce the volume of data to be processed by human users.

Software Packages for Knowledge Work

A number of software packages have been developed that extend the capabilities and improve the productivity of knowledge workers. These software packages may also be used by clerical workers, but the focus is on their use by knowledge workers.

TABLE 14.1 Software Packages for Knowledge Work and Use for Knowledge Work Activities

Software Package	Use for Knowledge Work Activities
Word processor with spell checker, grammar checker, and outliner. Extensions may include voice input to complement keyboard input and document scanning input.	Authoring of reports, memoranda, presentations, communications. Searching for stored documents. For clerical activities of formatting, input of data, filing and retrieving of text files, and list management.
Spreadsheet processor with modeling and statistical functions and graphics.	Analysis, modeling, communication, and presentation.
Communications package with email and fax.	Communication and coordination. Monitoring and searching for information.
Web browser for Internet or intranet, including capabilities to search the Web and access and search external databases.	Scanning for information. Monitoring for information. Searching for information. Coordination.
Presentation package for overheads, slide presentations, and so on.	Communications including activities that present results of knowledge work, persuade readers and listeners, and motivate to action.
Database package to build and/or access internal databases.	Scan, search, and monitor activities. Clerical activities of filing and retrieving data and formatting reports with retrieved data.
Personal information management software, including address book and personal scheduler.	Knowledge work activities of planning, organizing, time management, and scheduling.
Graphics package with charting, drawing, and graphics functions.	Modeling of processes by flowcharting, drawing, or sketching. Communication activities of presentation and persuading.
System management utility software that extends capabilities of operating system, including virus checkers, software removers, software updaters, compression and backup, and so forth.	Knowledge work management activities required to maintain capabilities to perform knowledge work.

The functionality of the packages supports the set of activities performed by knowledge workers. The major set of general software packages and the relationship of each to knowledge work activities are summarized in Table 14.1. The basic set consists of three distinct components:

1. Tools that enhance productivity of the individual knowledge worker (word processor, spreadsheets, email systems, Web browsers, presentation development tools, database management systems, and personal information management packages)
2. System management utility software that extends the capabilities of the operating system (virus checkers, compression and backup utilities, etc.)

TABLE 14.1 Continued

Software Package	Use for Knowledge Work Activities
Coordination software that provides coordination and communication with groups, including project scheduling, shared data access, group communication, collaborative authoring, and electronic meeting.	Knowledge work activities within a group of scanning, monitoring, searching, modeling, planning, organizing, scheduling, authoring, deciding, and communicating.
Knowledge management software that provides a shared repository for project reports, analyses, problem and solution commentaries, and so forth.	Scanning, monitoring; search, model, and formulate activities. The knowledge management software allows these activities to locate experience and knowledge in the organization or group.
Advanced: Scheduling and project management software.	Planning, organizing, and scheduling.
Advanced: On-line analytical processing (OLAP) software for exploration of multidimensional databases.	Scanning, monitoring, searching, and analyzing activities.
Advanced: Desktop publishing software with advanced capabilities for formatting reports and presentation of outputs.	Communicate activities and clerical activities of formatting outputs.
Advanced: Statistical software to extend capabilities of spreadsheet processor.	Modeling and analysis.
Advanced: Modeling software to extend capabilities of spreadsheet processor.	Formulate, model, analyze, and decide activities.

3. Group-oriented software that provides for coordination, communication, and knowledge management within and across work groups, including scheduling and project management capabilities

Software items that extend the functionality in the basic packages are on-line analytic processing software to explore multidimensional databases; desktop publishing to extend publishing capabilities of word processors; and two advanced packages that extend, where needed, the statistical and modeling capabilities of a spreadsheet processor.

Use of Information Technologies in Achieving Knowledge Work Effectiveness

Information technology features and functions are often multipurpose, providing support for both effectiveness and efficiency. Because the reasons for use of the technology may differ, the technologies are described in terms of the two strategies for effectiveness in this section. In the following section, the technologies are explained in terms of efficiency.

Technologies for Extending Scope, Depth, and Completeness of Knowledge Work Activities

Knowledge work activities such as information monitoring and search, formulating models for analysis, and performing analysis are limited by the technologies employed. For example, a knowledge worker using a manually prepared spreadsheet and a calculator is limited by the time required for manually entering, altering, and evaluating the spreadsheet. The error rates in manual entry and computation also affect the work. A software spreadsheet program reduces somewhat the time to enter a spreadsheet and lay out the spreadsheet analysis. The software dramatically reduces the time and error rate in changes, reformulations, examining effect of alternatives, and so forth. The technology changes the limits on spreadsheet analysis and therefore allows more extensive analysis by extending the scope of the analysis, and more intensive analysis by increasing the depth of analysis using different methods.

The extension of scope and depth is achieved with little or no increase in time required for performing analysis. Experience suggests that the productivity gains from doing analysis, such as a spreadsheet with software, have been applied to extending the scope and depth of analysis rather than reducing the knowledge work time applied to the analysis.

Effectiveness of knowledge work is also improved by completeness of the data and knowledge used and the information provided. Web technologies allow extensive searching of both traditional archives and current Web-based resources. One of the benefits of coordination information technology is the ability to combine activities that may have been divided and to share information during parallel activities by different people working on parts of the same problem. Knowledge management software enhances the ability to access information on prior experience and take advantage of accumulated organization knowledge.

Technology for Application of New Methods

At some point, increasing the scope, depth, and completeness of analysis and activities becomes dependent upon information technology because further improvements simply are not feasible without them. As an example, using spreadsheets to investigate alternatives in a "what-if" analysis is not feasible for problems of any complexity. "What-if" analysis is essentially a new method using technology. A second example is on-line information searching using Web browsers. A third example is on-line analytical processing, which provides temporal analysis not feasible with traditional tools.

Information Technology Functions and Features for Efficiency

The seven strategies for improved productivity through improved efficiency encompass both nontechnology changes, such as task design and organization structure, and technology changes. This section will describe the information technology functions and features that can be employed to improve productivity. The technology uses are organized in terms of the seven strategies.

Technology to Reduce Interface Time and Errors

The interface between the computer, its software, and the human user can be changed to reduce interface time and errors. The computer desktop can be organized to reduce access time. The applications most commonly used can be loaded when the computer is turned on. Time to switch among applications can be reduced by screen design and keyboard macros.

Applications can be tailored by selecting options that reduce time and error rates. For example, common operations can be mapped into keystrokes or onto icons. Some common operations can be changed to fit individual usage. As an example, a popular spreadsheet application can be tailored (using preferences) to change the direction of cursor movement after data are entered into a cell. The default option is to move the cursor down; a knowledge worker who commonly entered data across rows saves time and reduces errors by changing the default to move the cursor to the right on the same row. Although the savings with each entry are very small, the savings are repeated hundreds of times each day. Also, the frequency of errors is reduced. Errors are significant because of the correction time. In general, an error will take the time equivalent of several correct inputs because of recognition, deletion, and reentry.

Forms are an important software method for improving input performance in terms of both time and error rates. Input forms are prepared using the form facilities of the software package. For example, a form can be developed to input data into a spreadsheet or database. The advantage of the form is the layout of the input in a well-defined, labeled format that the user inputs in a natural order (without respect to the way the data are stored in the database or spreadsheet).

Technology to Reduce Process Learning Time and Dual Processing Losses

Process learning time is reduced by software versions that are compatible with prior versions. Work done using features of prior versions will be automatically converted to the new version. A software package may allow a user to employ the keystrokes and codes of a competing product and automatically convert files produced with competing software. On-line tutorials guide a user to learn new or upgraded software. On-line help facilities that respond to errors or inquiries reduce learning time.

Technology to Reduce Time and Effort to Structure Tasks and Format Outputs

The reuse of task structures and output formats is supported by storage and retrieval functions. It is enhanced by the software functions and features of templates and macros. A template saves the format of a document, spreadsheet, or database retrieval report. It is easily developed, stored, and retrieved. A new use employs the stored format. Templates are so useful that software packages often contain a number of suggested templates. Examples of word processing templates are standard documents replying to customers, making job offers, responding to complaints, and so forth. Examples of spreadsheet templates are expense reports, business plans, budget reports, and so forth.

Macros are programs employed within a package. The simplest form of macro is a recorded macro. A user turns on the macro recorder, executes a sequence of operations, and turns off the recorder. The resulting macro, when played, will execute the same sequence of operations. The macro may be stored and invoked from the list of macros, a menu item, a button, or keystrokes. A recorded macro is very effective when a user frequently repeats a set sequence of operations. The macro reduces both time to execute and errors in doing the operations. The disadvantage is that the recorded macro contains only a sequence of steps; it contains no selection logic.

Recorded macros may be modified by editing them to include selection logic. A macro may also be written using the macro language of a package. This is essentially a programming language. The investment to learn a macro language may be justified if many operations may be automated. Macros may also be supplied by vendors or by the information systems group if the macros benefit a number of users.

The concepts of reuse embodied in templates and macros may be incorporated in the features and functions of packages. For example, a database package will store retrievals and report formulations so that they can be reused.

Technology to Reduce Nonproductive Expansion of Work

Technology functions and features invite expansion of work. Planning and scheduling software can assist in establishing time limits for activities and suggest stopping rules to be applied. There is no technology that automates stopping rules. This is a knowledge work management problem.

Technology to Reduce Data and Knowledge Search and Storage Time and Costs

A strategy for storage management and a strategy for data and knowledge search can be supported by software functions and features. Because storage software allows a range of storage strategies, the technology is most effective when the storage strategy is designed to reduce time to store and time to locate and retrieve. A user defines a storage structure that makes it simple to recall where something should be stored and where it was stored for retrieval. This generally involves task-oriented or project-oriented storage with all the files or folders (spreadsheet, documents, retrievals) stored in the same directories. When a file or folder is stored, a description can be stored with it to help identify its contents. The directories are named to reflect the project or task. The software facilities support building a directory structure and changing it as needed. When a file or folder location is not remembered, search facilities are included in the software to locate a file or folder based on its name, words in its description, or its contents.

Search software (often termed search engines) is employed in locating sources of data and specific documents, spreadsheets, and so on. The technology of search engines is based on searching for individual words, sets of words, and strings with several words in a set order. The search can specify that a "hit" be based on any word or string (OR condition), must include all items (AND condition), or must exclude items if they contain some words or strings (NOT). The software may include additional logic functions. Some search facilities provide an indication of relevance by a score. This is true of most Web-based search engines. This provides some basis for constraining the examination of suggested items. When a retrieved item is selected, the search engine may suggest other documents like that one.

Many databases are multidimensional. They contain data with many different dimensions, including time. Such databases are difficult to analyze using traditional database tools. A special set of database tools—often termed on-line analytical processing, or OLAP—assist marketing and financial analysis of data in multidimensional databases. Moving averages, growth rates, period comparisons, and cumulative statistics are easily obtained.

Technology to Reduce Communication and Coordination Time and Costs

As group size increases, the time taken for communication and coordination rises exponentially. Software functions can be employed to reduce communication and coordination costs. Electronic communication allows messages to be sent to all members of a work group or all those requiring coordination. Scheduling software can coordinate the work schedules of a group. Shared data access allows group members to locate any data being used by the group and any work products being produced. Knowledge management software supports project or topic collaboration by storing and making available ideas and progress reports. Electronic meetings may be held instead of face-to-face meetings. In both electronic and face-to-face meetings, electronic meeting facilities assist in recording ideas, group evaluations of ideas, and recording the ideas and evaluations. Documents and spreadsheets may be worked on concurrently using collaborative authoring software that shows the work of different authors and manages versions.

Technology to Reduce Losses From Human Information Overload

Overload has traditionally been handled by presenting recipients of information with high-level reports that contain summarized data. A hierarchy of reports supports the high-level report so that a user can "drill down" through the reports to the detail supporting any item. The concept of compression or summarization is supported by software functions in database packages and spreadsheet processors. OLAP reduces information overload by automating complex search and analysis strategies.

An example of a software function to compress data is the cross tab function (also called pivot table or modeling desktop). Data items from a database or spreadsheet are summarized with subtotals and totals. Rows and columns are selected with subtotals and totals indicated. The output can be pivoted or rotated so that rows become columns and columns become rows. This functionality allows low-cost exploration by compressing large amounts of detail data in meaningful ways.

Summary

Significant differences in productivity between knowledge workers suggests opportunities for improvement using information technologies. Effectiveness and efficiency strategies can be employed to achieve productivity improvements. Information technologies are vital components of both strategies. These technologies include tools to enhance productivity of the individual knowledge worker, system management utility software, and group-oriented software.

The introduction of information technology for knowledge work productivity has implications for individuals and organizations. Knowledge workers as individuals have significant responsibility for being productive by applying productivity principles and developing skills in using the knowledge work functions and features of information and communication technologies. At the organizational level, management has responsibility for providing appropriate technology infrastructure with knowledge work functions and features, establishing organization forms, and providing training and help facilities so that individual workers and groups can employ effectiveness and efficiency strategies.

Note

1. This section is based on Davis and Naumann (1997), pp. 5-37.

References

Avison, D., Kendall, J. E., & DeGross, J. I. (Eds.). (1993). *Human, organizational, and social dimensions of information systems development.* Amsterdam: North Holland.
Davis, G. B., & Naumann, J. D. (1997). *Personal productivity with information technology.* New York: McGraw-Hill.
Drucker, P. F. (1978). *The age of discontinuity: Guidelines to our changing society.* New York: Harper and Row.
Drucker, P. F., Dyson, E., Handy, C., Saffo, P., & Senge, P. M. (1997, September-October). Looking ahead: Implications of the present. *Harvard Business Review,* pp. 18-24.
Orlikowski, W. J., Walsham, G., Jones, M. R., & DeGross, J. I. (Eds.). (1996). *Information technology and changes in organizational work.* London: Chapman & Hall.

Index

Acceptance, ix, 3, 38-41, 39 (table), 41 (table)
Alexa, 278
Animation in user interfaces, 6-7, 45-46, 67-69, 274
    abstraction and, 50-51, 67
    application of, 67-69
    data analysis, 63-67, 64-66 (tables)
    decision quality, hypotheses of, 54-55, 68, 69
    goal of, 49, 55
    GOMS (goals, operators, methods, and selection rules) model, 49
    image, 47-48
    interactivity, 51-52, 54
    properties of, 49-54, 50 (figure), 69
    research design/methodology, 55-62, 58 (figure), 59 (figure)
    research results, discussion of, 67-70
    task type/design, 53-54
    techniques of, 48
    transition/alteration, 51
    user perception/cognition, 52-53
Argus Clearinghouse, The, 36
Artificial intelligence (AI), 5-6, 5 (table), 8, 117
    autonomous intelligent machines (AIM), 131-133
    common sense and, 122-123
    data mining and, 134-135
    developing technologies, 135
    expert systems and, 130-131, 135
    genetic algorithms, 126, 135
    human-computer interfaces, 126-127
    knowledge acquisition, 121-122
    neural network models in, 125, 135
    optical character recognition (OCR), 128-129
    predictions concerning, 117-119, 136-137
    search space/speed and, 124
    sensory inputs/outputs, additional, 129
    speech processing, 127-128
    weak vs. strong, 119-120, 135

AUCNET, 308
AUGMENT, 77
Autonomous agent, 268
Autonomous intelligent machines (AIM):
    immobots, 132
    robots, 131
    softbots, 132-133
    World Wide Web and, 133

Bayesian profile, 33
Best match principle, 29
Bluetooth, Harald, 286
Bolt and boat task, 56-57
Bookmark managers, 266
Boolean vector space model, 27, 28, 33
Bots (spiders), 268, 269 (figure), 277, 278
Broadcasting, 273-274, 275 (figure)
Browser accelerators, 266
Bush, Vannevar, 76, 80

Client/server systems (CSS), x, 15
    data analysis, 331-332
    developer skills, 324-325, 330
    development of, 318-320, 335, 336-337
    end-user characteristics, 323-324, 330
    end-user involvement, 324, 330, 334-335
    end-user jobs, impact on, 321-322, 327
    end-user satisfaction, 322-323, 329-330, 334 (table)
    implementation of, 317-318
    management support of, 325-326, 330, 335-336
    research methodology, 326-332, 328-329 (tables)
    research results, 332-334, 333-334 (tables)
    success, measures of, 321, 321-323, 322 (figure)

system usage, 323, 328, 334 (table)
   theoretical model for study, 320-321
   variables, 323-326
Cognitive fit theory, 76, 94
Cognitive process. *See* Human
   understanding/information processing
Collaborative filtering systems, 24-25, 34-35
Communication media, 9, 10, 143-144
   appropriateness, determination of, 168-169
   experience and media choice, 150-151,
      155-156, 164-167, 165-167 (tables)
   media richness theory, 145-146, 150, 244
   media-task interaction and media choice,
      145-147
   new vs. old, appropriateness of, 159-164,
      160-162 (tables), 171
   organizational perspective and, 170-172
   planned behavior, theory of, 148-149
   research design/procedures, 152-156
   research results, 156-167, 157-158 (tables),
      160-162 (tables), 165-167 (tables),
      169-170
   social cognitive theory, 148
   social presence theory, 145, 155
   technology acceptance model, 149
Computer-mediated communication systems
   (CMCS), 241, 242-246, 256
Conference systems, 4, 12, 241-242, 274
   computer-mediated communication systems
      (CMCS), 241, 242-246, 256
   future of, 257-258
   MeetingWeb, 249-250, 250 (figure), 253, 257
   relational links in groups, 244-246, 250-251,
      251 (table), 252, 253 (table), 255 (table)
   research results, 251-253, 252-253 (tables)
   research study, 246-251, 247 (table), 250
      (figure), 251 (table)
   survey instrument, 259-260
   synchronous/asynchronous meetings,
      242-243, 244, 245-246
   TIP theory (Time-Interaction-Performance),
      244, 257
   virtual teams, creation of, 254-257
   virtual vs. face-to-face teams, 243-246,
      253-254, 254 (figure), 282
Consumer activity. *See* Electronic commerce
Content-based retrieval systems, 33-34
Cookies, 274, 276, 300
Cooperation-facilitating technologies, ix-x, 4
   communication media and, 10
   executive information systems, 11
   group support systems, 10-11

research and, 8-12, 9 (table)
web-based conferencing, 12
Corporations. *See* Organizations
CYC Project, 122-123

Data mining, 111-112, 112 (table), 113 (figure),
   134-135, 279
Data warehousing, 7-8, 99
   cost of, 108
   data, form/flow of, 105, 106 (figure)
   data marts, 108
   data mining/Knowledge Data Discovery
      (KDD), 111-112, 112 (table), 113
      (figure), 134-135
   decision support and, 7-8, 99-100, 106
   defined, 101-103, 103 (table)
   industry growth, 109-110, 110 (table)
   managerial perspective on, 113-115
   marketing, database, 112-113, 113 (table),
      114 (figure)
   on-line analytic processing (OLAP), 110-111
   on-line transaction processing (OLTP) and,
      106-107
   operational data store (ODS), 109
   origins of, 99-101
   parallel computing, 108, 124
   software architecture in, 106, 107 (figure)
   structure of, 103-105
   use mechanisms, 107
Decision support systems (DSS), 5, 6-7, 8,
   23-24, 45-46
   data warehousing and, 99-100, 106
   group support systems (GSS) and, 178-179
   See also Animation in user interfaces
Decision-supporting technologies, ix, 3-4, 277
   animation and, 6-7
   artificial intelligence, 8
   classification of, 24 (figure)
   data warehousing, 7-8
   hypertext and, 7
   objectives of, 23
   recommendation systems, 6
   research and, 4-8, 5 (table)
   See also Executive information systems
      (EIS); Information delivery systems
      (IDS); Recommendation systems
Deep Blue, 118
Digital Librarian's Award, 36
Digital Subscriber Line (DSL), 299
Distribution channels, 307-310, 310 (table)

Index

E-commerce. *See* Electronic commerce
Electronic commerce, x, 4, 6, 14, 310-311
   business governance in, 306-307
   business infrastructure, 293-295, 298
   consumer marketplace, 302-305, 304 (table)
   development of, 289-291
   distribution channels and, 307-310, 310 (table)
   electronic cash, 295
   hierarchical framework of, 291-298, 292 (table)
   infrastructure, limitations/asymmetries, 299-300
   infrastructure, technological, 291-293
   internet in, 292-293
   levels of functionality in, 25, 26 (figure)
   payment in, 301-302
   products/structures of, 296-298
   recommendation systems in, 25-27, 26 (figure)
   stability in, 21-22
   virtualization of products/processes, 305-306
Electronic data interchange (EDI), 289-290, 294-295
Electronic funds transfer systems (EFTS), 294, 295
Electronic meeting system (EMS), 10, 143
Emergence, x, 3
   barriers to, 16-18, 17 (figure)
   information technologies, x, 2
   technological, and research, 5 (table)
Enabling. *See* Cooperation-facilitating technologies; Infrastructure-enabling technologies
Englebart, Douglas, 76-77
Evolutionary agents, 270-272, 272 (figure), 279
Executive Information Systems (EIS), x, 4, 8, 11, 100, 106, 231-233, 279-280
   adopters vs. nonadopters, 222-227, 224-226 (tables), 228-230, 229 (table)
   adoption level/status, 208, 217, 218 (table), 224-227, 225-226 (tables), 229 (table), 230-231
   adoption profile, 206-208, 228
   contextual variables in adoption, 208-210, 210-213, 223 (table)
   development of, 206
   emergent perspective of, 205-206, 206 (table), 207
   empirical study, 213-222, 215-216 (tables), 218 (table), 220-221 (tables)
   environmental uncertainty and, 210-211, 218-219, 220 (table)
   information system departments and, 212-213
   innovation theory, 208
   organizational characteristics and, 211-212, 219-221, 221 (table)
   questionnaire, 234-236
   research analysis/results, 222-228
   research model/hypotheses, 210-213, 211 (figure)
Expert Systems, 121, 130-131, 320

FAB system, 37
Face-to-face teams. *See* Conference systems
FAQ (Frequently Asked Questions) databases, 35
Feigenbaum, Edward, 130-131

General Problem Solver, 121
GOMS (goals, operators, methods, and selection rules) model, 49
Group support systems (GSS), 4, 10-11
   access to information, 190-192
   access to persons, 196-197
   characteristics of, 179
   communication patterns, 191 (table), 197
   decision support systems (DSS), outgrowth of, 178-179
   decision making, participation in, 192-194
   influencing outcomes, 195-196
   organizational design/structure and, 177-178
   power and influence, 180-183, 191 (table)
   research methodology, 183-190, 201
   research overview, 179-180
   research results/discussion, 190-200, 191 (table), 201
   system use, purpose of, 191 (table), 197-198
   work practices, 191 (table), 198-199

Home directory task, 55-57
Human understanding/information processing, 75, 76, 80, 94
Human-computer interactivity, 7, 12, 49, 51-52, 54
   See also Artificial intelligence (AI)
Hyperlink-Induced Topic Search (HITS), 270
Hypersolver, 79
Hypertext, 3, 7, 75
   help systems, 4, 94
   history/definition of, 76-77

levels of, 77-78
problem-solving and, 75-76, 82, 83
research model/methodology, 81-88, 81 (figure), 85 (table), 87-88 (tables), 89 (figure)
research results/discussion, 88-94, 89-92 (tables)
research/studies on, 78-79
theoretical foundation, 79-80
transfer protocol (HTTP), 300

Individual Inc.'s First! Service, 26-27
Inference network, 28 (figure)
Information delivery systems (IDS), xi, 13-14, 265, 266, 284-285
 future implications of, 285-286
 managerial implications of, 281-282
 organizational push technology, 280-282
 societal implications of, 282-284
Information economy, 25-27, 26 (figure), 41
Information retrieval (IR), 27-28, 28 (figure)
 best match principle, 29
 content-based/rule-based, 33-34
 electronic commerce and, 29, 41-42
 recall/precision, 29, 40-41
 recommendation systems, comparison, 30, 42
 relevance feedback technique, 28, 29
Information systems (IS), 4, 93, 99, 209-210, 212-213, 318
Information technology (IT), 2
 adoption in organizations, 208
 barriers to emergence, 16-18, 17 (figure)
 research classification in, 3-4
 See also Knowledge work productivity systems
Infrastructure-enabling technologies, x, 4
 client-server systems, xi, 15
 electronic commerce, 14, 291-293
 information delivery systems, 13-14
 knowledge work productivity systems, 15-16
 research and, 12-16, 13 (table)
Innovation theory, 208
Interactivity, 7, 12, 49, 51-52, 54, 58-59
Intermediation, 25, 42, 308-309
Internet commerce, 292-293, 294
 business governance and, 306-307
 consumer marketplace, 302-305, 303 (table)
 infrastructure limitations, 299-300
Internet Society, 293
Invention/introduction, ix, 3

Kleinberg, J., 270
Knowledge:
 common sense, 122-123
 emergent, 121-122
 expert systems, 121, 130-131, 320
 representational, 121
Knowledge Data Discovery (KDD), 111-112, 112 (table), 113 (figure), 134
Knowledge work productivity systems, 15-16, 343
 defined, 344
 effectiveness, improvement of, 346-347, 346 (figure), 352
 efficiency, improvement of, 346 (figure), 347-349, 348 (figure), 353-356
 information technologies in, 351-356
 productivity differentials, 344-345, 356
 software packages for, 349-351, 350-351 (table)

Learning theory. *See* Human understanding/information processing
Life cycle. *See* Technological advancement life cycle
Linear/nonlinear links. *See* Hypertext; Problem-solving

Marketing:
 one-to-one, 26-27, 42
 relationship, 113, 114 (figure)
Massively Parallel Processor (MPP), 108
McCarthy, John, 118
McGrath, J. E., 244, 257
Media. *See* Communication media
Media richness theory, 145-146, 150, 244
MeetingWeb, 249-250, 250 (figure), 253, 257
Memex (memory extender), 76
Metaphors, 93
Meta-search tools, 269-270, 271 (figure)

Navigation interactivity, 54, 58-59, 278
Nelson, T. H., 77
NLS/AUGMENT, 77
Nonlinear system. *See* Hypertext; Problem-solving
Non-Uniform Memory Access (NUMA), 108
Nye, D. E., ix, 16

Index **363**

On-line analytical processing (OLAP), 99, 110-111, 134
On-line transaction processing (OLTP), 101, 106-107
Open Personalization (Profiling) Standard (OPS), 39
Operational data store (ODS), 109
Optical character recognition (OCR), 128-129
Organizations:
 boundaries-of-the-firm analysis, 306-307
 communication media and, 170-172
 context of, 10-11, 16
 electronic integration and, 289-290
 power and influence in, 180-183
 technological innovation in, 209, 210-213
 telecommunications capabilities and, 292-293
 See also Electronic commerce; Executive information systems (EIS); Group support systems (GSS); Information delivery systems (IDS)

Parallel computing, 108, 124
Parallel navigation interactivity, 7
Personal search engines, 269-270, 271 (figure)
PHOAKS (People Helping One Another Know Stuff), 35
Planned behavior, theory of, 148-149
Postman, N., 283
Power and influence, 180-181, 191 (table)
 access to information, 190-192
 access to persons, 196-197
 components of, 181-183
 decision-making, participation in, 192-194
 dimensions of, 183
 influencing opinions, 195-196
Prefcalc system, 33
Probabilistic retrieval models, 28
Problem-solving:
 cost-benefit theory, 94
 hypotheses of, 83
 metaphors in, 93
 nonlinear links in, 75-76, 93, 94
 performance/satisfaction, 83, 91-92
 problem tasks, 82
 research methodology, 84-88, 85 (table), 87-88 (tables), 89 (figure)
 research results/discussion, 88-94, 89-92 (tables)
 search spaces and, 124
Productivity. *See* Knowledge work productivity systems

Pull technologies, 13-14, 265-266, 267 (table)
 alpha-pull technology, 266-267, 268 (figure)
 beta-pull technology, 267-268, 269 (figure)
 delta-pull technology, 270-272, 272 (figure)
 gamma-pull technology, 268-270, 271 (figure)
 Hyperlink-Induced Topic Search (HITS), 270
 See also Information delivery systems (IDS)
Push technologies, 13-14, 265-266, 273 (table)
 Alexa, 278
 alpha-push technology, 273-274, 275 (figure)
 beta-push technology, 275-276, 276 (figure)
 delta-push technology, 277-280, 279 (figure)
 gamma-push technology, 276-277, 278 (figure)
 organizational use of, 280-282
 RealTime streaming protocol (RTSP), 274
 See also Information delivery systems (IDS)

RealTime streaming protocol (RTSP), 274
Reasoned action, theory of (TRA), 148, 149, 320
Recommendation systems, 4, 5 (table), 6
 acceptance, factors influencing, 38-41, 39 (table), 41 (table)
 application domains, 32 (table), 37 (table)
 architecture for, 30, 31 (figure)
 classification of, 32-33, 32 (table), 42
 collaborative systems, 34-35
 content-based systems, 33-34
 coping technologies and, 21-22, 22 (figure)
 cost-benefit analysis, 40-41, 41 (table)
 decision technology and, 23-25, 24 (figure)
 electronic commerce and, 25-27, 26 (figure)
 functions/capabilities of, 30-32
 hybrid systems, 36
 information retrieval and, 27-29, 28 (figure), 34
 managerial implications, 36-38, 37 (table)
 performance evaluation, 40-41
 recall/precision, 29, 40-41
 social consequences of, 42
 third-party expertise, 35-36
 utility-based techniques, 33
 See also Information retrieval
Recommender systems, 23-25, 24 (figure), 41
RediMaster, 84
Relationship marketing, 113, 114 (figure)
Relevance feedback techniques, 28, 30-31
Research:
 classification of, 3-4

cooperation-facilitating technologies and, 8-12, 9 (table)
decision-supporting technologies and, 4-8, 5 (table)
infrastructure-enabling technologies and, 12-16, 13 (table)
Robots. *See* Autonomous intelligent machines (AIM)
Rule-based retrieval systems, 34

Script theory, 79-80
Search engines, 267-268, 268-270, 268 (figure), 269 (figure), 271 (figure)
Secure Electronic Transaction (SET) protocol, 294
Secure messaging, 293-294
Simon, Herbert, 118, 123
Social cognitive theory, 148
Social development, 18
Social presence theory, 145
Societal revolution, 282-284
Speech recognition, 3, 127-128
Spiders (bots), 268, 269 (figure), 277
Spreading activation theory, 80
Stanford University digital library project, 37
Startpages, 276-277
Streaming protocol, 274
Sublime, technological, ix, 2, 3
Surfing the Web, 267
Surplus, technological, ix, 3
Symmetric Multiprocessors (SMP), 108
Syskill & Webert, 33
Systems implementation, 11

Teams. *See* Conference systems
Technological advancement life cycle, 1-2
  phases of, viii-ix, 3
  research classification, ix-x, 3-4
Technology acceptance model, 149
Third-party expertise, 35-36
TIP theory (Time-Interaction-Performance), 244, 257
Transaction processing systems, 105, 109, 134

Usenet, 35, 40
User interfaces. *See* Animation
User profile, 28, 30-31
Utility-based techniques, 33

Value-added networks (VANs), 292, 293, 305-306
Vector space model, 28, 33
Videoconferencing, 4, 274
Virtual teams. *See* Conference systems
Vision systems, 128-129
Vividness of Visual Imagery Questionnaire (VVIQ), 61

Webcasting, 273-274, 275 (figure), 279 (figure)
World Wide Web, 7, 12
  bookmark managers, 266
  bots and, 133, 268, 269 (figure), 277, 278
  broadcasting, 273-274, 275 (figure)
  browser accelerators, 266
  electronic commerce, x, 4, 6, 14, 25-27, 26 (figure), 29
  electronic meeting system (EMS), 10
  email, 4, 10
  evolutionary agent, 270-272, 272 (figure)
  information glut/coping technologies, 21-22, 22 (figure), 41-42
  internet commerce, 292-293, 294, 299-300
  navigation utility, 278
  nonlinear system and, 85-86
  recommendation systems within, 25-27, 26 (figure)
  rings, 267-268
  search engine technology, 267-268, 268-270, 269 (figure)
  streaming protocol, 274
  See also Client/server systems (CSS); Conference systems; Information delivery systems (IDS); Pull technologies; Push technologies

Xanadu project, 77

About the Editor

Kenneth E. Kendall, PhD, is Professor of Information Systems and Operations Technology in the School of Business-Camden, Rutgers University. He recently co-authored a text, *Systems Analysis and Design* (4th ed.) and coedited *The Impact of Computer Supported Technologies on Information Systems Development.* Additionally, he has had his research published in *MIS Quarterly, Management Science, Operations Research, Decision Sciences, Information & Management,* and many other journals. He is one of the founders of the International Conference on Information Systems (ICIS). He is the past Chair of IFIP Working Group 8.2 and is currently a Vice President for the Decision Sciences Institute. He is the MIS Editor for the *Journal of Management Systems*; a Functional Editor of MIS for *Interfaces*; and an Associate Editor for *Decision Sciences,* the *Information Systems Journal,* and the *Information Resources Management Journal.* Professor Kendall's research focuses on developing new tools for systems analysis and design and developing decision support systems applications.

About the Contributors

Deepinder S. Bajwa is Assistant Professor in the FMDS Department at Western Washington University. He received his MBA and DBA from Southern Illinois University at Carbondale. His research interests include executive information systems, diffusion of emerging information technologies, IS service quality, management of information technology, and total quality management. He has published his articles in *Decision Sciences, Decision Support Systems, Information Resources Management Journal,* and the proceedings of several national and international conferences. He is a member of the Decision Sciences Institute.

Gordon B. Davis is Honeywell Professor of Management Information Systems at the Carlson School of Management, University of Minnesota, Minneapolis. He is one of the principal founders and intellectual architects of the academic field of information systems. His book, *Management Information Systems: Conceptual Foundations, Structure, and Development* (1974; 1985) is recognized as a foundational classic in the field. He has published 19 other books and more than 200 journal articles. He is the Executive Editor of the *MIS Quarterly* and is on the editorial boards of numerous other journals. He serves as the USA representative to the International Federation for Information Processing (IFIP) Technical Committee 8 (Information Systems). He is the 1998 President of the Association for Information Systems. His doctorate is from Stanford University in business administration. He has been honored as a fellow of the Association for Computing Machinery.

Phillip Ein-Dor is Professor of Information Systems in the Faculty of Management, Tel Aviv University. He has a long-standing interest in artificial intelligence, beginning with his doctoral dissertation. He has been active in the series of workshops on Artificial Intelligence in Economics and Management, chairing AIEM4 and editing the proceedings. His main current research interests are (a) development of the Internet—intelligent agents, the Internet as immobot; (b) design and implementation of natural language query systems for accessing multiple, heterogeneous, multimedia databases; (c) applications of artificial intelligence to business problems; (d) representing commonsense business knowledge; and (e) government information technology policy and its effect on IT development and on the Internet. He was recently appointed founding editor of the *Journal of the*

Association for Information Systems and is currently engaged in designing the procedures for what will be a purely electronic journal and is intended to be the leader in its field.

Mark N. Frolick is Associate Professor of Management Information Systems in the Fogelman College of Business and Economics and a project manager with the FedEx Center for Cycle Time Research at the University of Memphis. His research, teaching, and consulting have emphasized executive information systems, data warehousing, cycle time reduction, and systems analysis and design. He has published extensively in numerous journals, including *MIS Quarterly, Journal of Management Information Systems, Decision Support Systems, Information & Management,* and *Decision Sciences.* He has more than 16 years' experience in the information systems field and has worked as an independent consultant for numerous Fortune 500 companies.

Cleotilde González is Associate Professor in the Department of Computer Engineering at Universidad de las Américas Puebla, México, where she is instrumental in the Laboratory of Interactive and Cooperative Technologies. She received a PhD in management information systems from Texas Tech University and is currently a postdoctoral research associate at Carnegie Mellon University. Her research interests are in animation, graphical and spatial representation of data, usability testing, and design of the user interface for supporting decision making.

Paul Gray is Professor and Founding Chair of the School of Information Science at Claremont Graduate University. He specializes in decision support systems and in data warehousing. He worked for 18 years in research and development organizations, including nine years at SRI International. Before coming to CGU in 1983, he was a professor at Stanford University, the Georgia Institute of Technology, the University of Southern California, and Southern Methodist University. He is the first editor of the *Communications of AIS.* He was president of the Institute of Management Sciences for 1992-1993, and was formerly president-elect, vice president, and secretary of the Institute. He is on the editorial board of several journals. He is the author of more than 100 journal articles and the author/editor of 12 books, most recently *Decision Support in the Data Warehouse* with H. J. Watson. He received his PhD in operations research from Stanford University.

Tor Guimaraes holds the Jesse E. Owen Chair of Excellence at Tennessee Technological University. He has a PhD in MIS from the University of Minnesota and an MBA from California State University, Los Angeles. Dr. Guimaraes was a professor and department chairman at St. Cloud State University, and before that, he was an assistant professor and director of the MIS Certificate Program at Case Western Reserve University. He has been the keynote speaker at numerous national and international meetings sponsored by organizations such as the Information Processing Society of Japan, Institute of Industrial Engineers, American Society for

Quality Control, IEEE, ASM, and Sales and Marketing Executives. He has consulted with many leading organizations, including TRW, American Greetings, AT&T, IBM, and the Department of Defense. Working with partners throughout the world, he has published more than 130 articles about the effective use and management of information systems and other technologies.

Ross Hightower is Assistant Professor of MIS in the College of Business Administration at the University of Central Florida. His research focuses on computer-mediated communication and information sharing in groups as well as adoption/diffusion of technology. His work has appeared in journals such as *Information Systems Research, Information and Management, Computers in Human Behavior,* and *Journal of Information Technology Management.* He received his doctorate in business administration from Georgia State University.

Magid Igbaria is Associate Professor of Management Information Systems at Claremont Graduate School and Tel Aviv University. He holds a BA in statistics and business administration and an MA in information systems and operations research from Hebrew University. He received his PhD in management information systems from Tel Aviv University. He has published articles on management of MIS functions, economics of computers, computer performance evaluation, charging of computer services, compumetrical approaches in MIS, and microcomputers in business in *Applied Statistics, Communications of the ACM, Computers & Operations Research, Information & Management, Journal of Management,* and others. His current research interests focus on economics of computers, management of information systems, career development of MIS professionals, and end-user computing.

George M. Kasper is Professor and Chair of the Department of Information Systems in the School of Business at Virginia Commonwealth University. Prior to this position, he was a professor of information systems at Texas Tech University. His research in decision support systems and user interface design has been published in many journals. He also serves as chair of the Special Interest Group on Management Information Systems (SIGMIS) of the ACM.

Julie E. Kendall, PhD, is Associate Professor of MIS in the School of Business-Camden, Rutgers University. She has published in *MIS Quarterly, Decision Sciences, Information & Management, Organization Studies,* and many other journals. Additionally, she has recently co-authored a college textbook with Kenneth E. Kendall, *Systems Analysis and Design* (4th ed.). She has also co-edited a book titled *Human, Organizational, and Social Dimensions of Information Systems Development* and has recently served as co-editor of a special issue on "Computers and Playfulness" for the ACM journal *The DATA BASE for Advances in Information Systems.* She is a functional editor of MIS for *Interfaces* and has served as an associate editor for *MIS Quarterly.* She is on the editorial boards of the *Journal of*

Management Systems and the *Journal of Database Management,* and she is on the editorial review board of the *Information Resource Management Journal.* Her research interests include developing innovative qualitative approaches for information systems researchers interested in systems analysis and design. She is currently working on hypermedia theory and applications.

Ruth C. King is Assistant Professor of Information Systems at the University of Illinois at Urbana-Champaign. She received her PhD in information systems from the University of Texas at Austin. Her research interests involve the strategic use of information systems in organizational context, computer-supported group collaboration, organizational communications with emerging technologies, and information systems professional development. She has published in *Information Systems Research, Decision Sciences, Journal of Management Information Systems, European Journal of Information Systems, Journal of Information Technology Management, Journal of High Technology Research,* and others. She has previously held a faculty appointment in the Katz Graduate School of Business, University of Pittsburgh.

J. David Naumann is Associate Professor of Management Information Systems in the Carlson School of Management at the University of Minnesota, where he received his doctorate. His research focuses on the process of information systems development. He has published articles in the leading MIS journals and co-authored a book, *Personal Productivity with Information Technology* (1997), with G. B. Davis. He is active nationally in MIS curriculum development. He designed and initiated the Web-accessible version of the international IS Faculty Directory, which contains more than 3,000 individual records. He teaches telecommunications, applications development, and systems analysis and design courses for MBAs and undergraduates.

Arun Rai is Associate Professor in the Department of Decision Sciences at Georgia State University. He was a faculty member in the Department of Management at Southern Illinois University at Carbondale for 7 years before joining Georgia State in the fall of 1997. He received his PhD from Kent State University in 1990. His present research interests include the diffusion, infusion, and impacts of information technology, information technology design for information and knowledge management, and management of unstructured processes such as innovation, product development, decision making, and systems development. He has published several articles on these and other related subjects in journals such as *Communications of the ACM, Decision Sciences, Decision Support Systems, European Journal of Information Systems, Journal of Management Information Systems, Omega,* and several others. He is the president of the Diffusion Interest Group on Information Technology (DIGIT) and is an associate editor for *MIS Quarterly* and *Information Resources Management Journal* and department editor of *Data Base for Advances in Information Systems.* He is a member of the Decision Sciences Institute, IN-

ORMS, Association for Information Systems, Beta Gamma Sigma, and Phi Kappa Phi.

Narender K. Ramarapu is Assistant Professor of computer information systems in the Accounting and CIS Department at the University of Nevada, Reno. He received his bachelor's degree in electronics engineering from Osmania University, Hyderabad, India, and an MBA and PhD in MIS from the University of Memphis. His current research is in the areas of information presentation, hypertext/hypermedia, global information systems, and emerging technologies. Nari has published in *Information and Management, International Journal of Information Management, Journal of Information Technology, Journal of Marketing Theory and Practice, Journal of Systems Management, International Journal of Operations and Production Management,* and others. In addition, he has articles and presentations in several national and international conferences, and he serves as an ad hoc reviewer for several academic journals.

Lutfus Sayeed is Associate Professor of MIS in the College of Business Administration, San Francisco State University. His research focuses on information sharing in groups using computer-mediated communication systems, adoption/diffusion of information technology, and impact of information technology. His work has appeared in journals such as *Information Systems Research, Information and Management, Computers in Human Behavior, Accounting, Management and Information Technologies,* and *Journal of Information Technology Management*. He received his doctorate in business administration from Georgia State University.

Edward A. Stohr is Director of the Center for Information Intensive Organizations at the Stern School. He holds a Bachelor of Civil Engineering degree from Melbourne University, Australia, and MBA and PhD degrees in Information Science from the University of California, Berkeley. For the period 1984 to 1995, he served as Chairman of the Information Systems Department at the Stern School of Business, New York University. In 1992, he served as chairman of the executive board of the International Conference on Information Systems (ICIS). He is on the editorial boards of several journals, including the *Journal of Information Systems Research, International Journal of Decision Support Systems,* and *Journal of Management Information Systems*. His research focuses on the problems of developing computer systems to support work and decision making in organizations.

Sivakumar Viswanathan is a doctoral student in the Information Systems Department at the Stern School of Business, New York University. He received his BS in electrical engineering and an MBA from the Indian Institute of Management, Bangalore, India. His research interests include the organizational impact of information technologies, financial information systems, and marketing issues in electronic commerce. He has presented papers at HICCS, ACM, AIS, IEEE, and DSI conferences.

Merrill Warkentin is Associate Professor and Coordinator of MIS in the College of Business Administration, Northeastern University in Boston, MA. His research primarily involving IT management, knowledge engineering, computer security, and electronic commerce, has appeared in such journals as *Decision Sciences, MIS Quarterly, Expert Systems, ACM Applied Computing Review, Journal of Computer Information Systems,* and *The Journal of Intelligent Technologies*. He has served as an associate editor and guest editor of several journals, and as a consultant to numerous companies and organizations. He has also been a featured speaker at more than 100 industry association meetings and is currently a national lecturer for the Association for Computing Machinery (ACM). He received his PhD in MIS from the University of Nebraska–Lincoln.

James C. Wetherbe is FedEx Professor of Excellence and Executive Director of the Center for Cycle Time Research at the University of Memphis, as well as professor of MIS and director of the MIS Research Center at the University of Minnesota. He is internationally known as a dynamic and entertaining speaker, author, and leading authority on the use of computers and information systems to improve organizational performance and competitiveness. He is particularly appreciated for his ability to explain complex technology in straightforward, practical terms that can be strategically applied by both executives and general management. He is the author of 17 highly regarded books, including *The Management of Information Systems*; *So, What's Your Point?*; *Systems Analysis and Design: Best Practices*; and his newest book *The World on Time: Management Principles That Made FedEx an Overnight Sensation*. In addition, he is the publisher of Cycle Time Research. Quoted often in leading business and information system journals, he has also authored more than 200 articles, writes regular columns, and serves as a consulting editor for publishing companies.

Ronald B. Wilkes is Chief Technology Advisor for Global Operations and Technology at Citicorp. He was an associate professor of management information systems in the Fogelman College of Business and Economics at the University of Memphis. He received a BSE from the University of Tennessee at Martin, an MBA from Memphis State University, and a PhD in management information systems from the University of Minnesota. His primary research interests are in management of information technology resources. He has published articles in *Information and Management, Information Systems Management, Journal of Strategic Information Systems, Journal of Computer Information Systems,* and *Information Strategy*. In addition, he has articles in several national and international conference proceedings, and he has written chapters for two books. He has consulted for a variety of organizations in both the public and private sectors on the management of information technology. He was vice president of systems for Data Communications Corporation, Memphis, and vice president of development for Cylix Communications, Memphis. He has served as president of the Memphis Chapter of the Society of Information Management.

Susan Rebstock Williams is Assistant Professor of Management Information Systems at Georgia Southern University. She holds a PhD in MIS from Oklahoma State University. Her current research interests include organizational impacts of emerging technologies, group support systems, and integrated management science applications. Previous research has been published in *International Journal of Computer Applications in Technology, International Journal of Information and Management Sciences,* and *Journal of Computer Information Systems.*

Rick L. Wilson is Director of the Master of Science in Telecommunications Management Program and the Fleming Companies, Inc., Professor of Technology Management at Oklahoma State University. He received his PhD in MIS from the University of Nebraska–Lincoln. His research interests include neural network applications, multicriteria decision making, emerging technologies, and management science applications. Previous publications include articles in *Communications of the ACM, Computers and Operations Research, Decision Support Systems, Information and Management, Interfaces, Strategic Management Journal,* and others.

Weidong Xia is a doctoral candidate at the Katz Graduate School of Business at the University of Pittsburgh. He was a faculty member and the deputy director of the Information Systems and Management Science Division at Beijing University of Aeronautics and Astronautics. His current research interests are management of information systems infrastructure, telecommunications, and end-user computing. He has published in *MIS Quarterly, Journal of End-User Computing,* and a number of international conference proceedings. He is also the coauthor of two textbooks on computer applications and information systems analysis and design.

Vladimir Zwass is Professor of Management Information Systems and Computer Science at Fairleigh Dickinson University, and also Seminar Associate at Columbia University. He holds a PhD in computer science from Columbia University and is the author of six books and several book chapters, including one in the *Encyclopaedia Britannica,* as well as a number of papers in various journals and conference proceedings. His recent research interests center on electronic commerce and organizational memory as a form of knowledge management. He has received several grants, consulted for a number of major corporations, and is a frequent speaker to national and international audiences. His most recent book is *Foundations of Information Systems* (1998). He is the founding editor-in-chief of the *Journal of Management Information Systems* and of the *International Journal of Electronic Commerce,* the first scholarly journal fully devoted to E-commerce.